EVERYDAY LIFE EDITION

The New Testament
A New Translation

By
JAMES MOFFATT
D.D., D.Litt.

ASSOCIATION PRESS
New York: 347 Madison Avenue
1919

PRINTED IN THE UNITED STATES OF AMERICA

PREFACE

In his essay on Protestantism, de Quincey has a characteristic paragraph upon the popular delusion that "every idea and word which exists, or has existed, for any nation, ancient or modern, must have a direct interchangeable equivalent in all other languages." No one who attempts to translate any part of the New Testament is likely to remain very long under such a delusion. Thus, there is no exact English equivalent for terms like λόγος and μυστήριον and δικαιοσύνη. The first of these I have simply transliterated once or twice; 'Logos' is at any rate less misleading than 'Word' would be to a modern reader. Even when an equivalent can be got for some New Testament term like ζωή or Ἅιδης, it cannot be used invariably. I have kept "Gentiles" for ἔθνη in cases where the contrast between Judaism and the outer world is prominent; if Kipling's "Recessional" was intelligible to modern readers, "Gentiles" here should not cause them undue difficulty. But now and then the Greek term carries a sense which can only be represented by our "pagans" or "heathen," and occasionally it is no more than "nations." This will serve as an illustration of the difficulties which confront a translator. But once the translation of the New Testament is freed from the influence of the theory of verbal inspiration, these difficulties cease to be so formidable. I have tried not to sacrifice the spirit to the letter. It is true, as de Quincey observes in the same essay, that "the great ideas of the Bible protect themselves. The heavenly truths, by their own imperishableness, defeat the mortality of languages with which for a moment they are associated." Still, this is a victory in which even the camp-followers or translators have a modest share. They can or they should further this linguistic triumph. Hellenistic Greek has its own defects, from the point of view of the classical scholar, but it is an eminently translatable language; and the evidence of papyrology shows it was more flexible than once was imagined. My intention, therefore, has been to produce a version which will to some degree represent the gains of recent lexical research and also prove readable. I have attempted to translate the New Testament exactly as one would render any piece of contemporary Hellenistic prose; in this way, students of the

v

original text may perhaps be benefited. But I hope also that the translation may fall into the hands of some who know how to freshen their religious interest in the meaning of the New Testament by reading it occasionally in some unauthorized English or foreign version, as well as into the hands of others who for various reasons neglect the Bible even as an English classic. This is a hope which, no doubt, is accompanied with some risks and fears. Every translation has to face a double ordeal. Some of its readers know the original, some do not, and both classes have to be met. "The English reader," as Dr. Rouse remarks, "may be quite competent to judge of a translation as literature and as intelligible or not intelligible, but he cannot judge of its accuracy. The scholar alone can judge of its accuracy, but (granting that he has literary taste) he knows the original too well to be independent of it, and hence cannot judge of the impression which the translation will make on the minds of those who are not scholars." If this is true of Homer, it is three times true of the New Testament. Any new translation starts under a special handicap. It appears to challenge in every line the rhythm and diction of an English classic, and this irritates many who have no knowledge of the original. *The old*, they say, *is better*. They are indifferent to the changes which recent grammatical research has necessitated in the translation of the aorist, the article, and the particles, for example, even since the Revised Version of 1881 was made. But intelligibility is more than associations, and to atone in part for the loss of associations I have endeavoured to make the New Testament, especially St. Paul's epistles, as intelligible to a modern English reader as any version that is not a paraphrase can hope to make them.

This raises one of the numerous points of difficulty that beset the translator. How far is he justified in modernizing an Oriental book? How far can he assume that certain turns of expression have become naturalized in English by the Authorized Version itself? I have never seen any satisfactory solution of this problem, and I have not been able to find one. However, it is superfluous to discuss such matters at length. This is not the place to develop any theories on the subject. What the general public cares for is a translator's practice rather than his principles, and students can easily detect the latter, or the lack of them, in the former.

I wish only to add this caution, that a translator appears to be more dogmatic than he really is. He must come down on one side of the fence or on the other. He has often to decide on a rendering, or even on the text of a passage, when his own mind is by no means clear and certain. In a number of cases, therefore, when the evidence is conflicting, I must ask scholars and students to believe that a line has been taken only after long thought and only with serious hesitation.

The translation has been made from the text recently issued by Von Soden of Berlin, but I have not invariably followed his arrangement and punctuation. Wherever I have felt obliged to adopt a different reading, this is noted at the foot of the page.

Quotations or direct reminiscences of the Old Testament are printed in italics.

The books are arranged for the convenience of the general reader in the order of the English Bible. This applies to the order of chapters as well. Thus the last four chapters of Second Corinthians appear in their usual canonical position instead of in what I believe to be their original position between First and Second Corinthians. The only exception I have made to this rule is in the case of some occasional transpositions either of verses or of paragraphs, for example, in the case of the Fourth Gospel. Any one who cares to look into the evidence for such changes will find it in my *Introduction to the Literature of the New Testament*.

Lastly, it is right to add that I have not consulted any other version of the New Testament in preparing this work, though probably echoes and reminiscences have clung to one's mind. The only version I have kept before me is the one I prepared thirteen years ago for my *Historical New Testament*. But the present version is not a revision of that. It is an independent work. I agreed to undertake it with sharp misgivings, but I trust that the spirit and method of its composition may at any rate do something to make some parts of the New Testament more intelligible to some readers.

JAMES MOFFATT.

CONTENTS

	PAGE
MATTHEW	1
MARK	52
LUKE	83
JOHN	136
ACTS	175
ROMANS	225
I. CORINTHIANS	247
II. CORINTHIANS	269
GALATIANS	283
EPHESIANS	290
PHILIPPIANS	297
COLOSSIANS	302
I. THESSALONIANS	307
II. THESSALONIANS	311
I. TIMOTHEUS	314
II. TIMOTHEUS	320
TITUS	324
PHILEMON	327
HEBREWS	329
JAMES	345

CONTENTS

	PAGE
I. PETER	351
II. PETER	357
I. JOHN	361
II. JOHN	367
III. JOHN	368
JUDAS	369
REVELATION	371

THE NEW TESTAMENT
A NEW TRANSLATION

THE GOSPEL ACCORDING TO
S. MATTHEW

1 The birth-roll of Jesus Christ, the son of David, the son of Abraham.
2 Abraham was the father of Isaac, Isaac the father of
3 Jacob, Jacob the father of Judah and his brothers, Judah the father of Perez and Zerah by Tamar, Perez the father
4 of Hezren, Hezron the father of Aram, Aram the father of Aminadab, Aminadab the father of Nahshon, Nahshon the
5 father of Salmon, Salmon the father of Boaz by Rahab, Boaz the father of Obed by Ruth, Obed the father of Jessai,
6 and Jessai the father of king David.
   David was the father of Solomon by Uriah's wife,
7 Solomon the father of Rehoboam, Rehoboam the father of
8 Abijah, Abijah the father of Asa, Asa the father of Jehoshaphat, Jehoshaphat the father of Joram, Joram the
9 father of Uzziah, Uzziah the father of Jotham, Jotham the
10 father of Ahaz, Ahaz the father of Hezekiah, Hezekiah the father of Manasseh, Manasseh the father of Amon,
11 Amon the father of Josiah, and Josiah the father of Jechoniah and his brothers at the period of the Babylonian
12 captivity. After the Babylonian captivity, Jechoniah was the father of Shealtiel, Shealtiel the father of Zerubbabel,
13 Zerubbabel the father of Abiud, Abiud the father of Elia-
14 kim, Eliakim the father of Azor, Azor the father of Zadok, Zadok the father of Achim, Achim the father of Eliud,
15 Eliud the father of Eleazar, Eleazar the father of Matthan,
16 Matthan the father of Jacob, Jacob the father of Joseph, and Joseph (to whom the virgin Mary was betrothed) the the father of Jesus, who is called 'Christ.'
17 Thus all the generations from Abraham to David number fourteen, from David to the Babylonian captivity fourteen, and from the Babylonian captivity to Christ fourteen.
18 The birth of [Jesus] Christ came about thus. His mother Mary was betrothed to Joseph, but before they came together she was discovered to be pregnant by the Holy
19 Spirit. As Joseph her husband was a just man but unwilling to disgrace her, he resolved to divorce her secretly;
20 but after he had planned this, there appeared an angel of the Lord to him in a dream saying, "Joseph, son of David, fear not to take Mary your wife home, for what is begotten
21 in her comes from the holy Spirit. She will bear a son,

1

and you will call him 'Jesus,' for he will save his people
22 from their sins." All this happened for the fulfilment of what the Lord had spoken by the prophet:
23 *The maiden will conceive and bear a son,
and his name will be called Immanuel*
24 (which may be translated, *God is with us*). So on waking from sleep Joseph did as the angel of the Lord had com-
25 manded him; he took his wife home, but he did not live with her as a husband till she bore a son, whom he called Jesus.

2 Now when Jesus was born at Bethlehem, belonging to Judaea, in the days of king Herod, magicians from the
2 East arrived at the Jerusalem, asking, "Where is the newly-born king of the Jews? We saw his star when it rose, and we
3 have come to worship him." The news of this troubled
4 king Herod and all Jerusalem as well; so he gathered all the high priests and scribes of the people and made inquiries of them about where the messiah was to be born.
5 They told him, "In Bethlehem belonging to Judaea: for thus it is written by the prophet:
6   *And you Bethlehem, in Judah's land,
    You are not least among the rulers of Judah:
    For a ruler will come from you,
    Who will shepherd Israel my people.*"
7 Then Herod summoned the magicians in secret and ascer-
8 tained from them the time of the star's appearance. He also sent them to Bethlehem, telling them, "Go and make a careful search for the child, and when you have found him
9 report to me, so that I can go and worship him too." The magicians listened to the king and then went their way. And the star they had seen rise went in front of them till
10 it stopped over the place where the child was. When they
11 caught sight of the star they were intensely glad. And on reaching the house they saw the child with his mother Mary, they fell down to worship him, and opening their caskets they offered him gifts of gold and frankincense
12 and myrrh. Then, as they had been divinely warned in a dream not to return to Herod, they went back to their own country by a different road.
13   After they had gone, there appeared an angel of the Lord to Joseph in a dream, saying, "Rise, take the child and his mother and flee to Egypt; stay there till I tell you. For Herod is going to search for the child and de-
14 stroy him." So he got up, took the child and his mother
15 by night, and went off to Egypt, where he stayed until the death of Herod. This was to fulfil what the Lord had said by the prophet: *I called my Son from Egypt.*

16 Then Herod saw the magicians had trifled with him, and he was furiously angry; he sent and slew all the male children in Bethlehem and in all the neighbourhood who were two years old or under, calculating by the time he 17 had ascertained from the magicians. Then the saying was fulfilled which had been uttered by the prophet Jeremiah:
18 *A cry was heard in Rama,*
weeping and sore lamentation—
Rachel weeping for her children,
and inconsolable because they are no more.
19 But when Herod died, there appeared an angel of the 20 Lord in a dream to Joseph in Egypt, saying, "Rise, take the child and his mother and go to the land of Israel, for 21 those who sought the child's life are dead." So he rose, took the child and his mother and went to the land of 22 Israel; but on hearing that Archelaus reigned over Judaea in place of his father Herod, he was afraid to go there and, by a divine injunction in a dream, withdrew to the region 23 of Galilee. He went and settled in a town called Nazaret, so that what had been said by the prophets might be fulfilled: 'He shall be called a Nazarene.'

3 In those days John the Baptist came on the scene, 2 preaching in the desert of Judaea, "Repent, the Reign 3 of heaven is near." (This was the man spoken of by the prophet Isaiah:
The voice of one who cries in the desert,
'Make the way ready for the Lord,
level the paths for him.')
4 This John had his clothes made of camel's hair, with a leather girdle round his loins; his food was locusts and wild 5 honey. Then Jerusalem and the whole of Judaea and all the 6 Jordan-district went out to him and got baptized by him in 7 the Jordan, confessing their sins. But when he noticed a number of the Pharisees and Sadducees coming for his baptism, he said to them, "You brood of vipers, who told 8 you to flee from the coming Wrath? Now, produce fruit that 9 answers to your repentance, instead of presuming to say to yourselves, 'We have a father in Abraham.' I tell you, God 10 can raise up children for Abraham from these stones! The axe is lying all ready at the root of the trees; any tree that is not producing good fruit will be cut down and thrown into the fire.
11 I baptize you with water for repentance,
but he who is coming after me is mightier,
and I am not fit even to carry his sandals;
he will baptize you with the holy Spirit and fire.
12 His winnowing-fan is in his hand,

he will clean out his threshing-floor,
his wheat he will gather into the granary,
but the straw he will burn with fire unquenchable."
13 Then Jesus came on the scene from Galilee, to get bap-
14 tized by John at the Jordan. John tried to prevent him;
"I need to get baptized by you," he said, "and you come
15 to me!" But Jesus answered him, "Come now, this is how
we should fulfil all our duty to God." Then John gave
16 in to him. Now when Jesus had been baptized, the moment he rose out of the water, the heavens opened and he
saw the Spirit of God coming down like a dove upon him.
17 And a voice from heaven said,
"This is my Son, the Beloved,
in him is my delight.'

4 THEN Jesus was led into the desert by the Spirit to be
2 tempted by the devil. He fasted forty days and forty
3 nights and afterwards felt hungry. So the tempter came
up and said to him, "If you are God's Son, tell these stones
4 to become loaves." He answered, "It is written,
Man is not to live on bread alone,
but on every word that issues from the mouth of God."
5 Then the devil conveyed him to the holy city and, placing
6 him on the pinnacle of the temple, said to him, "If you are
God's Son, throw yourself down; for it is written,
He will give his angels charge of you;
they will bear you on their hands,
lest you strike your foot against a stone."
7 Jesus said to him, "It is written again, *You shall not tempt*
8 *the Lord your God."* Once more the devil conveyed him
to an exceedingly high mountain and showed him all the
9 realms of the world and their grandeur; he said, "I will
give you all that if you will fall down and worship me."
10 Then Jesus told him, "Begone, Satan! it is written, *You*
must worship the Lord your God, and serve him alone."
11 At this the devil left him, and angels came up and ministered to him.
12 Now when Jesus heard that John had been arrested, he
13 withdrew to Galilee; he left Nazaret and settled at Capharnahum beside the lake, in the territory of Zebulun
14 and Naphtali—for the fulfilment of what had been said by
the prophet Isaiah:
15 *Land of Zebulun, land of Naphtali*
lying to the sea, across the Jordan,
Galilee of the Gentiles!
16 *The people who sat in darkness saw a great light,*
yea light dawned on those who sat in the land and the
shadow of death.

17 From that day Jesus began to preach, saying, "Repent, the Reign of heaven is near."
18 As he was walking along the sea of Galilee he saw two brothers, Simon (who is called Peter) and his brother Andrew, casting a net in the sea—for they were fishermen;
19 so he said to them, "Come, follow me, and I will make you
20 fish for men." And they dropped their nets at once and fol-
21 lowed him. Then going on from there he saw two other brothers, James the son of Zebedaeus and his brother John, mending their nets in the boat beside their father
22 Zebedaeus. He called them, and they left the boat and their father at once, and went after him.
23 Then he made a tour through the whole of Galilee, teaching in their synagogues, preaching the gospel of the Reign, and healing all the sickness and disease of the people.
24 The fame of him spread all through the surrounding country,* and people brought him all their sick, those who suffered from all manner of disease and pain, demoniacs, lunatics, and paralytics; he healed them all.
25 And he was followed by great crowds from Galilee and Decapolis and Jerusalem and Judaea and from across the Jordan.

5 So when he saw the crowds, he went up the hill, and
2 sat down; his disciples came up to him and he opened his lips and began to teach them. He said:
3 "Blessed are those who feel poor in spirit!
    the Realm of heaven is theirs.
4 Blessed are the mourners!
    they will be consoled.
5 Blessed are *the humble!*
    they will inherit the earth.
6 Blessed are those who hunger and thirst for goodness!
    they will be satisfied.
7 Blessed are the merciful!
    they will find mercy.
8 Blessed are the pure in heart!
    they will see God.
9 Blessed are the peacemakers!
    they will be ranked sons of God.
10 Blessed are those who have been persecuted for the sake of goodness!
    the Realm of heaven is theirs.
11 Blessed are you when men denounce you and persecute you and utter all manner of evil against you for my sake;
12 rejoice and exult in it, for your reward is rich in heaven; that is how they persecuted the prophets before you.

* I accept Blass's suggestion that Συρίαν here is a corruption of συνορίαν (see Mark i. 28), which is actually read by one uncial manuscript Γ.

13 You are the salt of the earth. But if salt becomes insipid, what can make it salt again? After that it is fit for nothing, fit only to be thrown outside and trodden by the feet of men.
14 You are the light of the world. A town on the top of a
15 hill cannot be hidden. Nor do men light a lamp to put it under a bowl; they put it on a stand and it shines for
16 all in the house. So your light is to shine before men, that they may see the good you do and glorify your Father in heaven.
17 Do not imagine I have come to destroy the Law or the
18 prophets; I have not come to destroy but to fulfil. (I tell you truly, till heaven and earth pass away not an iota, not a comma, will pass from the Law until it is all in force. Therefore
19 whoever relaxes a single one of these commands, were it
even one of the least, and teaches men so,
he will be ranked least in the Realm of heaven;
but whoever obeys them and teaches them,
20 he will be ranked great in the Realm of heaven.) For I tell you, unless your goodness excels that of the scribes and Pharisees, you will never get into the Realm of heaven.
21 You have heard how the men of old were told, '*Murder not:*
whoever murders must come up for sentence,*
22 whoever maligns his brother must come before the Sanhedrin,
whoever curses his brother must go to the fire of Gehenna.'
But I tell you, whoever is angry with his brother [without
23 cause] will be sentenced by God. So if you remember, even when offering your gift at the altar, that your brother has
24 any grievance against you, leave your gift at the very altar and go away; first be reconciled to your brother, then come back and offer your gift.
25 Be quick and make terms with your opponent, so long as you and he are on the way to court, in case he hands you over to the judge, and the judge to the jailer, and you
26 are thrown into prison; truly I tell you, you will never get out till you pay the last halfpenny of your debt.
27 You have heard how it used to be said, *Do not commit*
28 *adultery.* But I tell you, any one who even looks with lust at a woman has committed adultery with her already in his heart.

* I follow the suggestion that the second and third clauses of ver. 22 should be restored to what seems to be their original position as a rabbinic comment upon the closing words of ver. 21.

29 If your right eye is a hindrance to you,
pluck it out and throw it away:
better for you to lose one of your members
than to have all your body thrown into Gehenna.
30 And if your right hand is a hindrance to you,
cut it off and throw it away:
better for you to lose one of your members
than to have all your body thrown into Gehenna.
31 It used to be said, *Whoever divorces his wife must give*
32 *her a divorce-certificate.* But I tell you, anyone who divorces his wife for any reason except unchastity makes her an adulteress; and whoever marries a divorced woman commits adultery.
33 Once again, you have heard how the men of old were told, *'You must not forswear yourself but discharge your*
34 *vows to the Lord'.* But I tell you, you must not swear any oath,
neither by *heaven*,
for it *is the throne of God*,
35 nor by *earth*,
for it *is the footstool of his feet.*
nor by Jerusalem,
for it *is the city of the great King;*
36 nor shall you swear by your head,
for you cannot make a single hair white or black.
37 Let what you say be simply 'yes' or 'no';
whatever exceeds that springs from evil.
38 You have heard the saying, *An eye for an eye and a tooth for a tooth.*
39 But I tell you, you are not to resist an injury;
whoever strikes you on the right cheek,
turn the other to him as well;
40 whoever wants to sue you for your shirt,
let him have your coat as well;
41 whoever forces you to go one mile,
go two miles with him;
42 give to the man who begs from you,
and turn not away from him who wants to borrow.
43 You have heard the saying, *'You must love your neigh-*
44 *bour and hate your enemy.'* But I tell you, love your
45 enemies and pray for those who persecute you, that you may be sons of your Father in heaven:
he makes his sun rise on the evil and the good,
and sends rain on the just and the unjust.
46 For if you love only those who love you, what reward do you get for that?
do not the very taxgatherers do as much?

47 and if you only salute your friends, what is special about that?
do not the very pagans do as much?
48 *You must be perfect* as your heavenly Father is perfect.

6 Take care not to practise your charity before men in order to be noticed; otherwise you get no reward from your Father in heaven. No,
2 When you give alms,
make no flourish of trumpets like the hypocrites in the synagogues and the streets,
so as to win applause from men;
I tell you truly, they do get their reward.
3 When you give alms,
do not let your left hand know what your right hand is doing,
4 so as to keep your alms secret;
then your Father who sees what is secret will reward you openly.*
5 Also, when you pray, you must not be like the hypocrites,
for they like to stand and pray in the synagogues and at the street-corners,
so as to be seen by men;
I tell you truly, they do get their reward.
6 When you pray,
go into your room and shut the door,
pray to your Father who is in secret,
and your Father who sees what is secret will reward you.
7 Do not pray by idle rote like pagans,
for they suppose they will be heard the more they say;
8 you must not copy them;
your Father knows your needs before you ask him.
9 Let this be how you pray:
'our Father in heaven,
thy name be revered,
10 thy Reign begin,
thy will be done
on earth as in heaven!
11 give us to-day our bread for the morrow,
12 and forgive us our debts
as we ourselves have forgiven our debtors,
13 and lead us not into temptation
but deliver us from evil.'
14 For if you forgive men their trespasses,
then your heavenly Father will forgive you;

* Retaining ἐν τῷ φανερῷ, which has powerful support in the Old Latin and Syriac versions.

15 but if you do not forgive men,
   your Father will not forgive your trespasses either.
16 When you fast,
   do not look gloomy like the hypocrites,
   for they look woebegone to let men see they are fasting;
   I tell you truly, they do get their reward.
17 But when you fast,
   anoint your head and wash your face,
18 so that your fast may be seen not by men but by your
   Father who is in secret,
   and your Father who sees what is secret will reward
   you.
19 Store up no treasures for yourselves on earth,
   where moth and rust corrode,
   where thieves break in and steal:
20 store up treasures for yourselves in heaven,
   where neither moth nor rust corrode,
   where thieves do not break in and steal.
21 For where your treasure lies,
   your heart will lie there too.
22 The eye is the lamp of the body:
   so, if your Eye is generous,
   the whole of your body will be illumined,
23 but if your Eye is selfish,
   the whole of your body will be darkened.
   And if your very light turns dark,
   then—what a darkness it is!
24 No one can serve two masters:
   either he will hate one and love the other,
   or else he will stand by the one and despise the other—
   you cannot serve both God and Mammon.
25 Therefore I tell you,
   do not trouble about what you are to eat or drink in life,
   nor about what you are to put on your body;
   surely life means more than food,
   surely the body means more than clothes!
26 Look at the wild birds;
   they sow not, they reap not, they gather nothing in
   granaries,
   and yet your heavenly Father feeds them.
   Are you not worth more than birds?
27 Which of you can add an ell to his height by troubling
   about it?
28 And why should you trouble over clothing?
   Look how the lilies of the field grow;
   they neither toil nor spin,
29 and yet, I tell you, even Solomon in all his grandeur
   was never robed like one of them,

30 Now if God so clothes the grass of the field which blooms to-day and is thrown to-morrow into the furnace, will not he much more clothe you? O men, how little you trust
31 him! Do not be troubled, then, and cry, 'What are we to eat?' or 'what are we to drink?' or 'how are we to be
32 clothed?' (pagans make all that their aim in life) for your
33 heavenly Father knows quite well you need all that. Seek God's Realm and his goodness, and all that will be yours over and above.
34 So do not be troubled about to-morrow;
to-morrow will take care of itself.
The day's own trouble is quite enough for the day.

7 JUDGE not, that you may not be judged yourselves;
2 for as you judge so you will be judged,
and the measure you deal out to others will be dealt out to yourselves.
3 Why do you note the splinter in your brother's eye and
4 fail to see the plank in your own eye? How can you say to your brother, 'Let me take out the splinter from your
5 eye,' when there lies the plank in your own eye? You hypocrite! take the plank out of your own eye first, and then you will see properly how to take the splinter out of your brother's eye.
6 Do not give dogs what is sacred and do not throw pearls before swine, in case they trample them under foot and turn to gore you.
7 Ask and the gift will be yours,
seek and you will find,
knock and the door will open to you;
8 for every one who asks receives,
the seeker finds,
the door is opened to anyone who knocks.
9 Why, which of you, when asked by his son for a loaf, will hand him a stone?
10 Or, if he asks a fish, will you hand him a serpent?
11 Well, if for all your evil you know to give your children what is good,
how much more will your Father in heaven give good gifts to those who ask him?
12 Well then, whatever you would like men to do to you, do just the same to them; that is the meaning of the Law and the prophets.
13 Enter by the narrow gate:
for [the gate] is broad and the road is wide that leads to destruction,
and many enter that way.

14 But the road that leads to life is both narrow and close,
and there are few who find it.
15 Beware of false prophets; they come to you with the garb of sheep but at heart they are ravenous wolves.
16 You will know them by their fruit; do men gather grapes from thorns or figs from thistles? No,
17 every good tree bears sound fruit, but a rotten tree bears bad fruit;
18 a good tree cannot bear bad fruit, and a rotten tree cannot bear sound fruit.
20
19 So you will know them by their fruit.* Any tree that does not produce sound fruit will be cut down and thrown into the fire.
21 'It is not everyone who says to me 'Lord, Lord!', who will get into the Realm of heaven, but he who does the will
22 of my Father in heaven. Many will say to me at that Day, 'Lord, Lord, did we not prophesy in your name? did we not cast out daemons in your name? did we not perform many
23 miracles in your name?' Then I will declare to them, 'I never knew you; *depart from my presence, you workers of iniquity.*'
24 Now, everyone who listens to these words of mine and acts upon them will be like a sensible man who built his
25 house on rock. The rain came down, the floods rose, the winds blew and beat upon that house, but it did not fall,
26 for it was founded on rock. And everyone who listens to these words of mine and does not act upon them will be
27 like a stupid man who built his house on sand. The rain came down, the floods rose, the winds blew and beat upon that house, and down it fell—with a mighty crash."
28 When Jesus finished his speech, the crowds were as-
29 tounded at his teaching; for he taught them like an authority, not like their own scribes.

2 **8** WHEN he came down from the hill, he was followed by large crowds. A leper came up and knelt before him, saying, "If you only choose, sir, you can cleanse me";
3 so he stretched his hand out and touched him, with the words, "I do choose, be cleansed." And his leprosy was
4 cleansed at once. Then Jesus told him, "See, you are not to say a word to anybody; away and show yourself to the priest and offer the gift prescribed by Moses, to notify men."
5 When he entered Capharnahum an army-captain came

* Ver. 19 is repeated from iii. 10; to preserve the proper sequence of thought, it must be placed after ver. 20 as a link with the following paragraph.

S. MATTHEW VIII

6 up to him and appealed to him, saying, "Sir, my servant
7 is lying ill at home with paralysis, in terrible agony." He
8 replied, "I will come and heal him." The captain answered, "Sir, I am not fit to have you under my roof;
9 only say the word, and my servant will be cured. For though I am a man under authority myself, I have soldiers under me; I tell one man to go, and he goes, I tell another to come, and he comes, I tell my servant, 'Do this,' and
10 he does it." When Jesus heard that, he marvelled; "I tell you truly," he said to his followers, "I have never met
11 faith like this anywhere in Israel. Many, I tell you, will come *from east and west* and take their places beside
12 Abraham, Isaac, and Jacob in the Realm of heaven, while the sons of the Realm will pass* outside, into the darkness;
13 there men will wail and gnash their teeth." Then Jesus said to the captain, "Go; as you have had faith, your prayer is granted." And the servant was cured at that very hour.
14 On entering the house of Peter, Jesus noticed his
15 mother-in-law was down with fever, so he touched her hand; the fever left her and she rose and ministered to him.
16 Now when evening came they brought him many demoniacs, and he cast out the spirits with a word and
17 healed all the invalids—that the word spoken by the prophet Isaiah might be fulfilled, *He took away our sicknesses and he removed our diseases.*
18 When Jesus saw crowds round him he gave orders for
19 crossing to the other side. A scribe came up and said to
20 him, "Teacher, I will follow you anywhere"; Jesus said to him,
"The foxes have their holes,
   the wild birds have their nests,
but the Son of man has nowhere to lay his head."
21 Another of the disciples said to him, "Lord, let me go
22 and bury my father first of all"; Jesus said to him, "Follow me, and leave the dead to bury their own dead."
23 Then he embarked in the boat, followed by his disciples.
24 Now a heavy storm came on at sea, so that the boat was
25 buried under the waves. He was sleeping. So the disciples went and woke him up, saying, "Help, Lord, we are drown-
26 ing!" He said to them, "Why are you afraid? How little you trust God!" Then he got up and checked the winds and
27 the sea, and there was a great calm. Men marvelled at

* Reading ἐξελεύσονται with ℵ*, the Old Latin and Syriac versions, the Diatessaron, etc. The variant ἐκβληθήσονται represents a conventional term which would easily be substituted for the less common expression.

this; they said, "What sort of man is this? the very winds and sea obey him!"

28 When he reached the opposite side, the country of the Gadarenes, he was met by two demoniacs who ran out of the tombs; they were so violent that nobody could pass
29 along the road there. They shrieked, "Son of God, what business have you with us? Have you come here to tor-
30 ture us before it is time?" Now, some distance away,
31 there was a large drove of swine grazing; so the daemons begged him saying, "If you are going to cast us out, send
32 us into that drove of swine." He said to them, "Begone!" So out they came and went to the swine, and the entire droye rushed down the steep slope into the sea and per-
33 ished in the water. The herdsmen fled; they went off to the town and reported the whole affair of the demoniacs.
34 Then all the town came out to meet Jesus, and when they saw him they begged him to move out of their district.

9 So he embarked in the boat and crossed over to his
2 own town. There a paralytic was brought to him, lying on a pallet; and when Jesus saw the faith of the bearers he said to the paralytic, "Courage, my son! your
3 sins are forgiven." Some scribes said to themselves,
4 "The man is talking blasphemy!" Jesus saw what they were thinking and said, "Why do you think evil in your
5 hearts? Which is the easier thing, to say, 'Your sins are
6 forgiven,' or to say, 'Rise and walk'? But to let you see the Son of man has power on earth to forgive sins"—he then said to the paralytic, "Get up, lift your pallet, and
7 go home." And he got up and went home. The crowds
8 who saw it were awed and glorified God for giving such power to men.
9 As Jesus passed along from there, he saw a man called Matthew sitting at the tax-office; he said to him, "Follow me"; and he rose and followed him.
10 Jesus was at table indoors, and many taxgatherers and sinners had come to be guests with him and his disciples.
11 So when the Pharisees saw this, they said to his disciples, "Why does your teacher eat with taxgatherers and
12 sinners?" When Jesus heard it he said, "Those who are strong have no need of a doctor, but those who are ill.
13 Go and learn the meaning of this word, *I care for mercy not for sacrifice*. For I have not come to call just men but sinners."
14 Then the disciples of John came up to him and said, "Why do we and the Pharisees fast a great deal, and your disciples do not fast?"
15 Jesus said to them,

"Can friends at a wedding mourn so long as the bridegroom is beside them?
A time will come when the bridegroom is taken from them, and then they will fast.
16 No one sews a piece of undressed cloth on an old coat,
for the patch breaks away from it,
and the tear is made worse:
17 nor do men pour fresh wine into old wineskins,
otherwise the wineskins burst,
and the wine is spilt, the wineskins are ruined.
They put fresh wine into fresh wineskins,
and so both are preserved."
18 As he said this, an official came in and knelt before him, saying, "My daughter is just dead; do come and lay your
19 hand on her, and she will live." So Jesus rose and went
20 after him, accompanied by his disciples. Now a woman who had had a hemorrhage for twelve years came up
21 behind him and touched the tassel of his robe; what she said to herself was this, "If I can only touch his robe,
22 I will recover." Then Jesus turned round, and when he saw her he said, "Courage, my daughter, your faith has made you well." And the woman was well from that hour.
23 Now when Jesus reached the official's house and saw the flute-players and the din the crowd were making, he
24 said, "Be off with you; the girl is not dead but asleep."
25 They laughed at him. But after the crowd had been put out, he went in and took her hand, and the girl rose up.
26 The report of this went all over that country.
27 As Jesus passed along from there, he was followed by two blind men who shrieked, "Son of David, have pity on
28 us!" When he went indoors the blind men came up to him, and Jesus asked them, "Do you believe I can do
29 this?" They said, "Yes, sir." Then he touched their eyes and said, "As you believe, so your prayer is granted,"
30 and their eyes were opened. Jesus sternly charged them,
31 "See, nobody is to know of this." But they went out and
32 spread the news of him all over that country. As they went out, a dumb man was brought to him, who was pos-
33 sessed by a daemon, and when the daemon had been cast out, the dumb man spoke. Then the crowd marvelled; they said, "Such a thing has never been seen in Israel!" *
35 Then Jesus made a tour through all the towns and villages, teaching in their synagogues, preaching the gospel of the Reign, and healing every disease and com-

* Ver. 34 ('But the Pharisees said, "He casts out daemons by the prince of daemons" ') is to be omitted, with D, Syr.Sin., the Old Latin, the Diatessaron, etc. It is probably a later insertion from xii. 24 or Mark iii. 22, to prepare for xii. 24 f.

S. MATTHEW X

36 plaint. As he saw the crowds he was moved with pity for them; they were harassed and dejected, like sheep with-
37 out a shepherd. Then he said to his disciples, "The
38 harvest is rich, but the labourers are few; so pray the Lord of the harvest to send labourers to gather his harvest."

10 And summoning his twelve disciples he gave them power over unclean spirits, power to cast them out
2 and also to heal every disease and every ailment. These are the names of the twelve apostles: first Simon (who is called Peter) and Andrew his brother, James the son of
3 Zebedaeus and John his brother, Philip and Bartholomew, Thomas and Matthew the taxgatherer, James the son of Alphaeus and Lebbaeus whose surname is Thaddaeus,
4 Simon the Zealot and Judas Iscariot who betrayed him.
5 These twelve men Jesus despatched with the following
6 instructions, "Do not go among the Gentiles, rather make
7 your way to the lost sheep of the house of Israel. And preach as you go, tell men, 'The Reign of heaven is near.'
8 Heal the sick, raise the dead, cleanse lepers, cast out daemons; give without paying, as you have got without
9 paying; you are not to take gold or silver or coppers in
10 your girdle, nor a wallet for the road, nor two shirts, nor sandals, nor stick—the workman deserves his rations.
11 Whatever town or village you go into, find out a deserving inhabitant and stay with him till you leave.
12 When you enter the house, salute it;
13 if the household is deserving,
let your peace rest on it;
but if the household is undeserving,
let your peace return to you.
14 Whoever will not receive you or listen to your message, leave that house or town and shake off the very dust from
15 your feet. I tell you truly, on the day of judgment it will be more bearable for Sodom and Gomorra than for that town.
16 I am sending you out like sheep among wolves; so be
17 wise like serpents and guileless like doves. Beware of men, they will hand you over to sanhedrins and scourge
18 you in their synagogues, and you will be haled before governors and kings for my sake—it will be a testimony to
19 them and to the Gentiles. Now, when they bring you up for trial, do not trouble yourselves about how to speak or what to say; what you are to say will come to you at the
20 moment, for you are not the speakers, it is the Spirit of
21 your Father that is speaking through you. Brother will betray brother to death, the father will betray his child, *children will rise against their parents and put them to*

22 death, and you will be hated by all men on account of my name; but he will be saved who holds out to the very end.
23 When they persecute you in one town, flee to the next; truly I tell you, you will not have covered the towns of Israel before the Son of man arrives.
24 A scholar is not above his teacher,
nor a servant above his lord;
25 enough for the scholar to fare like his teacher,
and the servant like his lord.
If men have called the master of the house Beelzebul,
how much more will they miscall his servants!
26 Fear them not:—
nothing is veiled that shall not be revealed,
or hidden that shall not be known;
27 what I tell you in the dark, you must utter in the open,
what you hear in a whisper you must proclaim on the housetop.
28 Have no fear of those who kill the body but cannot kill the soul:
rather fear Him who can destroy both soul and body in Gehenna.
29 Are not two sparrows sold for a farthing?
Yet not one of them will fall to the ground unless your Father wills it.
30 The very hairs on your head are all numbered;
31 fear not, then, you are worth far more* than sparrows!
32 Everyone who will acknowledge me before men,
I will acknowledge him before my Father in heaven;
33 and whoever will disown me before men,
I will disown him before my Father in heaven.

34 Do not imagine I have come to bring peace on earth;
I have not come to bring peace but a sword.
35 I have come to set a man *against his father*,
a daughter against her mother,
a daughter-in-law against her mother-in-law;
36 yes, *a man's own household will be his enemies.*
37 He who loves father or mother more than me
is not worthy of me;
he who loves son or daughter more than me
is not worthy of me:
38 he who will not take his cross and follow after me
is not worthy of me.
39 He who has found his life will lose it,
and he who loses his life for my sake will find it.

* The πολλῶν of the text is either a corruption of πολλῷ or, as Wellhausen points out, a mistranslation of the Aramaic equivalent for that. 'The distinction is qualitative, not quantitative.'

40 He who receives you receives me,
and he who receives me receives Him who sent me.
41 He who receives a prophet because he is a prophet,
will receive a prophet's reward;
he who receives a good man because he is good,
will receive a good man's reward.
42 And whoever gives one of these little ones even a cup of
cold water because he is a disciple,
I tell you, he shall not lose his reward."

11 AFTER finishing these instructions to his twelve disciples, Jesus removed from there to teach and preach among their towns.
2 Now when John heard in prison what the Christ was
3 doing, he sent his disciples to ask him, "Are you the Com-
4 ing One? Or are we to look out for someone else?" Jesus answered them, "Go and report to John what you hear and
5 see: *the blind see*, the lame walk, lepers are cleansed, the
6 deaf hear, and the dead are raised.* And blessed is he who
7 is repelled by nothing in me!" As the disciples of John went away, Jesus proceeded to speak to the crowds about John:
"What did you go out to the desert to see?
A reed swayed by the wind?
8 Come, what did you go out to see?
A man arrayed in soft raiment?
The wearers of soft raiment are in royal palaces.
9 Come, why did you go out?
To see a prophet?
Yes, I tell you, and far more than a prophet.
10 This is he of whom it is written,
Here I send my messenger before your face
to prepare the way for you.
11 I tell you truly, no one has arisen among the sons of women who is greater than John the Baptist, and yet the
12 least in the Realm of heaven is greater than he is. From the days of John the Baptist till now the Realm of heaven
13 suffers violence, and the violent press into it. For all the
14 prophets and the law prophesied of it until John:—if you
15 care to believe it, he is the Elijah who is to come. He who has an ear, let him listen to this.
16 But to what shall I compare this generation? It is like children sitting in the marketplace, who call to their playmates,
17 'We piped to you and you would not dance,
we lamented and you would not beat your breasts.'

* Omitting καὶ πτωχοὶ εὐαγγελίζονται, which seems a harmonistic interpolation from Luke vii. 22. Matthew never uses εὐαγγελίζεσθαι.

18   For John has come neither eating nor drinking,
        and men say, 'He has a devil';
19   the Son of man has come eating and drinking,
        and men say, 'Here is a glutton and a drunkard,
          a friend of taxgatherers and sinners!'
      Nevertheless, Wisdom is vindicated by all that she does."
20   Then he proceeded to upbraid the towns where his many miracles had been performed, because they would not re-
21   pent. "Woe to you, Khorazin! Woe to you, Bethsaida! Had the miracles performed in you been performed in Tyre and Sidon, they would have repented long ago in sackcloth
22   and ashes. I tell you this, it will be more bearable for Tyre
23   and Sidon on the day of judgment than for you. And you, O Capharnahum! *Exalted to heaven? No, you will sink to Hades!*—for if the miracles performed in you had been performed in Sodom, Sodom would have lasted to this day.
24   I tell you, it will be more bearable for Sodom on the day of judgment than for you."
25   At that time Jesus spoke and said, "I praise thee, Father, Lord of heaven and earth, for hiding all this from the wise
26   and learned and revealing it to the simpleminded; yes, Father, I praise thee that such was thy chosen purpose.
27   All has been handed over to me by my Father:
        and no one knows the Son except the Father—
        nor does anyone know the Father except the Son,
        and he to whom the Son chooses to reveal him.
28   Come to me, all who are labouring and burdened,
        and I will refresh you.
29   Take my yoke upon you and learn from me,
        for I am gentle and humble in heart,
        and *you will find your souls refreshed;*
30   my yoke is kindly and my burden light."

12 At that time Jesus walked one sabbath through the cornfields, and as his disciples were hungry they
2 started to pull some ears of corn and eat them. When the Pharisees noticed it, they said to him, "Look at your disciples, they are doing what is not allowed on the sabbath."
3 He replied, "Have you not read what David did when he
4 and his men were hungry, how he went into the house of God, and there they ate *the loaves of the Presence* which neither he nor his men were allowed to eat, but only the
5 priests? Have you not read in the Law that the priests in the temple are not guilty when they desecrate the sabbath?
6 I tell you, One is here who is greater than the temple.
7 Besides, if you had known what this meant, *I care for mercy not for sacrifice,* you would not have condemned men

S. MATTHEW XII

8 who are not guilty. For the Son of man is Lord of the sabbath."
9 Then he moved on from there and went into their syn-
10 agogue. Now a man with a withered hand was there; so in order to get a charge against him they asked him, "Is
11 it right to heal on the sabbath?" He said to them, "Is there a man of you with one sheep, who will not catch hold of it
12 and lift it out of a pit on the sabbath, if it falls in? And how much more is a man worth than a sheep? Thus it is
13 right to do a kindness on the sabbath." Then he said to the man, "Stretch out your hand." He stretched it out, and
14 it was quite restored, as sound as the other. So the Pharisees withdrew and plotted against him, to destroy him;
15 but as Jesus knew of it he retired from the spot. Many
16 followed him, and he healed them all, charging them
17 strictly not to make him known—it was for the fulfilment of what had been said by the prophet Isaiah,
18 *Here is my servant whom I have selected,*
my Beloved in whom my soul delights;
I will invest him with my Spirit,
and he will proclaim religion to the Gentiles.
19 *He will not wrangle or shout,*
no one will hear his voice in the streets.
20 *He will not break the bruised reed,*
he will not put out the smouldering flax,
till he carries religion to victory:
21 *and the Gentiles will hope in his name.*
22 Then a blind and dumb demoniac was brought to him, and he healed him, so that the dumb man spoke and saw.
23 And all the crowds were amazed; they said, "Can this be
24 the Son of David?" But when the Pharisees heard of it they said, "This fellow only casts out daemons by Beelzebul
25 the prince of daemons." As Jesus knew what they were thinking, he said to them,
"Any realm divided against itself comes to ruin,
any city or house divided against itself will never stand;
26 and if Satan casts out Satan, he is divided against himself;
how then can his realm stand?
27 Besides, if I cast out daemons by Beelzebul,
by whom do your sons cast them out?
Thus they will be your judges.
28 But if I cast out daemons by the Spirit of God,
then the Reign of God has reached you already.
29 Why, how can anyone enter the strong man's house and plunder his goods, unless he first of all binds the strong man? Then he can plunder his house.

30 He who is not with me is against me,
and he who does not gather with me scatters.
31 I tell you therefore, men will be forgiven any sin and blasphemy,
but they will not be forgiven for blaspheming the Spirit.
32 Whoever says a word against the Son of man will be forgiven,
but whoever speaks against the holy Spirit will never be forgiven,
neither in this world nor in the world to come.
33 Either make the tree good and its fruit good,
or make the tree rotten and its fruit rotten;
for the tree is known by its fruit.
34 You brood of vipers, how can you speak good when you are evil?
For the mouth utters what the heart is full of.
35 The good man brings good out of his good store,
and the evil man brings evil out of his store of evil.
36 I tell you, men will have to account on the day of judgment for every light word they utter;
37 for by your words you will be acquitted,
and by your words you will be condemned."
38 Then some of the scribes and Pharisees said to him,
39 "Teacher, we would like to have some Sign from you." He replied to them,
"It is an evil and disloyal generation that craves a Sign,
but no Sign will be given to it except the Sign of the prophet Jonah;
40 for as Jonah *was three days and three nights in the belly of the whale,*
so the Son of man will be three days and three nights in the heart of the earth.
41 The men of Ninive will rise at the judgment with this generation and condemn it;
for when Jonah preached they did repent,
and here is One greater than Jonah.
42 The queen of the South will rise at the judgment with this generation and condemn it;
for she came from the ends of the earth to listen to the wisdom of Solomon,
and here is One greater than Solomon.
43 When an unclean spirit leaves a man, it roams through
44 dry places in search of refreshment and finds none. Then it says, 'I will go back to the house I left,' and when it comes it finds the house vacant, clean, and all in order.
45 Then it goes off to fetch seven other spirits worse than itself; they go in and dwell there, and the last state of that

man is worse than the first. This is how it will be with the present evil generation."
46 He was still speaking to the crowds when his mother and brothers came and stood outside; they wanted to speak to
48 him.* But he replied to the man who told him this, "Who
49 is my mother? and who are my brothers?" Stretching out his hand towards his disciples he said, "Here are my mother
50 and my brothers! Whoever does the will of my Father in heaven, that is my brother and sister and mother."

13 That same day Jesus went out of the house and seated
2 himself by the seaside; but, as great crowds gathered to him, he entered a boat and sat down, while all the crowd
3 stood on the beach. He spoke at some length to them in
4 parables, saying: "A sower went out to sow, and as he sowed some seeds fell on the road and the birds came and
5 ate them up. Some other seeds fell on stony soil where they had not much earth, and shot up at once because they had
6 no depth of soil; but when the sun rose they got scorched
7 and withered away because they had no root. Some other seeds fell among thorns, and the thorns sprang up and
8 choked them. Some other seeds fell on good soil and bore a crop, some a hundredfold, some sixty, and some thirtyfold.
9 He who has an ear, let him listen to this."
10 Then the disciples came up and said to him, "Why do you
11 speak in parables?" He replied, "Because it is granted you to understand the open secrets of the Realm of heaven, but it is not granted to these people.
12 For he who has, to him shall more be given and richly given,
but whoever has not, from him shall be taken even what he has.
13 This is why I speak to them in parables, because for all their seeing they do not see and for all their hearing they
14 do not hear or understand. In their case the prophecy of Isaiah is being fulfilled:
You will hear and hear but never understand,
you will see and see but never perceive.
15 *For the heart of this people is obtuse,*
their ears are heavy of hearing,
their eyes they have closed,
lest they see with their eyes and hear with their ears,

* Ver. 47, which is rightly omitted by ℵ*BL, the Old Latin and Syriac versions, etc., has been interpolated by an early copyist who wished to prepare for ver. 48 by using the material of Mark iii. 32. It runs thus: "And a man said to him, 'Here are your mother and brothers standing outside and wanting to speak to you.'"

*lest they understand with their heart and turn again
and I cure them.*
16 But blessed are your eyes for they see,
and your ears, for they hear!
17 I tell you truly, many prophets and good men have longed
to see what you see,
but they have not seen it;
and to hear what you hear,
but they have not heard it.
18
19 Now, listen to the parable of the sower. When anyone hears the word of the Realm and does not understand it, the evil one comes and snatches away what has been sown in his heart; that is the man who is sown 'on the road.'
20 As for him who is sown 'on stony soil,' that is the man who hears the word and accepts it at once with enthusiasm;
21 he has no root in himself, he does not last, but when the word brings trouble or persecution he is at once repelled.
22 As for him who is sown 'among thorns,' that is the man who listens to the word, but the worry of the world and the delight of being rich choke the word; so it proves un-
23 fruitful. As for him who is sown 'on good soil,' that is the man who hears the word and understands it; he bears fruit, producing now a hundredfold, now sixty, and now thirty-fold."
24 He put another parable before them. "The Realm of heaven," he said, "is like a man who sowed good seed in
25 his field, but while men slept his enemy came and resowed
26 weeds among the wheat and then went away. When the blade sprouted and formed the kernel, then the weeds ap-
27 peared as well. So the servants of the owner went to him and said, 'Did you not sow good seed in your field, sir?
28 How then does it contain weeds?' He said to them, 'An enemy has done this.' The servants said to him, 'Then
29 would you like us to go and gather them?' 'No,' he said, 'for you might root up the wheat when you were gathering
30 the weeds. Let them both grow side by side till harvest; and at harvest-time I will tell the reapers to gather the weeds first and tie them in bundles to be burnt, but to collect the wheat in my granary.'"
31 He put another parable before them. "The Realm of heaven," he said, "is like a grain of mustard-seed which a
32 man takes and sows in his field. It is less than any seed on earth, but when it grows up it is larger than any plant, it becomes a tree, so large that *the wild birds* come and *roost in its branches.*"
33 He told them another parable. "The Realm of heaven," he said, "is like dough which a woman took and buried in three pecks of flour, till all of it was leavened."

34 Jesus said all this to the crowds in parables; he never
35 spoke to them except in a parable—to fulfil what had been
said by the prophet,
I will open my mouth in parables,
I will speak out what has been hidden since the foundation of the world.
36 Then he left the crowds and went indoors. And his disciples came up to him saying, "Explain to us the parable of
37 the weeds in the field." So he replied, "He who sows the
38 good seed is the Son of man; the field is the world; the good seed means the sons of the Realm; the weeds are the sons
39 of the evil one; the enemy who sowed them is the devil; the harvest is the end of the world, and the reapers are
40 angels. Well then, just as the weeds are gathered and burnt
41 in the fire, so will it be at the end of the world; the Son of man will despatch his angels, and they will gather out of his Realm all who are hindrances and who practise iniquity,
42 and throw them into the furnace of fire; there men will
43 wail and gnash their teeth. Then the just will shine like the sun in the Realm of their Father. He who has an ear, let him listen to this.
44 The Realm of heaven is like treasure hidden in a field; the man who finds it hides it and in his delight goes and sells all he possesses and buys that field.
45 Again, the Realm of heaven is like a trader in search of
46 fine pearls; when he finds a single pearl of high price, he is off to sell all he possesses and buy it.
47 Again, the Realm of heaven is like a net which was
48 thrown into the sea and collected fish of every sort. When it was full, they dragged it to the beach and sitting down they gathered the good fish into vessels but flung away the
49 bad. So will it be at the end of the world. The angels will
50 go out and separate the evil from among the just and fling them into the furnace of fire; there men will wail and gnash their teeth.
51 Have you understood all this?" They said to him, "Yes."
52 So he said to them, "Well then, every scribe who has become a disciple of the Realm of heaven is like a householder who produces what is new and what is old from his stores."
53 Now when Jesus had finished these parables he set out
54 from there, and went to his native place, where he taught the people in the synagogue till they were astounded. They said, "Where did he get this wisdom and these
55 miraculous powers? Is this not the son of the joiner? Is not his mother called Mary, and his brothers James and
56 Joseph and Simon and Judas? Are not his sisters settled
57 here among us? Then where has he got all this?" So they were repelled by him. But Jesus said to them, "A

prophet never goes without honour except in his native
58 place and in his home." There he could not do many miracles owing to their lack of faith.

14 At that time Herod the tetrarch heard about the fame
2 of Jesus. And he said to his servants, "This is John
the Baptist; he has risen from the dead. That is why
miraculous powers are working through him."
3 For Herod had arrested John and bound him and put him
in prison on account of Herodias the wife of his brother
4 Philip, since John had told him, "You have no right to
5 her." He was anxious to kill him but he was afraid of the
6 people, for they held John to be a prophet. However, on
Herod's birthday, the daughter of Herodias danced in public
7 to the delight of Herod; whereupon he promised with an
8 oath to give her whatever she wanted. And she, at the
instigation of her mother, said, "Give me John the Baptist's
9 head this moment on a dish." The king was sorry, but
for the sake of his oath and his guests he ordered it to be
10 given her; he sent and had John beheaded in the prison,
11 his head was brought on a dish and given to the girl, and
12 she took it to her mother. His disciples came and removed
the corpse and buried him; then they went and reported it
to Jesus.
13 When Jesus heard it he withdrew by boat to a desert
place in private; but the crowds heard of it and followed
14 him on foot from the towns. So when he disembarked he
saw a large crowd, and out of pity for them he healed their
15 sick folk. When evening fell, the disciples came up to him
and said, "It is a desert place and the day is now gone;
send off the crowds to buy food for themselves in the vil-
16 lages." Jesus said to them, "They do not need to go away;
17 give them some food yourselves." They said, "We have
18 only five loaves with us and two fish." He said, "Bring
19 them here to me." Then he ordered the crowds to recline
on the grass, and after taking the five loaves and the two
fish he looked up to heaven, blessed them, and after breaking the loaves handed them to the disciples, and the dis-
20 ciples handed them to the crowds. They all ate and had
enough; besides, they picked up the fragments left over and
21 filled twelve baskets with them. The men who ate numbered about five thousand, apart from the women and children.
22 Then he made the disciples embark in the boat and cross
before him to the other side, while he dismissed the crowds;
23 after he had dismissed the crowds he went up the hill by
24 himself to pray. When evening came he was there alone, but
the boat was now in the middle of the sea, buffeted by the

25 waves (for the wind was against them). In the fourth watch
26 of the night he went to them, walking on the sea, but when
the disciples saw him walking on the sea they were terri-
27 fied; "It is a ghost," they said and shrieked for fear. Then
Jesus spoke to them at once; "Courage," he said, "it is I,
28 have no fear." Peter answered him, "Lord, if it is really you,
29 order me to come to you on the water." He said, "Come."
Then Peter got out of the boat and walked over the water
30 on his way to Jesus; but when he saw the strength of the
wind he was afraid and began to sink. "Lord," he shouted,
31 save me." Jesus at once stretched his hand out and caught
him, saying, "How little you trust me! Why did you
32 doubt?" When they got into the boat the wind dropped,
33 and the men in the boat worshipped him, saying, "You are
certainly God's Son."
34
35 On crossing over they came to land at Gennesaret. The
men of that place recognized him and sent all over the
surrounding country, bringing him all who were ill
36 and begging him to let them touch the mere tassel of his
robe—and all who touched it got perfectly well.

15 THEN Pharisees and scribes from Jerusalem came to
2 Jesus, saying, "Why do your disciples transgress the
tradition of the elders? They do not wash their hands
3 when they take their food." He replied, "And why do you
4 transgress the command of God with your traditions? God
enjoined, *Honour your father and mother*, and, *He who*
5 *curses his father or mother is to suffer death.* But you
say, whoever tells his father or mother, 'This money might
have been at your service but it is dedicated to God,'
6 need not honour his father or mother. So you have repealed
7 the law of God to suit your own tradition. You hypocrites! Isaiah made a grand prophecy about you when he
said,
8   *This people honours me with their lips,*
    but their heart is far away from me:
9   *vain is their worship of me,*
    for the doctrines they teach are but human precepts."
10 Then he called the crowd and said to them, "Listen, understand this:
11   it is not what enters a man's mouth that defiles him,
    what defiles a man is what comes out of his mouth."
12 Then the disciples came up and said to him, "Do you know
that the Pharisees have taken offence at what they hear
13 you say?" He replied, "Any plant that my heavenly Father
14 has not planted will be rooted up. Let them alone; they
are blind guides of the blind, and if one blind man leads
15 another, both of them will fall into a pit." Peter answered,

16 Explain this parable to us at anyrate." He said, "And are
17 you totally ignorant? Do you not see how all that enters
the mouth passes into the belly and is then thrown out
18 into the drain, while what comes out of the mouth comes
19 from the heart—and that is what defiles a man. For out
of the heart come evil designs, murder, adultery, sexual
20 vice, stealing, false witness, and slander. That is what
defiles a man; a man is not defiled by eating with hands
unwashed!"
21 Going away from there Jesus withdrew to the district of
22 Tyre and Sidon. And a woman of Canaan came out of these
parts and wailed, "Have pity on me, Lord, O Son of David!
23 My daughter is cruelly possessed by a daemon." But he
made no answer to her. Then his disciples came up and
pressed him, saying, "Send her away, she is wailing behind
24 us." He replied, "It was only to the lost sheep of the house
25 of Israel that I was sent." But she came and knelt before
26 him, saying, "Lord, do help me." He replied, "It is not
fair to take the children's bread and throw it to the dogs."
27 "No, sir," she said, "but even the dogs eat the crumbs that
28 fall from their master's table." At that Jesus replied, "O
woman, you have great faith; your prayer is granted as you
wish." And from that hour her daughter was cured.
29 Then Jesus removed from that country and went along
the sea of Galilee; he went up the hillside and sat there.
30 And large crowds came to him bringing the lame, and the
blind, the dumb, the maimed, and many others; they laid
31 them at his feet, and he healed them. This made the crowd
wonder, to see dumb people speaking,* the lame walking,
32 and the blind seeing. Then Jesus called his disciples and
said, "I am sorry for the crowd; they have been three days
with me now, and they have nothing to eat. I will not
send them away starving, in case they faint on the road."
33 The disciples said to him, "Where are we to get loaves
34 enough in a desert to satisfy such a crowd?" Jesus said to
them, "How many loaves have you got?" They said, "Seven,
35 and some little fish." So he ordered the crowd to recline on
36 the ground. He took the seven loaves and the fish and after
giving thanks he broke them and gave them to the disciples,
37 and the disciples to the crowds. So the people all ate and
were satisfied, and they picked up the fragments left over
38 and filled seven large baskets with them. The men who ate
numbered four thousand, apart from the children and the
39 women. Then he sent the crowd away, got into the boat and
went to the territory of Magadan.

* Leaving out the phrase κυλλοὺς ὑγιεῖς with ℵ, the Latin version, the Old Syriac, Origen, etc. Its insertion for harmonistic reasons is more likely than its omission.

S. MATTHEW XVI

16 Now the Pharisees and Sadducees came up and, in order to tempt him, asked him to show them a Sign
2 from heaven. He replied,
4 "It is an evil and disloyal generation that craves a Sign, and no Sign shall be given to it except the Sign of Jonah."*
Then he left them and went away.
5 When the disciples reached the opposite side, they found
6 they had forgotten to bring any bread. Jesus said to them, "See and beware of the leaven of the Pharisees and Sad-
7 ducees." They argued among themselves, "But we have not
8 brought any bread!" When Jesus noted this he said, "How little trust you have in me! Why all this talk, because you
9 have brought no bread? Do you not understand even yet? Do you not remember the five loaves of the five thousand
10 and how many baskets you took up? And the seven loaves of the four thousand and how many large baskets you took
11 up? Why do you not see that I was not speaking to you about bread? No, beware of the leaven of the Pharisees
12 and Sadducees." Then they realized that what he told them to beware of was not leaven† but the teaching of the Pharisees and Sadducees.
13 Now when Jesus came to the district of Caesarea Philippi he asked his disciples, "Who do people say the
14 Son of man is?" They told him, "Some say John the Baptist, others Elijah, others Jeremiah or one of the prophets."
15 He said to them, "And who do you say I am?" So Simon
16 Peter replied, "You are the Christ, the Son of the living
17 God." Jesus answered him, "You are a blessed man, Simon Bar-jona, for it was my Father in heaven, not flesh and
18 blood, that revealed this to you. Now I tell you, Peter is your name‡ and on this rock I will build my church; the
19 powers of Hades shall not succeed against it. I will give you the keys of the Realm of heaven;

---

* Three uncials (C D W) of the fifth century and several versions, including the Latin and the Syriac (Vulgate), together with the Diatessaron, insert at the beginning of this answer the following:
"When evening comes, you say, 'It will be fine,' for the sky is red; in the morning you say, 'It will be stormy to-day,' for the sky is red and cloudy. You know how to distinguish the look of the sky, but you cannot read the signs of the times."
The majority of the uncials, with the Old Syriac and Origen, rightly omit the passage as irrelevant to the original text.

† Omitting τῶν ἄρτων after ζύμης with strong support from the Old Latin and Syriac versions.

‡ English fails to bring out the play on the Greek word for "rock." The French version reproduces it : "Et moi je te dis aussi que tu es le Pierre, et sur cette pierre je battrai mon église."

whatever you prohibit on earth will be prohibited in heaven,
and whatever you permit on earth will be permitted in heaven."
20 Then he forbade the disciples to tell anyone he was the Christ.
21 From that time Jesus began to show his disciples that he had to leave for Jerusalem and endure great suffering at the hands of the elders and high priests and scribes, and
22 be killed and raised on the third day. Peter took him and began to reprove him for it; "God forbid, Lord," he said,
23 "This must not be." But he turned and said to Peter, "Get behind me, you Satan! You are a hindrance to me! Your
24 outlook is not God's but man's." Then Jesus said to his disciples, "If anyone wishes to come after me, let him deny himself, take up his cross, and to follow me;
25 for whoever wants to save his life will lose it, and whoever loses his life for my sake will find it.
26 What profit will it be if a man gains the whole world and forfeits his own soul? What will a man offer as an equiva-
27 lent for his soul? For the Son of man is coming in the glory of his Father with his angels, and then he will
28 reward everyone for what he has done. I tell you truly, there are some of those standing here who will not taste death till they see the Son of man coming himself to reign."

17 Six days afterwards Jesus took Peter, James and his brother John, and led them up a high hill by them-
2 selves; in their presence he was transfigured, his face shone like the sun, and his clothes turned white as light.
3 There appeared to them Moses and Elijah, who conversed
4 with Jesus. So Peter addressed Jesus and said, "Lord, it is a good thing we are here; if you like, I will put up three tents here, one for you, one for Moses, and one for Elijah."
5 He was still speaking when a bright cloud overshadowed them, and from the cloud a voice said,
"This is my Son, the Beloved,
in him is my delight:
listen to him."
6 When the disciples heard the voice they fell on their faces
7 in terror; but Jesus came forward and touched them, say-
8 ing, "Rise, have no fear." And on raising their eyes they
9 saw no one except Jesus all alone. As they went down the hill Jesus ordered them, "Tell this vision to nobody until
10 the Son of man is raised from the dead." The disciples inquired of him, "Then why do the scribes say that Elijah
11 has to come first?" He replied, "Elijah to come and
12 restore all things? Nay, I tell you Elijah has already

S. MATTHEW XVIII

come, but they have not recognized him—they have worked their will on him. And the Son of man will suffer at their
13 hands in the same way." Then the disciples realized he was speaking to them about John the Baptist.
14 When they reached the crowd, a man came up and knelt
15 to him. "Ah, sir," he said, "have pity on my son; he is an epileptic and he suffers cruelly, he often falls into the fire
16 and often into the water. I brought him to your disciples,
17 but they could not heal him." Jesus answered, "O faithless and perverse generation, how long must I still be with you? How long have I to bear with you? Bring him here
18 to me." So Jesus checked the daemon and it came out of
19 him, and from that hour the boy was healed. Then the disciples came to Jesus in private and said, "Why could
20 we not cast it out?" He said to them, "Because you have so little faith. I tell you truly, if you had faith the size of a grain of mustard-seed, you could say to this hill, 'Move from here to there,' and remove it would; nothing would be impossible for you."
22 When his adherents mustered in Galilee Jesus told them, "The Son of man is to be betrayed into the hands of men,
23 they will kill him, but on the third day he will be raised." They were greatly distressed at this.
24 When they reached Capharnahum, the collectors of the temple-tax came and asked Peter, "Does your teacher not
25 pay the temple-tax?" He said, "Yes." But when he went indoors Jesus spoke first; "Tell me, Simon," he said, "from whom do earthly kings collect customs or taxes? Is it
26 from their own people or from aliens?" "From aliens," he said. Then Jesus said to him, "So their own people are
27 exempt. However, not to give any offence to them, go to the sea, throw a hook in, and take the first fish you bring up. Open its mouth and you will find a five-shilling piece; take that and give it to them for me and for yourself."

2 **18** At that hour the disciples came and asked Jesus, "Who is greatest in the Realm of heaven?" So he
3 called a child, set it among them, and said, "I tell you truly, unless you turn and become like children, you will
4 never get into the Realm of heaven at all. Whoever humbles himself like this child, he is the greatest in the
5 Realm of heaven; and whoever receives a little child like
6 this for my sake, receives me. But whoever is a hindrance to one of these little ones who believe in me, better for him to have a great mill-stone hung round his neck and
7 be sunk in the deep sea. Woe to the world for hindrances! Hindrances have to come, but—woe to the man by whom the hindrance does come!

S. MATTHEW XVIII

8 If your hand or your foot is a hindrance to you, cut it off and throw it away;
better be maimed or crippled and get into Life,
than keep both feet or hands and be thrown into the everlasting fire.
9 If your eye is a hindrance to you, tear it out and throw it away;
better get into Life with one eye
than keep your two eyes and be thrown into the fire of Gehenna.
10 See that you do not despise one of these little ones; for I tell you, their angels in heaven always look on the face of my Father in heaven.
12 Tell me, if a man has a hundred sheep and one of them strays, will he not leave the ninety-nine sheep on the hills
13 and go in search of the one that has strayed? And if he happens to find it, I tell you he rejoices over it more than
14 over the ninety-nine that never went astray. So it is not the will of your Father in heaven that a single one of these little ones should be lost.
15 If your brother sins [against you], go and reprove him, as between you and him alone. If he listens to you, then you
16 have won your brother over; but if he will not listen, take one or two others along with you, so that *every case may be decided on the evidence of two or of three witnesses.*
17 If he refuses to listen to them, tell the church; and if he refuses to listen to the church, treat him as a pagan or a
18 taxgatherer. I tell you truly,
Whatever you prohibit on earth will be prohibited in heaven,
and whatever you permit on earth will be permitted in heaven.
19 I tell you another thing: if two of you agree on earth about anything you pray for, it will be done for you by my
20 Father in heaven. For where two or three have gathered in my name, I am there among them."
21 Then Peter came up and said to him, "Lord, how often is my brother to sin against me and be forgiven? Up to
22 seven times?" Jesus said to him, "Seven times? I say,
23 seventy times seven! That is why the Realm of heaven may be compared to a king who resolved to settle accounts
24 with his servants. When he began the settlement, a debtor
25 was brought in who owed him three million pounds; as he was unable to pay, his master ordered him to be sold, along with his wife and children and all he had, in pay-
26 ment of the sum. So the servant fell down and prayed him, 'Have patience with me, and I will pay you it all.'
27 And out of pity for that servant his master released him

28 and discharged his debt. But as that servant went away, he met one of his fellow-servants who owed him twenty pounds, and seizing him by the throat he said, 'Pay your
29 debt!' So his fellow-servant fell down and implored him,
30 saying, 'Have patience with me, and I will pay you.' But he refused; he went and had him thrown into prison, till
31 he should pay the debt. Now when his fellow-servants saw what had happened they were greatly distressed, and they went and explained to their master all that had happened.
32 Then his master summoned him and said, 'You scoundrel of a servant! I discharged all that debt for you, because
33 you implored me. Ought you not to have had mercy on
34 your fellow-servant, as I had on you?' And in hot anger his master handed him over to the torturers, till he should
35 pay him all the debt. My Father will do the same to you unless you each forgive your brother from the heart."

19 When Jesus finished saying this he moved from Galilee and went to the territory of Judaea that lies
2 across the Jordan. Large crowds followed him and he healed them there.
3 Then the Pharisees came up to tempt him. They asked,
4 "Is it right to divorce one's wife for any reason?" He replied, "Have you never read that He who *created them*
5 *male and female* from the beginning said,
Hence a man shall leave his father and mother,
and cleave to his wife,
and the pair shall be one flesh?
6 So they are no longer two, but one flesh. What God has
7 joined, then, man must not separate." They said to him, "Then why did Moses lay it down that we were to *divorce*
8 *by giving a separation-notice?*" He said to them, "Moses permitted you to divorce your wives, on account of the hardness of your hearts, but it was not so from the begin-
9 ning. I tell you, whoever divorces his wife except for unchastity and marries another woman, commits adultery; and he who marries a divorced woman commits adultery."
10 The disciples said to him, "If that is a man's position with
11 his wife, there is no good in marrying." He said to them, "True, but this truth is not practicable for everyone, it is only for those who have the gift.
12 There are eunuchs who have been eunuchs from their birth,
there are eunuchs who have been made eunuchs by men,
and there are eunuchs who have made themselves eunuchs for the sake of the Realm of heaven.
Let anyone practice it for whom it is practicable."
13 Then children were brought to him that he might lay his hands on them and pray over them. The disciples

S. MATTHEW XX

14 checked the people, but Jesus said to them, "Let the children alone, do not stop them from coming to me; the
15 Realm of heaven belongs to such as these." Then he laid his hands on them and went upon his way.
16 Up came a man and said to him, "Teacher, what good
17 deed must I do to gain life eternal?" He said to him, "Why do you ask me about what is good? One alone is good. But if you want to get into Life, keep the com-
18 mands." "Which?" he said. Jesus answered, "The commands, *you shall not kill, you shall not commit adultery,*
19 *you shall not steal, you shall not bear false witness, honour your father and mother,* and *you must love your neighbour*
20 *as yourself.*" The young man said, "I have observed all
21 these. What more is wanting?" Jesus said to him, "If you want to be perfect, go and sell your property, give the money to the poor and you shall have treasure in heaven;
22 then come and follow me." When the young man heard that, he went sadly away, for he had great possessions.
23 And Jesus said to his disciples, "I tell you truly, it will be difficult for a rich man to get into the Realm of heaven.
24 I tell you again, it is easier for a camel to get through a needle's eye than for a rich man to get into the Realm of
25 God." When the disciples heard this they were utterly astounded; they said, "Who then can possibly be saved?"
26 Jesus looked at them and said, "This is impossible for men,
27 but anything is possible for God." Then Peter replied, "Well, we have left our all and followed you. Now what
28 are we to get?" Jesus said to them, "I tell you truly, in the new world, when the Son of man shall sit on the throne of his glory, you who have followed me shall also sit on twelve
29 thrones to govern the twelve tribes of Israel. Everyone who has left brothers or sisters or father or mother or wife or children or lands or houses for my name's sake will get a hundred times as much and inherit life eternal.
30 Many who are first shall be last, and many who are last shall be first.

20 For the Realm of heaven is like a householder who went out early in the morning to hire labourers for
2 his vineyard; and after agreeing with the labourers to pay them a shilling a day he sent them into his vineyard.
3 Then, on going out at nine o'clock he noticed some other
4 labourers standing in the marketplace doing nothing; to them he said, 'You go into the vineyard too, and I will give
5 you whatever wage is fair.' So they went in. Going out again at twelve o'clock and at three o'clock, he did the
6 same thing. And when he went out at five o'clock he came upon some others who were standing; he said to them,
7 'Why have you stood doing nothing all the day?' 'Because

S. MATTHEW XX

nobody hired us,' they said. He told them, 'You go into
8 the vineyard too.' Now when evening came the master
of the vineyard said to his bailiff, 'Summon the labourers
and pay them their wages, beginning with the last
9 and going on to the first.'* When those who had been
10 hired about five o'clock came, they got a shilling each. So
when the first labourers came up, they supposed they would
11 get more; but they too got each their shilling. And on
12 getting it they grumbled at the householder. 'These last,'
they said, 'have only worked a single hour, and yet you
have ranked them equal to us who have borne the brunt
13 of the day's work and the heat!' Then he replied to one
of them, 'My man, I am not wronging you. Did you not
14 agree with me for a shilling? Take what belongs to you
and be off. I choose to give this last man the same as you.
15 Can I not do as I please with what belongs to me? Have
16 you a grudge because I am generous?' So shall the last
be first and the first last."
17 Now as Jesus was about to go up to Jerusalem he took
the twelve aside by themselves and said to them as they
18 were on the road, "We are going up to Jerusalem, and the
Son of man will be betrayed to the high priests and
19 scribes; they will sentence him to death and hand him
over to the Gentiles to be mocked and scourged and crucified; then on the third day he will be raised."
20 Then the mother of the sons of Zebedaeus came up to
21 him with her sons, praying him for a favour. He said to
her, "What do you want?" She said, "Give orders that my
two sons are to sit at your right hand and at your left in
22 your Realm." Jesus replied, "You do not know what you
are asking. Can you drink the cup I am going to drink?"
23 They said to him, "We can." "You shall drink my cup,"
said Jesus, "but it is not for me to grant seats at my right
hand and at my left; these belong to the men for whom
24 they have been destined by my Father." When the ten
25 heard of this, they were angry at the two brothers; but
Jesus called them and said,
"You know the rulers of the Gentiles lord it over them,
and their great men overbear them:
26   not so with you.
Whoever wants to be great among you must be your
    servant,
27 and whoever wants to be first among you must be your
    slave;
28 just as the Son of man has not come to be served but to
    serve,
and to give his life as a ransom for many."

* Note the connexion between this parable (ver. 16) and xix. 30.

29 As they were leaving Jericho a crowd followed him,
30 and when two blind men who were sitting beside the road heard Jesus was passing, they shouted, "O Lord, Son of
31 David, have pity on us!" The crowd checked them and told them to be quiet, but they shouted all the louder, "O
32 Lord, Son of David, have pity on us!" So Jesus stopped and called them. He said, "What do you want me to do
33 for you?" "Lord," they said, "we want our eyes opened."
34 Then Jesus in pity touched their eyes, and they regained their sight at once and followed him.

21 WHEN they came near Jerusalem and had reached Bethphage at the Hill of Olives, then Jesus des-
2 patched two disciples, saying to them, "Go to the village in front of you and you will at once find an ass tethered with a colt alongside of her; untether them and bring
3 them to me. If anyone says anything to you, you will say that the Lord needs them; then he will at once let them
4 go." This took place for the fulfilment of what had been spoken by the prophet,
5 *Tell the daughter of Sion,*
  'Here is your king coming to you,
  He is gentle and mounted on an ass,
  And on a colt the foal of a beast of burden.'
6 So the disciples went and did as Jesus told them;
7 they brought the ass and the colt and put their clothes on
8 them. Jesus seated himself on them, and the greater part of the crowd spread their clothes on the road, while others cut branches from the trees and strewed them on the road.
9 And the crowds who went in front of him and who followed behind shouted,
  "Hosanna to the Son of David!
  Blessed be he who comes in the Lord's name!
  Hosanna in high heaven!"
10 When he entered Jerusalem the whole city was in excite-
11 ment over him. "Who is this?" they said, and the crowds replied, "This is the prophet Jesus from Nazaret in Gali-
12 lee!" Then Jesus went into the temple of God and drove out all who were buying and selling inside the temple; he upset the tables of the money-changers and the stalls
13 of those who sold doves, and told them, "It is written, *My house shall be called a house of prayer*, but you make it *a den of robbers.*"
14 Blind and lame people came up to him in the temple and
15 he healed them. But when the high priests and scribes saw his wonderful deeds and saw the children who shouted in the temple, "Hosanna to the Son of David!" they were
16 indignant; they said to him, "Do you hear what they are

S. MATTHEW XXI 35

saying?" "Yes," said Jesus, "have you never read *Thou hast brought praise to perfection from the mouth of babes* 17 *and sucklings?*" Then he left them and went outside the city to Bethany, where he spent the night.
18 In the morning as he came back to the city he felt 19 hungry, and noticing a fig tree by the roadside he went up to it, but found nothing on it except leaves. He said to it, "May no fruit ever come from you after this!" And 20 instantly the fig tree withered up. When the disciples saw this they marvelled. "How did the fig tree wither 21 up in an instant?" they said. Jesus answered, "I tell you truly, if you have faith, if you have no doubt, you will not only do what has been done to the fig tree but even if you say to this hill, 'Take and throw yourself into the 22 sea,' it will be done. All that ever you ask in prayer you shall have, if you believe."
23 When he entered the temple, the high priests and elders of the people came up to him as he was teaching, and said, "What authority have you for acting in this way? Who 24 gave you this authority?" Jesus replied, "Well, I will ask you a question, and if you answer me, then I will tell 25 you what authority I have for acting as I do. Where did the baptism of John come from? From heaven or from men?" Now they argued to themselves, "If we say, 'From heaven,' he will say to us, 'Then why did you not believe 26 him?' And if we say, 'From men,' we are afraid of the 27 crowd, for they all hold that John was a prophet." So they answered Jesus, "We do not know." He said to them, "No more will I tell you what authority I have for acting 28 as I do. Tell me what you think. A man had two sons. He went to the first and said, 'Son, go and work in the 29 vineyard to-day'; he replied, 'I will go, sir,' but he did not 30 go. The man went to the second and said the same to him; he replied, 'I will not,' but afterwards he changed his 31 mind and did go. Which of the two did the will of the father?" They said, "The last." Jesus said to them, "I tell you truly, the taxgatherers and harlots are going into 32 the Realm of God before you. For John showed you the way to be good and you would not believe him; the taxgatherers and harlots believed him, and even though you saw that, you would not change your mind afterwards and believe him.
33 Listen to another parable. There was a householder who *planted a vineyard, put a fence round it, dug a wine-vat inside it, and built a watchtower:* then he leased it to vine-34 dressers and went abroad. When the fruit-season was near, he sent his servants to the vinedressers to collect his 35 fruit; but the vinedressers took his servants and flogged

S. MATTHEW XXII

36 one, killed another, and stoned a third. Once more he sent some other servants, more than he had sent at first,
37 and they did the same to them. Afterwards he sent them
38 his son; 'They will respect my son,' he said. But when the vinedressers saw his son they said to themselves, 'Here is the heir; come on, let us kill him and seize his inherit-
39 ance!' So they took and threw him outside the vineyard
40 and killed him. Now, when the owner of the vineyard
41 comes, what will he do to these vinedressers?" They replied, "He will utterly destroy the wretches and lease the vineyard to other vinedressers who will give him the
42 fruits in their season." Jesus said to them, "Have you never read in the scriptures,

The stone that the builders rejected
is the chief stone now of the corner:
this is the doing of the Lord,
and a wonder to our eyes?

43 I tell you therefore that the Realm of God will be taken from you and given to a nation that bears the fruits of the Realm.
44 [Everyone who falls on this stone will be shattered, and whoever it falls upon will be crushed.]"
45 When the high priests and Pharisees heard these parables
46 they knew he was speaking about them; they tried to get hold of him, but they were afraid of the crowds, as the crowds held him to be a prophet.

22 2 THEN Jesus again addressed them in parables. "The Realm of heaven," he said, "may be compared to a king who gave a marriage-banquet in honour of his son.
3 He sent his servants to summon the invited guests to the
4 feast, but they would not come. Once more he sent some other servants, saying, 'Tell the invited guests, here is my supper all prepared, my oxen and fat cattle are killed,
5 everything is ready; come to the marriage-banquet.' But they paid no attention and went off, one to his estate,
6 another to his business, while the rest seized his servants
7 and ill-treated them and killed them. The king was enraged; he sent his troops and destroyed those murderers
8 and burned up their city. Then he said to his servants, 'The marriage-banquet is all ready, but the invited guests
9 did not deserve it. So go to the byeways and invite anyone
10 you meet to the marriage-banquet.' And those servants went out on the roads and gathered all they met, bad and good alike. Thus the marriage-banquet was supplied
11 with guests. Now when the king came in to view his guests, he saw a man there who was not dressed in a
12 wedding-robe. So he said to him, 'My man, how did you

S. MATTHEW XXII

get in here without a wedding-robe?' The man was speech-
13 less. Then said the king to his servants, 'Take him hand
and foot, and throw him outside, out into the darkness;
14 there men will wail and gnash their teeth. For many
are invited but few are chosen.'"
15 Then the Pharisees went and plotted to trap him in talk.
16 They sent him their disciples with the Herodians, who
said, "Teacher, we know you are sincere and that you
teach the Way of God honestly and fearlessly; you do not
17 court human favour. Tell us, then, what you think about
18 this. Is it right to pay taxes to Caesar or not?" But
Jesus detected their malice. He said, "Why do you tempt
19 me, you hypocrites? Show me the coin for taxes." So
20 they brought him a shilling. Then Jesus said to them,
"Whose likeness, whose inscription is this?" "Caesar's,"
21 they said. Then he told them, "Give Caesar what belongs
22 to Caesar, give God what belongs to God." When they
heard that they marvelled; then they left him and went
away.
23 That same day some Sadducees came up to him, men who
24 hold there is no resurrection. They put this question to
24 him: "Teacher, Moses said that *if anyone dies without children, his brother is to espouse his wife and raise offspring
25 for his brother.* Now there were seven brothers in our number. The first married and died; as he had no children he
26 left his wife to his brother. The same happened with the
27 second and the third, down to the seventh. After them all,
28 the woman died. Now at the resurrection whose wife will
29 she be? They all had her." Jesus answered them, "You
go wrong because you understand neither the scriptures
30 nor the power of God. At the resurrection people neither
marry nor are married, they are like the angels of God in
31 heaven. And as for the resurrection of the dead, have you
32 not read what was said to you by God, *I am the God of
Abraham and the God of Isaac and the God of Jacob?* He
33 is not a God of dead people but of living." And when the
crowds heard it, they were astounded at his teaching.
34 When the Pharisees heard he had silenced the Sadducees,
35 they mustered their forces, and one of them, a jurist, put
36 a question in order to tempt him. "Teacher," he said, "what
37 is the greatest command in the Law?" He replied, "*You
must love the Lord your God with your whole heart, with
38 your whole soul, and with your whole mind.* This is the
39 greatest and chief command. There is a second like it: *you
40 must love your neighbour as yourself.* The whole Law
and the prophets hang upon these two commands."
41 As the Pharisees had mustered, Jesus put a question to
42 them. "Tell me," he said, "what you think about the Christ.

43 Whose son is he?" They said to him, "David's." He said to them, "How is it then that David in the Spirit calls him *Lord?*
44   *The Lord said to my Lord, 'Sit at my right hand,*
      till I put your enemies under your feet.'
45
46 If David calls him *Lord,* how can he be his son?" No one could make any answer to him, and from that day no one ventured to put another question to him.

23 Then Jesus spoke to the crowds and to his disciples.
2 "The scribes and Pharisees sit on the seat of Moses;
3 so do whatever they tell you, obey them, but do not do as
4 they do. They talk but they do not act. They make up heavy loads and lay them on men's shoulders but they will
5 not stir a finger to remove them. Besides, all they do is done to catch the notice of men; they make their phylac-
6 teries broad, they wear large tassels, they are fond of the best places at banquets and the front seats in the syna-
7 gogues; they like to be saluted in the marketplaces and to be called 'rabbi' by men.
8   But you are not to be called 'rabbi,'
    for One is your teacher, and you are all brothers;
9   you are not to call anyone 'father' on earth,
    for One is your heavenly Father;
10 nor must you be called 'leaders,'
    for One is your leader, even the Christ.
11 He who is greatest among you must be your servant.
12 Whoever uplifts himself will be humbled,
    and whoever humbles himself will be uplifted.
13 Woe to you, you impious scribes and Pharisees!
    you shut the Realm of heaven in men's faces;
    you neither enter yourselves,
    nor will you let those enter who are on the point of entering.
15 Woe to you, you impious scribes and Pharisees!
    you traverse sea and land to make a single proselyte,
    and when you succeed you make him a son of Gehenna twice as bad as yourselves.
16 Woe to you, blind guides that you are!
    you say, 'Swear by the sanctuary, and it means nothing;
    but swear by the gold of the sanctuary, and the oath is binding.'
17   You are senseless and blind! for which is the greater,
    the gold or the sanctuary that makes the gold sacred?
18   You say again, 'Swear by the altar, and it means nothing;
    but swear by the gift upon it, and the oath is binding.'
19   You are blind! for which is the greater,

S. MATTHEW XXIII

the gift or the altar that makes the gift sacred?
20 He who swears by the altar
swears by it and by all that lies on it;
21 he who swears by the sanctuary
swears by it and by Him who inhabits it;
22 he who swears by heaven
swears by the throne of God and by Him who sits upon it.
23 Woe to you, you impious scribes and Pharisees!
you tithe mint and dill and cummin,
and omit the weightier matters of the law,
justice and mercy and faithfulness;
these latter you ought to have practised—without omitting the former.
24 Blind guides that you are,
filtering away the gnat and swallowing the camel!
25 Woe to you, you irreligious scribes and Pharisees!
you clean the outside of the cup and the plate,
but inside they are filled with your rapacity and self-indulgence.
26 Blind Pharisee! first clean the inside of the cup,
so that the outside may be clean as well.
27 Woe to you, you irreligious scribes and Pharisees!
you are like tombs white-washed;
they look comely on the outside,
but inside they are full of dead men's bones and all manner of impurity.
28 So to men you seem just,
but inside you are full of hypocrisy and iniquity.
29 Woe to you, you irreligious scribes and Pharisees! You build tombs for the prophets and decorate the tombs of the
30 just, and you say 'If we had been living in the days of our fathers, we would not have joined them in shedding the
31 blood of the prophets.' So you are witnesses against yourselves, that you are sons of those who killed the prophets!
32 And you will fill up* the measure that your fathers filled.
33 You serpents! you brood of vipers! how can you escape
34 being sentenced to Gehenna? This is why I will send you prophets, wise men, and scribes, some of whom you will kill and crucify, some of whom you will flog in your synagogues
35 and persecute from town to town; it is that on you may fall the punishment for all the just blood shed on earth from the blood of Abel the just down to the blood of Zechariah the son of Barachiah, whom you murdered be-
36 tween the sanctuary and the altar. I tell you truly, it will all come upon this generation.

* Reading πληρώσετε with B, Syr.Sin.

37 O Jerusalem, Jerusalem! slaying the prophets and stoning those who have been sent to you! How often I would fain have gathered your children as a fowl gathers her
38 brood under her wings! But you would not have it! See,
39 *your House is left to you, desolate.* For I tell you, you will never see me again till you say, *Blessed be he who comes in the Lord's name."*

24 So Jesus left the temple and went on his way. His disciples came forward to point out to him the temple-
2 buildings, but he replied to them, "You see all this? I tell you truly, not a stone here will be left upon another, without being torn down."
3 So as he sat on the Hill of Olives the disciples came up to him in private and said, "Tell us, when will this happen? What will be the sign of your arrival and of the end of the
4 world?" Jesus replied, "Take care that no one misleads
5 you; for many will come in my name, saying 'I am the
6 Christ,' and they will mislead many. You will hear of wars and rumours of wars; see and do not be alarmed. *These*
7 *have to come,* but it is not the end yet. For *nation will rise against nation, and realm against realm;* there will be
8 famines and earthquakes here and there. All that is but
9 the beginning of the trouble. Then men will hand you over to suffer affliction, and they will kill you; you will be hated
10 by all the Gentiles on account of my name. And *many will be repelled* then, they will betray one another and hate one
11 another. Many false prophets will rise and mislead
12 many. And in most of you love will grow cold by the in-
13 crease of iniquity; but he will be saved who holds out to
14 the very end. This gospel of the Reign shall be preached all over the wide world as a testimony to all the Gentiles, and then the end will come.
15 So when you see *the appalling Horror* spoken of by the prophet Daniel, standing erect *in the holy place* (let the
16 reader note this), then let those who are in Judaea fly to
17 the hills; a man on the housetop must not go down to fetch
18 what is inside his house, and a man in the field must not
19 turn back to get his coat. Woe to women with child and to
20 women who give suck in those days! Pray that you may
21 not have to fly in winter or on the sabbath, for there will be *sore misery* then, *such as has never been from the begin-*
22 *ning of the world till now*—no and never shall be. Had not those days been cut short, not a soul would be saved alive; however, for the sake of the elect, those days will be cut short.
23 If anyone tells you at that time, 'Here is the Christ!' or,
24 'there he is!' do not believe it; for false Christs and *false*

S. MATTHEW XXIV

prophets will rise and *bring forward great* signs and *wonders,* so as to mislead the very elect,—if that were pos-
25 sible. (I am telling you this beforehand.)
26   If they tell you, 'Here he is in the desert,'
      do not go out;
      'here he is in the chamber,'
      do not believe it.
27   For like lightning that shoots from east to west,
      so will be the arrival of the Son of man.
28   Wherever the body lies,
      there will the vultures gather.
29   Immediately after the misery of those days
      the sun will be darkened,
      and the moon will not yield her light,
      the stars will drop from heaven
      and the orbs of the heavens will be shaken.
30 Then the Sign of the Son of man will appear in heaven; then *all tribes on earth* will wail, they will see *the Son of man coming on the clouds of heaven* with great power and
31 glory. He will despatch his angels *with a loud trumpet-call to muster* his elect *from the four winds, from the verge of heaven to the verge of earth.*
32   Let the fig tree teach you a parable. As soon as its branches turn soft and put out leaves, you know summer is
33 at hand; so, whenever you see all this happen, you may be sure He is at hand, at the very door.
34   I tell you truly, the present generation will not pass away
35 till all this happens. Heaven and earth will pass away, but my words will never pass away.
36   Now no one knows anything about that day or hour, not
37 even the angels in heaven, but only my Father. As were the days of Noah, so will the arrival of the Son of man be.
38 For as in the days before the deluge people ate and drank, married and were married, till the day *Noah entered the*
39 *ark;* and as they knew nothing till the deluge came and swept them all away; so will the arrival of the Son of man be.
40   Then there will be two men in the field,
      one will be taken and one will be left;
41   two women will be grinding at the millstone,
      one will be taken and one will be left.
42 Keep on the watch then, for you never know what day your
43 Lord will come. But be sure of this, that if the householder had known at what watch in the night the thief was com-ing, he would have been on the watch, he would not have
44 allowed his house to be broken into. So be ready your-selves, for the Son of man is coming at an hour you do not expect.

45 Now where is the trusty and thoughtful servant, whom his lord and master has set over his household to assign
46 them their supplies at the proper time? Blessed is that servant if his lord and master finds him so doing when he
47 arrives! I tell you truly, he will set him over all his prop-
48 erty. But if the* bad servant says to himself, 'My lord and
49 master is long of coming,' and if he starts to beat his fel-
50 low-servants and to eat and drink with drunkards, that servant's lord and master will arrive on a day when he does not expect him and at an hour which he does not know;
51 he will cut him in two and assign him the fate of the hypocrites. There men will wail and gnash their teeth.

25 Then shall the Realm of heaven be compared to ten maidens who took their lamps and went out to meet
2 the bridegroom and the bride. † Five of them were stupid
3 and five were sensible. For although the stupid took their
4 lamps, they took no oil with them, whereas the sensible
5 took oil in their vessels as well as their lamps. As the bridegroom was long of coming, they all grew drowsy and
6 went to sleep. But at midnight the cry arose, 'Here is the
7 bridegroom! Come out to meet him!' Then all the maidens
8 rose and trimmed their lamps. The stupid said to the sensible, 'Give us some of your oil, for our lamps are going
9 out.' But the sensible replied, 'No, there may not be enough for us and for you. Better go to the dealers and buy for
10 yourselves.' Now while they were away buying oil, the bridegroom arrived; those maidens who were ready accompanied him to the marriage-banquet, and the door was shut.
11 Afterwards the rest of the maidens came and said, 'Oh sir,
12 oh sir, open the door for us!' but he replied, 'I tell you
13 frankly, I do not know you.' Keep on the watch then, for you know neither the day nor the hour.
14 For the case is that of a man going abroad, who summoned his servants and handed over his property to them;
15 to one he gave twelve hundred pounds, to another five hundred, and to another two hundred and fifty; each got according to his capacity. Then the man went abroad.
16 The servant who had got the twelve hundred pounds at once went and traded with them, making another twelve hundred.
17 Similarly the servant who had got the five hundred pounds
18 made another five hundred. But the servant who had got the two hundred and fifty pounds went off and dug a hole

* Omitting [ἐκεῖνος], a harmonistic gloss from Luke xii. 45.

† The words καὶ τῆς νύμφης are added by D X*, the Latin and Syriac versions, etc. Their omission may have been due to the feeling of the later church that Jesus as the Bridegroom ought alone to be mentioned.

S. MATTHEW XXV 43

19 in the ground and hid his master's money. Now a long time afterwards the master of those servants came back and
20 settled accounts with them. Then the servant who had got the twelve hundred pounds came forward, bringing twelve hundred more; he said, 'You handed me twelve hundred pounds, sir; here I have gained another twelve hundred.'
21 His master said to him, 'Capital, you excellent and trusty servant! You have been trusty in charge of a small sum: I will put you in charge of a large sum. Come and share
22 your master's feast.' Then the servant with the five hundred pounds came forward. He said, 'You handed me five hundred pounds, sir; here I have gained another
23 five hundred.' His master said to him, 'Capital, you excellent and trusty servant! You have been trusty in charge of a small sum: I will put you in charge of a
24 large sum. Come and share your master's feast.' Then the servant who had got the two hundred and fifty pounds came forward. He said, 'I knew you were a hard man, sir, reaping where you never sowed and gathering
25 where you never winnowed. So I was afraid; I went and hid your two hundred and fifty pounds in the earth.
26 There's your money!' His master said to him in reply, 'You rascal, you idle servant! You knew, did you, that I reap where I have never sowed and gather where I have never
27 winnowed! Well then, you should have handed my money to the bankers and I would have got my capital with inter-
28 est when I came back. Take therefore the two hundred and fifty pounds away from him, give it to the servant who had the twelve hundred.
29 For to everyone who has shall more be given and richly given;
but from him who has nothing, even what he has shall be taken.
30 Throw the good-for-nothing servant into the darkness outside; there men will wail and gnash their teeth.
31 When the Son of man comes in his glory and *all the angels with him*, then he will sit on the throne of his glory,
32 and all nations will be gathered in front of him; he will separate them one from another, as a shepherd separates
33 the sheep from the goats, setting the sheep on his right
34 hand and the goats on his left. Then shall the King say to those on his right, 'Come, you whom my Father has blessed, come into your inheritance in the realm prepared for you from the foundation of the world.
35 For I was hungry and you fed me,
I was thirsty and you gave me drink,
I was a stranger and you entertained me,
36 I was unclothed and you clothed me,

I was ill and you looked after me,
I was in prison and you visited me.'
37 Then the just will answer,
'Lord, when did we see you hungry and fed you? or thirsty and gave you drink?
38 when did we see you a stranger and entertain you? or unclothed and clothed you?
39 when did we see you ill or in prison and visit you?'
40 The King will answer them, 'I tell you truly, in so far as you did it to one of these brothers of mine, even to the least
41 of them, you did it to me.' Then he will say to those on the left, 'Begone from me, you accursed ones, to the eternal fire which has been prepared for the devil and his angels!
42 For I was hungry but you never fed me,
I was thirsty but you never gave me drink,
43 I was a stranger but you never entertained me,
I was unclothed but you never clothed me,
I was ill and in prison but you never looked after me.'
44 Then they will answer too, 'Lord, when did we ever see you hungry or thirsty or a stranger or unclothed or ill or
45 in prison, and did not minister to you?' Then he will answer them, 'I tell you truly, in so far as you did not do it to one of these, even the least of them, you did not do it to me.'
46 So they shall depart to eternal punishment,
and the just to eternal life."

26 WHEN Jesus finished saying all this he said to his
2 disciples, "You know the passover is to be held two days after this; and the Son of man will be delivered up to be crucified."
3 Then the high priests and the elders of the people met in the palace of the high priest who was called Caiaphas
4 and took counsel together to get hold of Jesus by craft and
5 have him put to death. "Only," they said, "it must not be during the festival, in case of a riot among the people."
6 Now when Jesus was at Bethany in the house of Simon
7 the leper, a woman came up to him with an alabaster flask of expensive perfume which she poured over his head as
8 he lay at table. When the disciples saw this they were
9 angry. "What is the use of this waste?" they said; "the perfume might have been sold for a good sum, and the poor
10 might have got that." But Jesus was aware of what they said, and he replied, "Why are you annoying the woman?
11 It is a beautiful thing she has done to me. The poor you always have beside you, but you will not always have me.
12 In pouring this perfume on my body she has acted in view
13 of my burial. I tell you truly, wherever this gospel is

preached through all the world, men will speak of what she has done in memory of her."
14 Then one of the twelve called Judas Iscariot went
15 and said to the high priests, "What will you give me for betraying him to you?" And *they weighed out for him thirty*
16 *silver pieces.* From that moment he sought a good opportunity to betray him.
17 On the first day of unleavened bread the disciples of Jesus came up and said to him, "Where do you want us to prepare
18 for you to eat the passover?" He said, "Go into the city to so-and-so; tell him that the Teacher says, 'My time is near, I will celebrate the passover at your house with my dis-
19 ciples.'" So the disciples did as Jesus had told them and
20 prepared the passover. When evening came he lay at table
21 with the disciples, and as they were eating he said, "One
22 of you is going to betray me." They were greatly distressed at this, and each of them said to him, "Lord, surely it is
23 not me." He answered, "One who has dipped his hand into
24 the same dish as myself is going to betray me. The Son of man goes the road that the scripture has described for him, but woe to the man by whom the Son of man is betrayed!
25 Better that man had never been born!" Then Judas his betrayer said, "Surely it is not me, rabbi?" He said to him, "Is it not?"
26 As they were eating he took a loaf and after the blessing he broke it; then he gave it to the disciples saying, "Take
27 and eat this, it means my body." He also took a cup and after thanking God he gave it to them saying, "Drink of
28 it, all of you; this means my blood, the new *covenant-blood*,
29 shed for many, to win the remission of their sins. I tell you, after this I will never drink this produce of the vine till the day I drink it new with you in the Realm of my Father."
30 After the hymn of praise they went out to the Hill of
31 Olives. Then Jesus said to them, "You will all be disconcerted over me to-night; for it is written, *I will strike at the shepherd and the sheep of the flock will be scattered.*
32
33 But after my rising I will precede you to Galilee." Peter answered, "Supposing they are all disconcerted over you,
34 I will not be disconcerted." Jesus said to him, "I tell you truly, you will disown me three times this very night,
35 before the cock crows." Peter said to him, "Even though I have to die with you, I will never disown you." And all the disciples said the same thing.
36 Then Jesus came with them to a place called Gethsemane, and he told the disciples, "Sit here till I go over there and
37 pray." But he took Peter and the two sons of Zebedaeus along with him; and when he began to feel distressed and

38 agitated, he said to them, "*My heart is sad*, sad even to
39 death; stay here and watch with me." Then he went forward a little and fell on his face praying, "My father, if it is possible, let this cup pass me. Yet, not what I will but
40 what thou wilt." Then he went to the disciples and found them asleep; and he said to Peter, "So the three of you could
41 not watch with me for a single hour? Watch and pray, all of you, so that you may not slip into temptation. The
42 spirit is eager but the flesh is weak." Again he went away for the second time and prayed, "My Father, if this cup
43 cannot pass unless I drink it, thy will be done." And when he returned he found them asleep again, for their eyes
44 were heavy. So he left them and went back for the third
45 time, praying in the same words as before. Then he went to the disciples and said to them, "Still asleep? still resting? The hour is near, the Son of man is betrayed into the
46 hands of sinners. Come, get up and let us go. Here is my
47 betrayer close at hand!" While he was still speaking, up came Judas, one of the twelve, accompanied by a large mob with swords and clubs who had come from the high priests
48 and the elders of the people. Now his betrayer had given them a signal; he said, "Whoever I kiss, that is the man."
49 So he went up at once to Jesus; "Hail, rabbi!" he said, and
50 kissed him. Jesus said, "My man, do your errand." Then
51 they laid hands on Jesus and seized him. One of his companions put out his hand, drew his sword, and struck the
52 servant of the high priest, cutting off his ear. Then Jesus said to him, "Put your sword back into its place; all who
53 draw the sword shall die by the sword. What! do you think I cannot appeal to my Father to furnish me at this moment
54 with over twelve legions of angels? Only, how could the scriptures be fulfilled then—the scriptures that say this
55 must be so?" At that hour Jesus said to the crowds, "Have you sallied out to arrest me like a robber, with swords and clubs? Day after day I sat in the temple teaching, and you
56 never seized me. However, this has all happened for the fulfilment of the prophetic scriptures!"
57 Then all the disciples left him and fled; but those who had seized Jesus took him away to the house of Caiaphas the high priest, where the scribes and elders had gathered.
58 Peter followed him at a distance as far as the courtyard of the high priest, and when he got inside he sat down beside the attendants to see the end.
59 Now the high priests and the whole of the Sanhedrin tried to secure false witness against Jesus, in order to have him
60 put to death; but they could find none, although a number of false witnesses came forward. However, two men came
61 forward at last and said, "This fellow declared, 'I can

destroy the temple of God and build it in three days.'"
62 So the high priest rose and said to him, "Have you no reply
63 to make? What of this evidence against you?" Jesus said
nothing. Then the high priest addressed him, "I adjure you
by the living God, tell us if you are the Christ, the Son of
64 God!" Jesus said to him, "Even so! But I tell you, in future
you will all see *the Son of man seated at the right hand* of the
65 *Power, and coming on the clouds of heaven.*" Then the
high priest tore his dress and cried, "He has blasphemed!
What more evidence do we want? Look, you have heard
66 his blasphemy for yourselves! What is your view?" They
67 replied, "He is doomed to death." Then they spat in his
face and buffeted him, some of them cuffing him and crying,
68 "Prophesy to us, you Christ! tell us who struck you!"
69 Now Peter was sitting outside in the courtyard. A maidservant came up and said to him, "You were with Jesus the
70 Galilean too." But he denied it before them all. "I do not
71 know what you mean," he said. When he went out to the
gateway another maidservant noticed him and said to those
who were there, "This fellow was with Jesus the Nazarene."
72 Again he denied it; he swore, "I do not know the man."
73 After a little the bystanders came up and said to Peter,
"To be sure, you are one of them too. Why, your accent
74 betrays you!" At this he broke out cursing and swearing,
"I do not know the man." At that moment a cock crowed.
75 Then Peter remembered what Jesus had said, that 'before
the cock crows you will disown me three times.' And he
went outside and wept bitterly.

27 WHEN morning came, all the high priests and the
elders of the people took counsel against Jesus, so as
2 to have him put to death. After binding him, they led him
off and handed him over to Pontius Pilate the governor.
3 Then Judas his betrayer saw he was condemned, and
repented; he brought back the thirty silver pieces to the
4 high priests and elders, saying, "I did wrong in betraying
innocent blood." "What does that matter to us?" they said,
5 "it is your affair, not ours!" Then he flung down the
silver pieces in the temple and went off and hung himself.
6 The high priests took the money and said, "It would be
wrong to put this into the treasury, for it is the price of
7 blood." So after consulting they bought with it the Potter's
8 Field, to serve as a burying-place for strangers. That is
why the field is called to this day "The Field of Blood."
9 Then the word spoken by the prophet Jeremiah was fulfilled: *and I took the thirty silver pieces, the price of him
who had been priced, whom they had priced and expelled*

10 *from the sons of Israel; and I gave them for the potter's field, as the Lord had bidden me.*
11   Now Jesus stood before the governor, and the governor asked him, "Are you the king of the Jews?" Jesus replied,
12 "Certainly." But while he was being accused by the high
13 priests and elders, he made no reply. Then Pilate said to him, "Do you not hear all their evidence against you?"
14 But, to Pilate's great astonishment, he would not answer him a single word.
15   At festival time the governor was in the habit of releasing
16 any one prisoner whom the crowd chose. At that time they
17 had a notorious prisoner called Jesus* Bar-Abbas; so, when they had gathered, Pilate said to them, "Who do you want released? Jesus Bar-Abbas or Jesus the so-called 'Christ'?"
18 (He knew quite well that Jesus had been delivered up out
19 of envy. Besides, when he was seated on the tribunal, his wife had sent to tell him, "Do nothing with that innocent man, for I have suffered greatly to-day in a dream about
20 him.") But the high priests and elders persuaded the
21 crowds to ask Bar-Abbas and to have Jesus killed. The governor said to them, "Which of the two do you want
22 me to release for you?" "Bar-Abbas," they said. Pilate said, "Then what am I to do with Jesus the so-called
23 'Christ'?" They all said, "Have him crucified!" "Why," said the governor, "what has he done wrong?" But they shouted on more fiercely than ever, "Have him crucified!"
24 Now when Pilate saw that instead of him doing any good a riot was rising, he took some water and washed his hands in presence of the crowd, saying, "I am innocent of this
25 good man's blood. It is your affair!" To this all the people replied, "His blood be on us and on our children!"
26 Then he released Bar-Abbas for them; Jesus he scourged and handed over to be crucified.
27   Then the soldiers of the governor took Jesus into the prae-
28 torium and got all the regiment round him; they stripped
29 him and threw a scarlet mantle round him, plaited a crown of thorns and set it on his head, put a stick in his hand, and knelt before him in mockery, crying, "Hail, king of the
30 Jews!" They spat on him, they took the stick and struck
31 him on the head, and after making fun of him they stripped him of the mantle, put on his own clothes, and took him
32 off to be crucified. As they went out they met a Cyrenian
33 called Simon, whom they forced to carry his cross. When

---

* Adding here and in the following verse Ἰησοῦν with the Sinaitic (and Palestinian) Syriac version, some good minuscules, and manuscripts known to Origen. The evidence is discussed in Professor Burkitt's *Evangelion da-Mepharreshe*, ii. 277 f.

S. MATTHEW XXVII 49

they came to a place called Golgotha (meaning the place
34 of a skull), *they gave* him *a drink of wine* mixed *with*
35 *bitters;* but when he tasted it he would not drink it. Then
they crucified him, *distributed his clothes among them by*
36 *drawing lots,* and sat down there to keep watch over him.
37 They also put over his head his charge in writing,

THIS IS JESUS THE KING OF THE JEWS.

38 Two robbers were also crucified with him at that time, one
39 on the right hand and one on the left. Those who passed
40 by scoffed at him, nodding at him in derision and calling,
"You were to destroy the temple and build it in three days!
Save yourself, if you are God's Son! Come down from the
41 cross!" So, too, the high priests made fun of him with the
42 scribes and the elders of the people. "He saved others,"
they said, "but he cannot save himself! He the 'King of
Israel'! Let him come down now from the cross; then we
43 will believe in him! *His trust is in God?* Let God deliver
him now *if he cares for him!* He said he was the Son of
44 God!" The robbers who were crucified with him also denounced him in the same way.
45 Now from twelve o'clock to three o'clock darkness covered
46 all the land, and about three o'clock Jesus gave a loud cry,
"*Eli, eli, lema sabachthani*" (that is, My God, my God,
47 why hast thou forsaken me?) On hearing this some of
48 the bystanders said, "He is calling for Elijah." One of
them ran off at once and took a sponge, which he soaked
in vinegar and put on the end of a stick to give him
49 a drink. But the others said, "Stop, let us see if Elijah
does come to save him!" [Seizing a lance, another pricked
50 his side, and out came water and blood.] Jesus again uttered
51 a loud scream and gave up his spirit. And the curtain
of the temple was torn in two from top to bottom, the earth
52 shook, the rocks were split, the tombs were opened, and a
number of bodies of the saints who slept the sleep of death
53 rose up—they left the tombs after his resurrection and
entered the holy city and appeared to a number of people.
54 Now when the army-captain and his men who were watching Jesus saw the earthquake and all that happened, they
were dreadfully afraid; they said, "This man was certainly
55 a son of God!" There were also a number of women there
looking on from a distance, women who had followed Jesus
56 from Galilee and waited on him, including Mary of Magdala, Mary the mother of James and Joseph, and the mother
of the sons of Zebedaeus.
57 Now when evening came, a rich man from Arimathaea,
58 called Joseph, who had become a disciple of Jesus, went to
Pilate and asked him for the body of Jesus. Pilate then

59 ordered the body to be handed over to him. So Joseph took
60 the body, wrapped it in clean linen, and put it in his new tomb, which he had cut in the rock; then, after rolling a large boulder to the opening of the tomb, he went away.
61 Mary of Magdala and the other Mary were there, sitting opposite the tomb.
62 Next day (that is, on the day after the Preparation) the
63 high priests and Pharisees gathered round Pilate and said, "We remember, sir, that when this impostor was alive he
64 said, 'I will rise after three days.' Now then, give orders for the tomb to be kept secure till the third day, in case his disciples go and steal him and then tell the people, 'He has risen from the dead.' The end of the fraud will then
65 be worse than the beginning of it." Pilate said to them, "Take a guard of soldiers, go and make it as secure as you
66 can." So off they went and made the tomb secure by putting a seal on the boulder and setting the guard.

28 At the close of the sabbath, as the first day of the week was dawning, Mary of Magdala and the other
2 Mary went to look at the tomb. But a great earthquake took place; an angel of the Lord came down from heaven
3 and went and rolled away the boulder and sat on it. His appearance was like lightning and his raiment white as
4 snow. For fear of him the sentries shook and became like
5 dead men; but the angel addressed the women, saying, "Have no fear; I know you are looking for the crucified
6 Jesus. He is not here, he has risen, as he told you he would.
7 See, here is the place where he [the Lord] lay. Now be quick and go to his disciples, tell them he has risen from the dead and that 'he precedes you to Galilee; you shall see him
8 there.' That is my message for you." Then they ran quickly from the tomb in fear and great joy, to announce the news
9 to his disciples. And Jesus himself met them, saying, "Hail!" So they went up to him and caught hold of his
10 feet and worshipped him; then Jesus said to them, "Have no fear! Go and tell my brothers to leave for Galilee; they shall see me there."
11 While they were on their way, some of the sentries went into the city and reported all that had taken place to the
12 high priests, who, after meeting and conferring with the elders, gave a considerable sum of money to the soldiers
13 and told them to say that "his disciples came at night and
14 stole him when we were asleep." "If this comes to the ears of the governor," they added, "we will satisfy him and
15 see that you have no trouble about the matter." So the soldiers took the money and followed their instructions;

S. MATTHEW XXVIII 51

and this story has been disseminated among the Jews down to the present day.
16 Now the eleven disciples went to Galilee, to the hill where
17 Jesus had arranged to meet them. When they saw him
18 they worshipped him, though some were in doubt. Then Jesus came forward to them and said, "Full authority has
19 been given to me in heaven and on earth; go and make disciples of all nations, baptize them in the name of the
20 Father and the Son and the holy Spirit, and teach them to obey all the commands I have laid on you. And I will be with you all the time, to the very end of the world."

THE GOSPEL ACCORDING TO

S. MARK

1 The beginning of the gospel of Jesus Christ [the Son of God].
2 As it is written in the prophet Isaiah,
   Here I send my messenger before your face
   to prepare the way for you:
3 *the voice of one who cries in the desert,*
   'Make the way ready for the Lord,
   level the paths for him'—
4 John appeared baptizing in the desert and preaching a
5 baptism of repentance for the remission of sins; and the whole of Judaea and all the people of Jerusalem went out to him and got baptized by him in the Jordan river, con-
6 fessing their sins. John was dressed in camel's hair, with a leather girdle round his loins, and he ate locusts and
7 wild honey. He announced,
   "After me one who is mightier will come,
      and I am not fit to stoop and untie the string of his sandals:
8 I have baptized you with water,
      but he will baptize you with the holy Spirit."
9 Now it was in those days that Jesus arrived from Nazaret in Galilee and got baptized in the Jordan by John.
10 And the moment he rose from the water he saw the heavens cleft and the Spirit coming down upon him like a
11 dove; then said a voice from heaven,
   'Thou art my Son, the Beloved,
      in thee is my delight.'
12 Then the Spirit drove him immediately into the desert,
13 and in the desert he remained for forty days, while Satan tempted him; he was in the company of wild beasts, but angels ministered to him.
14 After John had been arrested Jesus went to Galilee
15 preaching the gospel of God; he said, "The time has now come, God's reign is near: repent and believe in the gospel."
16 Now as he passed along the sea of Galilee he saw Simon and Simon's brother Andrew netting fish in the sea—for
17 they were fishermen; so Jesus said to them, "Come, follow

S. MARK I 53

18 me and I will make you fish for men." At once they
19 dropped their nets and went after him. Then going on a
little further he saw James the son of Zebedaeus and his
brother John; they too were in their boat, mending their
20 nets; he called them at once, and they left their father
Zebedaeus in the boat with the crew and went to follow
him.
21 They then entered Capharnahum. As soon as the sabbath came, he at once began to teach in the synagogue;
22 and they were astounded at his teaching, for he taught
23 them like an authority, not like the scribes. Now there
was a man with an unclean spirit in their synagogue, who
24 at once shrieked out, "Jesus of Nazaret, what business
have you with us? Have you come to destroy us? We
25 know who you are, you are God's holy One." But Jesus
26 checked it; "Be quiet," he said, "come out of him." And
after convulsing him the unclean spirit did come out of
27 him with a loud cry. Then they were all so amazed that
they discussed it together, saying, "Whatever is this?"
"It's new teaching with authority behind it!" "He orders
28 even unclean spirits!" "Yes, and they obey him!" So
his fame at once spread in all directions through the whole
of the surrounding country of Galilee.
29 On leaving the synagogue they went straight to the house
of Simon and Andrew, accompanied by James and John.
30 Simon's mother-in-law was in bed with fever, so they told
31 him at once about her, and he went up to her and taking
her hand made her rise; the fever left her at once and
32 she ministered to them. Now when evening came, when
the sun set, they brought him all who were ill or possessed
33 by daemons—indeed the whole town was gathered at the
34 door—and he cured many who were ill with various diseases and cast out many daemons; but as the daemons
35 knew him he would not let them say anything. Then in
the early morning, long before daylight, he got up and went
36 away out to a lonely spot. He was praying there when
37 Simon and his companions hunted him out and discovered him; they told him, "Everybody is looking for
38 you," but he said to them, "Let us go somewhere else, to
the adjoining country-towns, so that I may preach there as
39 well; that is why I came out here." And he went
preaching in their synagogues throughout the whole of
Galilee, casting out daemons.
40 A leper came to him beseeching him on bended knee, say-
41 ing, "If you only choose, you can cleanse me;" so he
stretched his hand out in pity and touched him saying,
42 "I do choose, be cleansed." And the leprosy at once left
43 him and he was cleansed. Then he sent him off at once

44 with the stern charge, "See, you are not to say a word to anybody; away and show yourself to the priest and offer what Moses prescribed for your cleansing, to notify men."
45 But he went off and proceeded to proclaim it aloud and spread news of the affair both far and wide. The result was that Jesus could no longer enter any town openly; he stayed outside in lonely places, and people came to him from every quarter.

2 WHEN he entered Capharnahum again after some days it was reported that he was at home, and a large number at once gathered, till there was no more room for them, not even at the door. He was speaking the word to
3 them, when a paralytic was brought to him; four men
4 carried him, and as they could not get near Jesus on account of the crowd they tore up the roof under which he stood and through the opening they lowered the pallet
5 on which the paralytic lay. When Jesus saw their faith, he said to the paralytic, "My son, your sins are for-
6 given." Now there were some scribes sitting there who
7 argued in their hearts, "What does the man mean by talking like this? It is blasphemy! Who can forgive sins,
8 who but God alone?" Conscious at once that they were arguing to themselves in this way, Jesus asked them,
9 "Why do you argue thus in your hearts? Which is the easier thing, to tell the paralytic, 'Your sins are forgiven,'
10 or to tell him, 'Rise, lift your pallet, and go away'? But to let you see the Son of man has power on earth to forgive
11 sins"—he said to the paralytic, "Rise, I tell you, lift your
12 pallet, and go home." And he rose, lifted his pallet at once, and went off before them all; at this they were all amazed and glorified God saying, "We never saw the like of it!"
13 Then he went out again by the seaside, and all the crowd
14 came to him and he taught them. As he passed along he saw Levi the son of Alphaeus sitting at the tax-office; he said to him, "Follow me," and he rose and followed him.
15 Now Levi was at table in his own house, and he had many taxgatherers and sinners as guests along with Jesus and his disciples—for there were many of them among his
16 followers. So when some scribes of the Pharisees saw he was eating with sinners and taxgatherers they said to his disciples, "Why does he eat and drink with taxgatherers
17 and sinners?" On hearing this, Jesus said to them, "Those who are strong have no need of a doctor, but those who are ill:
I have not come to call just men but sinners."
18 As the disciples of John and of the Pharisees were ob-

S. MARK III

serving a fast, people came and asked him, "Why do John's disciples and the disciples of the Pharisees fast, and your
19 disciples do not fast?" Jesus said to them,
"Can friends at a wedding fast while the bridegroom is beside them?
As long as they have the bridegroom beside them they cannot fast.
20 A time will come when the bridegroom is taken from them; then they will fast, on that day.
21 No one stitches a piece of undressed cloth on an old coat,
otherwise the patch breaks away, the new from the old,
and the tear is made worse:
22 no one pours fresh wine into old wineskins,
otherwise the wine will burst the wineskins,
and both wine and wineskins are ruined."*
23 Now it happened that he was passing through the cornfields on the sabbath, and as the disciples made their way
24 through they began to pull the ears of corn. The Pharisees said to him, "Look at what they are doing on the sabbath!
25 That is not allowed." He said to them, "Have you never read what David did when he was in need and hungry,
26 he and his men? He went into the house of God (Abiathar was high priest then) and ate *the loaves of the Presence* which no one except the priests is allowed to eat, and also
27 shared them with his followers." And he said to them,
"The sabbath was made for man, not man for the sabbath:
28 so that the Son of man is Lord even over the sabbath."

3 Again he entered a synagogue. Now a man was there
2 whose hand was withered, and they watched to see if he would heal him on the sabbath, so as to get a charge
3 against him. He said to the man with the withered hand,
4 "Rise and come forward;" then he asked them, "Is it right to help or to hurt on the sabbath, to save life or to kill?"
5 They were silent. Then glancing round him in anger and vexation at their obstinacy he told the man, "Stretch out your hand." He stretched it out and his hand was quite
6 restored. On this the Pharisees withdrew and at once joined the Herodians in a plot against him, to destroy him.
7 Jesus retired with his disciples to the sea, and a large number of people from Galilee followed him; also a large

---

* Omitting ἀλλὰ οἶνονὰ νέον εἰς ἀσκοὺς καινούς, a harmonistic addition from the parallel passage in Luke v. 38 and Matthew ix. 17.

8 number came to him from Judaea, Jerusalem, Idumaea, the
other side of the Jordan, and the neighbourhood of Tyre
9 and Sidon, as they had heard of his doings. So he told his
disciples to have a small boat ready; it was to prevent
10 him being crushed by the crowd, for he healed so many
that all who had complaints were pressing on him to get
11 a touch of him. And whenever the unclean spirits saw
him they fell down before him, screaming, "You are the
12 Son of God!" But he charged them strictly and severely
not to make him known.
13 Then he went up the hillside and summoned the men he
14 wanted, and they went to him. He appointed twelve to be
15 with him, also that he might despatch them to preach with
16 the power of casting out daemons; there was Simon,
17 whom he surnamed Peter, James the son of Zebedaeus and
John the brother of James (he surnamed them Boanerges,
18 or "Sons of thunder"), Andrew, Philip, Bartholomew, Matthew, Thomas, James the son of Alphaeus, Thaddaeus,
19 Simon the zealot, and Judas Iscariot who betrayed him.
20 Then they went indoors, but the crowd gathered again,
21 so that it was impossible even to have a meal. And when
his family heard this, they set out to get hold of him, for
22 what they said was, "He is out of his mind." But the
scribes who had come down from Jerusalem said, "He has
Beelzebul," and "It is by the prince of daemons that he
23 casts out daemons." So he called them and said to them
by way of parable, "How can Satan cast out Satan?
24 If a realm is divided against itself,
 that realm cannot stand:
25 if a household is divided against itself,
 that household cannot stand:
26 and if Satan has risen against himself and is divided,
 he cannot stand, he comes to an end.
27 No one can enter the strong man's house and plunder
his goods unless first of all he binds the strong man; then
28 he can plunder his house. I tell you truly,
 the sons of men shall be forgiven all their sins,
 and all the blasphemies they may utter,
29 but whoever blasphemes against the holy Spirit is
 never forgiven,
 he is guilty of an eternal sin."
30 (This was because they said, "He has an unclean spirit.")
31 Then came his brothers and his mother, and standing out-
32 side they sent to call him; there was a crowd sitting round
him, and he was told, "Here are your mother and brothers
33 and sisters wanting you outside." He replied, "Who are
34 my mother and my brothers?" And glancing at those who
were sitting round him in a circle he said, "There are my

35 mother and my brothers! Whoever does the will of God, that is my brother and sister and mother."

4 Once more he proceeded to teach by the seaside, and a huge crowd gathered round him; so he entered a boat on the sea and sat down, while all the crowd stayed on
2 shore. He gave them many lessons in parables, and said to
3 them in the course of his teaching: "Listen, a sower went
4 out to sow, and as he sowed it chanced that some seed fell
5 on the road, and the birds came and ate it up; some other seed fell on stony soil where it had not much earth, and
6 it shot up at once because it had no depth of earth, but when the sun rose it got scorched and withered away,
7 because it had no root; some other seed fell among thorns, and the thorns sprang up and choked it, so it bore no crop;
8 some other seed fell on good soil and bore a crop that sprang up and grew, yielding at the rate of thirty, sixty,
9 and a hundredfold." He added, "Anyone who has ears to hear, let him listen to this."
10 When he was by himself his adherents and the twelve
11 asked him about the parable, and he said to them: "The open secret of the Realm of God is granted to you, but these outsiders get everything by way of parables, so that
12 *for all their seeing they may not perceive,*
and for all their hearing they may not understand,
lest they turn and be forgiven."
13 And he said to them, "You do not understand this parable?
14 Then how are you to understand the other parables? The
15 sower sows the word. As for those 'on the road,' when the seed is sown there—as soon as they hear it, Satan at once comes and carries off the word sown within them.
16 Similarly those who are sown 'on stony soil' are the people
17 who on hearing the word accept it* with enthusiasm; but they have no root in themselves, they do not last; the next thing is that when the word brings trouble or persecu-
18 tion, they are at once repelled. Another set are those
19 who are sown 'among thorns'; they listen to the word, but the worries of the world and the delight of being rich and all the other passions come in to choke the word; so it
20 proves unfruitful. As for those who were sown 'on good soil,' these are the people who listen to the word and take it in and bear fruit at the rate of thirty, sixty, and a hundredfold."
21 He also said to them,

* Omitting εὐθύς with D, the Sinaitic Syriac, some manuscripts of the Old Latin, etc. The tendency was to add Mark's εὐθύς rather than omit it, especially when it occurred as here in the Matthew-parallel (xiii. 20).

"Is a lamp brought to be placed under a bowl or a bed? Is it not to be placed upon the stand?
22 Nothing is hidden except to be disclosed, nothing concealed except to be revealed.
23
24 If anyone has an ear to hear, let him listen to this." Also he said to them, "Take care what you hear; the measure you deal out to others will be dealt out to yourselves, and you will receive extra.
25 For he who has, to him shall more be given; while as for him who has not, from him shall be taken even what he has."
26 And he said, "It is with the Realm of God as when a
27 man has sown seed on earth; he sleeps at night and rises by day, and the seed sprouts and shoots up—he knows not
28 how. (For the earth bears crops by itself, the blade first, the ear of corn next, and then the grain full in the ear.)
29 But whenever the crop is ready, he has the sickle put in at
30 once, as harvest has come." He said also, "To what can we compare the Realm of God? how are we to put it in a parable?
31 It is like a grain of mustard-seed—less than any seed on
32 earth when it is sown on earth; but once sown it springs up to be larger than any plant, throwing out such big branches that *the wild birds can roost under its shadow.*"
33 In many a parable like this he spoke the word to them, so
34 far as they could listen to it; he never spoke to them except by way of parable, but in private he explained everything to his own disciples.
35 That same day when evening came he said to them,
36 "Let us cross to the other side;" so, leaving the crowd, they took him just as he was in the boat, accompanied by
37 some other boats. But a heavy squall of wind came on, and the waves splashed into the boat, so that the boat
38 filled. He was sleeping on the cushion in the stern, so they woke him up saying, "Teacher, are we to drown, for all
39 you care?" And he woke up, checked the wind, and told the sea, "Peace, be quiet." The wind fell and there was
40 a great calm. Then he said to them, "Why are you afraid
41 like this? Have you no faith yet?" But they were overawed and said to each other, "Whatever can he be, when the very wind and sea obey him?"

5 THEN they reached the opposite side of the sea, the
2 country of the Gerasenes. And as soon as he stepped out of the boat a man from the tombs came to meet him, a man
3 with an unclean spirit who dwelt among the tombs; by this
4 time no one could bind him, not even with a chain, for he had often been bound with fetters and chains and had

snapped the chains and broken the fetters—nobody could
5 tame him. All night and day among the tombs and the
6 hills he shrieked and gashed himself with stones. On
catching sight of Jesus from afar he ran and knelt before
7 him, shrieking aloud, "Jesus, son of God most High, what
business have you with me? By God, I adjure you, do not
8 torture me." (For he had said, "Come out of the man,
9 you unclean spirit.") Jesus asked him, "What is your
10 name?" "Legion," he said, "there is a host of us." And
they begged him earnestly not to send them out of the
11 country. Now a large drove of swine was grazing there on
12 the hillside; so the spirits begged him saying, "Send us
13 into the swine, that we may enter them." And Jesus gave
them leave. Then out came the unclean spirits and entered the swine, and the drove rushed down the steep
slope into the sea (there were about two thousand of them)
14 and in the sea they were drowned. The herdsmen fled and
reported it to the town and the hamlets. So the people
15 came to see what had happened, and when they reached
Jesus they saw the lunatic sitting down, clothed and in his
sober senses—the man who had been possessed by 'Legion.'
16 That frightened them. And those who had seen it related
to them what had happened to the lunatic and the swine.
17 Then they began begging Jesus to leave their district.
18 As he was stepping into the boat the lunatic begged that
19 he might accompany him; but he said, "Go home to your
own people, and report to them all the Lord has done for
20 you and how he took pity on you." So he went off and
began to proclaim throughout Decapolis all that Jesus had
done for him; it made everyone astonished.
21 Now when Jesus had crossed in the boat to the other
side again, a large crowd gathered round him; so he
22 remained beside the sea. A president of the synagogue
called Jairus came up, and on catching sight of him fell
23 at his feet with earnest entreaties. "My little girl is
dying," he said, "do come and lay your hands on her that
24 she may recover and live." So Jesus went away with him.
Now a large crowd followed him; they pressed round him.
25 And there was a woman who had had a hemorrhage for
26 twelve years—she had suffered a great deal under a
number of doctors and had spent all her means but was
27 none the better; in fact she was rather worse. She heard
about Jesus, got behind him in the crowd, and touched his
28 robe; "if I can touch even his clothes," she said to her-
29 self, "I will recover." And at once the hemorrhage
stopped, and she felt in her body that she was cured of
30 her complaint. Jesus was at once conscious that some
healing virtue had passed from him, so he turned round

31 in the crowd and asked, "Who touched my clothes?" His
disciples said to him, "You see the crowd are pressing
32 round you, and yet you ask, 'Who touched me?'" But
33 he kept looking round to see who had done it, and the
woman, knowing what had happened to her, came forward
in fear and trembling and fell down before him, telling
34 him all the truth. He said to her, "Daughter, your faith
has made you well; go in peace and be free from your
35 complaint." He was still speaking when a message came
from the house of the synagogue-president, "Your daughter
is dead. Why trouble the teacher to come any further?"
36 Instantly Jesus ignored the remark and told the president,
37 "Have no fear, only believe." He would not allow anyone
to accompany him except Peter and James and John the
38 brother of James. So they reached the president's house,
where he saw a tumult of people wailing and making shrill
39 lament; and on entering he asked them, "Why make a
40 noise and wail? The child is not dead but asleep." They
laughed at him. However, he put them all outside and
taking the father and mother of the child as well as his
companions he went in to where the child was lying,
41 then he took the child's hand and said to her, "Talitha
koum"—which may be translated, "Little girl, I am telling
42 you to rise." The girl got up at once and began to walk
(she was twelve years old); and at once they were lost in
43 utter amazement. But he strictly forbade them to let
anyone know about it, and told them to give her something
to eat.

6 Leaving there he went to his native place, followed by
2 his disciples. When the sabbath came, he began to teach
in the synagogue, and the large audience was astounded.
"Where did he get all this?" they said. "What is the
meaning of this wisdom he is endowed with? And these
3 miracles, too, that his hands perform! Is this not the
joiner, the son of Mary and the brother of James and Joses
and Judas and Simon? Are not his sisters settled here
4 among us?" So they were repelled by him. Then Jesus
said to them, "A prophet never goes without honour except
in his native place and among his kinsfolk and in his
5 home." There he could not do any miracle, beyond laying
6 his hands on a few sick people and curing them. He was
astonished at their lack of faith.
7 Then he made a tour round the villages, teaching. And
summoning the twelve he proceeded to send them out two
8 by two; he gave them power over the unclean spirits, and
ordered them to take nothing but a stick for the journey,
9 no bread, no wallet, no coppers in their girdle; they were

to wear sandals, but not to put on two shirts, he said.
10 Also, he told them, "Wherever you enter a house, stay
11 there till you leave the place. And if any place will not receive you and the people will not listen to you, shake off the very dust under your feet when you leave, as a
12 warning to them." So they went out and preached re-
13 pentance; also they cast out a number of daemons and cured a number of sick people by anointing them with oil.
14 Now this came to the hearing of king Herod, for the name of Jesus had become well known; people said,* "John the Baptizer has risen from the dead, that is why
15 miraculous powers are working through him;" others said, "It is Elijah;" others again, "It is a prophet, like
16 one of the old prophets." But when Herod heard of it he
17 said, "John has risen, the John I beheaded." For this Herod had sent and arrested John and bound him in prison on account of his marriage to Herodias the wife of
18 his brother Philip; John had told Herod, "You have no
19 right to your brother's wife." Herodias had a grudge against him; she wanted him killed but she could not
20 manage it, for Herod stood in awe of John, knowing he was a just and holy man; so he protected John—he was greatly exercised when he listened to him, still he was
21 glad to listen to him. Then came a holiday, when Herod held a feast on his birthday for his chief officials and gen-
22 erals and the notables of Galilee. The daughter of Herodias went in and danced to them, and Herod and his guests were so delighted that the king said to the girl,
23 "Ask anything you like and I will give you it." He swore to her, "I will give you whatever you want, were it the half
24 of my realm." So she went out and said to her mother, "What am I to ask?" "John the Baptizer's head," she an-
25 swered. Then she hurried in at once and asked the king, saying, "I want you to give me this very moment John the
26 Baptist's head on a dish." The king was very vexed, but for the sake of his oaths and his guests he did not like to
27 disappoint her; so the king at once sent one of the guard with orders to bring his head. The man went and be-
28 headed him in the prison, brought his head on a dish, and gave it to the girl; and the girl gave it to her mother.
29 When his disciples heard of it they went and fetched his body and laid it in a tomb.
30 Now the apostles gathered to meet Jesus and reported to
31 him all they had done and taught. And he said to them, "Come away to some lonely spot and get a little rest" (for there were many people coming and going, and they could

* Reading ἔλεγον with B D and the Old Latin.

32 get no time even to eat). So they went away privately
33 in the boat to a lonely spot. However a number of people who saw them start and recognised them, got to the place before them by hurrying there on foot from all the towns.
34 So when Jesus disembarked he saw a large crowd, and out of pity for them, as they were like sheep without a shep-
35 herd, he proceeded to teach them at length. Then, as the day was far gone, his disciples came up to him, saying, "It
36 is a desert place and the day is now far gone; send them off to the farms and villages round about to buy some food
37 for themselves." He replied, "Give them some food, your- selves." They said, "Are we to go and buy ten pounds'
38 worth of food and give them that to eat?" He said, "How many loaves have you got? Go and see." When they found
39 out they told him, "Five, and two fish." Then he gave orders that they were to make all the people lie down
40 in parties on the green grass; so they arranged them-
41 selves in groups of a hundred and of fifty. And he took the five loaves and the two fish, and looking up to heaven he blessed them, broke the loaves in pieces which he handed to the disciples to set before them, and divided the two
42 fish among them all. They all ate and had enough;
43 besides, the fragments of bread and of fish which were
44 picked up filled twelve baskets. (The number of men who ate the loaves was five thousand.)
45 Then he made the disciples at once embark in the boat and cross before him towards Bethsaida, while he dis-
46 missed the crowd; and after saying goodbye to them he
47 went up the hill to pray. Now when evening came the boat was [far out] in the middle of the sea, and he was on the
48 land alone; but when he saw them buffeted as they rowed (for the wind was against them) he went to them about the
49 fourth watch of the night walking on the sea. He meant to pass them, but when they saw him walking on the sea they
50 thought it was a ghost and shrieked aloud—for they all saw him and were terrified. Then he spoke to them at
51 once; "Courage," he said, "it is I, have no fear." And he got into the boat beside them, and the wind dropped. They
52 were utterly astounded, for they had not understood the lesson of the loaves; their minds were dull.
53 On crossing over they came to land at Gennesaret and
54 moored to the shore. And when they had disembarked, the
55 people at once recognized Jesus; they hurried round all the district and proceeded to carry the sick on their pallets
56 wherever they heard that he was; whatever village or town or hamlet he went to, they would lay their invalids in the marketplace, begging him to let them touch even the tassel of his robe—and all who touched him recovered.

7 Now the Pharisees gathered to meet him, with some
2 scribes who had come from Jerusalem. They noticed
that some of his disciples ate their food with 'common'
3 (that is, unwashed) hands. (The Pharisees and all the
Jews decline to eat till they wash their hands up to the
4 wrist, in obedience to the tradition of the elders; they
decline to eat what comes from the market till they have
washed it; and they have a number of other traditions to
keep about washing cups and jugs and basins [and beds].)
5 Then the Pharisees and scribes put this question to him,
"Why do your disciples not follow the tradition of the
elders? Why do they take their food with 'common'
6 hands?" He said to them, "Isaiah made a grand prophecy
about you hypocrites—as it is written,
This people honours me with their lips,
but their heart is far away from me:
7 *vain is their worship of me,*
for the doctrines they teach are but human pre-
cepts.
8 You drop what God commands and hold to human tradi-
9 tion.* Yes, forsooth," he added, "you set aside what God
10 commands, so as to maintain your own tradition. Thus,
Moses said, *Honour your father and mother,* and, *He who*
11 *curses his father or mother is to suffer death.* But you
say that if a man tells his father or mother, 'This money
might have been at your service, but it is Korban' (that
12 is, dedicated to God), he is exempt, so you hold, from
13 doing anything for his father or mother. That is repeal-
ing the word of God in the interests of the tradition which
14 you keep up. And you do many things like that." Then he
called the crowd to him again and said to them, "Listen to
me, all of you, and understand this:—
15 nothing outside a man can defile him by entering him;
it is what comes from him that defiles him.
16 If anyone has ears to hear, let him listen to this."
17 Now when he went indoors away from the crowd, his
disciples asked him the meaning of this parabolic saying.
18 He said to them, "So you do not understand, either? Do
you not see how nothing outside a man can defile him by
19 entering him? It does not enter his heart but his belly
and passes from that into the drain" (thus he pronounced
20 all food clean). "No," he said, "it is what comes from a
21 man, that is what defiles him. From within, from the
22 heart of man, the designs of evil come: sexual vice, stealing, murder, adultery, lust, malice, deceit, sensuality, envy-

* Omitting βαπτισμοὺς ξεστῶν καὶ ποτηρίων καὶ ἄλλα παρόμοια τοιαῦτα πολλὰ ποιεῖτε.

23 ing, slander, arrogance, recklessness, all these evils issue from within and they defile a man."
24 Leaving there, he went away to the territory of Tyre and Sidon. He went into a house and wished no one to know
25 of it, but he could not escape notice; a woman heard of him, whose daughter had an unclean spirit, and she came
26 in and fell at his feet (the woman was a pagan, of Syrophœnician birth) begging him to cast the daemon out of
27 her daughter. He said to her, "Let the children be satisfied first of all; it is not fair to take the children's bread
28 and throw it to the dogs." She answered him, "No, sir, but under the table the dogs do pick up the children's
29 crumbs." He said to her, "Well, go your way; the daemon
30 has left your daughter, since you have said that." So she went home and found the child lying in bed and the daemon gone from her.
31 He left the territory of Tyre again and passed through Sidon to the sea of Galilee, crossing the territory of Decap-
32 olis. And a deaf man who stammered was brought to him, with the request that he would lay his hand on him.
33 So taking him aside from the crowd by himself, he put his fingers into the man's ears, touched his tongue with saliva,
34 and looking up to heaven with a sigh he said to him,
35 "Ephphatha" (which means, Open). Then his ears were [at once] opened and his tongue freed from its fetter—he began
36 to speak correctly. Jesus forbade them to tell anyone about it, but the more he forbade them the more eagerly
37 they made it public; they were astounded in the extreme, saying, "How splendidly he has done everything! He actually makes the deaf hear and the dumb speak!"

8 In those days, when a large crowd had again gathered and when they had nothing to eat, he called his dis-
2 ciples and said to them, "I am sorry for the crowd; they have been three days with me now, and they have nothing
3 to eat. If I send them home without food they will faint on the road. Besides, some of them have come a long
4 way." His disciples replied, "Where can one get loaves
5 to satisfy them in a desert spot like this?" He asked them, "How many loaves have you got?" They said,
6 "Seven." So he ordered the crowd to recline on the ground, and taking the seven loaves he gave thanks, broke them, and gave them to his disciples to serve out. They
7 served them out to the crowd, and as they also had a few small fish, he blessed them too and told the disciples to
8 serve them out as well. So the people ate and were satisfied, and they picked up seven baskets of fragments which
9 were left over. (There were about four thousand of them.)

10 Then he sent them away, embarked at once in the boat with his disciples, and went to the district of Dalmanutha.
11 Now the Pharisees came out and started to argue with him, asking him for a Sign from heaven, by way of tempt-
12 ing him. But he sighed in spirit and said, "Why does this generation demand a Sign? I tell you truly, no Sign shall be given this generation."
13 Then he left them, embarked again, and went away to the opposite side.
14 They had forgotten to bring any bread, and had only one
15 loaf with them in the boat. So he cautioned them, "See and beware of the leaven of the Pharisees and the leaven
16 of Herod." "Leaven?" they argued to themselves, "we
17 have no bread at all." He noted this and said to them, "Why do you argue you have no bread? Do you not see, do you not understand, even yet? Are you still dull of heart?
18 You have eyes, do you not see?
you have ears, do you not hear?
19 Do you not remember how many baskets full of fragments you picked up when I broke the five loaves for the five
20 thousand?" They said, "Twelve." "And how many basketfuls of fragments did you pick up when I broke the seven
21 loaves for the four thousand?" They said, "Seven." "Do you not understand now?" he said.
22 Then they reached Bethsaida. A blind man was brought
23 to him with the request that he would touch him. So he took the blind man by the hand and led him outside the village; then, after spitting on his eyes, he laid his hands
24 on him and asked him, "Do you see anything?" He began to see and said, "I can make out people, for I see them as
25 large as trees, moving." At this he laid his hands on his eyes once more, and the man stared in front of him; he
26 was quite restored and saw everything distinctly. And Jesus sent him home, saying, "Do not go even into the village."
27 Then Jesus and his disciples set off for the villages of Cæsarea Philippi; and on the road he inquired of his dis-
28 ciples, "Who do people say I am?" "John the Baptist," they told him, "though some say Elijah and others say you
29 are one of the prophets." So he inquired of them, "And who do you say I am?" Peter replied, "You are the
30 Christ." Then he forbade them to tell anyone about him.
31 And he proceeded to teach them that the Son of man had to endure great suffering, to be rejected by the elders and the high priests and the scribes, to be killed and after

32 three days to rise again; he spoke of this quite freely.
33 Peter took him and began to reprove him for it, but he turned on him and noticing his disciples reproved Peter, telling him, "Get behind me, you Satan! Your outlook is
34 not God's but man's." Then he called the crowd to him with his disciples and said to them, "If anyone wishes to follow me, let him deny himself, take up his cross, and so follow me;
35 for whoever wants to save his life will lose it, and whoever loses his life for my sake and the gospel's will save it.
36 What profit is it for a man to gain the whole world and
37 to forfeit his soul? What could a man offer as an equivafor his soul?
38 Whoever is ashamed of me and my words in this disloyal and sinful generation, the Son of man will be ashamed of him when he comes in the glory of his Father with the holy
9 angels. I tell you truly," he said, to them, "there are some of those standing here who will not taste death till they see the coming of God's Reign with power."
2 Six days afterwards Jesus took Peter, James and John, and led them up a high hill by themselves alone; in their
3 presence he was transfigured, and his clothes glistened white, vivid white, such as no fuller on earth could bleach
4 them. And Elijah along with Moses appeared to them, and
5 conversed with Jesus. So Peter addressed Jesus, saying, "Rabbi, it is a good thing we are here; let us put up three
6 tents, one for you, one for Moses, and one for Elijah" (for
7 he did not know what to say, they were so terrified). Then a cloud came overshadowing them, and from the cloud a voice said, "This is my Son, the Beloved, listen to him."
8 And suddenly looking round they saw no one there except
9 Jesus all alone beside them. As they went down the hill, he forbade them to tell anyone what they had seen, till
10 such time as the Son of man rose from the dead. This order they obeyed, debating with themselves what 'rising
11 from the dead' meant. So they put this question to him, "Why do the [Pharisees and] scribes say that Elijah has to
12 come first?" He said to them, "Elijah does come first, to restore all things; but what is written about the Son of man as well? This, that he is to endure great suffering
13 and be rejected. As for Elijah, I tell you he has come already, and they have done to him whatever they pleased
14 —as it is written of him." When they reached the disciples they saw a large crowd round them, and some
15 scribes arguing with them. On seeing him the whole
16 crowd was thunderstruck and ran to greet him. Jesus
17 asked them, "What are you discussing with them?" A

man from the crowd answered him, "Teacher, I brought
18 my son to you; he has a dumb spirit, and whenever it
seizes him it throws him down, and he foams at the
mouth and grinds his teeth. He is wasting away with it;
so I told your disciples to cast it out, but they could not."
19 He answered them, "O faithless generation, how long must
I still be with you? how long have I to bear with you?
20 Bring him to me." So they brought the boy to him, and
when the spirit saw Jesus it at once convulsed the boy;
he fell on the ground and rolled about foaming at the
21 mouth. Jesus asked his father, "How long has he been
22 like this?" "From childhood," he said; "it has thrown
him into fire and water many a time, to destroy him. If
you can do anything, do help us, do have pity on us."
23 Jesus said to him, "'If you can'! Anything can be done
24 for one who believes." At once the father of the boy cried
25 out, "I do believe; help my unbelief." Now as Jesus saw
that a crowd was rapidly gathering, he checked the unclean spirit. "Deaf and dumb spirit," he said, "leave him,
26 I command you, and never enter him again." And it did
come out, after shrieking aloud and convulsing him vio-
lently. The child turned like a corpse, so that most people
27 said, "he is dead"; but, taking his hand, Jesus raised
28 him and he got up. When he went indoors his disciples
asked him in private, "Why could we not cast it out?"
29 He said to them, "Nothing can make this kind come out but
prayer and fasting."
30 On leaving there they passed through Galilee. He did
31 not want anyone to know of their journey, for he was
teaching his disciples, telling them that the Son of man
would be betrayed into the hands of men, that they would
kill him, and that when he was killed he would rise again
32 after three days. But they did not understand what he
said, and they were afraid to ask him what he meant.
33 Then they reached Capharnahum. And when he was
indoors he asked them, "What were you arguing about
34 on the road?" They said nothing, for on the road they
had been disputing about which of them was the greatest.
35 So he sat down and called the twelve. "If anyone wants to
be first," he said to them, "he must be last of all and the
36 servant of all." Then he took a little child, set it among
them, and putting his arms round it said to them,
37 "Whoever receives one of these little ones in my name
receives me,
and whoever receives me receives not me but him who
sent me."
38 John said to him, "Teacher, we saw a man casting out
daemons in your name; but he does not follow us, and

39 so we stopped him." Jesus said, "Do not stop him; no one who performs any miracle in my name will be ready to
40 speak evil of me. He who is not against us is for us.
41 Whoever gives you a cup of water because you belong to Christ, I tell you truly, he shall not miss his reward.
42 And whoever is a hindrance to one of these little ones who believe, it were better for him to have a great millstone hung round his neck and be thrown into the sea.
43 If your hand is a hindrance to you, cut it off:
better be maimed and get into Life,
than keep your two hands and go to Gehenna, to the fire that is never quenched.
45 If your foot is a hindrance to you, cut it off:
better get into Life a cripple,
than keep your two feet and be thrown into Gehenna.
47 If your eye is a hindrance to you, tear it out:
better get into God's Realm with one eye,
than keep your two eyes and be thrown into Gehenna,
48 where *their worm never dies and the fire is never put out.*
49 Everyone has to be consecrated * by the fire of the discipline.
50 Salt is excellent:
but if salt is tasteless, how are you to restore its flavour?
Let there be 'salt between you';
be at peace with one another."

10 Then he left and went to the territory of Judaea over the Jordan. Crowds gathered to him again, and
2 again he taught them as usual. Now some Pharisees came up and asked him if a man was allowed to divorce
3 his wife. This was to tempt him. So he replied, "What
4 did Moses lay down for you?" They said, "Moses permitted a man *to divorce her by writing out a separation
5 notice.*" Jesus said to them, "He wrote you that com-
6 mand on account of the hardness of your hearts. But from the beginning, when God created the world,
Male and female, He created them:
7 *hence a man shall leave his father and mother,*
8 *and the pair shall be one flesh.*

* The Greek word ἁλισθήσεται literally means 'salted,' the metaphor being taken from the custom of using salt in sacrifices (cp. *e.g.* Levit. ii. 13; Josephus, *Antiquities*, iii. 9. 1). "There is fire to be encountered afterwards if not now; how much better to face it now and by self-sacrifice insure against the future" (Professor Menzies).

9 So they are no longer two, but one flesh. What God has
10 joined, then, man must not separate." Indoors, the dis-
11 ciples again asked him about this, and he said to them,
"Whoever divorces his wife and marries another woman
12 is an adulterer to the former, and she is an adulteress
if she divorces her husband and marries another
man."
13 Now people brought children for him to touch them,
14 and the disciples checked them; but Jesus was angry when
he saw this, and he said to them, "Let the children come
to me, do not stop them: the Realm of God belongs to such
15 as these. I tell you truly, whoever will not submit to the
Reign of God like a child will never get into it at all."
16 Then he put his arms round them, laid his hands on them
and blessed them.
17 As he went out on the road a man ran up and knelt
down before him. "Good teacher," he asked, "what must
18 I do to inherit life eternal?" Jesus said to him, "Why call
19 me 'good'? No one is good, no one but God. You know
the commands: *do not kill, do not commit adultery, do not
steal, do not bear false witness,* do not defraud, *honour
20 your father and mother.*" "Teacher," he said, "I have ob-
21 served all these commands from my youth." Jesus looked
at him and loved him. "There is one thing you want,"
he said; "go and sell all you have; give the money to the
poor and you will have treasure in heaven; then come, take
22 up the cross, and follow me." But his face fell at that, and he
23 went sadly away, for he had great possessions. Jesus looked
round and said to his disciples, "How difficult it is for
those who have money to get into the Realm of God!"
24 The disciples were amazed at what he said; so he repeated,
"My sons, how difficult it is [for those who rely on money]
25 to get into the Realm of God! It is easier for a camel to
get through a needle's eye than for a rich man to get into
26 the Realm of God." They were more astounded than ever;
they said to themselves, "Then who ever can be saved?"
27 Jesus looked at them and said, "For men it is impossible,
28 but not for God: anything is possible for God." Peter
29 began, "Well, we have left our all and followed you." Jesus
said, "I tell you truly, no one has left home or brothers or
sisters or mother or father or children or lands for my
30 sake and for the sake of the gospel, who does not get a
hundred times as much—in this present world homes,
brothers, sisters, mothers, children and lands, together
with persecutions, and in the world to come life eternal.
31 Many who are first will be last, and many who are last will
be first."
32 They were on the way up to Jerusalem, Jesus walking

in front of them: the disciples were in dismay and the company who followed were afraid. So once again he took the twelve aside and proceeded to tell them what was
33 going to happen to himself. "We are going up to Jerusalem," he said, "and the Son of man will be betrayed to the high priests and scribes; they will sentence him to
34 death and hand him over to the Gentiles, who will mock him, spit on him, scourge him, and kill him; then after three days he will rise again."
35 James and John, the sons of Zebedaeus, came up to him saying, "Teacher, we want you to do whatever we ask
36 you." So he said, "What do you want me to do for you?"
37 They said to him, "Give us seats, one at your right hand
38 and one at your left hand, in your glory." Jesus said, "You do not know what you are asking. Can you drink the cup I have to drink, or undergo the baptism I have to under-
39 go?" They said to him, "We can." Jesus said, "You shall drink the cup I have to drink and undergo the baptism
40 I have to undergo; but it is not for me to grant seats at my right or my left hand—these belong to the men for
41 whom they have been destined." Now when the ten heard
42 of this, they burst into anger at James and John; so Jesus called them and said,

"You know the so-called rulers of the Gentiles lord it over them,
and their great men overbear them:
43   not so with you.
Whoever wants to be great among you must be your servant,
44 and whoever of you wants to be first must be your slave;
45 for the Son of man himself has not come to be served but to serve,
and to give his life as a ransom for many."
46 Then they reached Jericho; and as he was leaving Jericho with his disciples and a considerable crowd, the son of Timaeus, Bartimaeus, the blind beggar who sat beside the
47 road, heard it was Jesus of Nazaret. So he started to
48 shout, "Son of David! Jesus! have pity on me." A number of the people checked him and told him to be quiet, but he shouted all the more, "Son of David, have pity on me!"
49 Jesus stopped and said, "Call him." Then they called the blind man and told him, "Courage! Get up, he is calling
50 you." Throwing off his cloak he jumped up and went to
51 Jesus. Jesus spoke to him and said, "What do you want me to do for you?" The blind man said, "Rabboni, I want
52 to regain my sight." Then Jesus said, "Go, your faith has made you well;" and he regained his sight at once and followed Jesus along the road.

S. MARK XI

11 Now when they came near Jerusalem, near Bethphage and Bethany, at the Hill of Olives, he despatched
2 two of his disciples, saying to them, "Go to the village in front of you. As soon as you enter it you will find a colt tethered, on which no one has ever sat; untether it
3 and bring it here. If anyone asks you, 'Why are you doing that?' say, 'The Lord needs it, and he will send it back
4 immediately.'" Off they went and found a colt tethered
5 outside a door in the street. They untethered it; but some of the bystanders said to them, "What do you mean by un-
6 tethering that colt?" So they answered as Jesus had told
7 them, and the men allowed them to go. Then they brought the colt to Jesus, and when they had put their clothes on
8 it Jesus seated himself. Many also spread their clothes on the road, while others strewed leaves cut from the
9 fields; and both those in front and those who followed shouted,
"*Hosanna!*
Blessed be he who comes in the Lord's name!
10 *Blessed be the Reign to come, our father David's reign: Hosanna in high heaven!*"
11 Then he entered Jerusalem, entered the temple, and looked round at everything; but as it was late he went away with the twelve to Bethany.
12 Next day, when they had left Bethany, he felt hungry,
13 and noticing a fig tree in leaf some distance away he went to see if he could find anything on it; but when he reached it he found nothing but leaves, for it was not
14 the time for figs. Then he said to it, "May no one ever eat fruit from you after this!" The disciples heard him say it.
15 Then they came to Jerusalem, and entering the temple he proceeded to drive out those who were buying and selling inside the temple; he upset the tables of the money-
16 changers and the stalls of those who sold doves, and would
17 not allow anyone to carry a vessel through the temple; also he taught them. "Is it not written," he asked, "*My house shall be called a house of prayer for all nations?*
18 *You have made it a den of robbers.*" This came to the ears of the scribes and high priests, and they tried to get him put to death, for they were afraid of him. But the multi-
19 tude were all astounded at his teaching. And when evening came he went outside the city.
20 Now as they passed in the morning they noticed the fig
21 tree had withered to the root. Then Peter remembered. "Rabbi," he said, "there is the fig tree you cursed, all
22 withered!" Jesus answered them, "Have faith in God!
23 I tell you truly, whoever says to this hill, 'Take and throw yourself into the sea,' and has not a doubt in his mind

but believes that what he says will happen, he will have
24 it done. So I tell you, whatever you pray for and ask,
25 believe you have got it and you shall have it. Also, whenever you stand up to pray, if you have anything against anybody, forgive him, so that your Father in heaven may forgive you your trespasses."
27 Once more they came to Jerusalem. And as he was walking within the temple the high priests and scribes and
28 elders came and asked him, "What authority have you for acting in this way? Who gave you authority to ac-
29 in this way?" Jesus said to them, "I am going to ask you a question. Answer this, and I will tell you what author-
30 ity I have for acting as I do. What about the baptism
31 of John? Was it from heaven or from men?" Now they
32 argued to themselves, "[What are we to say?] If we say, 'From heaven,' he will ask, 'Then why did you not believe him.' No, let us say, From men"—but they were afraid of the multitude, for the people all held John had been really
33 a prophet. So they replied to Jesus, "We do not know." Jesus said to them, "No more will I tell you what authority I have for acting as I do."

12 Then he proceeded to address them in parables. "A man *planted a vineyard, fenced it round, dug a trough for the winepress, and built a tower;* then he leased it to
2 vinedressers and went abroad. When the season came round he sent a servant to the vinedressers to collect from
3 the vinedressers some of the produce of the vineyard, but they took and flogged him and sent him off with nothing.
4 Once more he sent them another servant; him they
5 knocked on the head and insulted. He sent another, but they killed him. And so they treated many others; some
6 they flogged and some they killed. He had still one left, a beloved son; he sent him to them last, saying, 'They
7 will respect my son.' But these vinedressers said to themselves, 'Here is the heir; come on, let us kill him, and the
8 inheritance will be our own.' So they took and killed him,
9 and threw him outside the vineyard. Now what will the owner of the vineyard do? He will come and destroy the vinedressers, and he will give the vineyard to others.
10 Have you not even read this scripture?—
*The stone that the builders rejected is the chief stone now
   of the corner:*
11 *this is the doing of the Lord,
   and a wonder to our eyes."*
12 Then they tried to get hold of him, but they were afraid of the multitude. They knew he had meant the parable for them.

13 So they left him and went away. But they sent some of
the Pharisees and Herodians to him for the purpose of
14 catching him with a question. They came up and said to
him, "Teacher, we know you are sincere and fearless; you
do not court human favour, you teach the Way of God
15 honestly. Is it right to pay taxes to Caesar or not? Are
we to pay, or are we not to pay?" But he saw their trick
and said to them, "Why tempt me? Bring me a shilling.
16 Let me see it." So they brought one. He said, "Whose
likeness, whose inscription is this?" "Caesar's," they said.
17 Jesus said to them, "Give Caesar what belongs to Caesar,
give God what belongs to God." He astonished them.
18 Sadducees, men who hold there is no resurrection, also
19 came up and put a question to him. "Teacher," they said,
"Moses has written this law for us, that *if a man's brother
dies leaving a wife but no child, his brother is to take
20 the woman and raise offspring for his brother.* Now there
were seven brothers. The first married a wife and died
21 leaving no offspring: the second took her and died without
22 leaving any offspring: so did the third: none of the seven
23 left any offspring. Last of all the woman died too. At the
resurrection, when they rise, whose wife will she be? She
24 was wife to the seven of them." Jesus said to them, "Is
this not where you go wrong?—you understand neither the
25 scriptures nor the power of God. When people rise from
the dead they neither marry nor are married, they are
26 like the angels in heaven. As for the dead being raised,
have you not read in the book of Moses, at the passage on
the Bush, how God said to him, *I am the God of Abraham
27 and the God of Isaac and the God of Jacob?* He is not the
God of dead people but of living. You are far wrong."
28 Then a scribe came up, who had listened to the discussion.
Knowing Jesus had given them an apt answer, he put this
question to him, "What is the chief of all the commands?"
29 Jesus replied, "The chief one is: *Hear, O Israel, the Lord
30 our God is one Lord, and you must love the Lord your God
with your whole heart, with your whole soul, with your
31 whole mind, and with your whole strength.* The second is
this: *You must love your neighbour as yourself.* There is no
32 other command greater than these." The scribe said to him,
"Right, teacher! You have truly said, He is One, and there
33 is none else but Him. Also, to love him with the whole heart,
with the whole understanding, and with the whole strength,
and to love one's neighbour as oneself—that is far more than
34 all holocausts and sacrifices." Jesus noted his intelligent
answer and said to him, "You are not far off the Realm of
God." After that no one ventured to put any more questions to him.

35 And as Jesus taught in the temple he asked, "How can
36 the scribes say that the Christ is David's son? David himself said in the holy Spirit,
> The Lord said to my Lord, 'Sit at my right hand,
> till I make your enemies a footstool for your feet.'
37 David here calls him Lord. Then how can he be his son?"
Now the mass of the people listened with delight to him.
38 And in the course of his teaching he said, "Beware of the scribes! They like to walk about in long robes, to get
39 saluted in the marketplaces, to secure the front seats in
40 the synagogues and the best places at banquets; they prey upon the property of widows and offer long unreal prayers. All the heavier will their sentence be!"
41 Sitting down opposite the treasury, he watched the people putting their money into the treasury. A number of the
42 rich were putting in large sums, but a poor widow came up and put in two little coins amounting to a halfpenny.
43 And he called his disciples and said to them, "I tell you truly, this poor widow has put in more than all who have
44 put their money into the treasury; for they have all put in a contribution out of their surplus, but she has given out of her neediness all she possessed, her whole living."

13 As he went out of the temple one of his disciples said to him, "Look, teacher, what a size these stones and
2 buildings are!" Jesus said to him, "You see these great buildings? Not a stone shall be left on another, without being torn down."
3 And as he sat on the Hill of Olives opposite the temple, Peter and James and John and Andrew asked him in pri-
4 vate, "Tell us, when is this to happen? What will be the
5 sign for all this to be accomplished?" So Jesus began:
6 "Take care that no one misleads you:—many will come in
7 my name saying, 'I am he,' and mislead many. And when you hear of wars and rumours of war, do not be alarmed;
8 *these have to come, but it is not the end yet. For nation will rise against nation, and realm against realm;* there will be earthquakes here and there, and famines too. All
9 that is but the beginning of the trouble. Look to yourselves. Men will hand you over to Sanhedrins and you will be flogged in synagogues and brought before governors
10 and kings for my sake, to testify to them. (Ere the end,
11 the gospel must be preached to all nations.) Now when they carry you off to trial, do not worry beforehand about what you are to say; say whatever comes to your lips at the moment, for he who speaks is not you but the holy Spirit.
12 Brother will betray brother to death, the father will betray

S. MARK XIII

his child, *children will rise against their parents* and kill
13 them, and you will be hated by all men on account of my
name; but he will be saved who holds out to the very
end.
14 But whenever you see *the appalling Horror* standing
where he has no right to stand (let the reader note this),
15 then let those who are in Judaea fly to the hills; a man on
the housetop must not go down into the house or go inside
16 to fetch anything out of his house, and a man in the field
17 must not turn back to get his coat. Woe to women with
18 child and to women who give suck in those days! Pray
19 it may not be winter when it comes, for those days will be
days of *misery, the like of which has never been from the
beginning of God's creation until now*—no and never shall
20 be. Had not the Lord cut short those days, not a soul
would be saved alive; but he has cut them short for the
sake of the elect whom he has chosen.
21 If anyone tells you at that time, 'Look, here is the Christ,'
22 or, 'Look, there he is,' do not believe it; for false Christs
and *false prophets will* rise and *perform* signs and *wonders*
23 to mislead the elect if they can. Now take care! I am telling you of it all beforehand.
24 But when that misery is past, in those days,
*the sun will be darkened
and the moon will not yield her light,*
25 *the stars will drop from heaven,
and the orbs of the heavens will be shaken.*
26 Then they will see *the Son of man coming in the clouds*
27 *with great power and glory*. Then he will despatch his
angels and muster the elect from the four winds, from the
verge of earth to the verge of heaven.
28 Let the fig tree teach you a parable. As soon as its
branches turn soft and put out leaves, you know summer is
29 at hand; so, whenever you see this happen, you may be
sure He is at hand, at the very door.
30 I tell you truly, the present generation will not pass away
31 till all this happens. Heaven and earth will pass away,
but my words never.
32 Now no one knows anything about that day or hour, not
even the angels in heaven, not even the Son, but only the
33 Father. Take care, keep awake and pray; you never know
34 the time. It is like a man leaving his house to go abroad;
he puts his servants in charge, each with his work to do,
35 and he orders the porter to keep watch. Watch then, for
you never know when the Lord of the House will come, in
the late evening or at midnight or at cock-crow or in the
36 morning. Watch, in case he comes suddenly and finds you
37 asleep. Watch: I say it to you, and I say it to all."

14 The passover and the festival of unleavened bread fell two days later; so the high priests and scribes were trying how to get hold of him by craft and have him put
2 to death. "Only," they said, "it must not be during the festival; that would mean a popular riot."
3 Now when he was at Bethany in the house of Simon the leper, lying at table, a woman came up with an alabaster flask of pure nard perfume, which had cost a great sum; the flask she broke and poured the perfume over his head.
4 This angered some of those present. "What was the use
5 of wasting perfume like this? This perfume might have been sold for over three hundred shillings, and the poor
6 might have got that." So they upbraided her. But Jesus said, "Let her alone. Why are you annoying her? She has
7 done a beautiful thing to me. The poor you always have beside you, and you can be kind to them whenever you want;
8 but you will not always have me. She has done all she could—she has anticipated the perfuming of my body for
9 burial. I tell you truly, wherever the gospel is preached all over the world, men will speak of what she has done in memory of her."
10 Then Judas Iscariot, one of the twelve, went to the high
11 priests to betray him to them. They were delighted to hear it, and promised to pay him for it. Meantime he sought a good opportunity for betraying him.
12 On the first day of unleavened bread (the day when the paschal lamb was sacrificed) his disciples said to him, "Where do you want us to go and prepare for you to eat
13 the passover?" So he despatched two of his disciples, telling them, "Go into the city and you will meet a man carry-
14 ing a water-jar; follow him, and whatever house he goes into, tell the owner that the Teacher says, 'Where is my room, that I may eat the passover there with my disciples?'
15 He will show you a large room upstairs, with couches spread, all ready; prepare the passover for us there."
16 The disciples went away into the city and found it was as
17 he had told them. So they prepared the passover, and when
18 evening fell he arrived along with the twelve. As they were at table eating, Jesus said, "Truly I tell you, one of you is
19 going to betray me, one who is eating with me." They got distressed at this, and said to him one after another,
20 "Surely it is not me?" "Surely it is not me?" "One of the twelve," he told them, "one who is dipping into the same
21 dish as I am. The Son of man goes the road that the scripture has described for him, but woe to the man by whom the Son of man is betrayed! Better that man had
22 never been born!" And as they were eating he took a loaf and after the blessing he broke and gave it to them, saying,

23 "Take this, it means my body." He also took a cup and after thanking God he gave it to them, and they all drank
24 of it; he said to them, "This means my *covenant-blood*
25 which is shed for many; truly I tell you, I will never drink the produce of the vine again till the day I drink it new within the Realm of God."
26 After the hymn of praise they went out to the Hill of
27 Olives. Jesus said to them, "You will all be disconcerted, for it is written: *I will strike at the shepherd and the sheep*
28 *will be scattered*. But after my rising I will precede you to
29 Galilee." Peter said to him, "Though all are disconcerted,
30 I will not be." Jesus said to him, "I tell you truly, to-day you will disown me three times, this very night, before the
31 cock crows twice." But he persisted, "Though I have to die with you, I will never disown you." And they all said the same.
32 Then they came to a place called Gethsemane, and he
33 told his disciples, "Sit here till I pray." But he took Peter and James and John along with him; and as he began to
34 feel appalled and agitated, he said to them, "*My heart is*
35 *sad*, sad even to death; stay here and watch." Then he went forward a little and fell to the earth, praying that the
36 hour might pass away from him, if possible. "Abba, Father," he said, "Thou canst do anything. Take this cup away from me. Yet, not what I will but what thou wilt."
37 Then he came and found them asleep; so he said to Peter, "Are you sleeping, Simon? Could you not watch for a
38 single hour? Watch and pray, all of you, so that you may not slip into temptation. The spirit is eager but the flesh
39 is weak." Again he went away and prayed in the same
40 words as before; then he returned and found them once more asleep, for their eyes were heavy. They did not know
41 what to say to him. Then he came for the third time and said to them, "Still asleep? still resting? No more of that! The hour has come, here is the Son of man betrayed into
42 the hands of sinners. Come, get up, here is my betrayer
43 close at hand." At that very moment, while he was still speaking, Judas [Iscariot] one of the twelve came up accompanied by a mob with swords and clubs who had come
44 from the high priests and scribes and elders. Now his betrayer had given them a signal; he said, "Whoever I kiss, that is the man. Seize him and get him safely away."
45 So when he arrived he at once went up to him and said,
46 "Rabbi [rabbi]," and kissed him. Then they laid hands on
47 him and seized him, but one of the bystanders drew his sword and struck the servant of the high priest, cutting off
48 his ear. Jesus turned on them, saying, "Have you sallied out to arrest me like a robber, with swords and clubs?

49 Day after day I was beside you in the temple teaching, and you never seized me. However, it is to let the scriptures be fulfilled."
50 Then they left him and fled, all of them; one young man
51 did follow him, with only a linen sheet thrown round his
52 body, but when the [young] men seized him he fled away naked, leaving the sheet behind him.
53 They took Jesus away to the high priest, and all the high
54 priests and scribes and elders met there with him. Peter followed him at a distance till he got inside the courtyard of the high priest, where he sat down with the attendants to warm himself at the fire.
55 Now the high priests and the whole of the Sanhedrin tried to secure evidence against Jesus, in order to have him put to
56 death; but they could find none, for while many bore false
57 witness against him their evidence did not agree. Some got
58 up and bore false witness against him, saying, "We heard him say, 'I will destroy this temple made by hands, and in three days I will build another temple not made by hands.'
59 But even so the evidence did not agree. So the high priest
60 rose in their midst and asked Jesus, "Have you no reply to
61 make? What about this evidence against you?" He said nothing and made no answer. Again the high priest put a question to him. "Are you the Christ?" he said, "the Son of
62 the Blessed?" Jesus said, "I am. And, what is more, you will all see *the Son of man sitting at the right hand* of the
63 Power and *coming with the clouds of heaven*." Then the high priest tore his clothes and cried, "What more evidence
64 do we want? You have heard his blasphemy for yourselves. What is your mind?" They condemned him, all of them,
65 to the doom of death; and some of them started to spit on him and to blindfold him and buffet him, asking him, "Prophesy." The attendants treated him to cuffs and slaps.
66 Now as Peter was downstairs in the courtyard, a maid-
67 servant of the high priest came along, and when she noticed Peter warming himself she looked at him and said, "You
68 were with Jesus of Nazaret too." But he denied it. "I do not know," he said, "I have no idea what you mean." Then
69 he went outside into the passage. The cock crowed. Again the maidservant who had noticed him began to tell the by-
70 standers, "That fellow is one of them." But he denied it again. After a little the bystanders once more said to Peter, "To be sure, you are one of them. Why, you are a
71 Galilean!"* But he broke out cursing and swearing, "I
72 do not know the man you mean." At that moment the cock crowed for the second time. Then Peter remembered how

* Omitting [καὶ ἡ λαλιά σου ὁμοιάζει].

Jesus had told him, "Before the cock crows twice you will disown me thrice;" and he burst into tears.

15 Immediately morning came, the high priests held a consultation * with the elders and scribes and all the Sanhedrin, and after binding Jesus they led him off and
2 handed him over to Pilate. Pilate asked him, "Are you
3 the king of the Jews?" He replied, "Certainly." Then the high priest brought many accusations against him, and
4 once more Pilate asked him, "Have you no reply to make?
5 Look at all their charges against you." But, to the aston-
6 ishment of Pilate, Jesus answered no more. Now at festival time he used to release for them some prisoner whom they
7 begged from him. (There was a man called Bar-Abbas in prison, among the rioters who had committed murder dur-
8 ing the insurrection.) So the crowd pressed up and started
9 to ask him for his usual boon. Pilate replied, "Would you
10 like me to release the king of the Jews for you?" (For he knew the high priests had handed him over out of envy.)
11 But the high priests stirred up the crowd to get him to
12 release Bar-Abbas for them instead. Pilate asked them again, "And what am I to do with your so-called king of
13 the Jews?" Whereupon they shouted again, "Crucify him."
14 "Why," said Pilate, "what has he done wrong?" But they
15 shouted more fiercely than ever, "Crucify him!" So, as Pilate wanted to satisfy the crowd, he released Bar-Abbas for them; Jesus he handed over to be crucified, after he had scourged him.
16 The soldiers took him inside the courtyard (that is, the
17 praetorium) and got all the regiment together; then they dressed him in purple, put on his head a crown of thorns
18 which they had plaited, and began to salute him with,
19 "Hail, O king of the Jews!" They struck him on the head with a stick and spat upon him and bent their knees to
20 him in homage. Then, after making fun of him, they stripped off the purple, put on his own clothes, and took
21 him away to crucify him. They forced Simon a Cyrenian who was passing on his way from the country (the father
22 of Alexander and Rufus) to carry his cross, and they led him to the place called Golgotha (which means the place of
23 a skull). They offered him wine flavoured with myrrh,
24 but he would not take it. Then they crucified him and *distributed his clothes among themselves, drawing lots for*
25 *them to decide each man's share.* It was nine in the morn-
26 ing when they crucified him. The inscription bearing his charge was:
THE KING OF THE JEWS.

* Reading ποιήσαντες instead of ἑτοιμάσαντες.

27 They also crucified two robbers along with him, one at his
29 right and one at his left.* Those who passed by scoffed at
him, nodding at him in derision and calling, "Ha! You
were to destroy the temple and build it in three days!
30 Come down from the cross and save yourself!" So, too,
31 the high priests made fun of him to themselves with the
scribes; "he saved others," they said, "but he cannot save
32 himself! Let 'the Christ,' 'the king of Israel' come down
now from the cross! Let us see that and we will believe!"
Those who were crucified with him also denounced him.
33   When twelve o'clock came, darkness covered the whole
34 land till three o'clock, and at three o'clock Jesus gave a loud
cry, "Elôi, Elôi, lema sabachthanei" (which means, My
35 God, my God, why hast thou forsaken me?) On hearing
this some of the bystanders said, "Look, he is calling for
36 Elijah." One man ran off, soaked a sponge in vinegar, and put
it on the end of a stick to give him a drink, saying, "Come
37 on, let us see if Elijah does come to take him down!" But
38 Jesus gave a loud cry and expired. And the curtain of
39 the temple was torn in two, from top to bottom. Now when
the army-captain who stood facing him saw that he expired
in this way, he said, "This man was certainly a son of God."
40 There were some women also watching at a distance,
among them Mary of Magdala, Mary the mother of James
41 the younger and of Joses, and Salome, women who had followed him when he was in Galilee and waited on him, besides a number of other women who had accompanied him
to Jerusalem.
42   By this time it was evening, and as it was the day of
43 Preparation (that is, the day before the sabbath) Joseph
of Arimathaea, a councillor of good position who himself
was on the outlook for the Reign of God, ventured to go to
44 Pilate and ask for the body of Jesus. Pilate was surprised
that he was dead already; he summoned the captain and
45 asked if he had been dead some time, and on ascertaining
this from the captain he bestowed the corpse on Joseph.
46 He, after buying a linen sheet, took him down and swathed
him in the linen, laying him in a tomb which had been cut
out of the rock and rolling a boulder up against the opening
47 of the tomb. Now Mary of Magdala and Mary the mother
of Joses noted where he was laid.

16 And when the sabbath had passed Mary of Magdala,
Mary the mother of James, and Salome bought some
2 spices in order to go and anoint him; and very early on the

* Von Soden retains ver. 28 (cp. Luke xxii, 37): "So the scripture was fulfilled which says, *He was classed among criminals.*"

first day of the week they went to the tomb, after sunrise.
3 They said to themselves, "Who will roll away the boulder for us at the opening of the tomb?" (for it was a very large
4 boulder).* But when they looked they saw the boulder had
5 been rolled to one side, and on entering the tomb they saw a youth sitting on the right dressed in a white robe. They
6 were bewildered, but he said to them, "Do not be bewildered. You are looking for Jesus of Nazaret, who was crucified?
7 He has risen, he is not here. That is the place where he was laid. Go you and tell his disciples and Peter, 'He precedes you to Galilee; you shall see him there, as he told
8 you.'" And they fled out of the tomb, for they were seized with terror and beside themselves. They said nothing to anyone, for they were afraid of —.†

(a)

9 Now after he rose early on the first day of the week, he appeared first to Mary of Magdala out of whom he had cast
10 seven daemons. She went and reported it to those who had
11 been with him, as they mourned and wept; but although they heard he was alive and had been seen by her, they
12 would not believe it. After this he appeared in another form to two of them as they were walking on their way to
13 the country. They too went and reported it to the rest,
14 but they would not believe them either. Afterwards he appeared at table to the eleven themselves and reproached them for their unbelief and dulness of mind, because they had not believed those who saw him risen from the dead. [But they excused themselves, saying, "This age of lawlessness and unbelief lies under the sway of Satan, who will not allow what lies under the unclean spirits ‡ to understand the truth and power of God; therefore," they said to Christ, "reveal your righteousness now." Christ answered them, "The limit of years for Satan's power has now expired, but other terrors are at hand. I was delivered to death on behalf of sinners,§ that they might return to the truth and sin no more, that they might inherit that glory of righteousness which is spiritual and imperishable in

* Transposing the second clause of ver. 4 to the end of ver. 3.
† The following appendix represents a couple of second century attempts to complete the gospel. The passage within brackets in the first of these epilogues originally belonged to it, but was excised for some reason at an early date. Jerome quoted part of it, but the full text has only been discovered quite recently in codex W, the Freer uncial of the gospels.
‡ Or, the unclean things that lie under the control of spirits.
§ The Greek is obscure at this point.

15 heaven."] And he said to them, "Go to all the world and preach the gospel to every creature:
16 he who believes and is baptized shall be saved, but he who will not believe shall be condemned.
17 And for those who believe, these miracles will follow:
they will cast out daemons in my name,
they will talk in foreign tongues,
18 they will handle serpents,
and if they drink any deadly poison, it will not hurt them;
they will lay hands on the sick and make them well."
19 Then after speaking to them the Lord Jesus was taken
20 up to heaven and *sat down at the right hand of God*, while they went out and preached everywhere, the Lord working with them and confirming the word by the miracles that endorsed it.

(*b*)

But they gave Peter and his companions a brief account of all that had been enjoined. And after that, Jesus himself sent out by means of them from east to west the sacred and imperishable message of eternal salvation.

THE GOSPEL ACCORDING TO

S. LUKE

1 INASMUCH as a number of writers have essayed to draw
2 up a narrative of the established facts in our religion exactly as these have been handed down to us by the original eyewitnesses who were in the service of the Gospel Mes-
3 sage, and inasmuch as I have gone carefully over them all myself from the very beginning, I have decided, O Theophilus, to write them out in order for your excellency,
4 to let you know the solid truth of what you have been taught.

5 In the days of Herod king of Judaea there was a priest called Zechariah, who belonged to the division of Abijah; he had a wife who belonged to the daughters of Aaron, and
6 her name was Elizabeth. They were both just in the sight of God, blameless in their obedience to all the commands
7 and regulations of God; but they had no child, for Elizabeth was barren. Both of them were advanced in years.
8 Now while he was officiating before God in the due
9 course of his division, it fell to him by lot, as was the custom of the priesthood, to enter the sanctuary of the
10 Lord and burn incense, the mass of the people all remain-
11 ing in prayer outside at the hour of incense. And an angel of the Lord appeared to him, standing on the right side
12 of the altar of incense. When Zechariah saw him he was
13 troubled, and fear fell on him; but the angel said to him, "Fear not, Zechariah, your prayer has been heard; your wife Elizabeth will bear a son to you, and you must call his name John.
14   It will be joy and gladness for you,
    and many will rejoice over his birth:
15   for he shall be great in the sight of the Lord,
    he will drink neither wine nor strong drink,
    he will be filled with the holy Spirit from his very birth;
16   he will turn many of the sons of Israel to the Lord their God,
17   he will go in front of Him with the spirit and power *of Elijah*
    to turn the hearts of fathers to their children,

turning the disobedient to the wisdom of the just,
to make a people ready and prepared for the Lord."
18 Zechariah said to the angel, "But how am I to be sure of this? I am an old man myself, and my wife is advanced
19 in years." The angel replied, "I am Gabriel, I stand before God; I have been sent to speak to you and to tell you
20 this good news. But you will be silent and unable to speak till the day this happens, because you have not believed what I told you; it will be accomplished, for all that, in due time."
21 Now the people were waiting for Zechariah and wonder-
22 ing that he stayed so long inside the sanctuary. When he did come out he could not speak to them, so they realized that he had seen a vision in the sanctuary; he made signs
23 to them and remained dumb. Then, after his term of service had elapsed, he went home.
24 After those days his wife Elizabeth conceived; and for
25 five months she concealed herself. "The Lord has done this for me," she said, "he has now deigned to remove my reproach among men."
26 In the sixth month the angel Gabriel was sent by God
27 to a town in Galilee called Nazaret, to a maiden who was betrothed to a man called Joseph, belonging to the house of
28 David. The maiden's name was Mary. The angel went in and said to her, "Hail, O favoured one! the Lord be with
29 you!" At this she was startled; she thought to herself,
30 whatever can this greeting mean? But the angel said to her, "Fear not, Mary, you have found favour with God.
31 You are to conceive and bear a son, and you must call his name Jesus.
32 He will be great, he will be called the Son of the Most High,
and the Lord God will give him *the throne of David his father;*
33 *he will reign* over the house of Jacob *for ever, and to his reign there will be no end.*"
34 "How can this be?" said Mary to the angel, "I have no
35 husband." The angel answered her, "The holy Spirit will come upon you, the power of the Most High will overshadow you; hence what is born *will be called holy,* Son of
36 God. Look, there is your kinswoman Elizabeth! Even she has conceived a son in her old age, and she who was called
37 barren is now in her sixth month; for *with God nothing*
38 *is ever impossible.*" Mary said, "I am here to serve the Lord. Let it be as you have said." Then the angel went away.
39 In those days Mary started with haste for the hill-
40 country, for a town of Judah; she entered the house of
41 Zechariah and saluted Elizabeth, and when Elizabeth heard

the salutation of Mary, the babe leapt in her womb. Then
42 Elizabeth was filled with the holy Spirit; she called out
with a loud cry,
"Blessed among women are you, and blessed is the fruit of
your womb!
43 What have I done to have the mother of my Lord come to
44 me? Why, as soon as the sound of your salutation reached
45 my ears, the babe leapt for joy within my womb. And
blessed is she who believed that the Lord's words to her
46 would be fulfilled." Then Mary said
"*My soul* magnifies *the Lord,*
47 . *My spirit has joy in God my Saviour:*
48 *for he has considered the humiliation of his servant.*
From this time forth all generations will call me blessed,
49 for He who is Mighty has done great things for me.
His name is holy,
50 *his mercy is on generation after generation,*
for those who reverence him.
51 He has done a deed of might *with his arm,*
he has scattered the proud with their purposes,
52 *princes he has dethroned* and *the poor he has uplifted,*
53 *he has satisfied the hungry with good things* and *sent
the rich away empty.*
54 *He has succoured his servant Israel,*
mindful of his mercy—
55 *as he promised our fathers,*
to have mercy on Abraham and his offspring for ever."
56 Mary stayed with her about three months and then returned home.
57 Now the time for Elizabeth's delivery had elapsed, and
58 she gave birth to a son. When her neighbours and kinsfolk heard of the Lord's great mercy to her they rejoiced
59 with her, and on the eighth day came to circumcise the
child. They were going to call it by the name of its father
60 Zechariah, but the mother told them, "No, the child is to
61 be called John." They said to her, "None of your family is
62 called by that name." Then they made signs to the father,
63 to find out what he wanted the child to be called, and he
asked for a writing-tablet and wrote down, "His name is
64 John," to the astonishment of all. Instantly his mouth
was opened, his tongue loosed, and he spoke out blessing
65 God. Then fear fell on all their neighbours, and all these
events were talked of through the whole of the hill-country
66 of Judaea. All who heard of it bore it in mind; they said,
"Whatever will this child become?" For the hand of the
Lord was indeed with him.
67 And Zechariah his father was filled with the holy Spirit;
he prophesied in these words,

S. LUKE II

68 *"Blessed be the Lord the God of Israel,*
   for he has cared for his people and wrought them redemption;
69 *he has raised up a strong saviour for us*
   in the house of his servant David—
70 *as he promised of old by the lips of his prophets—*
71   *to save us from our foes and from the hand of all who hate us,*
72 *to deal mercifully with our fathers*
   and to be mindful of his holy covenant,
73   *of the oath he swore to Abraham our father,*
74   *that freed from fear and from the hand of our foes*
75 *we should worship him in holiness and uprightness*
   all our days within his presence.
76 *And you, my child, shall be called a prophet of the Most High;*
   for you shall go in front of the Lord to make his ways ready,
77 *to bring his people the knowledge of salvation*
   through the remission of their sins—
78 *by the tender mercy of our God,*
   who will make the Dawn visit us from on high,
79 *to shine on those who sit in darkness and in the shadow of death,*
   to guide our steps into the way of peace."
80 And the child grew, he became strong in the Spirit and remained in the desert till the day when he made his appearance before Israel.

2 Now in those days an edict was issued by Caesar
2 Augustus for a census of the whole world. (This was the first census, and it took place when Quirinius was gov-
3 ernor of Syria.) So everyone went to be registered, each
4 at his own town, and as Joseph belonged to the house and family of David he went up from Galilee to Judaea, from
5 the town of Nazaret to David's town called Bethlehem, to
6 be registered along with Mary his wife. She was pregnant, and while they were there the days elapsed for her de-
7 livery; she gave birth to her firstborn son, and as there was no room for them inside the khan she wrapped him
8 up and laid him in a stall for cattle. There were some shepherds in the district who were out in the fields keep-
9 ing guard over their flocks by night; and an angel of the Lord flashed upon them, the glory of the Lord shone all
10 round them. They were terribly afraid, but the angel said to them, "Have no fear. This is good news I am bringing you, news of a great joy that is meant for all the People.

11 To-day you have a saviour born in the town of David,
12 the Lord messiah. And here is a proof for you: you will
find a baby wrapped up and lying in a stall for cattle."
13 Then a host of heaven's army suddenly appeared beside
the angel extolling God and saying,
14 "Glory to God in high heaven,
and peace on earth for men whom he favours!"
15 Now when the angels had left them and gone away to
heaven, the shepherds said to one another, "Let us be off
to Bethlehem to see this thing that the Lord has told us
16 of." So they made haste and discovered Mary and Joseph
17 and the baby lying in the stall for cattle. When they saw
this they told people about the word which had been
18 spoken to them about the child; all who heard it were
19 astonished at the story of the shepherds, and as for Mary,
20 she treasured it all up and mused upon it. Then the shepherds went away back, glorifying and extolling God for all they had heard and seen as they had been told they would.
21 When the eight days had passed for his circumcision, he was named Jesus—the name given by the angel before he had been conceived in the womb.
22 When the days for their purification in terms of the Mosaic law had elapsed, they brought him up to Jeru-
23 salem to present him to the Lord (as it is written in the law of the Lord: *every male that opens the womb must be*
24 *considered consecrated to the Lord*) and also to offer the sacrifice prescribed in the law of the Lord, *a pair of turtle-*
25 *doves or two young pigeons*. Now there was a man in Jerusalem called Symeon, an upright and devout man, who was on the outlook for the Consolation of Israel. The holy
26 Spirit was upon him; indeed it had been revealed to him by the holy Spirit that he was not to see death before
27 he had seen the Lord messiah. By an inspiration of the Spirit he came to the temple, and when the parents of the child Jesus carried him in to perform the customary regu-
28 lations of the law for him, then Symeon took him in his arms, blessed God, and said,
29 "Now, Master, thou canst let thy servant go,
and go in peace, as thou didst promise;
30 for mine eyes *have seen thy saving power*
31 which thou hast prepared *before the face of all the peoples*,
32 *to be a light of revelation for the Gentiles*
and *a glory to thy people Israel.*"
33 His father and mother were astonished at these words
34 about him, but Symeon blessed them, and to his mother Mary he said, "This child is destined for the downfall as

well as for the rise of many a one in Israel; destined to be a Sign for man's attack—to bring out the secret aims of
35 many a heart. And your own soul will be pierced by a spear."
36 There was also a prophetess, Hannah the daughter of Phanuel, who belonged to the tribe of Asher; she was advanced in years, having lived seven years with her hus-
37 band after her girlhood and having been a widow for eighty-four years. She was never away from the temple;
38 night and day she worshipped, fasting and praying. Now at that very hour she came up, and she offered praise to God and spoke of him to all who were on the outlook for the redemption of Jerusalem.
39 When they had finished all the regulations of the law of the Lord, they returned to Galilee, to their own town of
40 Nazaret. And the child grew and became strong; he was filled with wisdom, and the favour of God was on him.
41 Every year his parents used to travel to Jerusalem at the
42 passover festival; and when he was twelve years old they
43 went up as usual to the festival. After spending the full number of days they came back, but the boy Jesus stayed behind in Jerusalem. His parents did not know of this;
44 they supposed he was in the caravan and travelled on for a day, searching for him among their kinsfolk and ac-
45 quaintances. Then, as they failed to find him, they came
46 back to Jerusalem in search of him. Three days later they found him in the temple, seated among the teachers, listen-
47 ing to them and asking them questions, till all his hearers
48 were amazed at the intelligence of his own answers. When his parents saw him they were astounded, and his mother said to him, "My son, why have you behaved like this to us? Here have your father and I been looking for you
49 anxiously!" "Why did you look for me?" he said, "Did you
50 not know I had to be at my Father's house?" But they
51 did not understand what he said. Then he went down along with them to Nazaret, and did as they told him.
52 His mother treasured up everything in her heart. And Jesus *increased* in wisdom and in stature, and *in favour with God and man.*

3 Now in the fifteenth year of the reign of Tiberius Caesar, when Pontius Pilate was governor of Judaea, Herod being tetrarch of Galilee, Philip his brother tetrarch of the country of Ituraea and Trachonitis, and Lysias
2 tetrarch of Abilene, during the high priesthood of Annas and Caiaphas the word of God came to John the son
3 of Zechariah in the desert; and he went into all the Jordan-district preaching a baptism of repentance for the

S. LUKE III

4 remission of sins—as it is written in the book of the sayings of the prophet Isaiah,
The voice of one who cries in the desert,
'Make the way ready for the Lord,
level the paths for him.
5 Every valley shall be filled up,
every hill and mound laid low,
the crooked made straight,
the rough roads smooth;
6 so shall all flesh see the saving power of God.'
7 To the crowds who came out to get baptized by him John said, "You brood of vipers, who told you to flee from the
8 coming Wrath? Now, produce fruits that answer to your repentance, instead of beginning to say to yourselves, 'We have a father in Abraham.' I tell you, God can raise up
9 children for Abraham from these stones! The axe is lying all ready at the root of the trees; any tree that is not producing good fruit will be cut down and thrown into the fire."
10 The crowds asked him, "Then what are we to do?"
11 He replied, "Let everyone who possesses two shirts share with him who has none, and let him who has food do like-
12 wise." Taxgatherers also came to get baptized, and they
13 said to him, "Teacher, what are we to do?" He said to
14 them, "Never exact more than your fixed rate." Soldiers also asked him, "And what are we to do?" He said to them, "Never extort money, never lay a false charge, but be content with your pay."
15 Now as people's expectations were roused and as everybody thought to himself about John, "Can he be the
16 Christ," John said to them all,
"I baptize you with water,
but after me one who is mightier will come,
and I am not fit to untie the string of his sandals;
he will baptize you with the holy Spirit and fire.
17 His winnowing-fan is in his hand to purge his threshing-floor,
to gather the wheat into his granary
and burn the straw with fire unquenchable."
18 Thus with many another appeal he spoke his message
19 to the people. But Herod the tetrarch, who had been reproved by him for Herodias his brother's wife as well as for all the wickedness that he, Herod, had committed,
20 crowned all by shutting John up in prison.
21 Now when all the people had been baptized and when Jesus had been baptized and was praying, heaven opened
22 and the holy Spirit descended in bodily form like a dove upon him; and a voice came from heaven,

"Thou art my son, the Beloved,
to-day have I become thy father." *
23 At the outset Jesus was about thirty years of age; he
was the son, as people supposed, of Joseph, the son of
24 Heli, the son of Matthat, the son of Levi, the son of Melchi,
25 the son of Jannai, the son of Joseph, the son of Mattathias,
the son of Amos, the son of Nahum, the son of Esli,
26 the son of Naggai, the son of Maath, the son of Mattathias, son of Semein, the son of Josech, the son of
27 Joda, the son of Joanan, the son of Rhesa, the son of
28 Zerubbabel, the son of Shealtiel, the son of Neri, the son of
Melchi, the son of Addi, the son of Kosam, the son of
29 Elmadam, the son of Er, the son of Jesus, the son of
30 Eliezer, the son of Jorim, the son of Matthat, the son of
Symeon, the son of Judas, the son of Joseph, the son of
31 Jonam, the son of Eliakim, the son of Melea, the son of
Menna, the son of Mattatha, the son of Nathan, the son
32 of David, the son of Jessai, the son of Jobed, the son of
33 Boaz, the son of Sala, the son of Nahshon, the son of
Aminadab, the son of Admin, the son of Arni, the son of
34 Hezron, the son of Perez, the son of Judah, the son of
Jacob, the son of Isaac, the son of Abraham, the son of
35 Terah, the son of Nachor, the son of Serug, the son of
36 Reu, the son of Peleg, the son of Eber, the son of Sala, the
son of Kainan, the son of Arphaxad, the son of Shem, the
37 son of Noah, the son of Lamech, the son of Methuselah,
the son of Enoch, the son of Jared, the son of Maleleel, the
38 son of Kainan, the son of Enos, the son of Seth, the son of
Adam, the son of God.

4 FROM the Jordan Jesus came back full of the holy
Spirit, and for forty days he was led by the Spirit in the
2 desert, while the devil tempted him. During these days he
3 ate nothing, and when they were over he felt hungry. The
devil said to him, "If you are God's son, tell this stone to
4 become a loaf." Jesus replied to him, "It is written, *Man
5 is not to live on bread alone.*" Then he lifted Jesus up
and showed him all the realms of the universe in a single
6 instant; and the devil said to him, "I will give you all their
power and grandeur, for it has been made over to me and
7 I can give it to anyone I choose. If you will worship
8 before me, then it shall all be yours." Jesus answered him,
"It is written, *You must worship the Lord your God, and
9 serve him alone.*" Then he brought him to Jerusalem

* Reading ἐγὼ σήμερον γεγέννηκά σε, with D, the Old Latin, Justin, Clement, Tyconius, etc. In the other MSS it has been altered, for harmonistic reasons.

and placing him on the pinnacle of the temple said to
him, "If you are God's son, throw yourself down from this;
10 for it is written,
> He will give his angels charge of you,
11 and
> They will bear you on their hands,
> lest you strike your foot against a stone."
12 Jesus answered him, "It has been said, You shall not tempt
13 the Lord your God." And after exhausting every kind of
temptation the devil left him till a fit opportunity arrived.
14 Then Jesus came back in the power of the Spirit to
Galilee, and the news of him spread over all the surround-
15 ing country. He taught in their synagogues and was glori-
16 fied by all. Then he came to Nazaret, where he had been
brought up, and on the sabbath he entered the synagogue
17 as was his custom. He stood up to read the lesson and
was handed the book of the prophet Isaiah; on opening the
book he came upon the place where it was written,
18 > The Spirit of the Lord is upon me:
> for he has consecrated me to preach the gospel to the
> poor,
> he has sent me to proclaim release for captives
> and recovery of sight for the blind,
> to set free the oppressed,
19 > to proclaim the Lord's year of favour.
20 Then, folding up the book, he handed it back to the
attendant and sat down. The eyes of all in the synagogue
21 were fixed on him, and he proceeded to tell them that
22 "To-day, this scripture is fulfilled in your hearing." All
spoke well of him and marvelled at the gracious words
that came from his lips; they said, "Is this not Joseph's
23 son?" So he said to them, "No doubt you will repeat to
me this proverb, 'Doctor, cure yourself!' 'Do here in your
own country all we have heard you did in Capharnahum.'"
24 He added, "I tell you truly, no prophet is ever welcome
25 in his native place. I tell you for a fact,
> In Israel there were many widows during the days of
> Elijah,
> when the sky was closed for three years and six
> months,
> when a great famine came over all the land:
26 > yet Elijah was not sent to any of these,
> but only to a widow woman at Zarephath in Sidon.
27 > And in Israel there were many lepers in the time of the
> prophet Elisha,
> yet none of these was cleansed,
> but only Naaman the Syrian."
28 When they heard this, all in the synagogue were filled

29 with rage; they rose up, put him out of the town, and brought him to the brow of the hill on which their town
30 was built, in order to hurl him down. But he made his way through them and went off.
31 Then he went down to Capharnahum, a town of Galilee,
32 and on the sabbath he taught the people; they were astounded at his teaching, for his word came with author-
33 ity. Now in the synagogue there was a man possessed by the spirit of an unclean daemon, who shrieked aloud,
34 "Ha! Jesus of Nazaret, what business have you with us? Have you come to destroy us? I know who you are, you
35 are God's holy One!" But Jesus checked it, saying, "Be quiet, come out of him." And after throwing him down before them the daemon did come out of him without doing
36 him any harm. Then amazement came over them all; they talked it over among themselves, saying, "What does this mean? He orders the unclean spirits with authority
37 and power, and they come out!" And a report of him spread over all the surrounding country.
38 When he got up to leave the synagogue he went to the house of Simon. Simon's mother-in-law was laid up with a severe attack of fever, so they asked him about her;
39 he stood over her and checked the fever, and it left her.
40 Then she instantly got up and ministered to them. At sunset all who had any people ill with any sort of disease brought them to him; he laid his hands on everyone and
41 healed them. From many people daemons were also driven out, clamouring aloud, "You are God's son!" But he checked them and refused to let them say anything, as
42 they knew he was the Christ. When day broke he went away out to a lonely spot, but the crowds made inquiries about him, came to where he was, and tried to keep
43 him from leaving them. He answered them, "I must preach the glad news of the Reign of God to the other
44 towns as well, for that is what I was sent to do." So he went preaching through the synagogues of Judaea.

5 Now as the crowd were pressing on him to listen to the
2 word of God, he saw, as he stood beside the lake of Gennesaret, two boats on the shore of the lake; the fishermen
3 had disembarked and were washing their nets. So he entered one of the boats, which belonged to Simon, and asked him to push out a little from the land. Then he sat
4 down and taught the people from the boat. When he stopped speaking, he said to Simon, "Push out to the deep
5 water and lower your nets for a take." Simon replied, "Master, we worked all night and got nothing! However,
6 I will lower the nets at your command." And when they

did so, they enclosed a huge shoal of fish, so that their
7 nets began to break. Then they made signals to their
mates in the other boat to come and assist them. They
8 came and filled both the boats, till they began to sink. But
when Simon Peter saw it he fell at the knees of Jesus, cry-
9 ing, "Lord, leave me; I am a sinful man." For amazement
had seized him and all his companions at the take of fish
10 they had caught; as was the case with James and John, the
sons of Zebedaeus, who were partners of Simon. Then said
Jesus to Simon, "Have no fear; from now your catch will
11 be men." Then they brought the boats to land, and leaving all they followed him.
12 When he was in one of their towns there was a man full
of leprosy who, on seeing Jesus, fell on his face and besought him, "If you only choose, sir, you can cleanse me."
13 So he stretched his hand out and touched him, with the
words, "I do choose, be cleansed." And the leprosy at once
14 left him. Jesus ordered him not to say a word to anybody,
but to "Go off and show yourself to the priest, and offer
whatever Moses prescribed for your cleansing, to notify
15 men." But the news of him spread abroad more and more;
large crowds gathered to hear him and to be healed of their
16 complaints, while he kept in lonely places and prayed.
17 One day he was teaching, and near him sat Pharisees
and doctors of the Law who had come from every village
of Galilee and Judaea as well as from Jerusalem. Now the
power of the Lord was present for the work of healing.
18 Some men came up carrying a man who was paralysed; they
tried to carry him inside and lay him in front of Jesus,
19 but when they could not find any means of getting him in,
on account of the crowd, they climbed to the top of the
house and let him down through the tiles, mattress and all,
20 among the people in front of Jesus. When he saw their
21 faith he said, "Man, your sins are forgiven you." Then the
scribes and Pharisees began to argue, "Who is this blasphemer? Who can forgive sins, who but God alone?"
22 Conscious that they were arguing to themselves, Jesus
23 addressed them, saying, "Why argue in your hearts? Which
is the easier thing, to say, 'Your sins are forgiven,' or to
24 say, 'Rise and walk'? But to let you see the Son of man
has power on earth to forgive sins"—he said to the paralysed man, "Rise, I tell you, lift your mattress and go
25 home." Instantly he got up before them, lifted what he
26 had been lying on, and went home glorifying God. And all
were seized with astonishment; they glorified God and were
filled with awe, saying, "We have seen incredible things today."
27 On going outside after this he noticed a taxgatherer called

28 29 Levi sitting at the tax-office and said to him, "Follow me"; he rose, left everything and followed him. Levi held a great banquet for him in his house; there was a large company present of taxgatherers and others who were guests
30 along with them. But the Pharisees and their scribes complained to his disciples, "Why do you eat and drink with
31 taxgatherers and sinners?" Jesus replied to them, "Healthy people have no need of a doctor, but those who are ill:
32 I have not come to call just men but sinners to repentance."
33 They said to him, "The disciples of John fast frequently and offer prayers, as do the disciples of the Pharisees; but
34 your adherents eat and drink." Jesus said to them, "Can you make friends at a wedding fast while the bridegroom is beside them?
35 A time will come when the bridegroom is taken from them, and then they will fast at that time."
36 He also told them a parable:
"No one tears a piece from a new cloak and sews it on an old cloak;
otherwise he will tear the new cloak,
and the new piece will not match with the old.
37 No one pours fresh wine into old wineskins;
otherwise the fresh wine will burst the wineskins,
the wine will be spilt and the wineskins ruined.
38 No, fresh wine must be poured into new wineskins.
39 Besides, no one wants new wine [immediately] after drinking old;
'The old,' he says, 'is better.'"

6 ONE sabbath it happened that as he was crossing the cornfields his disciples pulled some ears of corn and ate
2 them, rubbing them in their hands. Some of the Pharisees said, "Why are you doing what is not allowed on the sab-
3 bath?" But Jesus answered them, "And have you never read what David did when he and his men were hungry?
4 He went into the house of God, took *the loaves of the Presence* and ate them, giving them to his men as well—bread
5 that no one is allowed to eat except the priests." And he said to them, "The Son of man is lord even over the sabbath."
6 Another sabbath he happened to go into the synagogue and teach. Now a man was there who had his right hand
7 withered, and the scribes and Pharisees watched to see if he would heal on the sabbath, so as to discover some charge
8 against him. He knew what was in their minds; so he told

the man with the withered hand, "Rise and stand forward."
9 He rose and stood before them. Then Jesus said to them, "I ask you, is it right on the sabbath to help or to hurt,
10 to save life or to kill?" And glancing round at them all in anger he said to the man, "Stretch out your hand." He
11 did so, and his hand was quite restored. This filled them with fury, and they discussed what they could do to Jesus.
12 It was in these days that he went off to the hillside to
13 pray. He spent the whole night in prayer to God, and when day broke he summoned his disciples, choosing twelve of
14 them, to whom he gave the name of 'apostles': Simon (to whom he gave the name of Peter), Andrew his brother,
15 James, John, Philip, Bartholomew, Matthew, Thomas, James the son of Alphaeus, Simon (who was called 'the Zealot'),
16 Judas the son of James, and Judas Iscariot (who turned
17 traitor). With them he came down the hill and stood on a level spot. There was a great company of his disciples with him, and a large multitude of people from all Judaea, from Jerusalem, and from the coast of Tyre and Sidon, who had come to hear him and to get cured of their diseases.
18 Those who were annoyed with unclean spirits also were
19 healed. Indeed the whole of the crowd made efforts to touch him, for power issued from him and cured everybody.
20 Then, raising his eyes he looked at his disciples and said: "Blessed are you poor!
   the Realm of God is yours.
21 Blessed are you who hunger to-day!
   you shall be satisfied.
   Blessed are you who weep to-day!
   you shall laugh.
22 Blessed are you when men will hate you,
   when they will excommunicate you and denounce you
      and defame you as wicked on account of the Son
      of man;
23   rejoice on that day and leap for joy!
   rich is your reward in heaven—
   for their fathers did the very same to the prophets.
24 But woe to you rich folk!
   you get all the comforts you will ever get.
25 Woe to you who have your fill to-day!
   you will be hungry.
   Woe to you who laugh to-day!
   you will wail and weep.
26 Woe to you when all men speak well of you!
   that is just what their fathers did to the false
      prophets.
27 I tell you, my hearers,
   love your enemies, do good to those who hate you;

28   bless those who curse you, pray for those who abuse you.
29   If a man strikes you on the one cheek,
         offer him the other as well:
         if anyone takes your coat,
         do not deny him your shirt as well;
30   give to anyone who asks you,
         and do not ask your goods back from anyone who has taken them.
31   As you would like men to do to you,
         so do to them.
32   If you love only those who love you, what credit is that to you?
         Why, even sinful men love those who love them.
33   If you help only those who help you, what merit is that to you?
         Why, even sinful men do that.
34   If you only lend to those from whom you hope to get something, what credit is that to you?
         Even sinful men lend to one another, so as to get a fair return.
35   No, you must love your enemies and help them,
         you must lend to them without expecting any return;
         then you will have a rich reward,
         you will be sons of the Most High—
         for he is kind even to the ungrateful and the evil.
36   Be merciful,
         as your Father is merciful.
37   Also, judge not, and you will not be judged yourselves:
         condemn not, and you will not be condemned:
         pardon, and you will be pardoned yourselves:
38   give, and you will have ample measure given you—
         they will pour into your lap measure pressed down,
         shaken together, and running over;
         for the measure you deal out to others will be dealt back to yourselves."
39   He also told them a parabolic word:
"Can one blind man lead another?
         will they not both fall into a pit?
40   A scholar is not above his teacher:
         but if he is perfectly trained he will be like his teacher.
41 Why do you note the splinter in your brother's eye and
42 fail to see the plank in your own eye? How dare you say to your brother, 'Brother, let me take out the splinter that is in your eye,' and you never notice the plank in your own eye? You hypocrite! take the plank out of your own eye first, and then you will see properly to take out the splinter in your brother's eye.

43 No sound tree bears rotten fruit,
nor again does a rotten tree bear sound fruit:
44 each tree is known by its fruit.
Figs are not gathered from thorns,
and grapes are not plucked from a bramble-bush.
45 The good man produces good from the good stored in his heart,
and the evil man evil from his evil:
for a man's mouth utters what his heart is full of.
46
47 Why call me, 'Lord, Lord!' and obey me not? Everyone who comes to me and listens to my words and acts upon
48 them, I will show you whom he is like. He is like a man engaged in building a house, who dug deep down and laid his foundation on the rock; when a flood came, the river dashed against that house but could not shake it, for it
49 had been well built. He who has listened and has not obeyed is like a man who built a house on the earth with no foundation; the river dashed against it and it collapsed at once, and the ruin of that house was great."

7 WHEN he had finished what he had to say in the hearing of the people, he went into Capharnahum.
2 Now there was an army-captain who had a servant ill whom he valued very highly. This man was at the point
3 of death; so, when the captain heard about Jesus, he sent some Jewish elders to him, asking him to come and make
4 his servant well. When they reached Jesus they asked him earnestly to do this. "He deserves to have this favour
5 from you," they said, "for he is a lover of our nation; it
6 was he who built our synagogue." So Jesus went with them. But he was not far from the house when the captain sent some friends to tell him, "Do not trouble yourself,
7 sir, I am not fit to have you under my roof, and so I did not consider myself fit even to come to you. Just say the word,
8 and let my servant be cured. For though I am a man under authority myself, I have soldiers under me; I tell one man to go, and he goes, I tell another to come, and he comes,
9 I tell my servant, 'Do this,' and he does it." When Jesus heard this he marvelled at him, and turning to the crowd that followed he said, "I tell you, I have never met faith
10 like this anywhere even in Israel." Then the messengers went back to the house and found the sick servant was quite well.
11 It was shortly afterwards that he made his way to a town called Nain, accompanied by his disciples and a large
12 crowd. Just as he was near the gate of the town, there was a dead man being carried out; he was the only son of

his mother, and she was a widow. A large crowd from the
13 town were with her. And when the Lord saw her, he felt
14 pity for her and said to her, "Do not weep." Then he went
forward and touched the bier; the bearers stopped, and he
15 said, "Young man, I bid you rise." Then the corpse sat up
and began to speak; and Jesus gave him back to his mother.
16 All were seized with awe and glorified God. "A great
prophet has appeared among us," they said, "God has visited
17 his people." And this story of Jesus spread through the
whole of Judaea and all the surrounding country.
18
19 John's disciples reported all this to him. So John summoned two of his disciples and sent them to ask the Lord,
"Are you the Coming One? Or are we to look out for some-
20 one else?" When the men reached Jesus they said, "John
the Baptist has sent us to you to ask if you are the Coming
21 One or if we are to look out for someone else?" Jesus at
that moment was healing many people of diseases and
complaints and evil spirits; he also bestowed sight on many
22 blind folk. So he replied, "Go and report to John what
you have seen and heard; that *the blind see*, the lame walk,
lepers are cleansed, the deaf hear, the dead are raised, and
23 *to the poor the gospel is preached*. And blessed is he who
24 is repelled by nothing in me!" When John's messengers
had gone, he proceeded to speak to the crowds about John:
"What did you go out to the desert to see?
A reed swayed by the wind?
25 Come, what did you go out to see?
A man arrayed in soft robes?
Those who are gorgeously dressed and luxurious live
in royal palaces.
26 Come, what did you go out to see? A prophet?
Yes, I tell you, and far more than a prophet.
27 This is he of whom it is written,
Here I send my messenger before your face,
to prepare the way for you.
28 I tell you, among the sons of women there is none greater
than John, and yet the least in the Realm of God is greater
29 than he is." (On hearing this all the people and the taxgatherers acknowledged the justice of God, as they had been
30 baptized with the baptism of John; but the Pharisees and
jurists, who had refused his baptism, frustrated God's
purpose for themselves.)
31 "To what then shall I compare the men of this generation?
What are they like?
32 Like children sitting in the marketplace and calling to
one another,
'We piped to you and you would not dance,
we lamented and you would not weep.'

33 For John the Baptist has come, eating no bread and
drinking no wine,
and you say, 'He has a devil';
34 the Son of man has come eating and drinking,
and you say, 'Here is a glutton and a drunkard,
a friend of taxgatherers and sinners!'
35 Nevertheless, Wisdom is vindicated by all her children."
36 One of the Pharisees asked him to dinner, and entering
37 the house of the Pharisee he reclined at table. Now there
was a woman in the town who was a sinner, and when she
found out that Jesus was at table in the house of the
38 Pharisee she brought an alabaster flask of perfume and
stood behind him at his feet in tears; her tears began to
wet his feet, so she wiped them with the hair of her head,
pressed kisses on them, and anointed them with the per-
39 fume. When his host the Pharisee noticed this, he said to
himself, "If he was a prophet he would know what sort of
a woman this is who is touching him; for she is a sinner."
40 Then Jesus addressed him. "Simon," he said, "I have some-
41 thing to say to you." "Speak, teacher," he said. "There
was a moneylender who had two debtors; one owed him
42 fifty pounds, the other five. As they were unable to pay,
he freely forgave them both. Tell me, now, which of them
43 will love him most?" "I suppose," said Simon, "the man
44 who had most forgiven." "Quite right," he said. Then
turning to the woman he said to Simon, "You see this
woman? When I came into your house,
you never gave me water for my feet,
while she has wet my feet with her tears and wiped them
with her hair;
45 you never gave me a kiss,
while ever since she came in she has kept pressing
kisses on my feet;
46 you never anointed my head with oil,
while she has anointed my feet with perfume.
47 Therefore I tell you, many as her sins are, they are forgiven, for her love is great; whereas he to whom little is
48 forgiven has but little love." And he said to her, "Your
49 sins are forgiven." His fellow guests began to say to them-
50 selves, "Who is this, to forgive even sins?" But he said to
the woman, "Your faith has saved you; go in peace."

8 SHORTLY afterwards he went travelling from one town
and village to another preaching and telling the good
news of the Reign of God; he was accompanied by the
2 twelve and by some women who had been healed of evil
spirits and illnesses, Mary called Magdalene (out of whom
3 seven daemons had been driven), Joanna the wife of Chuza

the chancellor of Herod, Susanna, and a number of others,
4 who ministered to him out of their means. As a large
crowd was gathering and as people were resorting to him
from town after town, he addressed them in a parable.
5 "A sower went out to sow his seed. And as he sowed,
some seed fell on the road and was trampled down,
and the wild birds ate it up;
6 some other seed dropped on the rock,
but it withered away when it sprang up because it had
no moisture;
7 some other seed fell among thorns,
and the thorns sprang up along with it and choked it;
8 some other seed fell on sound soil,
and springing up bore a crop, a hundredfold."
When he said this he called out, "He who has an ear, let
9 him listen to this." The disciples questioned him about
10 the meaning of the parable; so he said, "It is granted you
to understand the open secrets of the Reign of God, but the
others get it in parables, so that
for all their seeing they may not see,
and for all their hearing they may not understand.
11 This is what the parable means. The seed is the word
12 of God. Those 'on the road' are people who hear; but then
the devil comes and carries off the word from their heart,
13 that they may not believe and be saved. Those 'on the
rock' are people who on hearing the word welcome it with
enthusiasm, but they have no root; they believe for a
14 while and fall away in the hour of trial. As for the seed
that fell among thorns, that means people who hear but
who go and get choked with worries and money and the
15 pleasures of life, so that they never ripen. As for the seed
in the good soil, that means those who hear and hold fast
the word in a good and sound heart and so bear fruit stedfastly.
16 No one lights a lamp and hides it under a vessel or puts
it below the bed:
he puts it on a stand so that those who come in can see
the light.
17 For nothing is hidden that shall not be disclosed,
nothing concealed that shall not be known and revealed.
18 So take care how you listen;
for he who has, to him shall more be given,
while as for him who has not, from him shall be taken
even what he thinks he has."
19 His mother and brothers reached him but they were un-
20 able to join him for the crowd. Word was brought to him
that "your mother and brothers are standing outside; they
21 wish to see you." But he answered, "My mother and

S. LUKE VIII 101

brothers are those who listen to the word of God and obey it."
22 It happened on one of these days that he embarked in a boat alone with his disciples and said to them, "Let us
23 cross to the other side of the lake." So they set sail. During the voyage he fell asleep. But when a gale of wind came down on the lake and they were being swamped and in peril,
24 they went and woke him up. "Master, master," they cried, "we are drowning!" So he woke up and checked the wind
25 and the surf; they ceased and there was a calm. Then he said to them, "Where is your faith?" They marvelled in awe, saying to one another, "Whatever can he be? He gives orders to the very winds and water, and they obey
26 him!" They put in at the country of the Gergesenes, on the
27 shore facing Galilee. As he stepped out on land he was met by a man from the town who had daemons in him; for a long while he had worn no clothing, and he stayed not in
28 a house but among the tombs. On catching sight of Jesus he shrieked aloud and prayed him with a loud cry, "Jesus, son of God most High, what business have you with me?
29 Do not torture me, I beg of you." (For he had charged the unclean spirit to come out of the man. Many a time when it had seized hold of him, he had been fastened secure in fetters and chains, but he would snap his bonds
30 and be driven by the daemon into the desert.) So Jesus asked him, "What is your name?" "Legion," he said, for
31 a number of daemons had entered him. And they begged
32 him not to order them off to the abyss. Now a considerable drove of swine was grazing there on the hillside, so the daemons begged him for leave to enter them. He gave
33 them leave, and the daemons came out of the man and went into the swine; the drove rushed down the steep slope
34 into the lake and were suffocated. When the herdsmen saw what had occurred they fled and reported it to the town
35 and the hamlets. The people came out to see what had occurred and when they reached Jesus they discovered the man whom the daemons had left, seated at the feet of Jesus,
36 clothed and sane. That frightened them. They got a report
37 from those who had seen how the lunatic was cured, and then all the inhabitants of the surrounding country of the Gergesenes asked him to leave them, they were so seized with terror. He embarked in the boat and went back.
38 The man whom the daemons had left begged that he might accompany him. Jesus, however, sent him away, saying,
39 "Go home and describe all that God has done for you." So he went off to proclaim through the whole town all that Jesus had done for him.
40 On his return Jesus was welcomed by the crowd; they

41 were all looking out for him. A man called Jairus came, who was a president of the synagogue, and falling at the
42 feet of Jesus entreated him to come to his house, for he had an only daughter about twelve years old and she was
43 dying. As Jesus went the crowds kept crushing him, and a woman who had had a hemorrhage for twelve years *
44 which no one could cure, came up behind him and touched the tassel of his robe. Her hemorrhage instantly ceased.
45 Jesus said, "Who touched me?" As everyone denied it, Peter and his companions said, "Master, the crowds are all
46 round you pressing hard!" Jesus said, "Somebody did
47 touch me, for I felt power had passed from me." So when the woman saw she had not escaped notice she came trembling, and falling down before him she told before all the people why she had touched him and how she had been
48 instantly cured. "Daughter," he said to her, "your faith has
49 made you well; depart in peace." He was still speaking when someone came from the house of the synagogue-president to say, "Your daughter is dead. Do not trouble
50 the teacher any further." But when Jesus heard it he said to him, "Have no fear, only believe and she shall get well."
51 When he reached the house he would not allow anyone to come in with him except Peter and James and John, and
52 the child's father and mother. Everyone was weeping and bewailing her, but he said, "Stop weeping; she is not dead
53 but asleep." They laughed at him, knowing that she was
54 dead. But he took her hand and called to her, "Rise, little
55 girl." And her spirit returned, she got up instantly, and
56 he ordered them to give her something to eat. Her parents were amazed, but he charged them not to tell anyone what had happened.

9 CALLING the twelve apostles together he gave them power and authority over all daemons as well as to heal diseases.
2 He sent them out to preach the Reign of God and to cure
3 the sick. And he told them, "Take nothing for the journey, neither stick nor wallet nor bread nor silver, and do not
4 carry two shirts. Whatever house you go into, stay there
5 and leave from there. Whoever will not receive you, leave that town and shake off the very dust from your feet as a
6 testimony against them." So they went out from village to village preaching the gospel and healing everywhere.
7 When Herod the tetrarch heard all that was going on, he was quite at a loss; for some said that John had risen from
8 the dead, some that Elijah had appeared, and others that

* Omitting ἰατροῖς προσαναλώσασα ὅλον τὸν βίον with BD arm. Syr.Sin. sah.

S. LUKE IX

9 one of the ancient prophets had arisen. Herod said, "John
I beheaded. But who is this, of whom I hear such tales?"
And he made efforts to see him.
10 Then the apostles came back and described all they had
done to Jesus. He took them and retired in private to a
11 town called Bethsaida, but the crowds learned this and
followed him. He welcomed them, spoke to them of the
Reign of God, and cured those who needed to be healed.
12 Now as the day began to decline the twelve came up to him
and said, "Send the crowd off to lodge in the villages and
farms around and get provisions there, for here we are in
13 a desert place." He said to them, "Give them some food
yourselves." They said, "We have only got five loaves and
two fish. Unless—are we to go and buy food for the whole
14 of this people?" (There were about five thousand men of
them.) He said to his disciples, "Make them lie down in
15 rows of about fifty." They did so, and made them all lie
16 down. Then taking the five loaves and the two fish and
looking up to heaven he blessed them, broke them in pieces
and handed them to the disciples to set before the crowd.
17 And they all ate and had enough. What they had left over
was picked up, twelve baskets full of fragments.
18 Now it happened that while he was praying by himself
his disciples were beside him. So he inquired of them,
19 "Who do the crowds say I am?" They replied, "John the
Baptist, though some say Elijah and some say that one of
20 the ancient prophets has arisen." He said to them, "And
who do you say I am?" Peter replied, "The Christ of God."
21 Then he forbade them strictly to tell this to anyone.
22 The Son of man, he said, has to endure great suffering, to
be rejected by the elders and high priests and scribes, to
be killed, and on the third day to be raised.
23 He said to all, "If anyone wishes to come after me, let
him deny himself, take up his cross day after day, and so
follow me;
24 for whoever wants to save his life will lose it,
and whoever loses his life for my sake, he will save it.
25 What profit will it be for a man to gain the whole world
26 and lose or forfeit himself? For whoever is ashamed of
me and my words, of him will the Son of man be ashamed
when he comes in his glory and in the glory of the Father
27 and of the holy angels. I tell you plainly, there are some
of those standing here who will not taste death till they see
the Reign of God."
28 It was about eight days after he said this, when he took
Peter, John, and James, and went up the hillside to pray.
29 While he was praying the appearance of his face altered and
30 his dress turned dazzling white. There were two men con-

31 versing with him, Moses and Elijah, who appeared in a vision of glory and said he must go through with his death
32 and departure at Jerusalem. Now Peter and his companions had been overpowered with sleep, but on waking up they saw his glory and the two men who were standing
33 beside him. When they were parting from him, Peter said to Jesus, "Master, it is a good thing we are here; let us put up three tents, one for you, one for Moses, and one for
34 Elijah" (not knowing what he was saying). As he spoke, a cloud came and overshadowed them. They were awe-
35 struck as they passed into the cloud, but a voice came from the cloud, "This is my Son, my Chosen one; listen to him."
36 When the voice ceased, they found themselves alone with Jesus. And in those days they kept silence and told nobody anything of what they had seen.
37 Next day, when they came down the hill, a large crowd
38 met him. "Teacher," shouted a man from the crowd, "look
39 at my son, I beg of you, for he is my only boy, and a spirit gets hold of him till he suddenly shrieks; it convulses him till he foams; indeed it will hardly leave off
40 tearing him to pieces. I begged your disciples to cast it
41 out, but they could not." Jesus answered, "O faithless and perverse generation, how long must I still be with you and
42 bear with you? Fetch your son here." Before the boy could reach Jesus, the daemon dashed him down and convulsed him, but Jesus checked the unclean spirit, cured the boy,
43 and handed him back to his father. And all were astounded at this grand display of God. But while all marvelled at
44 all he did, he said to his disciples, "Let these words sink into your ears: 'the Son of man is to be betrayed into the
45 hands of men.'" But they did not understand this saying—indeed it was kept a secret from them, to prevent them from fathoming it—and they were afraid to ask him about this saying.
46 A dispute arose among them as to which of them was
47 the greatest. Jesus knew the dispute that occupied their minds, so he took hold of a little child and set it by his
48 side; then he said to them,
"Whoever receives this little child in my name receives me, and whoever receives me receives him who sent me.
For it is the lowliest of you all who is great."
49 John said to him, "Master, we saw a man casting out daemons in your name, but we stopped him because he is
50 not a follower of ours." Jesus said to him, "Do not stop him;* he who is not against you is for you."
51 As the time for his assumption was now due, he set his

* Omitting [οὐ γάρ ἐστιν καθ' ὑμῶν].

S. LUKE X

52 face for the journey to Jerusalem. He sent messengers
in front of him. They went and entered a Samaritan vil-
53 lage to make preparations for him, but the people would not
receive him because his face was turned in the direction of
54 Jerusalem. So when the disciples James and John saw
this, they said, "Lord, will you have us bid *fire come down*
55 *from heaven and consume them?*" But he turned and
56 checked them. Then they journeyed to another village.
57 And as they journeyed along the road a man said to him,
58 "I will follow you anywhere." Jesus said to him,
"The foxes have their holes,
 the wild birds have their nests,
 but the Son of man has nowhere to lay his head."
59 He said to another man, "Follow me"; but he said, "Let me
60 go and bury my father first of all." Jesus said to him,
"Leave the dead to bury their own dead; you go and spread
61 the news of the Reign of God." Another man also said to
him, "I will follow you, Lord. But let me first say good-bye
62 to my people at home." Jesus said to him, "No one is any
use to the Reign of God who puts his hand to the plough
and then looks behind him."

10 After that the Lord commissioned other seventy disciples, sending them in front of him two by two to
every town and place that he intended to visit himself.
2 He said to them, "The harvest is rich, but the labourers are
few; so pray the Lord of the harvest to send labourers to
3 gather his harvest. Go your way; I am sending you out
4 like lambs among wolves. Carry no purse, no wallet, no
5 sandals. Do not stop to salute anybody on the road. Whatever house you enter, first say, 'Peace be to this household!'
6 Then, if there is a soul there breathing peace, your peace
will rest on him; otherwise it will come back to you.
7 Stay at the same house, eating and drinking what the people provide (for the workman deserves his wages); you
8 are not to shift from one house to another. Wherever you
are received on entering any town, eat what is provided for
9 you, heal those in the town who are ill, and tell them, 'The
10 Reign of God is nearly on you.' But wherever you are not
received on entering any town, go out into the streets of
11 the town and cry, 'The very dust of your town that clings to
us we wipe off from our feet as a protest. But mark this,
12 the Reign of God is near!' I tell you, on the great Day it
will be more bearable for Sodom than for that town.
13 Woe to you, Khorazin! woe to you, Bethsaida! Had the
miracles performed in you been performed in Tyre and
Sidon, they would long ago have been sitting penitent in
14 sackcloth and ashes. But it will be more bearable for

15 Tyre and Sidon at the judgment than for you. And you,
O Capharnahum! *Exalted to heaven? No, you will sink
to Hades!*
16 He who listens to you listens to me,
 he who rejects you rejects me,
 and he who rejects me rejects him who sent me."
17 The seventy came back with joy. "Lord," they said, "the
18 very daemons obey us in your name." He said to them,
"Yes, I watched Satan fall from heaven like a flash of
19 lightning. I have indeed given you the power of *treading
on serpents* and scorpions and of trampling down all the
20 power of the Enemy; nothing shall injure you. Only,
 do not rejoice because the spirits obey you:
 rejoice because your names are enrolled in heaven."
21 He thrilled with joy at that hour in the holy Spirit, saying, "I praise thee, Father, Lord of heaven and earth, for concealing this from the wise and learned and revealing it to the simple-minded; yes, Father, I praise thee that such was thy chosen purpose." Then turning to the disciples he said,
22 "All has been handed over to me by my Father:
 · and no one knows who the Son is except the Father,
 or who the Father is except the Son,
 and he to whom the Son chooses to reveal him."
Then turning to the disciples he said privately,
23 "Blessed are the eyes that see what you see!
24 For I tell you many prophets and kings have desired to
 see what you see,
 but they have not seen it;
 and to hear what you hear,
 but they have not heard it."
25 Now a jurist got up to tempt him. "Teacher," he said,
26 "what am I to do to inherit life eternal?" He said to him,
"What is written in the law? What do you read there?"
27 He replied, *"You must love the Lord your God with your
whole heart, with your whole soul, with your whole
strength, and with your whole mind. Also your neighbour
28 as yourself."* "A right answer!" said Jesus; *"do that and
29 you will live."* Anxious to make an excuse for himself,
however, he said to Jesus, "But who is my neighbour?"
30 Jesus rejoined, "A man going down from Jerusalem to
Jericho fell among robbers who stripped and belaboured
31 him and then went off leaving him half-dead. Now
it so chanced that a priest was going down the same
road, but on seeing him he went past on the opposite side.
32 So did a Levite who came to the spot; he looked at him
33 but passed on the opposite side. However a Samaritan
traveller came to where he was and felt pity when he saw

34 him; he went to him, bound his wounds up, pouring oil and wine into them, mounted him on his own steed, took
35 him to an inn, and attended to him. Next morning he took out a couple of shillings and gave them to the innkeeper, saying, 'Attend to him, and if you are put to any extra
36 expense I will refund you on my way back.' Which of these three men, in your opinion, proved a neighbour to the man
37 who fell among the robbers?" He said, "The man who took pity on him." Jesus said to him, "Then go and do the same."
38 In the course of their journey he entered a certain village, and a woman called Martha welcomed him to her house.
39 She had a sister called Mary, who seated herself at the feet
40 of the Lord to listen to his talk. Now Martha was so busy attending to them that she grew worried; she came up and said, "Lord, is it all one to you that my sister has left me to do all the work alone? Come, tell her to lend me a hand."
41 The Lord answered her, "Martha, Martha,* Mary has chosen the best dish, and she is not to be dragged away from it."

11 He was praying at a certain place, and when he stopped one of his disciples said to him, "Lord, teach
2 us to pray, as John taught his disciples." He said to them, "When you pray, say, Father,
    thy name be revered,
    thy Reign begin;
3   give us our bread for the morrow day by day,
4   and forgive us our sins
    for we do forgive everyone who has offended us;
    and lead us not into temptation."
5 And he said to them, "Suppose one of you has a friend, and you go to him at midnight and say to him, 'Friend, let me
6 have three loaves; for a friend of mine travelling has come
7 to my house and I have nothing to set before him.' And suppose he answers from the inside, 'Don't bother me; the door is locked by this time, and my children are in bed
8 with me. I can't get up and give you anything.' I tell you, though he will not get up and give you anything because you are a friend of his, he will at least rise and give you
9 whatever you want, because you persist. So I tell you,
    ask and the gift will be yours,
    seek and you will find,
    knock and the door will open to you;

* Omitting, with D, Syr.$^{Sin.}$ and the majority of the old Latin manuscripts μεριμνᾶς ... χρεία (D adding θορυβάζῃ). I translate μερίδα by 'dish,' to bring out the point and play of the saying. Jesus means that Mary has chosen well in selecting the nourishment of his teaching.

10   for everyone who asks receives,
        the seeker finds,
          the door is opened to anyone who knocks.
11   What father among you, if asked by his son for a loaf,
        will hand him a stone?
          Or, if asked for a fish, will hand him a serpent instead
            of a fish?
12   Or, if asked for an egg, will he hand him a scorpion?
13   Well, if for all your evil you know to give your children
        what is good,
          how much more will your Father give the holy Spirit
            from heaven to those who ask him?"
14 He was casting out a dumb daemon, and when the daemon
had gone out the dumb man spoke. The crowds marvelled,
15 but some of them said, "It is by Beelzebul the prince of
16 daemons that he casts out daemons." Others by way of
tempting him demanded he should give them a Sign from
17 heaven. He knew what they were thinking about, so he
said to them,
   "Any realm divided against itself comes to ruin,
      house after house falls down;
18   and if Satan is divided against himself,
      how can his realm stand?
   You say I am casting out daemons by Beelzebul?
19   If I cast out daemons by Beelzebul,
      by whom do your sons cast them out?
   Thus they will be your judges.
20   But if it is by the finger of God that I cast daemons out,
      then the Reign of God has reached you already.
21 When the strong man in armour guards his homestead, his
22 property is undisturbed; but when a stronger man attacks
and conquers him, he seizes the panoply on which he relied
and divides up the spoil.
23   He who is not with me is against me,
      and he who does not gather with me scatters.*
24 When an unclean spirit leaves a man, it roams through dry
places in search of refreshment. As it finds none, then it
25 says, 'I will go back to the house I left,' and when it comes
26 it finds the house clean and in order. Then it goes off to
fetch seven other spirits worse than itself; they go in and
dwell there, and the last state of that man is worse than
the first."
27   While he was saying this, a woman shouted to him out
of the crowd, "Blessed is the womb that bore you, and the

---

* Omitting με, which von Soden inserts within brackets from ℵL 33 and a few other authorities.

28 breasts you sucked!" But he said, "Blessed rather are those who hear and who observe the word of God!"
29 As the crowds were thronging to him, he proceeded to say,
"This is an evil generation: it demands a Sign,
but no Sign will be given to it except the Sign of Jonah;
30 for as Jonah was a Sign to the Ninivites,
so shall the Son of man be to this generation.
31 The queen of the South will rise at the judgment with the men of this generation and condemn them;
for she came from the ends of the earth to listen to the wisdom of Solomon,
and here is One greater than Solomon.
32 The men of Ninive will rise at the judgment with this generation and condemn it;
for when Jonah preached they did repent,
and here is One greater than Jonah.
33 No one lights a lamp to put it in a cellar or under a bowl,
but on a stand, so that those who come in can see the light.
Your eye is the lamp of the body:
when your eye is sound,
then the whole of your body has light,
but if your eye is diseased,
then your body is darkened.
35 (Look! perhaps your very light is dark.)
36 So if your whole body has light, without any corner of it in darkness, it will be lit up entirely, as when a lamp lights you with its rays."
37 When he finished speaking, a Pharisee asked him to take a meal in his house; so he went in and lay down at table.
38 The Pharisee was astonished to see that he had not
39 washed before the meal, but the Lord said to him,
"You Pharisees do clean the outside of the cup and the plate,
but your inner life is filled with rapacity and malice.
40 Foolish men! did not He who made the outside make the inside of things too?
41 Better cleanse * what is within; then nothing will be unclean for you.

* The ordinary text δότε ἐλεημοσυνην (" give alms ") represents the Aramaic *zakki*. But the Aramaic *dakki* (" purify " or " cleanse") suits the context better, and Wellhausen plausibly suggests that Luke has confused " these two verbs which differ very little in sound and originally are identical."

42 But woe to you Pharisees!
      you tithe mint and rue and every vegetable,
      but justice and the love of God you disregard;
        these latter you ought to have practised—without omitting the former.
43 Woe to you Pharisees!
      you love the front bench in the synagogues
      and salutations in the marketplaces.
44 Woe to you!
      you are like unsuspected tombs;
      men walk over them unawares."
45 One of the jurists said to him, "Teacher, when you say
46 this you are insulting us as well." He said,
      "And woe to you jurists! you load men with irksome burdens,
      and you will not put a single finger to their burdens.
47   Woe to you! you build tombs for the prophets whom your own fathers killed:
48   thus you testify and consent to what your fathers did,
      for they killed and you build.
49 This is why the Wisdom of God said, 'I will send them prophets and apostles, some they will kill and some they
50 will persecute'; it was that the blood of all the prophets shed from the foundation of the world might be charged
51 upon this generation, from the blood of Abel down to the blood of Zechariah who was slain between the altar and the House of God—yes, I tell you, it will all be charged upon this generation.
52   Woe to you jurists! you have taken the key that unlocks the door of knowledge;
      you have not entered yourselves,
      and you have stopped those who were entering."
53 After he had gone away, the scribes and Pharisees commenced to follow him up closely and cross-question him
54 on many points, lying in ambush to catch a word from his lips.

12 Meanwhile as the crowd was gathering in its thousands till they trod on one another, he proceeded to say to his disciples first of all, "Be on your guard against the leaven of the Pharisees, which is hypocrisy.
2   Nothing is hidden that shall not be revealed,
      or concealed that shall not be made known.
3   So all you utter in the dark will be heard in the light,
      and what you whisper in chambers will be proclaimed on the housetops.
4 I tell you, my friends,

have no fear of those who kill the body but after that can do no more;
5 I will show you whom to fear—
fear Him who after he has killed has power to cast you into Gehenna.
Yes, I tell you, fear Him.
6 Are not five sparrows sold for two farthings?
Yet not one of them is forgotten by God.
7 But the very hairs on your head are all numbered;
fear not, you are worth far more * than sparrows.
8 I tell you, whoever acknowledges me before men,
the Son of man will acknowledge him before the angels of God;
9 and he who disowns me before men
will be disowned before the angels of God.
10 Everyone also who says a word against the Son of man will be forgiven for it,
but he who blasphemes against the holy Spirit will never be forgiven.
11 When they bring you before synagogues and the magistrates and authorities, do not trouble yourselves about how
12 to defend yourselves or what to say, for the holy Spirit will teach you at that hour what you should say."
13 A man out of the crowd said to him, "Teacher, tell my
14 brother to give me my share of our inheritance"; but he said to him, "Man, who made me a judge or arbitrator over
15 your affairs?" Then he said to them, "See and keep clear of covetousness in every shape and form, for a man's life is not part of his possessions because he has ample wealth."
16 And he told them a parable. "A rich man's estate bore
17 heavy crops. So he debated, 'What am I to do? I have
18 no room to store my crops.' And he said, 'This is what I will do. I will pull down my granaries and build larger
19 ones, where I can store all my produce and my goods. And I will say to my soul, "Soul, you have ample stores laid up for many a year; take your ease, eat, drink and be merry."'
20 But God said to him, 'Foolish man, this very night your soul is wanted; and who will get all you have prepared?'
21 So fares the man who lays up treasure for himself instead
22 of gaining the riches of God." To his disciples he said, "Therefore I tell you,
do not trouble about what you are to eat in life,
nor about what you are to put on your body;
23 life is something more than food,
and the body is something more than clothes.
24 Look at the crows! they neither sow nor reap,

* See above, on p. 16.

no storehouse or granary have they,
and yet God feeds them.
How much more are you worth than birds?
25 Which of you can add an ell to his height by troubling about it?
26 and if you cannot manage even this, why trouble over other things?
27 Look how the lilies neither spin nor weave;
and yet, I tell you, even Solomon in all his grandeur was never robed like one of them.
28 Now if God so clothes grass, which blooms to-day in the field and is thrown to-morrow into the furnace, will he not much more clothe you? O men, how little you trust him!
29
30 So do not seek food and drink and be worried; pagans make food and drink their aim in life, but your Father
31 knows quite well you need that; only seek his Realm, and
32 it will be yours over and above. Fear not, you little flock, for your Father is delighted to give you the Realm.
33 Sell what you possess and give it away in alms,
make purses for yourselves that never wear out:
get treasure in heaven that never fails,
that no thief can get at, no moth destroy.
34 For where your treasure lies,
your heart will lie there too.
35
36 Keep your loins girt and your lamps lit, and be like men who are expecting their lord and master on his return from a marriage-banquet, so as to open the door for him
37 at once when he comes and knocks. Blessed are those servants whom the lord and master finds awake when he comes! I tell you truly, he will gird himself, make them recline at table, and come forward to wait on them.
38 Whether he comes in the second or the third watch of the
39 night and finds them thus alert, blessed are they! Be sure that if the householder had known at what hour the thief was coming,* he would not have allowed his house to be
40 broken into. So be ready yourselves, for the Son of man
41 is coming at an hour you do not expect." Peter said, "Lord, are you telling this parable for us, or is it for all
42 and sundry?" The Lord said, "Well, where is the trusty, thoughtful steward whom the lord and master will set over his establishment to give out supplies at the proper
43 time? Blessed is that servant if his lord and master finds
44 him so doing when he arrives! I tell you plainly, he will
45 set him over all his property. But if that servant says to himself, 'My lord and master is long of arriving,' and if

* Omitting [ἐγρηγόρησεν ἄν, καὶ], a harmonistic gloss from Matthew xxiv. 43.

he starts to beat the menservants and maidservants, to eat
46 and drink and get drunk, that servant's lord and master
will arrive on a day when he does not expect him and
at an hour which he does not know; he will cut him in
two and assign him the fate of unbelievers.
47 The servant who knew his lord and master's orders and
did not prepare * for them,
will receive many lashes;
48 whereas he who was ignorant and did what deserves a
beating,
will receive few lashes.
He who has much given him
will have much required from him,
and he who has much entrusted to him
will have all the more demanded of him.
49 I have come to throw fire on earth.
Would it were kindled already!
50 I have a baptism to undergo.
How I am distressed till it is all over!
51 You think I am here to make peace on earth?
No, I tell you, it is dissension.
52 After this there will be five at issue in one house,
three divided against two and two against three,
53 father against son and *son against father*,
mother against daughter and *daughter against mother*,
mother-in-law against daughter-in-law and *daughter-in-law against mother-in-law*."
54 And to the crowds he said,
"When you see a cloud rise in the west,
you say, 'There is a shower coming,'
and so it is:
55 when you feel the south wind blow,
you say, 'There will be heat,'
and so it is.
56 You hypocrites, you know how to decipher the look of
earth and sky;
how is it you cannot decipher the meaning of this era?
57 And why do you not yourselves settle what is right?
58 Thus, when you go before the magistrate with your opponent, do your utmost to get quit of him on the way there,
in case he hales you before the judge; then the judge will
hand you over to the jailer and the jailer will throw you
59 in prison. I tell you, you will never get out till you pay
the last farthing of your debt."

* Omitting ἢ ποιήσας with L, the majority of the old Latin manuscripts, the Syriac and Armenian versions, etc. The ordinary text is complete.

13 It was at this time that some people came to tell him about the Galileans whose blood Pilate had
2 mingled with their sacrifices. But he replied to them,
"Do you think, because they suffered this, that these Galileans were worse sinners than the rest of the Galileans?
3 I tell you, no;
unless you repent you will all perish as they did.
4 Or those eighteen men killed by the fall of the tower at Siloam?—
do you think they were worse offenders than the rest of the residents in Jerusalem?
5 I tell you, no;
unless you repent you will all perish as they did."
6 And he told this parable. "A man had a fig tree planted in his vineyard; he came in search of fruit on it but he
7 found none. So he said to the vinedresser, 'Here have I come for three years in search of fruit on this fig tree without finding any; cut it down, why should it take up
8 space?' But the man replied, 'Leave it for this year, sir,
9 till I dig round about it and put in manure. Then it may bear fruit next year. If not, you can have it cut down.'"
10 When he was teaching in one of the synagogues on the
11 sabbath, there was a woman who for eighteen years had suffered weakness from an evil spirit; indeed she was bent
12 double and quite unable to raise herself. Jesus noticed her and called to her, "Woman, you are released from your
13 weakness." He laid his hands on her, and instantly she
14 became erect and glorified God. But the president of the synagogue was annoyed at Jesus healing on the sabbath, and he said to the crowd, "There are six days for work to be done; come during them to get healed, instead of on
15 the sabbath." The Lord replied to him, "You hypocrites, does not each of you untether his ox or ass from the stall
16 on the sabbath and lead it away to drink? And this woman, a daughter of Abraham, bound by Satan for all these eighteen years, was she not to be freed from her
17 bondage on the sabbath?" As he said this, all his opponents were put to shame, but all the crowd rejoiced over all his
18 splendid doings. So he said,
"What is the Reign of God like?
to what shall I compare it?
19 It is like a grain of mustard-seed which a man took and put into his orchard, where it grew up and became a tree,
20 and *the wild birds roosted in its branches*." He added, "To
21 what shall I compare the Reign of God? It is like dough which a woman took and buried in three pecks of flour, till all of it was leavened."

S. LUKE XIV

22 On he went, teaching from one town and village to an-
23 other, as he made his way to Jerusalem. A man said to
him, "Is it only a few, sir, who are saved?" So he said
24 to them, "Strive to get in through the narrow door, for I tell
25 you many will try to get in and not be able, once the
master of the House has got up and closed the door. You
may stand outside and knock at the door, crying, 'Lord,
open for us,' but he will answer you, 'I do not know where
26 you come from.' You will then proceed to say, 'But we ate
and drank in your presence, and you taught in our streets!'
27 'I tell you,' he will say, 'I do not know where you come
28 from; *begone every one of you, you evildoers.*' There you
will wail and gnash your teeth, to see Abraham, Isaac,
Jacob and all the prophets inside the Realm of God and
29 yourselves thrown out. Yes, and people will come *from
east and west* and north and south to their places at the
feast within the Realm of God.
30   Some are last who will be first,
     and some are first who will be last."
31   Just then some Pharisees came up to tell him, "Get
32 away from here, for Herod intends to kill you." "Go and
tell that fox," he replied, "I cast out daemons and perform
cures to-day and to-morrow, and on the third day I com-
33 plete my task! But I must journey on, to-day, to-morrow,
and the next day; it would never do for a prophet to perish
34 except in Jerusalem! O Jerusalem, Jerusalem, slaying the
prophets and stoning those who have been sent to you!
How often I would fain have gathered your children as a
fowl gathers her brood under her wings! But you would
35 not have it! *See, your House is left to yourselves.* I
tell you, you will never see me till the day comes when
you say, *Blessed be he who comes in the Lord's name.*"

14 Now when he entered the house of a ruler who
belonged to the Pharisees to take a meal, they
2 watched him closely. In front of him there was a man who
3 had dropsy; so Jesus asked the jurists and Pharisees, "Is
4 it right to heal on the sabbath or not?" They held their
peace. Then Jesus took hold of the man and cured him
5 and sent him off. "Which of you," he said to them, "when
an ass or an ox has fallen into a well, will not pull him
6 out at once upon the sabbath day?" This they could not
7 dispute. He also told a parable to the guests, when he
8 observed how they picked out the best places. "When anyone invites you to a marriage-banquet," he said, "never lie
down in the best place, in case a more distinguished guest
9 than yourself has been invited; then the host will tell you,
'Make room for him,' and you will proceed in shame to

10 take the lowest place. No, when you are invited, go and recline in the lowest place, so that when your host comes in he will tell you, 'Move higher up, my friend.' Then you will be honoured before your fellow guests.
11 For everyone who uplifts himself will be humbled, and he who humbles himself will be uplifted."
12 He also said to his host, "When you give a dinner or supper, do not ask your friends or your brothers or your relatives or your rich neighbours, in case they
13 invite you back again and you get repaid. No, when you give a banquet, invite the poor, the maimed,
14 the lame, and the blind. Then you will be blessed; for as they have no means of repaying you, you will be repaid
15 at the resurrection of the just." Hearing this, one of his fellow guests said to him, "Blessed is he who feasts in the
16 Realm of God!" Jesus said to him, "There was a man who was giving a large supper, to which he had invited a
17 number of guests. At the hour for supper he sent his servant to tell the guests, 'Come, things are all ready.'
18 But they all alike proceeded to decline. The first said to him, 'I have bought a farm and I am obliged to go and look
19 at it. Pray consider me excused.' The second said, 'I have bought five pair of oxen and I am going to try them. Pray
20 consider me excused.' Another said, 'I have married a
21 wife; that is why I cannot come.' The servant went and reported this to his master. Then the master of the house was enraged, and said to his servant, 'Quick, go out to the streets and lanes of the town and bring in the poor, the
22 maimed, the blind, and the lame.' When the servant announced, 'Your order has been carried out, sir, but there
23 is still room,' the master said to the servant, 'Go out to the roads and hedges and make people come in, to fill
24 up my house. For I tell you that not one of those who were invited shall taste my supper.'"
25 There were large crowds travelling with him; so he turned and said to them,
26 "If anyone comes to me and does not hate his father and mother and wife and children and brothers and sisters, aye and his own life,
he cannot be a disciple of mine;
27 whoever does not carry his own cross and come after me, he cannot be a disciple of mine.
28 For which of you wants to build a tower and does not first sit down to calculate the expense, to see if he has enough
29 money to complete it?—in case, after he has laid the foundation and then is unable to finish the building, all
30 the spectators start to make fun of him, saying, 'This
31 fellow started to build but he could not finish it.' Or what

king sets out to fight against another king without first setting down to deliberate whether with ten thousand men he can encounter the king who is attacking him with twenty
32 thousand? If he cannot, when the other is still at a distance he will send an embassy to do homage to him.
33 So with everyone of you who will not part with all his goods—
he cannot be a disciple of mine.
34 Salt is excellent indeed: but if salt becomes insipid, what
35 will restore its flavour? It is no use for either soil or dunghill, it is flung out. He who has an ear let him listen to this."

2 15 Now the taxgatherers and sinners were all approaching him to listen to him, but the Pharisees and the scribes complained, "He welcomes sinners and eats along
3 with them!" So he told them this parable, "Which of
4 you with a hundred sheep, if he loses one, does not leave the ninety-nine in the desert and go after the lost one till
5 he finds it? When he finds it he puts it on his shoulders
6 with joy, and when he gets home he gathers his friends and neighbours: 'Rejoice with me,' he says to them, 'for I have
7 found the sheep I lost.' So, I tell you, there will be joy in heaven over a single sinner who repents, more than
8 over ninety-nine good people who do not need to repent. Or again, suppose a woman has ten shillings. If she loses one of them, does she not light a lamp and scour the house
9 and search carefully till she finds it? And when she finds it she gathers her women-friends and neighbours, saying,
10 'Rejoice with me, for I have found the shilling I lost.' So, I tell you, there is joy in the presence of the angels of God over a single sinner who repents."

11 He also said: "There was a man who had two sons,
12 and the younger said to his father, 'Father, give me the share of the property that falls to me.' So he divided his
13 means among them. Not many days later, the younger son sold off everything and went abroad to a distant land,
14 where he squandered his means in loose living. After he had spent his all, a severe famine set in throughout that
15 land, and he began to feel in want; so he went and attached himself to a citizen of that land, who sent him to his fields
16 to feed swine. And he was fain to fill his belly with the pods the swine were eating; no one gave him anything.
17 But when he came to his senses he said, 'How many hired men of my father have more than enough to eat, and here
18 am I perishing of hunger! I will be up and off to my father, and I will say to him, "Father, I have sinned
19 against heaven and before you; I don't deserve to be called

your son any more; only make me like one of your hired
20 men.'" So he got up and went off to his father. But
when he was still far away his father saw him and felt
pity for him and ran to fall upon his neck and kiss him.
21 The son said to him, 'Father, I have sinned against heaven
and before you; I don't deserve to be called your son any
22 more.' But the father said to his servants, 'Quick, bring
the best robe and put it on him, give him a ring for his
23 hand and sandals for his feet, and bring the fatted calf,
24 kill it, and let us eat and be merry; for my son here was
dead and he has come to life, he was lost and he is found.'
25 So they began to make merry. Now his elder son was out
in the field, and as he came near the house he heard music
26 and dancing; so, summoning one of the servants, he asked
27 what this meant. The servant told him, 'Your brother
has arrived, and your father has killed the fatted calf
28 because he has got him back safe and sound.' This angered
him, and he would not go in. His father came out and
29 tried to appease him, but he replied, 'Look at all the years
I have been serving you! I have never neglected any of
your orders, and yet you have never given me so much
30 as a kid, to let me make merry with my friends. But as
soon as this son of yours arrives, after having wasted your
31 means with harlots, you kill the fatted calf for him!' The
father said to him, 'My son, you and I are always together,
32 all I have is yours. We could not but make merry and
rejoice, for your brother here was dead and has come to
life again, he was lost but he has been found.'"

16 He also said to the disciples: "There was a rich man
who had a factor, and this factor, he found, was
2 accused of misapplying his property. So he summoned
him and said, 'What is this I hear about you? Hand in
3 your accounts; you cannot be factor any longer.' The
factor said to himself, 'What am I to do now that my
master is taking the factorship away from me? I am too
4 weak to dig, I am ashamed to beg. Ah, I know what I
will do, so that people will welcome me to their houses
5 when I am deposed from the factorship.' So he summoned
every single one of his master's debtors. He asked the
6 first, 'How much are you owing to my master?' 'A hundred
barrels of oil,' he said. The factor told him, 'Here is your
7 bill; sit down at once and enter fifty barrels.' Then he
asked another, 'And how much do you owe?' 'A hundred
quarters of wheat,' he said. 'Here is your bill,' said the
8 factor, 'just enter eighty.' Well, the master praised the
dishonest factor for looking ahead; for the children of this
world look further ahead in dealing with their own genera-

S. LUKE XVI 119

9 tion than the children of Light. And I tell you, use mammon, dishonest as it is, to make friends for yourselves, so that when you die * they may welcome you to the eternal abodes.
10 He who is faithful with a trifle is also faithful with a large trust,
and he who is dishonest with a trifle is also dishonest with a large trust.
11 So if you are not faithful with dishonest mammon, how can you ever be trusted with true Riches?
12 And if you are not faithful with what belongs to another, how can you ever be given what is your own?
13 No servant can serve two masters:
either he will hate the one and love the other,
or else he will stand by the one and despise the other—
you cannot serve both God and Mammon."
14 Now the Pharisees who were fond of money heard all
15 this, and they sneered at him. So he told them, "You are the people who get men to think you are good, but God knows what your hearts are! What is lofty in the view of man is loathsome in the eyes of God.
16 The Law and the prophets lasted till John; since then the good news of the Realm of God is preached, and anyone
17 presses in. Yet it is easier for heaven and earth to pass away than for an iota of the Law to lapse.
18 Anyone who divorces his wife and marries another woman commits adultery,
and he who marries a divorced woman commits adultery.
19 There was a rich man, clad in purple and fine linen, who
20 lived sumptuously every day. Outside his door lay a poor
21 man called Lazarus; he was a mass of ulcers, and fain to eat up the crumbs that fell from the rich man's table. (The
22 very dogs used to come and lick his ulcers.) Now it happened that the poor man died, and he was carried by the angels to Abraham's bosom. The rich man died too, and was
23 buried. And as he was being tortured in Hades he raised his eyes and saw Abraham far away with Lazarus in his
24 bosom; so he called out, 'Father Abraham, take pity on me, send Lazarus to dip his fingertip in water and cool my tongue,
25 for I am in anguish in these flames.' But Abraham said, 'Remember, my son, you got all the bliss when you were alive, just as Lazarus got the ills of life; he is in comfort
26 now, and you are in anguish. Besides all that, a great gulf yawns between us and you, to keep back those who want to cross from us to you and also those who want to pass

---

* Reading ἐκλίπητε or ἐκλείπητε with ℵ^{ca}, the bulk of the Latin manuscripts, the Harklean Syriac, etc.

27 from you to us.' Then he said, 'Well, father, I beg you to
28 send him to my father's house, for I have five brothers; let him bear testimony to them, that they may not come to
29 this place of torture as well.' 'They have got Moses and the
30 prophets,' said Abraham, 'they can listen to them.' 'No, father Abraham,' he said, 'but if someone only goes to them
31 from the dead, they will repent.' He said to him, 'If they will not listen to Moses and the prophets, they will not be convinced, not even if one rose from the dead."

17 To his disciples he said, "It is inevitable that hindrances should come, but woe to the man by whom they
2 come; it would be well for him to have a millstone hung round his neck and be flung into the sea, rather than prove
3 a hindrance to one of these little ones! Take heed to yourselves. If your brother sins, check him, and if he
4 repents forgive him. Even if he sins against you seven times in one day and turns to you seven times saying, 'I
5 repent,' you must forgive him." The apostles said to the
6 Lord, "Give us more faith!" The Lord said, "If you had faith the size of a grain of mustard-seed, you would say to this mulberry tree, 'Be uprooted and planted in the
7 sea,' and it would obey you. Which of you, with a servant out ploughing or shepherding, will say to him when he comes in from the field, 'Come at once and take your place
8 at table'? Will the man not rather say to him, 'Get something ready for my supper; gird yourself and wait on me till I eat and drink; then you can eat and drink yourself'?
9
10 Does he thank the servant for doing his bidding? Well, it is the same with you; when you have done all you are bidden, say, 'We are but servants;* we have only done our duty.'"

11 Now it happened in the course of his journey to Jeru-
12 salem that he passed between Samaria and Galilee. On entering one village he was met by ten lepers who stood at
13 a distance and lifted up their voice, saying, "Jesus, master,
14 have pity on us." Noticing them he said, "Go and *show yourselves to the priests.*" And as they went away they
15 were cleansed. Now one of them turned back when he saw
16 he was cured, glorifying God with a loud voice; and he fell on his face at the feet of Jesus and thanked him. The man
17 was a Samaritan. So Jesus said, "Were all the ten not
18 cleansed? Where are the other nine? Was there no one to return and give glory to God except this foreigner?"

* Omitting ἀχρεῖοι with Syr.Sin. followed by most recent editors. The emphasis falls on the simple fact of being slaves, not on any distinction between good and bad slaves.

19 And he said to him, "Get up and go, your faith has made you well."
20 On being asked by the Pharisees when the Reign of God was coming, he answered them, "The Reign of God is not
21 coming as you hope to catch sight of it; no one will say, 'Here it is' or 'There it is,' for the Reign of God is now in
22 your midst." To his disciples he said, "There will come days when you will long and long in vain to have even one
23 day of the Son of man. Men will say, 'See, here he is!' 'See, there he is!' but do not go out or run after them,
24 for like lightning that flashes from one side of the sky to the other,
so will the Son of man be on his own day.
25 But he must first endure great suffering and be rejected
26 by the present generation. And just as it was in the days of Noah, so will it be in the days of the Son of man;
27 they were eating, drinking, marrying and being married, till the day *Noah entered the ark*—then came the deluge
28 and destroyed them all. Or just as it was in the days of Lot; they were eating, drinking, buying, selling, planting
29 and building, but on the day that Lot left Sodom *it rained fire and brimstone from heaven* and destroyed them all.
30 So will it be on the day the Son of man is revealed.
31 On that day, if a man is on the housetop and his goods inside the house, he must not go down to fetch them out;
32 nor must a man in the field *turn back* (remember Lot's wife).
33 Whoever tries to secure his life will lose it, and whoever loses it will preserve it.
34 On that night, I tell you,
there will be two men in the one bed,
the one will be taken and the other left;
35 two women will be grinding together,
the one will be taken and the other left."
37 They asked him, "Where, Lord?"
And he said to them,
"Where the body is lying,
there the vultures will gather."

18 He also told them a parable about the need of always
2 praying and never losing heart. "In a certain town," he said, "there was a judge who had no reverence for God
3 and no respect even for man. And in that town there was a widow who used to go and appeal to him for 'Justice
4 against my opponent!' For a while he would not, but afterwards he said to himself, 'Though I have no reverence for
5 God and no respect even for man, still, as this widow is bothering me, I will see justice done to her—not to have

6 her for ever coming and pestering me.' Listen," said the
7 Lord, "to what this unjust judge says! And will not God
see justice done to his elect who cry to him by day and
8 night? Will he be tolerant to their opponents? I tell you,
he will quickly see justice done to his elect! And yet, when
the Son of man does come, will he find faith on earth?"
9 He also told the following parable to certain persons who
were sure of their own goodness and looked down upon
10 everybody else. "Two men went up to pray in the temple;
11 one was a Pharisee and the other was a taxgatherer. The
Pharisee stood up and prayed by himself as follows; 'I
thank thee, O God, I am not like the rest of men, thieves,
12 rogues, and immoral, or even like yon taxgatherer. Twice
13 a week I fast; on all my income I pay tithes.' But the taxgatherer stood far away and would not lift even his eyes to
heaven, but beat his breast, saying, 'O God, have mercy on
14 me for my sins!' I tell you, he went home accepted by God
rather than the other man;
for everyone who uplifts himself will be humbled,
and he who humbles himself will be uplifted."
15 Now people even brought their infants for him to touch
them; when the disciples noticed it they checked them,
16 but Jesus called for the infants. "Let the children come
to me," he said, "do not stop them: the Realm of God be-
17 longs to such as these. I tell you truly, whoever will not
submit to the Reign of God like a child will never get into
it at all."
18 Then a ruler asked him, "Good teacher, what am I to do
19 to inherit life eternal?" Jesus said to him, "Why call me
20 'good'? No one is good, no one but God. You know the
commands: *do not commit adultery, do not kill, do not steal,
do not bear false witness, honour your father and mother.*"
21 He said, "I have observed all these commands from my
22 youth." When Jesus heard this he said to him, "You lack
one thing more; sell all you have, distribute the money
among the poor and you will have treasure in heaven; then
23 come and follow me." But when he heard that, he was
24 vexed, for he was extremely rich. So Jesus looked at him
and said, "How difficult it is for those who have money
25 to enter the Realm of God! Why, it is easier for a camel
to get through a needle's eye than for a rich man to get
26 into the Realm of God." His hearers said, "Then whoever
27 can be saved?" He said, "What is impossible for men is
28 possible for God." Peter said, "Well, we have left our
29 homes and followed you!" He said to them, "I tell you
truly, no one has left home or wife or brothers or parents
30 or children for the sake of the Realm of God, who does not
receive ever so much more in this present world, and in the

31 world to come life eternal." Then he took the twelve aside and told them, "We are going up to Jerusalem, and all the predictions of the prophets regarding the Son of man will
32 be fulfilled; he will be betrayed to the gentiles, mocked,
33 illtreated, and spat on; they will scourge him and kill him,
34 but he will rise again on the third day." However, they did not understand a word of this; indeed the saying was hidden from them, and they did not know what he meant.
35 As he approached Jericho, it chanced that a blind man
36 was seated beside the road begging. When he heard the
37 crowd passing he inquired what was the matter, and they
38 told him that Jesus the Nazarene was going by. So he
39 shouted, "Jesus, Son of David, have pity on me!" The people in front checked him and told him to be quiet, but he shouted all the more, "Son of David, have pity on me!"
40 So Jesus stopped and ordered them to bring him, and asked
41 him when he approached, "What do you want me to do for you?" "Lord," he said, "I want to regain my sight."
42 And Jesus said to him, "Regain your sight; your faith has
43 made you well." Instantly he regained his sight and followed him, glorifying God. And all the people gave praise to God when they saw this.

19 Then he entered Jericho. And as he passed through
2 it, there was a man called Zacchaeus, the head of the
3 taxgatherers, a wealthy man, who tried to see what Jesus was like; but he could not, on account of the crowd—
4 for he was small of stature. So he ran forward and climbed into a sycomore tree to get a sight of him, as he
5 was to pass that road. But when Jesus reached the spot he looked up and said to him, "Zacchaeus, come down at
6 once, for I must stay at your house to-day." He came down
7 at once and welcomed him gladly. But when they saw this, everyone began to mutter that he had gone to be
8 the guest of a sinner. So Zacchaeus stopped and said to the Lord, "I will give the half of all I have, Lord, to the poor, and if I have cheated anybody I will give him back
9 four times as much." And Jesus said of him, "To-day salvation has come to this house, since Zacchaeus here is a
10 son of Abraham. For the Son of man has come to seek
11 and save the lost." He went on to tell a parable in their hearing, as he was approaching Jerusalem and as they
12 imagined God's Reign would instantly come into view. "A nobleman," he said, "went abroad to obtain royal power
13 for himself and then return. He first called his ten servants, giving them each a five-pound note, and telling them,
14 'Trade with this till I come back.' Now his people hated him and sent envoys after him to say, 'We object to him

15 having royal power over us.' However he secured the royal power and came home. Then he ordered the servants to be called who had been given the money, that he
16 might find out what business they had done. The first came up saying, 'Your five pounds has made other fifty, sir.'
17 'Capital,' he said, 'you excellent servant! because you have proved trustworthy in a trifle, you are placed over ten
18 towns.' Then the second came and said, 'Your five pounds
19 has made twenty-five, sir.' To him he said, 'And you are
20 set over five towns.' Then the next came and said, 'Here is
21 your five pounds, sir; I kept it safe in a napkin, for I was afraid of you, you are such a hard man—picking up what you never put down, and reaping what you never sowed.'
22 He replied, 'You rascal of a servant, I will convict you by what you have said yourself. You knew, did you, that I was a hard man, picking up what I never put down, and
23 reaping what I never sowed! Why then did you not put my money into the bank, so that I could have got it with
24 interest when I came back?' Then he said to the bystanders, 'Take the five pounds from him and give it to the
25 man with fifty.' 'Sir,' they said, 'he has fifty already!'
26 'I tell you,
  to everyone who has shall more be given,
    but from him who has nothing, even what he has shall
    be taken.
27 And now for these enemies of mine who objected to me reigning over them—bring them here and slay them in my presence.'"

28 With these words he went forward on his way up to
29 Jerusalem. When he was near Bethphage and Bethany at the hill called the Olive-Orchard, he despatched two of his
30 disciples, saying, "Go to the village in front, and on entering it you will find a colt tethered on which no one ever
31 has sat; untether it and bring it. If anyone asks you, 'Why are you untethering it?' this is what you will say,
32 'The Lord needs it.'" The messengers went off and found
33 the colt exactly as he had told them. As they were untethering it, the owners said to them, "Why are you un-
34 tethering the colt?" And they said, "Because the Lord
35 needs it." So they brought it to Jesus, and throwing their
36 clothes on the colt they mounted Jesus upon it. As he went forward they spread their clothes under him on the road;
37 and as he was now close to the descent from the Hill of Olives, all the multitude of the disciples started joyfully to praise God with a loud voice for all * they had seen,
38 saying,

* Omitting δυνάμεων with the old Syriac version, which preserves the original text περὶ πάντων εἶδον λέγοντες.

"Blessed be the king who comes in the Lord's name!
Peace in heaven and glory in the High places!"
39 Some Pharisees in the crowd said to him, "Check your
40 disciples, teacher." But he replied, "I tell you, if they were
41 to keep quiet, the very stones would shout." And when he
42 saw the city, as he approached, he wept over it, saying,
"Would that you too knew even to-day on what your peace
43 depends! But no, it is hidden from you! A time is coming
for you when your enemies will throw up ramparts round
44 you and encircle you and besiege you on every side and
raze you and your children within you to the ground, leaving not one stone upon another within you—and all because
you would not understand when God was visiting you."
45 Then he went into the temple and proceeded to drive out
46 those who were selling. "It is written," he told them,
"*my house shall be a house of prayer*, but you have made
it *a den of robbers.*"
47 Day after day he taught within the temple. The high
priests and scribes tried to have him put to death, and so
48 did the leaders of the people, but they could not discover
what was to be done, for the whole of the people hung upon
his lips.

20 One day, when he was teaching the people in the temple and preaching the gospel, up came the priests
2 and scribes along with the elders. "Tell us," they said,
"what authority you have for acting in this way? Who
3 was it that gave you this authority?" He answered them,
4 "Well, I will ask you a question. Tell me, did the baptism of
5 John come from heaven or from men?" Now they reasoned to themselves, "If we say, 'From heaven,' he will
6 ask, 'Why did you not believe him?' And if we say, 'From
men,' the whole of the people will stone us, for they are
7 convinced John was a prophet." So they answered that
8 they did not know where it came from. Jesus said to them,
"No more will I tell you what authority I have for acting
as I do."
9 Then he proceeded to tell the people the following
parable. "A man *planted a vineyard,* leased it to vine-
10 dressers, and went abroad for some time. When the season
came round he sent a servant to the vinedressers to receive
part of the produce of the vineyard, but the vinedressers
11 flogged him and sent him off with nothing. He proceeded
to send another servant, and they flogged him too, insulted
12 him and sent him off with nothing. Then he sent still a
third, but this one they wounded and threw outside.
13 Said the owner of the vineyard, 'What shall I do?' I will
14 send my beloved son; perhaps they will respect him.' But

when the vinedressers saw him, they argued to themselves, 'Here is the heir, let us kill him, so that the inheritance
15 may be ours.' And they threw him outside the vineyard and killed him. Now what will the owner of the vineyard
16 do to them? He will come and kill these vinedressers and give the vineyard to others." When they heard that, they
17 said, "God forbid!" But he looked at them and said, "Then what does this scripture mean?—
*The stone that the builders rejected
is the chief stone now of the corner.*
18 Everyone who falls on that stone will be shattered, and whoever it falls upon will be crushed."
19 At that hour the scribes and high priests tried to lay hands on him, but they were afraid of the people. They
20 knew he had meant this parable for them. So watching their chance they sent spies who pretended to be honest persons, in order to seize on what he said and get him handed over to the authority and jurisdiction of the gov-
21 ernor. They put this question to him, "Teacher, we know you are straight in what you say and teach, you do not
22 look to human favour but teach the Way of God honestly. Is
23 it right for us to pay tribute to Caesar or not?" But
24 he noted their knavery and said to them, "Show me a shilling. Whose likeness and inscription does it bear?"
25 "Caesar's," they replied. "Well then," he said to them, "give Caesar what belongs to Caesar, give God what belongs
26 to God." So they could not seize on what he said before the people, and marvelling at his reply they said nothing.
27 Some of the Sadducees came up, who deny any resurrec-
28 tion, and put a question to him. "Teacher," they said, "Moses has written this law for us, that *if a man's married brother dies and is childless, his brother is to take*
29 *the woman and raise offspring for his brother.* Well, there were seven brothers. The first married a wife and
30
31 died childless. The second and the third took her, as indeed all the seven did, dying and leaving no children.
32
33 Afterwards the woman died too. Now at the resurrection whose wife will she be? She was wife to the seven of them."
34 Jesus said to them, "People in this world marry and are
35 married, but those who are considered worthy to attain yonder world and the resurrection from the dead neither
36 marry nor are married, for they cannot die any more; they are equal to angels and by sharing in the resurrection they
37 are sons of God. And that the dead are raised has been indicated by Moses in the passage on the Bush, when he calls *the Lord 'God of Abraham and God of Isaac and God of*
38 *Jacob.'* God is not a God of dead people but of living, for
39 all live to him." Some of the scribes declared, "Teacher,

40 that was a fine answer!" They no longer dared to put any
41 question to him. But he said to them, "How can people
42 say that the Christ is David's son? Why, David himself
says in the book of psalms,
The Lord said to my Lord, 'Sit at my right hand,
43 *till I make your enemies a footstool for your feet.'*
44 David then calls him *Lord*. So how can he be his son?"
45 And in the hearing of all the people he said to his disciples,
46 "Beware of the scribes! They like to walk about in long
robes, they are fond of getting saluted in the market-places,
of securing the front seats in the synagogues and the best
47 places at banquets; they prey upon the property of widows
and offer long unreal prayers. All the heavier will their
sentence be!"

21 LOOKING up he saw the rich putting their gifts into
2 the treasury, and noticed a poor widow putting two
3 little coins in. He said, "I tell you plainly, this poor
4 widow has put in more than them all; for these people
all contributed out of their surplus, but she has given out
of her neediness all her living."
5 Some were speaking of the temple with its ornamenta-
6 tion of splendid stones and votive gifts, but he said, "As
for what you see, there are days coming when not a stone
7 will be left upon another, without being torn down." So
they asked him, "Teacher, and when will this happen?
8 What will be the sign for this to take place?" He said,
"Take care that you are not misled; for many will come
in my name saying, 'I am he' and 'the time is near'—do
9 not go after them. And when you hear of wars and dis-
turbances, do not be scared; *these have to come* first,
10 but the end is not at once." Then he said to them,
"Nation will rise against nation, and realm against realm,
11 there will be great earthquakes with famine and pestilence
here and there, there will be awful portents and great
12 signs from heaven. But before all that, men will lay hands
on you and persecute you, handing you over to synagogues
and prisons; you will be dragged before kings and gov-
13 ernors for the sake of my name. That will turn out an
14 opportunity for you to bear witness. So resolve to yourselves that you will not rehearse your defence beforehand,
15 for I will give you words and wisdom that not one of your
16 opponents will be able to meet or refute. You will be
betrayed by your very parents and brothers and kinsmen
17 and friends, and some of you will be put to death. You
18 will be hated by all on account of my name; but not a
19 hair of your head will perish. Hold out stedfast and you
win your souls.

20 But whenever you see Jerusalem surrounded by armies,
21 then be sure her desolation is not far away. Then let those who are in Judaea fly to the hills, let those who are in the city escape, and let not those who are in the country
22 come in to the city; for these are *the days of the divine Vengeance*, in fulfilment of all that is written in scripture.
23 Woe to women with child and to women who give suck in those days, for sore anguish will come upon the land
24 and Wrath on this people; they will fall by the edge of the sword, they will be carried prisoners to all nations, and *Jerusalem will be under the heel of the Gentiles* till the
25 period of the Gentiles expires. And there will be signs in sun and moon and stars, while on earth the nations will be in dismay with bewilderment *at the roar of sea and*
26 *waves,* men swooning with panic and foreboding of what is to befall the universe. For *the orbs of the heavens will*
27 *be shaken,* and then they will see *the Son of man coming*
28 *in a cloud* with power and great glory. But when these things begin to happen, look up and raise your heads, for
29 your release is not far distant." And he told them a
30 parable. "Look at the fig tree and indeed all the trees; as soon as they put out their leaves, you can see for yourselves
31 that summer is at hand. So, whenever you see all this happen, be sure the Reign of God is at hand.
32 I tell you truly, the present generation will not pass
33 away till all this happens. Heaven and earth will pass away, but my words never.
34 Take heed to yourselves in case your hearts get overpowered by dissipation and drunkenness and worldly anxieties, and so that Day catches you suddenly like *a*
35 *trap.* For it will come *upon* all *dwellers on* the face of all
36 *the earth.* From hour to hour keep awake, praying that you may succeed in escaping all these dangers to come and in standing before the Son of man."
37 By day he taught in the temple, but at night he went outside the city and passed the night on the hill called
38 the Olive-Orchard. And all the people used to come early in the morning to listen to him in the temple.

22 Now the feast of unleavened bread which is called
2 the passover was near. The high priests and scribes were trying how to get him put to death (for they were
3 afraid of the people), and Satan entered Judas called
4 Iscariot, a member of the twelve, who went off to discuss with the high priests and commanders how he could betray
5 him to them. They were delighted and agreed to pay him
6 for it. He assented to this and sought a good opportunity for betraying him to them in the absence of the crowd.

7 Then came the day of unleavened bread when the paschal
8 lamb had to be sacrificed. So Jesus despatched Peter and
John, saying, "Go and prepare the passover for us that
9 we may eat it." They asked him, "Where do you want us
10 to prepare it?" He said to them, "When you enter the city
you will meet a man carrying a water-jar: follow him to
11 the house he enters, and tell the owner of the house, 'The
Teacher asks you, Where is the room in which I can eat
12 the passover with my disciples?' Then he will show you
a large room upstairs with couches spread; make your
13 preparations there." They went off and found it was as
14 he had told them. So they prepared the passover, and
when the hour came he took his place, with the apostles
15 beside him. He said to them, "I have longed eagerly to
16 eat this passover with you before I suffer, for I tell you I
will never eat the passover again till the fulfilment of it in
17 the Reign of God." And he took a cup which was handed
to him, gave thanks to God and said, "Take this and dis-
18 tribute it among yourselves, for I tell you I will never
drink the produce of the vine again till such time as God's
19 Reign comes." Then he took a loaf and after thanking
God he broke it and gave it to them, saying, "This means
my body given up for your sake; do this in memory of
20 me." So too he gave them the cup after supper, saying,
"This cup means the new *covenant* ratified *by* my *blood*
21 shed for your sake. But the hand of my betrayer is on
22 the table beside me! The Son of man moves to his end
indeed as it has been decreed, but woe to the man by whom
23 he is betrayed!" And they began to discuss among themselves which of them could possibly be going to do such a
24 thing. A quarrel also rose among them as to which of
25 them could be considered the greatest. But Jesus said to
them,
"The kings of the Gentiles rule over them,
and their authorities take the name of 'Benefactor':
26 not so with you.
He who is greatest among you must be like the youngest,
and he who is chief like a servant.
27 Which is the greatest, guest or servant? Is it not the
guest?
But I am among you as a servant.
28 It is you who have stood by me through my trials;
29 so, even as my Father has assigned me royal power,
30 I assign you the right of eating and drinking at my table in
my Realm and of sitting on thrones to rule the twelve
31 tribes of Israel. Simon, Simon, Satan has claimed the
32 right to sift you all like wheat, but I have prayed that your
own faith may not fail. And you in turn must be a

33 strength to your brothers." "Lord," he said, "I am ready
34 to go with you to prison and to death." Jesus said, "I tell
you, Peter, the cock will not crow to-day before you have
35 three times denied that you know me." And he said to
them, "When I sent you out with neither purse nor wallet
nor sandals, did you want for anything?" "No," they said,
36 "for nothing." Then he said to them, "But he who has a
purse must take it now, and the same with a wallet; and
he who has no sword must sell his coat and buy one.
37 For I tell you, this word of scripture must be fulfilled in
me: *he was classed among criminals*. Yes, there is an end
38 to all that refers to me." "Lord," they said, "here are two
swords!" "Enough! Enough!" he answered.
39 Then he went outside and made his way to the Hill of
Olives, as he was accustomed. The disciples followed him,
40 and when he reached the spot he said to them, "Pray that
41 you may not slip into temptation." He withdrew about a
42 stone's throw and knelt in prayer, saying, "Father, if it
please thee, take this cup away from me. But thy will, not
43 mine, be done." [And an angel from heaven appeared to
44 strengthen him; he fell into an agony and prayed with
greater intensity, his sweat dropping to the ground like
45 clots of blood.] Then rising from prayer he went to the
46 disciples, only to find them asleep from sheer sorrow. He
said to them, "Why are you sleeping? Get up and pray
47 that you may not slip into temptation." While he was still
speaking, there came a mob headed by the man called
Judas, one of the twelve. He approached in order to kiss
48 Jesus, but Jesus said to him, "Judas! would you betray
49 the Son of man with a kiss?" Now when the supporters
of Jesus saw what was going to happen, they said, "Lord,
50 shall we strike with our swords?" And one of them did
strike the servant of the high priest, cutting off his right
51 ear. Jesus said, "Let me do this at least," and cured him
52 by touching his ear. Then he said to the high priests and
commanders of the temple and elders who had appeared
to take him, "Have you sallied out to arrest me like a
53 robber, with swords and clubs? Day after day I was
beside you in the temple, and you never stretched a hand
against me. But this is your hour, and the dark Power
has its way."
54 Then they arrested him and led him away inside the
house of the high priest. Peter followed at a distance and
55 sat down among some people who had lit a fire in the
56 courtyard and were sitting round it. A maidservant who
noticed him sitting by the fire took a long look at him and
57 said, "That fellow was with him too." But he disowned
58 him, saying, "Woman, I know nothing about him." Shortly

afterwards another man noticed him and said, "Why, you
59 are one of them!" "Man," said Peter, "I am not." About
an hour had passed when another man insisted, "That
fellow really was with him. Why, he is a Galilean!"
60 "Man," said Peter, "I do not know what you mean." In-
61 stantly, just as he was speaking, the cock crowed; the
Lord turned round and looked at Peter, and then Peter
remembered what the Lord had told him, that 'Before cock-
62 crow to-day you will disown me three times.' And he
went outside and wept bitterly.
63 Meantime the men who had Jesus in custody flogged him
64 and made fun of him; blindfolding him they would ask
65 him, "Prophesy, tell us who struck you?" And many another insult they uttered against him.
66 When day broke, the elders of the people all met along
with the high priests and scribes, and had him brought
67 before their Sanhedrin. They said to him, "Tell us if you
are the Christ." He said to them, "You will not believe
68 me if I tell you, and you will not answer me when I put
69 a question to you. But after this *the Son of man will be
70 seated at God's right hand* of power." "Are you the Son of
God then?" they all said. "Certainly," he replied, "I am."
71 So they said, "What more evidence do we need? We have
heard it from his own lips."

23 Then the whole body of them rose and led him to
2 Pilate. They proceeded to accuse him, saying, "We
have discovered this fellow perverting our nation, for-
bidding tribute being paid to Cæsar, and alleging he is king
3 messiah." Pilate asked him, "Are you the king of the
4 Jews?" He replied, "Certainly." And Pilate said to the
high priests and the crowds, "I cannot find anything crim-
5 inal about him." But they insisted, "He stirs up the people
by teaching all over Judaea. He started from Galilee and
6 now he is here." When Pilate heard that, he asked if the
7 man was a Galilean, and ascertaining that he came under
the jurisdiction of Herod, he remitted him to Herod, who
8 himself was in Jerusalem during those days. Herod was
greatly delighted to see Jesus; he had long wanted to see
him, because he had heard about him and also because
9 he hoped to see him perform some miracle. But though
he put many questions to him, Jesus gave him no answer.
10 Meanwhile the high priests and scribes stood and accused
11 him with might and main. Then Herod and his troops
scoffed at him and made fun of him, and after arraying
12 him in a bright robe he remitted him to Pilate. Herod and
Pilate, became friends that day—previously they had been
at enmity.

13 Then summoning the high priests and rulers and the
14 people, Pilate said to them, "You brought me this man as
being an inciter to rebellion among the people. I have
examined him before you and found nothing criminal about
15 him, for all your accusations against him. No, nor
has Herod, for he has remitted him to us. He has
16 done nothing, you see, that calls for death; so I
18 shall release him with a whipping."* But they shouted one
and all, "Away with him! Release Bar-Abbas for us!"
19 (This was a man who had been put into prison on account
of a riot which had taken place in the city and also on a
20 charge of murder.) Again Pilate addressed them, for he
21 wanted to release Jesus, but they roared, "To the cross,
22 to the cross with him!" He asked them a third time, "But
what crime has he committed? I have found nothing about
him that deserves death; so I shall release him with a
23 whipping." But they loudly urged their demand that he
should be crucified, and their shouts carried the day.
24 Pilate gave sentence that their demand was to be carried
25 out; he released the man they wanted, the man who had
been imprisoned for riot and murder, and Jesus he handed
over to their will.
26 As they led him off they caught hold of Simon a Cyrenian
on his way from the country and laid the cross on him to
27 carry after Jesus. He was followed by a large multitude
of the people and also of women who beat their breasts and
28 lamented him; but Jesus turned to them and said, "Daughters of Jerusalem, weep not for me but weep for yourselves
29 and for your children! For there are days coming when
the cry will be,
'Blessed are the barren,
the wombs that never have borne
and the breasts that never have suckled!'
30 Then will people say *to the mountains, 'Fall on us!' and
to the hills, 'Cover us.'*
31 For if this is what they do when the wood is green,
what will they do when the wood is dry?"
32 Two criminals were also led out with him to be executed,
33 and when they came to the place called The Skull they
crucified him there with the criminals, one at his right
34 and one at his left. Jesus said, "Father, forgive them, they do
not know what they are doing." Then they *distributed his
35 clothes among themselves by drawing lots.* The people
stood and looked on, and even the rulers sneered at him,
saying, "He saved others, let him save himself, if he is the

* Omitting [ἀνάγκην δὲ εἶχεν ἀπολύειν αὐτοῖς κατὰ ἑορτὴν ἕνα] as an explanatory and harmonistic gloss.

36 Christ of God, the Chosen One!" The soldiers made fun
37 of him too by coming up and handing him vinegar, saying,
38 "If you are the king of the Jews, save yourself." (For
there was an inscription over him in Greek and Latin
and Hebrew characters,

THIS IS THE KING OF THE JEWS.)

39 One of the criminals who had been hung also abused him,
saying, "Are you not the Christ? Save yourself and us as
40 well." But the other checked him, saying, "Have you no
fear even of God? You are suffering the same punishment
41 as he. And we suffer justly; we are getting what we
42 deserve for our deeds. But he has done no harm." And
he added, "Jesus, do not forget me when you come to
43 reign." "I tell you truly," said Jesus, "you will be in
paradise with me this very day."
44 By this time it was about twelve o'clock, and darkness
45 covered the whole land till three o'clock, owing to an
eclipse of the sun; the curtain in the middle of the temple
46 was torn in two. Then with a loud cry Jesus said, "Father,
I trust my spirit to thy hands," and with these words he
47 expired. When the army-captain saw what had happened,
he glorified God, saying, "This man was really innocent."
48 And when all the crowds who had collected for the sight
saw what had happened, they turned away beating their
49 breasts. As for *his acquaintances, they were all standing
at a distance* to look on, with the women who had accompanied him from Galilee.
50 Now there was a man called Joseph, a member of
51 council but a good and just man who had not voted for
their plan of action; he belonged to Arimathaea, a Jewish
town, and he was on the outlook for the Reign of God.
52 This Joseph went to Pilate and asked him for the body
53 of Jesus. He then took it down, wrapped it in linen, and
put it in a tomb cut out of the rock, where no one had yet
54 been buried. It was the day of the Preparation and the
55 sabbath was just dawning. So the women who had accompanied him from Galilee and who had followed Joseph,
56 noted the tomb and the position of the body; then they
went home and prepared spices and perfumes.

24 ON the sabbath they rested in obedience to God's
command, but on the first day of the week at early
dawn they took the spices they had prepared and went to
2 the tomb. The boulder they found rolled away from the
3 tomb, but when they went inside they could not find the
4 body of the Lord Jesus. They were puzzling over this,
5 when two men flashed on them in dazzling raiment. They

were terrified and bent their faces to the ground, but the men said to them, "Why do you look among the dead for
6 him who is alive? He is not here, he has risen. Remember
7 how he told you when he was still in Galilee that the Son of man had to be betrayed into the hands of sinful men
8 and be crucified and rise on the third day." Then they
9 remembered what he had said, and turning away from the tomb they reported all this to the eleven and all the others.
10 (It was Mary of Magdala, Joanna, and Mary the mother of James who with the rest of the women told this to the
11 apostles.) But this story of the women seemed in their opinion to be nonsense; they would not believe them.
12 Peter did get up and run to the tomb, but when he looked in he saw nothing except the linen bandages; so he went away home wondering what had happened.
13 That very day two of them were on their way to a village
14 called Emmaus about seven miles from Jerusalem. They
15 were conversing about all these events, and during their conversation and discussion Jesus himself approached and
16 walked beside them, though they were prevented from
17 recognizing him. He said to them, "What is all this you are debating on your walk?" They stopped, looking down-
18 cast, and one of them, called Cleopas, answered him, "Are you a lone stranger in Jerusalem, not to know what has
19 been happening there?" "What is that?" he said to them. They replied, "All about Jesus of Nazaret! To God and all the people he was a prophet strong in action and utter-
20 ance, but the high priests and our rulers delivered him up
21 to be sentenced to death and crucified him. Our own hope was that he would be the redeemer of Israel; but he is dead,
22 and that is three days ago! Though some women of our number gave us a surprise; they were at the tomb early in
23 the morning and could not find his body, but they came to tell us they had actually seen a vision of angels who de-
24 clared he was alive. Some of our company did go to the tomb and found things exactly as the women had said,
25 but they did not see him." He said to them, "O foolish men, with hearts so slow to believe, after all the prophets
26 have declared! Had not the Christ to suffer thus and so
27 enter his glory?" Then he began with Moses and all the prophets and interpreted to them the passages referring
28 to himself throughout the scriptures. Now they approached the village to which they were going. He pretended to be
29 going further on, but they pressed him, saying, "Stay with us, for it is getting towards evening and the day has now
30 declined." So he went in to stay with them. And as he lay at table with them he took the loaf, blessed it, broke it
31 and handed it to them. Then their eyes were opened and

S. LUKE XXIV

they recognized him, but he vanished from their sight.
32 And they said to one another, "Did not our hearts glow within us when he was talking to us on the road, opening
33 up the scriptures for us?" So they got up and returned that very hour to Jerusalem, where they found the eleven
34 and their friends all gathered, who told them that the Lord had really risen and that he had appeared to Simon.
35 Then they related their own experience on the road and how they had recognized him when he broke the loaf.
36 Just as they were speaking He stood among them [and said
37 to them, "Peace to you!"] They were scared and terrified,
38 imagining it was a ghost they saw; but he said to them, "Why are you upset? Why do doubts invade your mind?
39 Look at my hands and feet. It is I! Feel me and see; a
40 ghost has not flesh and bones as you see I have." [With
41 these words he showed them his hands and feet.] Even yet they could not believe it for sheer joy; they were lost
42 in wonder. So he said to them, "Have you any food here?"
43 And when they handed him a piece of broiled fish, he took
44 and ate it in their presence. Then he said to them, "When I was still with you, this is what I told you, that whatever is written about me in the law of Moses and the prophets
45 and the psalms must be fulfilled." Then he opened their
46 minds to understand the scriptures. "Thus," he said, "it is written that the Christ has to suffer and rise from the
47 dead on the third day, and that repentance and the remission of sins must be preached in his name to all nations,
48 beginning from Jerusalem. To this you must bear testi-
49 mony. And I will send down on you what my Father has promised; wait in the city till you are endued with power
50 from on high." He led them out as far as Bethany; then,
51 lifting his hands, he blessed them. And as he blessed them
52 he parted from them [and was carried up to heaven]. They [worshipped him and] returned with great joy to Jeru-
53 salem, where they spent all their time within the temple, blessing God.

THE GOSPEL ACCORDING TO

S. JOHN

1 THE Logos existed in the very beginning,
the Logos was with God,
the Logos was divine.
2 He was with God in the very beginning:
3 through him all existence came into being,
no existence came into being apart from him.
4 In him life lay,
and this life was the Light for men:
5 amid the darkness the Light shone,
but the darkness did not master it.
6 A man appeared, sent by God, whose name was John:
7 he came for the purpose of witnessing, to bear testimony to the Light, so that all men might believe by means of
8 him. He was not the Light; it was to bear testimony to
9 the Light that he appeared. The real Light, which enlightens every man, was coming then into the world:
10 he entered the world—
the world which existed through him—
yet the world did not recognize him;
11 he came to what was his own,
yet his own folk did not welcome him.
12 On those who have accepted him, however, he has conferred the right of being children of God, that is, on those
13 who believe in his Name, who owe this birth of theirs to God, not to human blood, nor to any impulse of the flesh or
14 of man. So the Logos became flesh and tarried among us; we have seen his glory—glory such as an only son enjoys from his father—seen it to be full of grace and reality.
15 (John testified to him with the cry, 'This was he of whom I said, my successor has taken precedence of me, for he
16 preceded me.') For we have all been receiving grace after
17 grace from his fulness; while the Law was given through Moses, grace and reality are ours through Jesus Christ.
18 Nobody has ever seen God, but God has been unfolded by the divine One, the only Son,* who lies upon the Father's breast.
19 Now here is John's testimony. When the Jews of Jeru-

* Although θεός ('the divine one') is probably more original than the variant reading υἱός, μονογενής (see ver. 14) requires some such periphrasis in order to bring out its full meaning here.

salem despatched priests and Levites to ask him, "Who are
20 you?" he frankly confessed—he did not deny it, he frankly
21 confessed, "I am not the Christ." They asked him, "Then
what are you? Elijah?" He said, "I am not." "Are you
22 the Prophet?" "No," he answered. "Then who are you?"
they said; "tell us, so that we can give some answer to
those who sent us. What have you to say for yourself?"
23 He said, "I am
the voice of one who cries in the desert,
'level the way for the Lord'—
24 as the prophet Isaiah said." Now it was some of the
25 Pharisees who had been sent to him; so they asked him,
saying, "Then why are you baptizing people, if you are
26 neither the Christ nor Elijah nor the Prophet?" "I am
baptizing with water," John replied, "but my successor
27 is among you, One whom you do not recognize, and I
28 am not fit to untie the string of his sandal." This took
place at Bethany on the opposite side of the Jordan, where
John was baptizing.
29 Next day he observed Jesus coming towards him and
exclaimed, "Look, there is the lamb of God, who is to
30 remove the sin of the world! That is he of whom I said,
'The man who is to succeed me has taken precedence of
31 me, for he preceded me.' I myself did not recognize him;
I only came to baptize with water, in order that he might
32 be disclosed to Israel." And John bore this testimony also:
"I saw the Spirit descend like a dove from heaven and rest
33 on him. I myself did not recognize him, but He who sent
me to baptize with water told me, 'He on whom you see the
Spirit descending and resting, that is he who baptizes with
34 the holy Spirit.' Now I did see it, and I testify that he
is the Son of God."

35 Next day again John was standing with two of his dis-
36 ciples; he gazed at Jesus as he walked about, and said,
37 "Look, there is the lamb of God!" The two disciples heard
38 what he said and went after Jesus. Now Jesus turned,
and when he observed them coming after him, he asked
them, "What do you want?" They replied, "Rabbi" (which
may be translated, 'teacher'), "where are you staying?" He
39 said to them, "Come and see." So they went and saw
where he stayed, and stayed with him the rest of that day
40 —it was then about four in the afternoon. One of the
two men who heard what John said and went after Jesus
41 was Andrew, the brother of Peter. In the morning* he met
his brother Simon and told him, "We have found the

* The Greek word (πρωΐ) has been misread in nearly all the MSS.
for "first" (πρῶτον); see the note in Mrs. A. S. Lewis's *Old Syriac*
Gospels (1910), pp. xxviii–xxix.

42 messiah" (which may be translated, 'Christ'). He took
him to Jesus; Jesus gazed at him and said, "You are
Simon, the son of John? Your name is to be Cephas"
(meaning 'Peter' or 'rock').
43 Next day Jesus determined to leave for Galilee; there
44 he met Philip and told him, "Follow me." Now Philip
belonged to Bethsaida, the same town as Andrew and
45 Peter; he met Nathanael and told him, "We have found
him whom Moses wrote about in the Law, and also the
prophets—it is Jesus, the son of Joseph, who comes from
46 Nazaret." "Nazaret!" said Nathanael, "can anything good
47 come out of Nazaret?" "Come and see," said Philip. Jesus
saw Nathanael approaching and said of him, "Here is a
48 genuine Israelite! There is no guile in him." Nathanael
said to him, "How do you know me?" Jesus answered,
"When you were under that fig tree, before ever Philip
49 called you, I saw you." "Rabbi," said Nathanael, "you are
50 the Son of God, you are the king of Israel!" Jesus
answered, "You believe because I told you I had seen you
51 under that fig tree? You shall see more than that." He
said to him, "Truly, truly I tell you all,* you shall see
heaven open wide and *God's angels ascending and descending* upon the Son of man."

2 Two days later a wedding took place at Cana in Galilee;
2 the mother of Jesus was present, and Jesus and his
3 disciples had also been invited to the wedding. As the
wine ran short, the mother of Jesus said to him, "They
4 have no wine." "Woman," said Jesus, "what have you to
5 do with me? My time has not come yet." His mother said
6 to the servants, "Do whatever he tells you." Now six stone
water-jars were standing there, for the Jewish rites of
7 'purification,' each holding about twenty gallons. Jesus
said, "Fill up the jars with water." So they filled them to
8 the brim. Then he said, "Now draw some out, and take it
9 to the manager of the feast." They did so; and when the
manager of the feast tasted the water which had become
wine, not knowing where it had come from (though the
10 servants who had drawn it knew), he called the bridegroom and said to him, "Everybody serves the good wine
first, and then the poorer wine after people have drunk
11 freely; you have kept the good wine till now." Jesus performed this, the first of his Signs, at Cana in Galilee, thereby displaying his glory; and his disciples believed in him.
12 After this he travelled down to Capharnahum, with his

* I insert the word ' all ', to make it clear that the ' you ' of ver. 51
is plural. The promise is more than a personal word to Nathanael.
Omit [ἀπ' ἄρτι].

S. JOHN II

mother and brothers and his disciples; they stayed there for a few days.*
22 After this Jesus and his disciples went into the country of Judaea, where he spent some time with them baptizing.
23 John was also baptizing at Aenon near Salim, as there was plenty of water there, and people came to him and
24 were baptized (John had not yet been thrown into prison).
25 Now a dispute arose between John's disciples and a Jew over
26 the question of 'purification'; and they came and told John, "Rabbi, the man who was with you on the opposite side of the Jordan, the man to whom you bore testimony—here
27 he is, baptizing, and everybody goes to him!" John answered, "No one can receive anything except as a gift from
28 heaven. You can bear me out, that I said, 'I am not the Christ'; what I said was, 'I have been sent in advance of
29 him.' He who has the bride is the bridegroom; the bridegroom's friend, who stands by and listens to him, is heartily glad at the sound of the bridegroom's voice. Such
30 is my joy, and it is complete. He must wax, I must wane."
13 Now the Jewish passover was near, so Jesus went up
14 to Jerusalem. There he found, seated inside the temple, dealers in cattle, sheep and pigeons, also money-changers.
15 Making a scourge of cords, he drove them all, sheep and cattle together, out of the temple, scattered the coins of the
16 brokers and upset their tables, and told the pigeon-dealers, "Away with these! My Father's house is not to be turned
17 into a shop!" (His disciples recalled the scripture saying,
18 *I am consumed with zeal for thy house.*) Then the Jews accosted him with the words, "What sign of authority
19 have you to show us, for acting in this way?" Jesus replied, "Destroy this sanctuary and I will raise it up in
20 three days." "This sanctuary took forty-six years to build," the Jews retorted, "and you are going to raise it up in
21 three days!" He meant the sanctuary of his body, how-
22 ever, and when the disciples recalled what he had said, after he had been raised from the dead, they believed the scripture and the word of Jesus.

23 When he was in Jerusalem at the festival of the passover, many people believed in his name, as they witnessed
24 the Signs which he performed. Jesus, however, would not
25 trust † himself to them; he knew all men, and required no evidence from anyone about human nature; well did he know what was in human nature.

* Transposing iii. 22–30 to its true position between ii. 12 and ii. 13.
† The Vulgate is able to preserve the assonance of the word 'trust' here and 'believe' in ver. 23: "multi crediderunt in nomine eius. . . . Iesus non credebat semet ipsum eis."

S. JOHN III

3 Now there was a Pharisee named Nicodemus, who belonged to the Jewish authorities; he came one night to Jesus and said, "Rabbi, we know you have come from God to teach us, for no one could perform these Signs of yours unless God were with him." Jesus replied, "Truly, truly I tell you, no one can see God's Realm unless he is born from above." Nicodemus said to him, "How can a man be born when he is old? Can he enter his mother's womb over again and be born?" Jesus replied, "Truly, truly I tell you, unless one is born of water and the Spirit, he cannot enter God's Realm. What is born of the flesh is flesh: what is born of the Spirit is Spirit. Do not wonder at me telling you, 'You must all be born from above.' The wind blows where it wills; you can hear its sound, but you never know where it has come from or where it goes: it is the same with everyone who is born of the Spirit." Nicodemus answered, "How can that be?" Jesus replied, "You do not understand this?—you, a teacher in Israel! Truly, truly I tell you, we are speaking of what we do understand, we testify to what we have actually seen—and yet you refuse our testimony. If you will not believe when I speak to you about things on earth, how will you believe if I speak to you about things in heaven? And yet the Son of man, descended from heaven, is the only one who has ever ascended into heaven. Indeed the Son of man must be lifted on high, just as Moses lifted up the serpent in the desert, that everyone who believes in him may have eternal life. For God loved the world so dearly that he gave up his only Son, so that everyone who believes in him may have eternal life, instead of perishing. God did not send his Son into the world to pass sentence on it, but to save the world by him. He who believes in him is not sentenced; he who will not believe is sentenced already, for having refused to believe in the name of the only Son of God. And this is the sentence of condemnation, that the Light has entered the world and yet men have preferred darkness to light. It is because their actions have been evil; for anyone whose practices are corrupt loathes the light and will not come out into it, in case his actions are exposed, whereas anyone whose life is true comes out into the light, to make it plain that his actions have been divinely prompted.

31 He who comes from above is far above all others; he who springs from earth belongs to earth and speaks of earth; he who comes from heaven [is far above all others. He] is testifying to what he has seen and heard, and yet no one accepts his testimony. Whoever does accept it, certifies to the truth of God. For he whom God has sent utters

S. JOHN IV

the words of God—God gives him the Spirit in no sparing
35 measure; the Father loves the Son and has given him
36 control over everything. He who believes in the Son has
eternal life, but he who disobeys the Son shall not see
life—God's anger broods over him."

4 Now when the Lord learned that the Pharisees had
heard of Jesus gaining and baptizing more disciples
2 than John (though Jesus himself did not baptize, it was
3 his disciples), he left Judaea and went back to Galilee.
4 He had to pass through Samaria, and in so doing he
5 arrived at a Samaritan town called Sychar; it lay near the
6 territory which Jacob had given to his son Joseph, and
Jacob's spring was there. Jesus, exhausted by the journey,
sat down at the spring, just as he was. It was about noon,
7 and a Samaritan woman came to draw water. Jesus said
8 to her, "Give me a drink" (his disciples had gone to the
9 town to buy some food). The Samaritan woman said,
"What? You* are a Jew, and you ask me for a drink—me,
a Samaritan!" (Jews do not associate with Samaritans.)
10 Jesus answered, "If you knew what is the free gift of God
and who is asking you for a drink, you would have asked
him instead, and he would have given you 'living' water."
11 "Sir," said the woman, "you have nothing to draw water
with, and it is a deep well; where do you get your 'living'
12 water? Are you a greater man than Jacob, our ancestor?
He gave us this well, and he drank from it, with his sons
13 and his cattle." Jesus answered, "Anyone who drinks this
14 water will be thirsty again, but anyone who drinks the
water I shall give him will never thirst any more; the
water I shall give him will turn into a spring of water
15 welling up to eternal life." "Ah, sir," said the woman,
"give me this water, so that I need not thirst or come all
16 this road to draw water." Jesus said to her, "Go and call
17 your husband, then come back here." The woman replied,
"I have no husband." Jesus said to her, "You were right
18 in saying, 'I have no husband'; you have had five husbands,
and he whom you have now espoused is not your husband.
19 That was a true word." "Sir," said the woman, "I see
20 you are a prophet. Now our ancestors worshipped on this
mountain, whereas you Jews declare the proper place for
21 worship is at Jerusalem." "Woman," said Jesus, "believe
me, the time is coming when you will be worshipping the
22 Father neither on this mountain nor at Jerusalem. You

* The Greek word for ' you ' (in the singular) occurs oftener in the
Fourth gospel than in all the first three gospels put together. Dr.
E. A. Abbott regards this as an indication of the evangelist's tendency
'to lay stress on personality, and to express personality in dialogue.'

S. JOHN IV

are worshipping something you do not know; we are worshipping what we do know—for salvation comes from the
23 Jews. But the time is coming, it has come already, when the real worshippers will worship the Father in Spirit and in reality; for these are the worshippers that the Father
24 wants. God is Spirit, and his worshippers must worship
25 him in Spirit and in reality." The woman said to him, "Well, I know messiah (which means Christ) is coming.
26 When he arrives, he will explain it all to us." "I am messiah," said Jesus, "I who am talking to you."
27 At this point his disciples came up; they were surprised that he was talking to a woman, but none of them said,
28 "What is it?" or, "Why are you talking to her?" Then the woman left her water-pot, and going off to the town told
29 the people, "Come here, look at a man who has told me
30 everything I ever did! Can he be the Christ?" They
31 set out from the town on their way to him. Meanwhile the
32 disciples pressed him, saying, "Rabbi, eat something." But he said to them, "I have food, of which you know nothing."
33 So the disciples asked each other, "Can anyone have
34 brought him something to eat?" Jesus said, "My food is to do the will of him who sent me, and to accomplish his
35 work. You have a saying, have you not, 'Four months yet, then harvest'? Look round, I tell you; see, the fields are
36 white for harvesting! The reaper is already getting his wages and harvesting for eternal life, so that the sower
37 shares the reaper's joy. That proverb, 'One sows and an-
38 other reaps,' holds true here: I sent you to reap a crop for which you did not toil; other men have toiled, and you
39 reap the profit of their toil." Now many Samaritans belonging to that town believed in him on account of the woman's testimony, "He told me everything I ever did."
40 So when the Samaritans arrived, they pressed him to stay
41 with them; he did stay there two days, and far more of
42 them believed on account of what he said himself. As they told the woman, "We no longer believe on account of what you said; we have heard for ourselves, we know that he is really the Saviour of the world."
43 When the two days were over, he left for Galilee
44 (for Jesus himself testified that a prophet enjoys no honour
45 in his own country); on reaching Galilee, he was welcomed by the Galileans, who had seen all he did at the festival in Jerusalem—for they too had gone to the festival.
46 Once more he came to Cana in Galilee, where he had turned the water into wine. There was a royal official,
47 whose son was lying ill at Capernaum; when he heard that Jesus had arrived in Galilee from Judaea, he went to him and begged him to come down and cure his

48 son, who was at the point of death. Jesus said to
him, "Unless you see signs and wonders, you never
49 will believe." The official said, "Come down, sir, before
50 my boy is dead." Jesus told him, "Go yourself, your son
is alive." The man believed what Jesus told him, and
51 started on his journey. And on the road his servants met
52 him with the news that his boy was alive. So he asked
them at what hour he had begun to improve; they told
53 him, "Yesterday at one o'clock the fever left him." Then
the father realized that it had left him at the very time
when Jesus had said to him, "Your son is alive"; and he
54 became a believer with all his household. This was the
second Sign which Jesus performed again after leaving
Judaea for Galilee.

5 AFTER this there was a festival of the Jews, and Jesus
2 went up to Jerusalem. Now in Jerusalem there is a
bath beside the sheep-pool, which is called in Hebrew Beth-
3 zatha; it has five porticoes, where a crowd of invalids used
to lie, the blind, the lame, and folk with shrivelled limbs
4 [waiting for the water to bubble. For an angel used to
descend from time to time into the bath, and disturb the
water; whereupon the first person who stepped in after
the water was disturbed was restored to health, no matter
5 what disease he had been afflicted with]. * Now one man
was there, whose illness had lasted thirty-eight years.
6 Jesus saw him lying, and knowing he had been ill for a
long while he said to him, "Do you want your health
7 restored?" The invalid replied, "Sir, I have nobody to put
me into the bath, when the water is disturbed; and while
I am getting down myself, someone else gets in before
8 me." Jesus said to him, "Get up, lift your mat, and walk."
9 And instantly the man got well, lifted his mat, and started
to walk.
10 Now it was the sabbath on that day. So the Jews said
to the man who had been cured, "This is the sabbath, you
11 have no right to be carrying your mat." He replied, "But
the man who healed me, he told me, 'Lift your mat and
12 walk'." They questioned him, "Who was it that told you,
13 'Lift it and walk'?" Now the man who had been healed
did not know who it was, for (owing to the crowd on the
14 spot) Jesus had slipped away. Later on Jesus met him in
the temple, and said to him, "See, you are well and strong;
commit no more sins, in case something worse befalls you."
15 Off went the man and told the Jews it was Jesus who had

* The words in brackets, omitted by von Soden, represent a passage which is absent from many important versions and manuscripts.

16 healed him. And this was why the Jews persecuted Jesus,
17 because he did things like this on the sabbath. The reply of Jesus was, "As my Father has continued working to
18 this hour, so I work too." But this only made the Jews more eager to kill him, because he not merely broke the sabbath but actually spoke of God as his own Father,
19 thereby making himself equal to God. So Jesus made this answer to them: "Truly, truly I tell you, the Son can do nothing of his own accord, nothing but what he sees the Father doing; for whatever he does, the Son also does the
20 same. The Father loves the Son and shows him all that he is doing himself. He will show him still greater deeds
21 than these, to make you wonder; for as the Father raises the dead and makes them live, so the Son makes anyone
22 live whom he chooses. Indeed the Father passes judgment on no one; he has committed the judgment which deter-
23 mines life or death entirely to the Son, that all men may honour the Son as they honour the Father. (He who does not honour the Son does not honour the Father who sent
24 him.) Truly, truly I tell you, he who listens to my word and believes him who sent me has eternal life; he will incur no sentence of judgment, he has already passed from
25 death across to life. Truly, truly I tell you, the time is coming, it has come already, when the dead will listen to the voice of the Son of God, and those who listen will
26 live; for as the Father has life in himself, so too he has
27 granted the Son to have life in himself, and also granted
28 him authority to act as judge, since he is Son of man. Do not wonder at this; for there is a time coming when all
29 who are in the tombs will listen to his voice and come out, the doers of good to be raised to life, ill-doers to be raised for the sentence of judgment.
30 I can do nothing of my own accord; I pass judgment on men as I am taught by God, and my judgment is just, because my aim is not my own will but the will of him
31 who sent me. If I testify to myself, then my evidence is
32 not valid; I have Another to bear testimony to me, and I
33 know the evidence he bears for me is valid. You sent to
34 John, and he bore testimony to the truth (though I accept no testimony from man—I only speak of this testimony,
35 that you may be saved); he was a burning and a shining lamp, and you chose to rejoice for a while in his light.
36 But I possess a testimony greater than that of John, for the deeds which the Father has granted me to accomplish, the very deeds on which I am engaged, are my testimony
37 that the Father has sent me. The Father who sent me has also borne testimony to me himself; but his voice you have
38 never heard, his form you have never seen, his word you

have not kept with you, because you do not believe him
39 whom he sent. You search the scriptures, imagining you
40 possess eternal life in their pages—and they do testify to
41 me—but you refuse to come to me for life. I accept no
42 credit from men, but I know there is no love to God in you;
43 here am I, come in the name of my Father, and you will
not accept me: let someone else come in his own name,
44 and you will accept him! How can you believe, you who
accept credit from one another instead of aiming at the
45 credit which comes from the only God? Do not imagine
I am going to accuse you to the Father; Moses is your
46 accuser, Moses who is your hope! For if you believed
Moses you would believe me, since it was of me that he
47 wrote. But if you do not believe what he wrote, how will
you ever believe what I say?"
15 The Jews were amazed, saying, "How can this un-
16 educated fellow manage to read?" Jesus told them in
reply, "My teaching is not my own but his who sent me;
17 anyone who chooses to do his will, shall understand
whether my teaching comes from God or whether I am
18 talking on my own authority. He who talks on his own
authority aims at his own credit, but he who aims at the
credit of the person who sent him, he is sincere, and there
19 is no dishonesty in him. Did not Moses give you the Law?
—and yet none of you honestly obeys the Law. Else, why
20 do you want to kill me?" The crowd replied, "You are
21 mad. Who wants to kill you?" Jesus answered them, "I
have only performed one deed, and yet you are all amazed
22 at it. Moses gave you the rite of circumcision (not that
it came from Moses, it came from your ancestors); and
23 you will circumcise a man upon the sabbath. Well, if a
man gets circumcised upon the sabbath, to avoid breaking
the Law of Moses, are you enraged at me for curing, not
24 cutting, the entire body of a man upon the sabbath? Give
over judging by appearances; be just."*

6 AFTER this Jesus went off to the opposite side of the sea
2 of Galilee (the lake of Tiberias), followed by a large
crowd on account of the Signs which they had seen him per-
3 form on sick folk. Now Jesus went up the hill and sat
4 down there with his disciples. (The passover, the Jewish
5 festival, was at hand.) On looking up and seeing a large
crowd approaching, he said to Philip, "Where are we to
6 buy bread for all these people to eat?" (He said this to
test Philip, for he knew what he was going to do himself.)
7 Philip answered, "Seven pounds' worth of bread would

* Restoring vii. 15–24 to this, its original position in the gospel.

S. JOHN VI

not be enough for them, for everybody to get even a
8 morsel." One of his disciples, Andrew the brother of Simon
9 Peter, said to him, "There is a servant here, with five
barley-cakes and a couple of fish; but what is that among
10 so many?" Jesus said, "Get the people to lie down." Now
there was plenty of grass at the spot, so the men lay down,
11 numbering about five thousand. Then Jesus took the
loaves, gave thanks to God, and distributed them to those
who were reclining; so too with the fish, as much as they
12 wanted. And when they were satisfied, he said to the
disciples, "Gather up the pieces left over, so that nothing
13 may be wasted." They gathered them up, and filled twelve
baskets with pieces of the five loaves left over from the
14 meal. Now when the people saw the Sign he had performed,
they said, "This really is the Prophet who is to come into
15 the world!" Whereupon Jesus perceived they meant to
come and seize him to make a king of him; so he withdrew by himself to the hill again.
16 When evening came, his disciples went down to the sea,
17 and embarking in a boat they started across the sea for
Capharnahum. By this time it was dark, Jesus had not
18 reached them yet, and the sea was getting up under a
19 strong wind. After rowing about three or four miles they
saw Jesus walking on the sea and nearing the boat. They
20 were terrified, but he said to them, "It is I, have no fear";
21 so they agreed to take him on board, and the boat instantly
reached the land they were making for.
22 Next day the crowd which had been left standing on
the other side of the sea bethought them that only one boat
had been there, and that Jesus had not gone aboard with
23 his disciples, who had left by themselves. So, as some
boats from Tiberias had put in near the spot where they
24 had eaten bread after the Lord's thanksgiving, and as the
crowd saw that neither Jesus nor his disciples were there,
they embarked in the boats themselves and made for
25 Capharnahum in search of Jesus. When they found him
on the other side of the sea, they said, "Rabbi, when did
26 you get here?" Jesus answered them, "Truly, truly I tell
you, it is not because you saw Signs that you are in quest
of me, but because you ate these loaves and had your fill.
27 Work for no perishing food, but for that lasting food which
means eternal life; the Son of man will give you that,
28 for the Father, God, has certified him." Then they asked
him, "What must we do to perform the works of God?"
29 Jesus replied to them, "This is the work of God, to believe
30 in him whom God has sent." "Well then," they said, "what
is the Sign you perform, that we may see it and believe
31 you? What work have you to show? Our ancestors ate

manna in the desert: as it is written, *He gave them bread*
32 *from heaven to eat.*" Then said Jesus, "What Moses gave
you was not the bread from heaven; it is my Father who
33 gives you the real bread from heaven—for the bread of God
is what comes down from heaven and gives life to the
34 world." "Ah, sir," they said to him, "give us that bread
35 always." Jesus said, "I am the bread of life; he who
comes to me will never be hungry, and he who believes in
36 me will never be thirsty again. But, as I told you, though
37 you have seen me, you do not believe. All those will come
to me who are the Father's gift to me, and never will I
38 reject one of them; for I have come down from heaven
not to carry out my own will but the will of him who
39 sent me, and the will of him who sent me is that I lose
none of those who are his gift to me, but that I raise them
40 all up on the last day. It is the will of my Father that
everyone who sees the Son and believes in him should
possess eternal life, and that I should raise him up on
the last day."
41 Now the Jews murmured at him for saying, "I am the
42 bread which has come down from heaven." They said, "Is
this not Jesus the son of Joseph? We know his father
and mother. How can he claim now, 'I have come down
43 from heaven'?" Jesus replied to them, "Stop murmur-
44 ing to yourselves. No one is able to come to me unless
he is drawn by the Father who sent me (and I will raise
45 him up on the last day). In the prophets it is written,
and they will be all instructed by God; everyone who has
listened to the Father and learned from him, comes to me.
46 Not that anyone has seen the Father—he only, who is
47 from God, he has seen the Father. Truly, truly I tell you,
48 the believer has eternal life. I am the bread of life.
49 Your ancestors ate manna in the desert, but they died;
50 the bread that comes down from heaven is such that one
51 eats of it and never dies. I am the living bread which
has come down from heaven; if anyone eats of this bread,
he will live for ever; and more, the bread I will give is
my flesh, given for the life of the world."
52 The Jews then wrangled with one another, saying, "How
53 can he give us his flesh to eat?" So Jesus said to them,
"Truly, truly I tell you, unless you eat the flesh of the Son
of man and drink his blood, you have no life within you.
54 He who feeds on my flesh and drinks my blood possesses
55 eternal life (and I will raise him up on the last day), for
56 my flesh is real food and my blood is real drink. He
who feeds on my flesh and drinks my blood remains within
57 me, as I remain within him. Just as the living Father
sent me and I live by the Father, so he who feeds on me

58 will also live by me. Such is the bread which has come down from heaven: your ancestors ate their bread and died, but he who feeds on this bread will live for ever."
59 This he said as he taught in the synagogue at Capharnahum.
60 Now many of his disciples, on hearing it, said, "This is hard to take in! Who can listen to talk like this?"
61 Jesus, inwardly conscious that his disciples were murmur-
62 ing at it, said to them, "So this upsets you? Then what if you were to see the Son of man ascending to where he
63 formerly existed? What gives life is the Spirit: flesh is of no avail at all. The words I have uttered to you are
64 spirit and life. And yet there are some of you who do not believe" (for Jesus knew from the very first who the
65 unbelieving were, and who was to betray him; that was why* he said 'I tell you that no one is able to come to me unless he is allowed by the Father').
66 After that, many of his disciples drew back and would
67 not associate with him any longer. So Jesus said to the
68 twelve, "You do not want to go, too?" Simon Peter answered him, "Lord, who are we to go to? You have got
69 words of eternal life, and we believe, we are certain, that
70 you are the holy One of God." Jesus answered them, "Did I not choose you, the twelve? And yet one of you is a devil!"
71 (He meant Judas the son of Simon Iscariot; for Judas was to betray him—and he was one of the twelve.)

7 AFTER this Jesus moved about in Galilee; he would not move in Judaea, because the Jews were trying to kill him.
2
3 Now the Jewish festival of booths was near, so his brothers said to him, "Leave this and go across into Judaea,
4 to let your disciples witness what you can do; for nobody who aims at public recognition ever keeps his actions secret. Since you can do these deeds, display yourself to
5 the world" (for even his brothers did not believe in him).
6 Jesus said to them, "My time has not come yet, but your
7 time is always at hand; the world cannot hate you, but it
8 hates me because I testify that its deeds are evil. Go up to the festival yourselves; I am not going up to this festi-
9 val, for my time has not arrived yet." So saying he stayed
10 on in Galilee. But after his brothers had gone up to the festival, he went up too, not publicly but as it were
11 privately. At the festival the Jews were in quest of him,

* Reading διὰ τοῦτο ἔλεγεν, with e (so Blass and Merx), instead of ἔλεγεν διὰ τοῦτο.

S. JOHN VII

12 saying, "Where is he?" And the crowd disputed about him
hotly; some said, "He is a good man," but others said,
13 "No, he is misleading the people." For fear of the Jews,
however, nobody spoke of him in public.
14 When the festival was half over, Jesus went up to the
25 temple and began to teach.* Then said some of the Jeru-
26 salemites, "Is this not the man they want to kill? Yet
here he is, opening his lips in public, and they say nothing
to him! Can the authorities have really discovered that
27 he is the Christ? No, we know where this man comes
from; but when the Christ does come, no one will know
28 where he comes from." So Jesus cried aloud, as he was
teaching in the temple, "You know me? you know where
I come from? But I have not come on my own initiative;
I am sent, and sent by Him who is real. You do not
29 know Him, but I know Him, because I have come from
30 Him and He sent me." So they tried to arrest him; but
no one laid hands on him, because his time had not come
31 yet. Indeed many of the people believed in him, saying,
"When the Christ does come, will he perform more Signs
32 than this man?" The Pharisees heard the people discussing Jesus in this way, so the high priests and the Pharisees
33 despatched attendants to arrest him. Then said Jesus, "I
will be with you a little longer, then I go to Him who
34 sent me; you will search for me but you will not find me,
35 and where I go, you cannot come." The Jews said to
themselves, "Where is he going, that we will not find him?
Is he off to the Dispersion among the Greeks, to teach the
36 Greeks? What does he mean by saying, 'You will search
for me but you will not find me, and where I go, you
cannot come'?"
37 Now on the last day, the great day, of the festival, Jesus
stood and cried aloud, "If anyone is athirst, let him come
38 to me and drink; he who believes in me—out of his body,
39 as scripture says, streams of living water will flow" (he
meant by this the Spirit which those who believed in him
were to receive:—as yet there was no Spirit, because
40 Jesus had not been glorified yet). On hearing this some
of the people said, "This really is the Prophet"; others
41 said, "He is the Christ"; but others said, "No, surely the
42 Christ does not come from Galilee? Does not scripture
say it is *from the offspring of David, from* David's village
43 of *Bethlehem*, that the Christ is to come?" So the people
44 were divided over him; some wanted to arrest him, but
45 no one laid hands on him. Then the attendants went back
to the high priests and Pharisees, who asked them, "Why

* See note, p. 145.

46 have you not brought him with you?" The attendants
47 replied, "No man ever spoke as he does." The Pharisees
48 retorted, "Are you misled as well? Have any of the au-
49 thorities or of the Pharisees believed in him? As for this
50 mob, with its ignorance of the Law—it is accursed!" Nicodemus, one of their number (the same who had come to
51 him before), said to them, "But surely our Law does not condemn the accused before hearing what he has to say
52 and ascertaining his offence?" They answered him, "And are you from Galilee, too? Search and you will see that no prophet ever springs from Galilee."

53
2 8 [And every one of them went home, but Jesus went to the Hill of Olives. Early in the morning he returned to the temple, the people all came to him, and he sat down
3 and taught them. The scribes and Pharisees brought a woman who had been caught in the act of committing
4 adultery, and making her stand forward they said to him, "Teacher, this woman was caught in the very act of com-
5 mitting adultery. Now Moses has commanded us in the
6 Law to stone such creatures; but what do you say?" (They said this to test him, in order to get a charge against him.) Jesus stooped down, and began to write with his finger
7 on the ground; but as they persisted with their question, he raised himself and said to them, "Let the innocent
8 among you throw the first stone at her"; then he
9 stooped down again and wrote on the ground. And on hearing what he said, they went away one by one, beginning with the older men, till Jesus was left alone with the
10 woman standing before him. Looking up, Jesus said to her, "Woman, where are they? Has no one condemned
11 you?" She said, "No one, sir." Jesus said, "Neither do I; be off, and never sin again."]*

12 Then Jesus again addressed them, saying, "I am the light of the world: he who follows me will not walk in
13 darkness, he will enjoy the light of life." So the Pharisees said to him, "You are testifying to yourself; your evidence
14 is not valid." Jesus replied to them, "Though I do testify to myself, my evidence is valid, because I know where I have come from and where I am going to—whereas you do not know where I have come from or where I am going to.
15
16 You judge by the outside. I judge no one; and though I do judge, my judgment is true, because I am not by my-
17 self—there is myself and the Father who sent me. Why, it is written in your own Law that the evidence of two
18 persons is valid: I testify to myself, and the Father who

---

* It is uncertain to which, if any, of the canonical gospels this fragment of primitive tradition originally belonged.

19 sent me also testifies to me." "Where is your Father?" they said. Jesus replied, "You know neither me nor my Father; if you had known me you would have known my
20 Father also." These words he spoke in the treasury, as he was teaching in the temple, but no one arrested him, because his time had not come yet.
21 Then he said to them again, "I go away, and you will search for me, but you will die in your sin; where I go,
22 you cannot come." So the Jews said, "Will he kill himself? Is that why he says, 'Where I go, you cannot come'?"
23 He said to them, "You are from the world below; I am from the world above: you belong to this world, I do not
24 belong to this world. So I told you, you would die in your sins; for unless you believe who I am, you will die in your
25 sins." They said, "Who are you?" Jesus replied, "Why
26 should I talk to you at all? I have a great deal to say about you and many a judgment to pass upon you; but he who sent me is true, and so I tell the world what I have
27 learned from him." They did not understand he was
28 speaking to them about the Father; so Jesus said, "When you have lifted up the Son of man, you will know then who I am, and that I do nothing of my own accord, but
29 speak as the Father has taught me. He who sent me is at my side; he has not left me alone; for I always do what
30 pleases him." As he said this, a number believed in him.
31 So Jesus addressed the Jews who had believed him, saying, "If you abide by what I say, you are really disciples
32 of mine: you will understand the truth, and the truth will
33 set you free." "We are Abraham's offspring," they retorted, "we have never been slaves to anybody. What do you mean
34 by saying, 'You will be free'?" Jesus replied, "Truly, truly
35 I tell you, everyone who commits sin is a slave.* Now the slave does not remain in the household for all time; the
36 son of the house does. So, if the Son sets you free, you
37 will be really free. I know you are Abraham's offspring! Yet you want to kill me, since my word makes no headway
38 among you! I speak of what I have seen with my Father,
39 and you act as you have learned from your father." They answered him, "Abraham is our father." "If you are Abraham's children," said Jesus, "then do as Abraham did;
40 but now you want to kill me—to kill a man who has told you the truth, the truth I have learned from God. Abraham
41 did not do that. You do the deeds of your father." They said to him, "We are no bastards: we have one father, even
42 God." Said Jesus, "If God were your father, you would

* Omitting τῆς ἁμαρτίας with D, some evidence from the Latin and Syriac versions, etc. It is a gloss which disturbs the sense of the passage.

love me, for I came here from God; I did not come of my
own accord, I was sent by him. Why do you not understand my speech? Because you are unable to listen to
what I am saying. You belong to your father the devil,
and you want to do what your father desires; he was a
slayer of men from the very beginning, and he has no
place in the truth because there is no truth in him: when
he tells a lie, he is expressing his own nature, for he is a
liar and the father of lies. It is because I tell the truth,
that you do not believe me. Which of you can convict me
of sin? If I tell the truth, why do you not believe me?
He who belongs to God listens to the words of God; you
do not listen to them, because you do not belong to
God." The Jews retorted, "Are we not right in saying you
are a Samaritan, you are mad?" Jesus replied, "I am not
mad: I honour my Father and you dishonour me. However, I do not aim at my own credit; there is One who
cares for my credit, and he is judge. Truly, truly I tell
you, if anyone holds to what I say, he will never see death."
The Jews said to him, "Now we are sure you are mad.
Abraham is dead, and so are all the prophets; and you
declare, 'If anyone holds to what I say, he will never taste
death'! Are you greater than our father Abraham? He
is dead, and the prophets are dead. Who do you claim
to be?" Jesus replied, "Were I to glorify myself, my glory
would be nothing; it is my Father who glorifies me; you
say 'He is our God,' but you do not understand him. I
know him. Were I to say, 'I do not know him,' I would be
a liar like yourselves; but I do know him and I hold to
his word. Your father Abraham exulted that he was to
see my Day: he did see it and he rejoiced." Then said the
Jews to him, "You are not fifty years old, and Abraham
has seen you?"* "Truly, truly I tell you," said Jesus, "I
have existed before Abraham was born." At this they
picked up stones to throw at him, but Jesus concealed himself and made his way out of the temple.

9 As he passed along he saw a man who had been blind
from his birth; and his disciples asked him, "Rabbi, for
whose sin—for his own or for his parents'—was he born
blind?" Jesus replied, "Neither for his own sin nor for his
parents'—it was to let the work of God be illustrated in
him. While daylight lasts, we must be busy with the work
of God: night comes, when no one can do any work. When

* Reading ἑώρακέν σε with ℵ and the Sinaitic Syriac, etc.—"leçon plus
naturelle peut-être que la leçon commune, mais qui a pu choquer, parce
qu'elle semble mettre Abraham au-dessus du Christ" (Loisy).

6 I am in the world, I am light for the world." With
these words he spat on the ground and made clay with the
7 saliva, which he smeared on the man's eyes, saying, "Go
and wash them in the pool of Siloam" (Siloam meaning
'sent'). So off he went and washed them, and went home
8 seeing. Whereupon the neighbours and those to whom he
had been a familiar sight as a beggar, said, "Is this not
9 the man who used to sit and beg?" Some said, "It is";
others said, "No, but it is like him." He said, "I am the
10 man." So they asked him, "How were your eyes opened?"
11 He replied, "The man they call Jesus made some clay
and smeared my eyes with it and told me, 'Go and wash
them in Siloam'; so I went and washed them, and I got
12 my sight." "Where is he?" they asked; he answered, "I
13 do not know." They brought him before the Pharisees,
14 this man who had once been blind. Now it was on the
sabbath day that Jesus had made clay and opened his
15 eyes. So the Pharisees asked him again how he had
regained his sight, and he told them, "He smeared some
clay on my eyes, and I washed them, and now I can see."
16 Then said some of the Pharisees, "This man is not from
God, for he does not keep the sabbath"; others said, "How
can a sinner perform such Signs?" They were divided on
17 this. So they asked the blind man once more, "What have
you to say about him, for opening your eyes?" The man
18 replied, "I say he is a prophet." Now the Jews would
not believe he had been born blind and had regained his
sight, till they summoned the parents of the man who had
19 regained his sight and asked them, "Is this your son,
the son you declare was born blind? How is it that he
20 can see now?" His parents answered, "This is our son,
21 and he was born blind; we know that. But how he can
see to-day, we do not know, nor do we know who opened his
eyes. Ask himself; he is of age, he can speak for him-
22 self." (His parents said this because they were afraid of
the Jews; for the Jews had already agreed that anyone
who confessed him to be Christ should be excommunicated.
23 That was why the man's parents said, "He is of age, ask
24 himself.") So the man born blind was summoned a second
time, and told, "Now give God the praise; this man, we
25 know quite well, is only a sinner." To which he replied,
"I do not know whether he is a sinner; one thing I do
26 know, that once I was blind and now I can see." "What
did he do to you?" they repeated; "How did he open your
27 eyes?" He retorted, "I have told you that already, and you
would not listen to me. Why do you want to hear it over
28 again? Do you want to be disciples of his?" Then they
stormed at him: "You are his disciple, we are disciples of

S. JOHN X

29 Moses! We know God spoke to Moses, but we do not know
30 where this fellow comes from." The man replied to them,
"Well, this is astonishing! You do not know where he
31 comes from, and yet he has opened my eyes! God, we
know, does not listen to sinners; he listens to anyone who
32 is devout and who obeys his will. It is unheard of, since
the world began, that anyone should open a blind man's
33 eyes. If this man were not from God, he could do noth-
34 ing." They retorted, "And so you would teach us—you,
35 born in utter depravity!" Then they expelled him. Jesus
heard that they had expelled him, and on meeting him he
36 said, "You believe in the Son of man?" * "Who is that,
sir?" said the man, "tell me, that I may believe in him."
37 "You have seen him," Jesus said, "he is talking to you."
38 He said, "I do believe, Lord"—and he worshipped him.
39 Then said Jesus, "It is for judgment that I have come into
this world, to make the sightless see, to make the seeing
40 blind." On hearing this the Pharisees who were beside
41 him asked, "And are we blind?" Jesus replied, "If you
were blind, you would not be guilty; but, as it is, you
19 claim to have sight—and so your sin remains." †
20   The Jews were again divided over these words. A num-
21 ber of them said, "He is mad. Why listen to him?" Others
said, "These are not a madman's words. Can a madman
open the eyes of the blind?"

22   Then came the festival of Dedication at Jerusalem; it
23 was winter, and Jesus used to walk inside the temple, in
24 the portico of Solomon. So the Jews gathered round him
and asked, "How long are you going to keep us in sus-
25 pense? If you are the Christ, tell us plainly." Jesus
replied, "I have told you, but you do not believe; the deeds
26 I do in the name of my Father testify to me, but you do
27 not believe, because you do not belong to my sheep. My
28 sheep listen to my voice, and I know them and they follow
me; and I give them eternal life; they will never perish,
29 and no one will snatch them out of my hand. My Father
who ‡ gave me them is stronger than all, and no one can
snatch anything out of the Father's hand.

10 Truly, truly I tell you, he who does not enter the
sheepfold by the gate but climbs up somewhere else,
2 he is a thief and a robber; he who enters by the gate is
3 the shepherd of the sheep. The gate-keeper opens the

* Reading ἀνθρώπου instead of θεοῦ.
† Transposing x. 19–29, for the sake of sequence, to the close of ch. ix.
‡ Reading ὅς . . . μείζων with A 1, the Syriac versions, etc.

gate for him, and the sheep listen to his voice; he calls his
4 sheep by name and leads them out. When he has brought
all his sheep outside, he goes in front of them, and the
5 sheep follow him because they know his voice; they will
not follow a stranger, they will run from him, because they
6 do not know the voice of strangers." Jesus told them this
allegory, but they did not understand what he was saying
7 to them; so he said to them again, "Truly, truly I tell you,
8 I am the shepherd * of the sheep; all who ever came before me have been thieves and robbers—but the sheep
9 would not listen to them. (I am the Gate; whoever enters
by me will be saved, he will go in and out and find pas-
10 ture.) The thief only comes to steal, to slay, and to destroy: I have come that they may have life and have it to
11 the full. I am the good shepherd; a good shepherd lays
12 down his own life for the sheep. The hired man, who is
not the shepherd and does not own the sheep, deserts them
when he sees the wolf coming; he runs away, leaving the
13 wolf to tear and scatter them, just because he is a hired
14 man, who has no interest in the sheep. I am the good
15 shepherd, I know my sheep and my sheep know me (just
as the Father knows me and I know the Father,) and I
16 lay down my life for the sheep. I have other sheep, too,
which do not belong to this fold; I must bring them also,
and they will listen to my voice; so it will be one flock,
17 one shepherd. This is why my Father loves me, because
18 I lay down my life to take it up again. No one takes it
from me, I lay it down of my own accord: I have power
to lay it down and also power to take it up again; I have
30 my Father's orders for this. I and my Father are one—."
31 The Jews again caught up stones to stone him. Jesus
32 replied, "I have let you see many a good deed of God; for
33 which of them do you mean to stone me?" The Jews retorted, "We mean to stone you, not for a good deed, but for
blasphemy, because you, a mere man, make yourself God."
34 Jesus answered, "Is it not written in your Law, 'I said,
35 you are gods'? If the Law said they were gods, to whom
the word of God came—and scripture cannot be broken—
36 do you mean to tell me, whom the Father consecrated and
sent into the world, 'You are blaspheming,' because I said,
37 'I am God's Son'? If I am not doing the deeds of my
38 Father, do not believe me; but if I am, then believe the
deeds, though you will not believe me—that you may learn
and understand that the Father is in me and I am in the

---

* ὁ ποιμὴν must be read here instead of ἡ θύρα, for the sake of the
sense, although it seems to have been preserved by the Sahidic version
alone.

S. JOHN XI

39 Father." Once more they tried to arrest him, but he
40 escaped their hands and went across the Jordan, back to
41 the spot where John had baptized at first. There he
stayed; and many came to him, saying, "John did not perform any Sign, but all he ever said about this man was
42 true." And many believed in him there.

11 Now there was a man ill, Lazarus of Bethany—the vil-
2 lage of Mary and her sister Martha. (The Mary whose
brother Lazarus was ill was the Mary who anointed the Lord
5 with perfume and wiped his feet with her hair.) Jesus loved
3 Martha and her sister and Lazarus;* so the sisters sent to
4 him, saying, "Lord, he whom you love is ill." When Jesus
heard it, he said, "This illness is not to end in death; the
end of it is the glory of God, that the Son of God may be
6 glorified thereby." So, when he heard of the illness, he
7 stayed where he was for two days; then, after that, he said
8 to the disciples, "Let us go back to Judaea." "Rabbi,"
said the disciples, "the Jews were trying to stone you only
9 the other day; are you going back there?" Jesus replied,
"Are there not twelve hours in the day?
If one walks during the day he does not stumble,
for he sees the light of this world:
10 but if one walks during the night he does stumble,
for the light is not in him."
11 This he said, then added, "Our friend Lazarus has fallen
12 asleep; I am going to waken him." "Lord," said the dis-
13 ciples, "if he has fallen asleep, he will get better." Jesus,
however, had been speaking of his death; but as they
14 imagined he meant natural sleep, he then told them plainly,
15 "Lazarus is dead; and for your sakes I am glad I was not
there, that you may believe. Come now, let us go to him."
16 Whereupon Thomas (called 'the Twin') said to his fellow-
disciples, "Let us go too, let us die along with him!"
17 Now when Jesus arrived, he found that Lazarus had
20 been buried for four days.† Then Martha, hearing of the
arrival of Jesus, went out to meet him, while Mary sat at
21 home. Said Martha to Jesus, "Had you been here, Lord,
22 my brother would not have died. But now—well, I know
23 whatever you ask God for, he will grant you." Jesus said
24 to her, "Your brother will rise again." "I know," said
Martha, "he will rise at the resurrection, on the last day."
25 Jesus said to her, "I am myself resurrection and life:

* I venture to restore ver. 5 to what appears to have been its original
position between vers. 2 and 3.
† Another case of displacement; vers. 18 and 19 seem originally to
have lain between vers. 30 and 31.

S. JOHN XI

he who believes in me will live, even if he dies,
26 and no one who lives and believes in me will ever die.
27 You believe that?" "Yes, Lord," she said, "I do believe you
    are the Christ, the Son of God, who was to come into the
28 world"—and with these words she went off to call her
    sister Mary, telling her secretly, "The Teacher is here,
29 and he is calling for you." So, on hearing this, Mary rose
30 hurriedly and went to him. Jesus had not entered the
    village yet, he was still at the spot where Martha had
18 met him. Now as Bethany is not far from Jerusalem, only
19 about two miles away, a number of Jews had gone to con-
31 dole with Martha and Mary about their brother; and when
    the Jews who were condoling with her inside the house
    noticed her rise hurriedly and go out, they followed her,
32 as they imagined she was going to wail at the tomb. But
    when Mary came to where Jesus was and saw him, she
    dropped at his feet, crying, "Had you been here, Lord,
33 my brother would not have died." Now when Jesus saw
    her wailing and saw the Jews who accompanied her wail-
34 ing, he chafed in spirit and was disquieted. "Where have
35 you laid him?" he asked. They answered, "Come and
36 see, sir." Jesus burst into tears. Whereupon the Jews
37 said, "See how he loved him!"—though some of them
    asked, "Could he not have prevented him from dying, when
38 he could open a blind man's eyes?" This made Jesus chafe
    afresh, so he went to the tomb; it was a cave with a boulder
39 to close it. Jesus said, "Remove the boulder." "Lord,"
    said Martha, the dead man's sister, "he will be stinking
40 by this time; he has been dead four days." "Did I not tell
    you," said Jesus, "if you will only believe, you shall see
41 the glory of God?" Then they removed the boulder, and
    Jesus, lifting his eyes to heaven, said, "Father, I thank
42 thee for listening to me. (I knew thou wouldst always
    listen to me, but I spoke on account of the crowd around,
43 that they might believe thou hast sent me.)" So saying,
44 he exclaimed with a loud cry, "Lazarus, come out!" Out
    came the dead man, his feet and hands swathed in band-
    ages, and his face tied up with a towel. Jesus said, "Untie
    him, and let him move."
45 Now a number of the Jews who had come to visit Mary
46 and who witnessed what he had done, believed in him. But
    some of them went off to the Pharisees and told them what
47 Jesus had done; whereupon the high priests and the
    Pharisees called a meeting of the Sanhedrin. "Whatever
    is to be done?" they said. "The fellow is performing a
48 number of Signs. If we let him alone, like this, every-
    body will believe in him, and then the Romans will come
49 and suppress our holy Place and our nation." But one of

them, Caiaphas, who was high priest that year, said, "You
50 know nothing about it—you do not understand it is in
your own interests that one man should die for the People,
51 instead of the whole nation being destroyed." (He did
not say this simply of his own accord; he was high priest
that year, and his words were a prophecy that Jesus was
52 to die for the nation, and not merely for the nation but
53 to gather into one the scattered children of God.) So from
54 that day their plan was to kill him. Accordingly Jesus no
longer appeared in public among the Jews, but withdrew
to the country adjoining the desert, to a town called
Ephraim; there he stayed with the disciples.

55 Now the passover of the Jews was near, and many people
went up from the country to Jerusalem, to purify them-
56 selves before the passover. They looked out for Jesus, and
as they stood in the temple they said to one another, "What
do you think? Do you think he will not come up to the
57 festival?" (The high priests and the Pharisees had given
orders that they were to be informed, if anyone found
out where he was, so that they might arrest him.)

12 Six days before the festival, Jesus came to Bethany,
where Lazarus stayed (whom Jesus had raised from
2 the dead). They gave a supper for him there; Martha
waited on him, and Lazarus was among those who reclined
3 at table beside him. Then Mary, taking a pound of expensive perfume, real nard, anointed the feet of Jesus and
wiped his feet with her hair, till the house was filled with
4 the scent of the perfume. One of his disciples, Judas Is-
5 cariot (who was to betray him), said, "Why was not this
perfume sold for ten pounds, and the money given to the
6 poor?" (Not that he cared for the poor; he said this
because he was a thief, and because he carried the money-
7 box and pilfered what was put in.) Then said Jesus, "Let
her alone, let her keep what she has for the day of my
8 burial. You have always the poor beside you, but you
have not always me."
9 Now the great mass of the Jews learned he was there,
and they came not only on account of Jesus but to see
10 Lazarus whom he had raised from the dead. So the high
11 priests planned to kill Lazarus as well, since it was owing
to him that a number of the Jews went away and believed
in Jesus.
12 Next day the great mass of people who had come up for
13 the festival heard that Jesus was entering Jerusalem, and
taking palm-branches they went out to meet him, shouting,
"*Hosanna!*

S. JOHN XII

*Blessed be he who comes in the Lord's name,
the king of Israel!"*
14 And Jesus came across a young ass and seated himself on it; as it is written,
15 *Fear not, daughter of Sion;
here is your king coming,
seated on an ass's colt.*
16 (His disciples did not understand this at first; but when Jesus was glorified, then they remembered this had been
17 written of him and had happened to him.) Now the people who were with him when he called Lazarus from the tomb and raised him from the dead, testified to it;
18 and that was why the crowd went out to meet him, because
19 they heard he had performed this Sign. Then said the Pharisees to one another, "You see, you can do nothing! Look, the world has gone after him."
20 Now there were some Greeks among those who had come
21 up to worship at the festival; they came to Philip of Beth-saida in Galilee and appealed to him, saying, "Sir, we want
22 to see Jesus." Philip went and told Andrew; Andrew and
23 Philip went and told Jesus. And Jesus answered, "The
24 hour has come for the Son of man to be glorified. Truly, truly I tell you, unless a grain of wheat falls into the earth and dies, it remains a single grain; but if it dies, it bears
25 rich fruit. He who loves his life loses it, and he who cares not for his life in this world will preserve it for eternal life.
26   If anyone serves me, let him follow me,
      and where I am, there shall my servant be also:
      if anyone serves me,
      my Father will honour him.
27 *My soul is now disquieted.* What am I to say? 'Father,
save me from this hour'? Nay, it is something else that
28 has brought me to this hour: I will say, 'Father, glorify thy name.'" Then came a voice from heaven, "I have
29 glorified it, and I will glorify it again." When they heard the sound, the people standing by said it had thundered;
30 others said, "An angel spoke to him." Jesus answered,
31 "This voice did not come for my sake but for yours. Now is this world to be judged; now the Prince of this world
32 will be expelled. But I, when I am lifted up from the
33 earth, will draw all men to myself." (By this he indicated
34 the kind of death he was to die.) So the people answered, "We have learned from the Law that the Christ is to remain for ever; what do you mean by saying that the Son of man must be lifted up? Who is this Son of man?"
35 Then Jesus said to them, "The Light will shine among you for a little longer yet; walk while you have the Light,

S. JOHN XIII

that the darkness may not overtake you. He who walks
36 in the dark does not know where he is going. While you
have the Light, believe in the Light, that you may be sons
44 of the Light." * And Jesus cried aloud, "He who believes
45 in me believes not in me but in him who sent me, and he
46 who beholds me beholds him who sent me. I have come
as light into the world, that no one who believes in me
47 may remain in the dark. If anyone hears my words and
does not keep them, it is not I who judge him; for I have
48 not come to judge the world but to save the world. He
who rejects me and will not receive my words has indeed
a judge: the word I have spoken will judge him on the
49 last day, for I have not spoken of my own accord—the
Father who sent me, he it was who ordered me what to say
50 and what to speak. And I know his orders mean eternal
life. Therefore when I speak, I speak as the Father has
36 told me." With these words Jesus went away and hid
from them.
37 Now for all the Signs he had performed before them,
38 they did not believe in him—that the word spoken by the
prophet Isaiah might be fulfilled:
Lord, who has believed what they heard from us?
And to whom has the arm of the Lord been revealed?
39 This was why they could not believe; for Isaiah again
said,
40 *He has blinded their eyes*
and made their hearts insensible,
to prevent them seeing with their eyes and understand-
ing with their hearts and turning for me to cure
them.
41 (Isaiah said this because he saw his glory and spoke of
42 him.) Still, a number even of the authorities believed in
him, though they would not confess it on account of the
43 Pharisees, in case of being excommunicated; they preferred the approval of men to the approval of God.

13 Now before the passover festival Jesus knew the time
had come for him to pass from this world to the
Father. He had loved his own in this world and he loved
2 them to the end; so at supper, knowing that though the
devil had suggested to Judas Iscariot, Simon's son, to
3 betray him, the Father had put everything into his hands
—knowing that he had come from God and was going to
4 God, he rose from table, laid aside his robe, and tied a
5 towel round him, then poured water into a basin, and

* Restoring vers. 44–50 to their original position in the middle of
ver. 36.

S. JOHN XIII

began to wash the feet of the disciples, wiping them with
6 the towel he had tied round him. He came to Simon
7 Peter. "Lord," said he, "you to wash my feet!" Jesus answered him, "You do not understand just now what I am
8 doing, but you will understand it later on." Said Peter, "You will never wash my feet, never!" "Unless I wash
9 you," Jesus replied, "you will not share my lot." "Lord," said Simon Peter, "then wash not only my feet but my
10 hands and head." Jesus said, "He who has bathed only needs to have his feet washed; he is clean all over. And
11 you are clean—but not all of you" (he knew the traitor;
12 that was why he said, "You are not all clean"). Then, after washing their feet and putting on his robe, he lay down again. "Do you know," he said to them, "what I
13 have been doing to you? You call me Teacher and Lord,
14 and you are right: that is what I am. Well, if I have washed your feet, I who am your Lord and Teacher, you
15 are bound to wash one another's feet; for I have been setting you an example, that you should do what I have
16 done to you. Truly, truly I tell you, a servant is not greater than his master, nor is a messenger greater than
17 he who sent him. If you know all this, blessed are you if
18 you really do it. When I say 'you,' I do not mean you all; I know the men of my choice, and I made my choice that this scripture might be fulfilled, *he who eats my bread has*
19 *lifted up his heel against me.* I am telling you this now, before it occurs, so that when it has occurred you may
20 believe who I am. (Truly, truly I tell you,

he who receives anyone I send receives me,

and he who receives me receives him who sent me.)"
21 On saying this Jesus was disquieted in spirit: he testified and said, "Truly, truly I tell you, one of you will betray
22 me." The disciples looked at each other, at a loss to know
23 which of them he meant. As one of his disciples was reclining on his breast—he was the favourite of Jesus—
24 Peter nodded to him, saying, "Tell us who he means."
25 The disciple just leant back on the breast of Jesus and said,
26 "Lord, who is it?" Jesus answered, "The man I am going to give this piece of bread to, when I dip it in the dish." Then he took the piece of bread, dipped it, and gave it to
27 Judas, the son of Simon Iscariot; and when he took the bread, at that moment Satan entered him. Then Jesus
28 told him, "Be quick with what you have to do." (None of
29 those at table understood why he said this to him; some of them thought that as Judas kept the money-box, Jesus told him to buy what they needed for the festival or to
30 give something to the poor.) So Judas went out immediately after taking the bread. And it was night.

S. JOHN XV

31 When he had gone out, Jesus said,*

15 "I AM the real Vine, and my Father is the vine-
2 dresser; he cuts away any branch on me which is not
bearing fruit, and cleans every branch which does bear
3 fruit, to make it bear richer fruit. You are already clean
4 by the word I have spoken to you. Remain in me, as I
remain in you: just as a branch cannot bear fruit
by itself, without remaining on the vine, neither
5 can you, unless you remain in me. I am the vine,
you are the branches. He who remains in me, as I in him,
bears rich fruit (because apart from me you can do noth-
6 ing). If anyone does not remain in me he is thrown aside
like a branch and he withers up; then the branches are
7 gathered and thrown into the fire to be burned. If you
remain in me and my words remain in you, then ask what-
8 ever you like and you shall have it. As you bear rich fruit
and prove yourselves my disciples, my Father is glorified.
9 As the Father has loved me, so I have loved you; remain
10 within my love. If you keep my commands you will
remain within my love, just as I have kept my Father's
commands and remain within his love.
11 I have told you this, that my joy may be within you and
12 your joy complete. This is my command: you are to love
13 one another as I have loved you. To lay life down for his
14 friends, man has no greater love than that. You are
15 my friends—if you do what I command you; I call you
servants no longer, because a servant does not know what
his master is doing: I call you friends, because I have im-
16 parted to you all that I have learned from my Father. You
have not chosen me; it is I who have chosen you, appoint-
ing you to go and bear fruit—fruit that lasts, so that the
Father may grant you whatever you ask in my name.
17 This is what I command you, to love one another.
18 If the world hates you, remember it hated me first.
19 If you belonged to the world, the world would love what it
owned; it is because you do not belong to the world,
because I have chosen you from the world, that the world
20 hates you. Remember what I told you, 'A servant is not
greater than his master.'
If they persecuted me, they will persecute you;
if they hold to my word, they will hold to yours.
21 They will do all this to you on account of my name,
22 because they know not him who sent me. They would
not be guilty, if I had not come and spoken to them; but,

---

* Chapters xv. and xvi. are restored to their original position in
the middle of ver. 31.

S. JOHN XVI

23 as it is, they have no excuse for their sin—he who hates
24 me hates my Father also. They would not be guilty, if I had not done deeds among them such as no one has ever done; but, as it is, they have seen—and they have hated—
25 both me and my Father. It is that the word written in their Law may be fulfilled: *they hated me for no cause.*

26 When the Helper comes, whom I will send to you from the Father, even the Spirit of truth which issues from the
27 Father, he will bear witness to me; and you too are witnesses, for you have been with me from the very beginning.

16 I have told you all this, to keep you from being
2 repelled. They will excommunicate you; indeed the time is coming when anyone who kills you will imagine he
3 is performing a service to God. This they will do to you, because they have not known the Father nor me.
4 I have told you all this, so that when the time for it arrives, you may remember what I said to you. I did not tell you about this at the beginning, because I was with
5 you then; but now I am going to him who sent me. And
6 yet not one of you asks, 'Where are you going?' No, your
7 heart is full of sorrow at what I have told you. Yet—I am telling you the truth—my going is for your good. If I do not depart, the Helper will not come to you; whereas if I
8 go, I will send him to you. And when he comes, he will convict the world, convincing men of sin, of righteousness,
9 and of judgment: of sin, because they do not believe in
10 me; of righteousness, because I go to the Father and you
11 see me no more; of judgment, because the Prince of this
12 world has been judged. I have still much to say to you,
13 but you cannot bear it just now. However, when the Spirit of truth comes, he will lead you into all the truth; for he will not speak of his own accord, he will say whatever he
14 is told, and he will disclose to you what is to come. He will glorify me, for he will draw upon what is mine and
15 disclose it to you. All that the Father has is mine; that is why I say, 'he will draw upon what is mine and disclose it to you.'
16 In a little while, you will behold me no longer; then,
17 after a little, you shall see me." So some of his disciples said to one another, "What does he mean by telling us, 'In a little while, you shall behold me no longer; then, after a little, you shall see me'? and, 'I go to the Father'?"
18 They said, "What is the meaning of 'In a little'? We do
19 not understand what he is saying." Jesus knew they wanted to ask him; so he said to them, "Is this what you are discussing together, why I said, 'In a little while, you will not see me: then, after a little, you shall see me'?

S. JOHN XVI

20 Truly, truly, I tell you, you will be wailing and lamenting while the world is rejoicing; you will be sorrowful, but
21 then your sorrow will be changed into joy. When a woman is in labour she is sorry, for her time has come; but when the child is born she remembers her anguish no longer, for joy that a human being has been born into the world.
22 So with you. Just now you are in sorrow, but I shall see you again and your heart will rejoice—with a joy that no one can take from you.
23 And on that day you will not ask me any questions. Truly, truly I tell you, whatever you ask the Father, he
24 will give you in my name; hitherto you have asked nothing in my name; ask and you will receive, that your joy
25 may be full. I have told you this in figures, but the time is coming when I shall speak to you in figures no longer;
26 I shall let you know plainly about the Father. On that day you will ask in my name, and I do not say to you I
27 will ask the Father on your behalf; for the Father loves you himself, because you have loved me and believed that
28 I came forth from God. From the Father I came and I entered the world; again, I leave the world and I go to
29 the Father." His disciples said, "Now, you are talking
30 plainly at last, not speaking in figures. Now we are sure you know everything, and need no one to put questions to you. This makes us believe you have come forth from
31 God." Jesus replied, "You believe it, at last? Behold, the
32 time is coming, it has come already, when you will be scattered to your homes, every one of you, leaving me alone. But I am not alone, for the Father is with me.
33 I have said all this to you that in me you may have peace; in the world you have trouble, but courage! I have conquered the world.*

31 "Now at last the Son of man is glorified, and in him
32 God is glorified: [if God is glorified in him,] God will
33 glorify him in Himself and glorify him at once. My dear children, I am only to be with you a little longer; then you will look for me, and, as I told the Jews I tell you now,
34 where I go you cannot come. I give you a new command, to love one another—as I have loved you, you are to love one
35 another. By this everyone will recognize that you are my
36 disciples, if you have love one for another." "Lord," said Simon Peter, "where are you going?" Jesus replied, "I am going where you cannot follow me at present; later on you
37 will follow me." "Lord," said Peter, "why cannot I follow
38 you just now? I will lay down my life for you." Jesus replied, "Lay down your life for me? Truly, truly I tell

* The sequence of xiii. 31 is now resumed (see above, note on p. 160).

you, before the cock crows, you will have disowned me thrice over.

14 Let not your hearts be disquieted; you believe—
2 believe in God and also in me. In my Father's house there are many abodes; were it not so, would I have told
3 you I was going to prepare a place for you? And when I go and prepare a place for you, I will come back and take
4 you to be with me, so that you may be where I am. And
5 you know the way to where I am going." "Lord," said Thomas, "we do not know where you are going, and how
6 are we to know the way?" Jesus said to him, "I am the real and living way: no one comes to the Father except
7 by means of me. If you knew me, you would know my Father too. You know him now and you have seen him."
8 "Lord," said Philip, "let us see the Father; that is all we
9 want." Jesus said to him, "Philip, have I been with you all this time, and yet you do not understand me? He who has seen me has seen the Father. What do you mean by
10 saying, 'Let us see the Father'? Do you not believe I am in the Father and the Father is in me? The words I speak to you all I do not speak of my own accord; it is the Father who remains ever in me, who is performing his own deeds.
11 Believe me, I am in the Father and the Father is in me:—
12 or else, believe because of the deeds themselves. Truly, truly I tell you, he who believes in me will do the very deeds I do, and still greater deeds than these. For I am going to
13 the Father, and I will do whatever you ask in my name,
14 that the Father may be glorified in the Son; I will do what-
15 ever you ask me in my name. If you love me you will
16 keep my commands, and I will ask the Father to give you
17 another Helper to be with you for ever, even the Spirit of truth: the world cannot receive him, because it neither sees nor knows him, but you know him, because he remains
18 with you and will be within you. I will not leave you
19 forlorn; I am coming to you. A little while longer and the world will see me no more; but you will see me
20 because I am living and you will be living too. You will understand, on that day, that I am in my Father and you
21 are in me and I am in you. He who possesses my commands and obeys them is he who loves me, and he who loves me will be loved by my Father, and I will love him
22 and appear to him." "Lord," said Judas (not Judas Iscariot), "why is it that you are to appear to us, and not to
23 the world?" Jesus answered, "If anyone loves me he will obey my word, and my Father will love him, and we will
24 come to him and take up our abode with him. He who does not love me does not obey my word; and what you

S. JOHN XVII

hear me say is not my word but the word of the Father who sent me.
25 I have told you all this while I am still with you,
26 but the Helper, the holy Spirit whom the Father will send in my name, will teach you everything and recall to you
27 everything I have said. Peace I leave to you, my peace I give to you; I give it not as the world gives its 'Peace!'
28 Let not your hearts be disquieted or timid. You heard me tell you I was going away and coming back to you; if you loved me, you would rejoice that I am going to the Father —for the Father is greater than I am.
29 I tell you this now, before it occurs, so that, when it does
30 occur, you may believe. I will no longer talk much with you, for the Prince of this world is coming. He has no
31 hold on me; his coming will only serve to let the world see that I love the Father and that I am acting as the Father ordered. Rise, let us be going."

17 So Jesus spoke; then, lifting his eyes to heaven, he said: "Father, the time has now come; glorify thy Son
2 that thy Son may glorify thee, since thou hast granted him power over all flesh to give eternal life to all whom thou
3 hast given to him. And this is eternal life, that they know thee, the only real God, and him whom thou hast sent, even
4 Jesus Christ. I have glorified thee on earth by accom-
5 plishing the work thou gavest me to do; now, Father, glorify me in thy presence with the glory which I enjoyed
6 in thy presence before the world began. I have made thy Name known to the men whom thou hast given to me
7 from the world (thine they were, and thou gavest them to me), and they have held to thy word. They know now
8 that whatever thou hast given me comes from thee, for I have given them the words thou gavest me and they have received them; they are now sure that I came from thee and believe that thou didst send me.
9 I pray for them—not for the world but for those whom
10 thou hast given me do I pray; for they are thine (all mine is thine and thine is mine), and I am glorified in them.
11 I am to be in the world no longer, but they are to be in the world; I come to thee. Holy Father, keep them by the power of thy Name which thou hast given me, that they
12 may be one as we are one. When I was with them, I kept them by the power of thy Name which thou hast given me; I guarded them, and not one of them perished—only the son of perdition, that the
13 scripture might be fulfilled. But now I come to thee (I speak thus in the world that they may have my joy com-
14 plete within them). I have given them thy word, and the

world has hated them because they do not belong to the
15 world any more than I belong to the world. I pray not
that thou wilt take them out of the world, but that thou
16 wilt keep them from the evil one. They do not belong to
17 the world any more than I belong to the world. Con-
18 secrate them by thy truth: thy word is truth. As thou
hast sent me into the world, so have I sent them into the
19 world, and for their sake I consecrate myself that they
may be consecrated by the truth.
20 Nor do I pray for them alone, but for all who believe in
21 me by their spoken word; may they all be one! As thou,
Father, art in me and I in thee, so may they be in us—
22 that the world may believe thou hast sent me. Yea, I
have given them the glory thou gavest me, that they may
23 be one as we are one—I in them and thou in me—that
they may be made perfectly one, so that the world may
recognize that thou hast sent me and hast loved them as
24 thou hast loved me. Father, it is my will that these, thy
gift to me, may be beside me where I am, to behold my
glory which thou hast given me, because thou lovedst me
25 before the foundation of the world. O just Father, though
the world has not known thee, I have known* thee, and
26 they have known that thou hast sent me; so have I
declared, so will I declare, thy Name to them, that the love
with which thou hast loved me may be in them, and I in
them."

18 Having said this, Jesus went out with his disciples
across the Kidron ravine to an orchard, which he
2 entered in the company of his disciples. Judas the traitor
also knew the spot, for Jesus and his disciples often met
3 there. So after procuring troops and some attendants
belonging to the high priests and the Pharisees, Judas went
4 there with lanterns and torches and weapons. Then Jesus,
who knew everything that was to happen to him, came
forward and asked them, "Who are you looking for?"
5 "Jesus the Nazarene," they replied. Jesus said, "I am he."
6 (And Judas the traitor was standing beside them.) When
he said, "I am he," they fell back and dropped to the
7 ground; so he asked them once more, "Who are you looking
8 for?" And when they replied, "Jesus the Nazarene," he
answered, "I told you that I am he; if it is me you are
9 looking for, let these men get away" (this was to fulfil
his own word: 'I did not lose a single one of those whom

---

* The English perfect is the least inadequate rendering of the Greek
aorist here. Luther, however, prefers the present. " Ich kenne Dich,
und diese erkennen...."

10 thou didst give me'). Then Simon Peter, who had a sword, drew it and struck the high priest's servant, cutting off
11 his right ear (the servant's name was Malchus); whereupon Jesus said to Peter, "Sheathe your sword. Am I not to drink the cup which the Father has handed me?"
12 So the troops and their commander and the Jewish
13 attendants seized Jesus, bound him, and brought him first of all to Annas (for Annas was the father-in-law of Caia-
14 phas, who was high priest that year—the Caiaphas who had advised the Jews that it was for their interests that
19 one man should die for the people).* Then the high priest questioned Jesus about his disciples and about his
20 teaching. Jesus answered, "I have spoken openly to the world; I have always taught in the synagogues and in the temple, where all Jews gather; I have said nothing in
21 secret. Why ask me? Ask my hearers what I have said
22 to them; they know what I said." As he said this, one of the attendants who stood by gave him a blow, saying, "Is
23 that how you answer the high priest?" "If I have said anything wrong," replied Jesus, "prove it; if I said what
24 was true, why strike me?" Then Annas had him bound
15 and sent him to Caiaphas the high priest. Simon Peter followed Jesus along with another disciple; and as this disciple was an acquaintance of the high priest, he passed
16 into the courtyard of the high priest with Jesus, while Peter stood outside at the door. Then this other disciple, who was an acquaintance of the high priest, came out and spoke to the woman at the door, and brought Peter inside.
17 The maidservant at the door then said to Peter, "Are you
18 not one of this fellow's disciples?" He said, "No." Now the servants and the attendants were standing and warming themselves at a charcoal fire which they had lit (for it was cold), and Peter also stood beside them and warmed
25 himself. They asked him, "Are you not one of his dis-
26 ciples?" He denied it, saying, "No." Said one of the high priest's servants, a kinsman of the man whose ear had been cut off by Peter, "Did I not see you with him in the
27 orchard?" Again Peter denied it. And at that very moment the cock crowed.
28 Then from the house of Caiaphas they took Jesus to the praetorium. (It was early morning.) They would not enter the praetorium themselves, in case of being cere-
29 monially defiled, for they wanted to eat the passover; so Pilate came outside to them and asked, "What charge do
30 you bring against this man?" They retorted, "If he had not been a criminal, we would not have handed him over

* Transposing vers. 19–24 to a position between vers. 14 and 15.

31 to you." Then said Pilate, "Take him yourselves, and sentence him according to your own Law." The Jews said,
32 "We have no right to put anyone to death" (that the word of Jesus might be fulfilled, by which he had indicated the
33 kind of death he was to die). So Pilate went back inside the praetorium and called Jesus, saying, "Then you are
34 king of the Jews?" Jesus replied, "Are you saying this of your own accord, or did other people tell you about me?"
35 "Am I a Jew?" said Pilate. "Your own nation and the high priests have handed you over to me. What have
36 you done?" Jesus replied, "My realm does not belong to this world; if my realm did belong to this world, my men would have fought to prevent me being handed over to
37 the Jews. No, my realm lies elsewhere." "So you are a king?" said Pilate, "you!" "Certainly," said Jesus, "I am a king. This is why I was born, this is why I came into the world, to bear testimony to the truth. Everyone who
38 belongs to the truth listens to my voice." "Truth!" said Pilate, "what is truth!" With these words he went outside to the Jews again and told them, "I cannot find anything
39 wrong about him. But it is your custom that I should release a prisoner for you at the passover. Is it your will
40 that I release you the king of the Jews?" Again they yelled, "No, not him! Bar-Abbas!" Now Bar-Abbas was a robber.

2 **19** Then Pilate took Jesus and had him scourged. And the soldiers twisted some thorns into a crown and put
3 it on his head, and arrayed him in a purple robe, marching up to him and shouting, "Hail, king of the Jews!"—and
4 striking him. Again Pilate went out and said to them, "Look, I am bringing him out to you. Understand, I can-
5 not find anything wrong about him." So out came Jesus, wearing the crown of thorns and the purple robe; and
6 Pilate said, "Here the man* is!" Now when the high priests and their attendants saw him, they yelled, "Crucify him, crucify him!" Pilate said, "Take him and crucify
7 him yourselves! I find nothing wrong about him." The Jews retorted, "But we have a Law, and by [our] Law he is bound to die, because he has made himself out to be
8 God's Son." Now when Pilate heard that, he was still
9 more afraid; he went inside the praetorium again and asked Jesus, "Where do you come from?" Jesus made no
10 reply. Then Pilate said, "You will not speak to me? Do you not know it is in my power to release you or to crucify

* The unconscious force of Pilate's words, it has been suggested, might be brought out by rendering either " Here is *the* man! " or, " Here is the Man! "

11 you?" Jesus answered, "You would have no power over me, unless it had been granted you from above. So you
12 are less guilty than he who betrayed me to you." This made Pilate anxious to release him, but the Jews yelled, "If you release him, you are no friend of Caesar's! Any-
13 one who makes himself a king is against Caesar!" On hearing this, Pilate brought Jesus out and seated him on the tribunal at a spot called the 'mosaic pavement'—the
14 Hebrew name is Gabbatha (it was the day of Preparation for the passover, about noon). "There is your king!" he
15 said to the Jews. Then they yelled, "Off with him! Off with him! Crucify him!" "Crucify your king?" said Pilate. The high priests retorted, "We have no king but
16 Caesar!" Then Pilate handed him over to them to be crucified.
17 So they took Jesus, and he went away, carrying the cross by himself, to the spot called the 'place' of the
18 skull'—the Hebrew name is Golgotha; there they crucified him, along with two others, one on each side and Jesus
19 in the middle. Pilate had written an inscription to be put on the cross; what he wrote was, JESUS THE NAZARENE,
20 THE KING OF THE JEWS. Now many of the Jews read this inscription, for the place where Jesus had been crucified was close to the city; besides, the inscription was in
21 Hebrew, Latin, and Greek. So the Jewish high priests said to Pilate, "Do not write, THE KING OF THE JEWS; write,
22 HE SAID I AM THE KING OF THE JEWS." Pilate replied, "What I have written, I have written."
23 Now when the soldiers crucified Jesus they took his clothes and divided them into four parts, one for each soldier. But as the tunic was seamless, woven right down
24 in a single piece, they said to themselves, "Don't let us tear it. Let us draw lots to see who gets it" (that the scripture might be fulfilled,
they distributed my clothes among them,
and drew lots for my raiment).
This was what the soldiers did.
25 Now beside the cross of Jesus stood his mother and his mother's sister, Mary the wife of Clopas, and Mary of
26 Magdala. So when Jesus saw his mother and his favourite disciple standing near, he said to his mother, "Woman,
27 there is your son!" Then he said to the disciple, "Son, there is your mother!" And from that hour the disciple
28 took her to his home. After that, as Jesus knew that everything was now finished and fulfilled, he said (to fulfil the
29 scripture), "*I am thirsty.*" A jug full of vinegar was lying there; so they put a sponge full of vinegar on a spear and
30 held it to his lips. And when Jesus took the vinegar, he

S. JOHN XX

said, "It is finished," bowed his head, and gave up his spirit.
31 Now, as it was the day of Preparation, in order to prevent the bodies remaining on the cross during the sabbath (for that sabbath-day was a great day), the Jews asked Pilate to have the legs broken and the bodies removed.
32 So the soldiers went and broke the legs of the first man and
33 of the other man who had been crucified along with him; but when they came to Jesus and saw he was dead already,
34 they did not break his legs; only, one of the soldiers pricked his side with a lance, and out came blood and
35 water in a moment. He who saw it has borne witness (his witness is true; God knows he is telling the truth),
36 that you may believe. For this took place that the scripture might be fulfilled,
 Not a bone of him will be broken.
37 And another scripture also says,
 They shall look on him whom they have impaled.
38 After this, Joseph of Arimathaea, a disciple of Jesus but a secret disciple—for fear of the Jews—asked Pilate for permission to remove the body of Jesus. And Pilate
39 allowed him. So he went and removed the body, accompanied by Nicodemus (he who had first come to Jesus by night) who brought a mixture of myrrh and aloes, about
40 a hundred pounds of it; they took and wrapped up the body of Jesus in the spices and in bandages, according to
41 the Jewish custom of burial. Now at the spot where he had been crucified there was an orchard, and in the orchard
42 a new tomb where no one had yet been laid; so they put Jesus there, since it was the Jewish day of Preparation, seeing that the tomb was close by.

20 ON the first day of the week Mary of Magdala went early to the tomb, when it was still dark; but as she
2 saw the boulder had been removed from the tomb, she ran off to Simon Peter and to the other disciple, the favourite of Jesus, telling them, "They have taken the master out of the tomb, and we do not know where they have put
3 him!" So Peter and the other disciple set out for the
4 tomb; they both started to run, but the other disciple ran
5 ahead, faster than Peter, and got to the tomb first. He glanced in and saw the bandages lying on the ground,
6 but he did not go inside. Then Simon Peter came after him, and went inside the tomb; he noticed not only that
7 the bandages were lying on the ground but that the napkin which had been round his head was folded up by itself,
8 instead of lying beside the other bandages. Upon this the other disciple, who had reached the tomb first, went inside

9 too, and when he saw for himself he was convinced. (For as yet they did not understand the Scripture that he must
10 rise from the dead.) Then the disciples returned home;
11 but Mary stood sobbing outside the tomb. As she sobbed,
12 she glanced inside the tomb and noticed two angels in white, sitting where the body of Jesus had lain, one at the
13 head and one at the feet. "Woman," they said to her, "why are you sobbing?". She said, "Because they have taken away my master, and I do not know where they
14 have put him!" With these words she turned round and noticed Jesus standing—though she did not know it was
15 Jesus. "Woman," said Jesus, "why are you sobbing? Who are you looking for?" Supposing he was the gardener, she said, "Oh, sir, if you carried him away, tell me where you
16 put him, and I will remove him." "Mary!" said Jesus. She started round and said, "Rabboni!" (a Hebrew word
17 meaning 'teacher'). Jesus said, "Cease clinging to me. I have not ascended yet to the Father, but go to my brothers and tell them, 'I am ascending to my Father and yours,
18 to my God and yours.'" Away went Mary of Magdala to the disciples with the news, "I have seen the Lord!"—telling them what he had said to her.
19 On the evening of that same day—the first day of the week—though the disciples had gathered within closed doors for fear of the Jews, Jesus entered and stood among
20 them, saying, "Peace be with you!" So saying he showed them his hands and his side; and when the disciples saw
21 the Lord, they rejoiced. Jesus then repeated, "Peace be with you! As the Father sent me forth, I am sending
22 you forth." And with these words he breathed on them,
23 and added, "Receive the holy Spirit! If you remit the sins of any, they are remitted: if you retain them, they are retained."
24 Now Thomas, one of the twelve, who was called 'the
25 Twin,' was not with them when Jesus came; and when the rest of the disciples told him, "We have seen the Lord," he said, "Unless I see his hands with the mark of the nails, and put my finger where the nails were, and put my
26 hand into his side, I refuse to believe it." Eight days afterwards his disciples were together again, and Thomas with them. Though the doors were closed, Jesus entered
27 and stood among them, saying, "Peace be with you!" Then he said to Thomas, "Look at my hands, put your finger here; and put your hand here into my side; cease your
28 unbelief and believe." Thomas answered him, "My Lord
29 and my God!" Jesus said to him, "You believe because you have seen me? Blessed be those who believe though they have never seen me."

S. JOHN XXI

30 Many another Sign did Jesus perform in presence of his
31 disciples, which is not recorded in this book; but these
Signs are recorded so that you may believe Jesus is the
Christ, the Son of God, and believing may have life through
his Name.

21 AFTER that, Jesus disclosed himself once more to the
disciples at the sea of Tiberias. It was in this way.
2 Simon Peter, Thomas (who was called 'the Twin'),
Nathanael from Cana in Galilee, the two sons of Zebedaeus,
3 and two other disciples of his, were all together. Simon
Peter said to them, "I am going to fish." They said, "We
are coming with you too." Off they went and embarked
4 in the boat, but that night they caught nothing. Now at
break of day Jesus was standing on the beach (though the
5 disciples did not know it was Jesus). "Lads," said Jesus,
6 "have you got anything?" "No," they answered. So he
told them, "Throw your net on the right of the boat, and
you will have a take." At this they threw the net, and
7 now they could not haul it in for the mass of fish. So the
disciple who was Jesus' favourite said to Peter, "It is the
Lord!" Hearing it was the Lord, Simon Peter threw on
his blouse (he was stripped for work) and jumped into the
8 water, while the rest of the disciples came ashore in the
punt (they were not far from land, only about a hundred
9 yards), dragging their netful of fish. When they got to
land, they saw a charcoal fire burning, with fish cooking
10 on it, and some bread. Jesus said to them, "Bring some
11 of the fish you have just caught." So Peter went aboard
and hauled the net ashore, full of large fish, a hundred
and fifty three of them; but for all their number the net
12 was not torn. Jesus said, "Come and breakfast." (Not
one of the disciples dared to ask him who he was; they
13 knew it was the Lord.) Jesus went and took the bread
14 and gave it to them, and the fish too. This was the third
time, now, that Jesus appeared to the disciples after rising
from the dead.
15 Then after breakfast Jesus said to Simon Peter, "Simon,
son of John, do you love me more than the others do?"
"Why, Lord," he said, "you know I love you." "Then feed
16 my lambs," said Jesus. Again he asked him, for the second
time, "Simon, son of John, do you love me?" "Why, Lord,"
he said, "you know I love you." "Then be a shepherd to
17 my sheep," said Jesus. For the third time he asked him,
"Simon, son of John, do you love me?" Now Peter was
vexed at being asked a third time, "Do you love me?" So
he replied; "Lord, you know everything, you can see I
18 love you." Jesus said, "Then feed my sheep. Truly, truly

I tell you, you put on your own girdle and went wherever you wanted, when you were young; but when you grow old, you will stretch out your hands for someone to gird you, and you will be taken where you have no wish to go"
19 (he said this to indicate the kind of death by which Peter
20 would glorify God); then he added, "Follow me." Peter turned round and saw that the favourite disciple of Jesus was following, the disciple who had leant on his breast at supper and put the question, "Lord, who is to betray you?"
21 So, on catching sight of him, Peter said to Jesus, "And
22 what about him, Lord?" Jesus replied, "If I choose that he should survive till I come back, what does that matter to
23 you? Follow me yourself." This started the report among the brotherhood that the said disciple was not to die. Jesus, however, did not say he was not to die; what he said was, "If I choose that he should survive till I come back, what does that matter to you?"
24 This was the disciple who bears testimony to these facts and who wrote them down; his testimony, we know, is true.
25 Now there is much else that Jesus did—so much, that if it were written down in detail, I do not suppose the world itself could hold the written records.

THE
ACTS OF THE APOSTLES

1 In my former volume, Theophilus, I treated all that
2 Jesus began by doing and teaching down to the day when,
after issuing his orders by the holy Spirit to the disciples
3 whom he had chosen, he was taken up to heaven. After
his sufferings he had shown them that he was alive by
a number of proofs, revealing himself to them for forty
4 days and discussing the affairs of God's Realm. Also,
as he ate with them, he charged them not to leave Jerusalem but to wait for what the Father promised—"for what
5 you have heard me speak of," said he; "for John baptized
with water, but not many days after this you shall be
6 baptized with the holy Spirit." Now when they met, they
asked him, "Lord, is this the time you are going to restore
7 the Realm to Israel?" But he told them, "It is not for
you to know the course and periods of time that the Father
8 has fixed by his own authority. You will receive power
when the holy Spirit comes upon you, and you will be my
witnesses at Jerusalem, throughout all Judaea and Samaria,
9 and to the end of the earth." On saying this he was lifted
up while they looked on, and a cloud took him out of sight.
10 As he went up, their eyes were fixed on heaven; but just
11 then two men stood beside them dressed in white, who
said, "Men of Galilee, why do you stand looking up to
heaven? This Jesus who has been taken from you into
heaven will come back, just as you have seen him depart
12 to heaven." Then they made their way back to Jerusalem
from the hill called 'The Olive-Orchard'; it is close to
13 Jerusalem, only a sabbath day's journey from it. On entering the city they went to the upper room where they were
in the habit of meeting; there were Peter, John, James,
Andrew, Philip and Thomas, Bartholomew and Matthew,
James (the son of Alphaeus) and Simon who had been a
14 Zealot, with Judas the son of James. All these men resorted with one mind to prayer, together with the women,
with Mary the mother of Jesus and with his brothers.
15 Now during these days Peter stood up among the
brothers (there was a crowd of about a hundred and
16 twenty persons all together). "My brothers," said he, "it
had to be fulfilled, that scripture which the holy Spirit
uttered beforehand by the lips of David with regard to
Judas who acted as guide to those who arrested Jesus.
17 Judas did enter our number, he did get his allotted share

18 of this our ministry. With the money paid him for his
crime he purchased an estate; but swelling up he burst in
19 two, and all his bowels poured out—a fact which became
known to all the residents in Jerusalem, so that the estate
got the name, in their language, of Akeldamach or The
20 Ground of Blood. Now it is written in the book of psalms,
Desolate be his residence,
may no one dwell in it:
also,
let another man take over his charge.
21 Well then, of the men who have been associated with us
all the time the Lord Jesus went in and out among us,
22 from the baptism of John down to the day when he was
taken up from us—of these men one must join us as a
23 witness to his resurrection." So they brought forward
two men, Joseph called Bar-Sabbas (surnamed Justus) and
24 Matthias; and they prayed, "O Lord, who readest the hearts
of all, do thou single out from these two men him whom
25 thou hast chosen to fill the place in this apostolic ministry
26 which Judas left in order to go to his own place." Then
they cast lots for them, and the lot fell upon Matthias,
who was assigned his position with the eleven apostles.

2 During the course of the day of Pentecost they were all
together, when suddenly there came a sound from heaven
like a violent blast of wind, which filled the whole house
3 where they were seated. They saw tongues like flames dis-
4 tributing themselves, one resting on the head of each, and
they were all filled with the holy Spirit—they began to
speak in foreign tongues, as the Spirit enabled them to
5 express themselves. Now there were devout Jews from
6 every nation under heaven staying in Jerusalem. So when
this sound was heard, the multitude gathered in bewilderment, for each heard them speaking in his own language.
7 All were amazed and astonished. "Are these not all
8 Galileans," they said, "who are speaking? Then how is it
9 that each of us hears them in his own native tongue? Par-
thians, Medes, Elamites, residents in Mesopotamia, in
10 Judaea and Cappadocia, in Pontus and Asia, in Phrygia
and Pamphylia, in Egypt and the districts of Libya round
11 Cyrene, visitors from Rome, Jews and proselytes, Cretans
and Arabians, we hear these men talking of the triumphs
12 of God in our own languages!" They were all amazed and
quite at a loss. "What can it mean?" they said to one an-
13 other. Some others sneered, "They are brim-full of new
14 wine!" But Peter stood up along with the eleven, and
raising his voice he addressed them thus: "Men of Judaea
and residents in Jerusalem, let every one of you understand

15 this—attend to what I say: these men are not drunk, as
16 you imagine. Why, it is only nine in the morning! No, this is what was predicted by the prophet Joel—
17 In the last days, saith God, *then will I pour out my Spirit
upon all flesh,
your sons and daughters shall prophesy,
your young men shall see visions,
your old men shall dream dreams:*
18 on *my very slaves and slave-girls in those days will I
pour out my Spirit,*
and they shall prophesy.
19 *And I will display wonders in heaven* above
and signs *on earth* below,
blood and fire and vapour of smoke:
20 *the sun shall be changed into darkness
and the moon into blood,
ere the great, open Day of the Lord arrives.*
21 *And everyone who invokes the name of the Lord shall be
saved.*
22 Men of Israel, listen to my words. Jesus the Nazarene, a man accredited to you by God through miracles, wonders, and signs which God performed by him among you (as
23 you yourselves know), this Jesus, betrayed in the predestined course of God's deliberate purpose, you got wicked
24 men to nail to the cross and murder; but God raised him by checking the pangs of death. Death could not hold
25 him. For David says of him,
*I saw the Lord before me evermore;
lest I be shaken, he is at my right hand.*
26 *My heart is glad,
my tongue exults,
my very flesh will rest in hope,*
27 *because thou wilt not forsake my soul in the grave,
nor let thy holy one suffer decay.*
28 *Thou hast made known to me the paths of life,
thou wilt fill me with delight in thy presence.*
29 Brothers, I can speak quite plainly to you about the patriarch David; he died and was buried and his tomb re-
30 mains with us to this day. (He was a prophet; he knew God *had sworn an oath to him that he would seat one of*
31 *his descendants on his throne;* * so he spoke with a prevision of the resurrection of the Christ, when he said that he was not forsaken in the grave nor did his flesh *suffer*
32 *decay.* This Jesus God raised, as we can all bear witness.
33 Uplifted then by God's right hand, and receiving from the Father the long-promised holy Spirit, he has poured on us

---

* Omitting [τὸ κατὰ σάρκα ἀναστήσειν τὸν Χριστὸν].

34 what you now see and hear.) For it was not David who ascended to heaven; David says,
The Lord said to my Lord, 'Sit at my right hand,
35 *till I make your enemies a footstool for your feet'.*
36 So let all the house of Israel understand beyond a doubt that God has made him both Lord and Christ, this very
37 Jesus whom you have crucified." When they heard this, it went straight to their hearts; they said to Peter and the rest of the apostles, "Brothers, what are we to do?"
38 "Repent," said Peter, "let each of you be baptized in the name of Jesus Christ for the remission of your sins; then
39 you will receive the gift of the holy Spirit. For the promise is meant for you and for your children and *for all who are far off, for anyone whom the Lord* our God
40 *may call to himself.*" And with many another appeal he urged and entreated them. "Save yourselves," he cried,
41 "from this crooked generation!" So those who accepted what he said were baptized; about three thousand souls
42 were brought in, that day. They devoted themselves to the instruction given by the apostles and to fellowship,
43 breaking bread and praying together. Awe fell on everyone, and many wonders and signs were performed by the
44 apostles [in Jerusalem]. The believers * all kept together;
45 they shared all they had with one another, they would sell their possessions and goods and distribute the proceeds
46 among all, as anyone might be in need. Day after day they resorted with one accord to the temple and broke bread together in their own homes; they ate with a glad
47 and simple heart, praising God and looked on with favour by all the people. Meantime the Lord added the saved daily to their number. †

3 PETER and John were on their way up to the temple
2 for the hour of prayer at three in the afternoon, when a man lame from birth was carried past, who used to be laid every day at what was called the 'Beautiful Gate' of the temple, to ask alms from those who entered the temple.
3 When he noticed that Peter and John meant to go into
4 the temple, he asked them for alms. Peter looked at him
5 steadily, as did John, and said, "Look at us." The man
6 attended, expecting to get something from them. But Peter said, "I have no silver or gold, but I will give you what I do have. In the name of Jesus Christ the Nazarene,
7 [get up and] walk!" And catching him by the right hand

* Omitting [φόβος τε ἦν μέγας ἐπὶ πάντας, καὶ].

† Omitting [τῇ ἐκκλησίᾳ], although the omission makes it difficult to get the above sense, or indeed any, out of the Greek.

he raised him. Instantly his feet and ankles grew strong,
8 he leapt to his feet, started to walk, and accompanied
them into the temple, walking, leaping, and praising God.
9 When all the people saw him walking and praising God,
10 and when they recognized this was the very man who used
to sit and beg at the Gate Beautiful, they were lost in awe
11 and amazement at what had happened to him. As he clung
to Peter and John, all the people rushed awestruck to
12 them in what was called Solomon's portico. But when
Peter saw this, he said to the people, "Men of Israel, why
are you surprised at this? Why do you stare at us, as if
we had made him walk by any power or piety of ours?
13 *The God of Abraham and the God of Isaac and the God
of Jacob, the God of our fathers has glorified* Jesus *his
servant,* whom you delivered up and repudiated before
14 Pilate. Pilate had decided to release him, but you repudiated the Holy and Just One; the boon you asked was
15 a murderer, and you killed the pioneer of Life. But God
16 raised him from the dead, as we can bear witness. (He it
is who has given strength to this man whom you see and
know, by faith in His name; it is the faith He inspires
which has made the man thus hale and whole before you
17 all.) Now I know, brothers, that you acted in ignorance,
18 like your rulers—though this was how God fulfilled what
he had announced beforehand by the lips of all the
19 prophets, namely the sufferings of his Christ. Repent then,
and turn to have your sins blotted out, so that a breathing-
20 space may be vouchsafed you, and that the Lord may send
21 Jesus your long-decreed Christ, who must be kept in
heaven till the period of the great Restoration. Ages ago
22 God spoke of this by the lips of his holy prophets; for
Moses said,
*The Lord our God will raise up a prophet for you from
among your brotherhood, as he raised me:
you must listen to whatever he may tell you.*
23 *Any soul that will not listen to this prophet shall be
exterminated from the People;*
24 and all the prophets who have spoken since Samuel and
25 his successors have also announced these days. Now you
are the sons of the prophets and of the covenant which
God made with your fathers when he said to Abraham,
all families on earth shall be blessed in your offspring.
26 It was for you first that God raised up his Servant, and
sent him to bless you by turning each of you from your
wicked ways."

4 While they were speaking to the people, they were
surprised by the priests, the commander of the temple,
2 and the Sadducees, who were annoyed at them teaching

the people and proclaiming Jesus as an instance of resurrection from the dead. They laid hands on them and, as
it was now evening, put them in custody till next morning. (A number of those who heard them speak believed,
bringing up their numbers to [about] five thousand.)

5 Next morning a meeting was held in Jerusalem of their
rulers, elders and scribes, which was attended by the
high priest Annas, by Caiaphas, John, Alexander, and all
the members of the high priest's family. They made the
men stand before them and inquired, "By what authority,
in whose name, have you* done this?" Then Peter, filled
with the holy Spirit, said to them: "Rulers of the people
and elders of Israel, if we are being cross-examined to-day
upon a benefit rendered to a cripple, upon how this man
got better, you and the people of Israel must all understand
that he stands before you strong and well, thanks to the
name of Jesus Christ the Nazarene whom you crucified and
whom God raised from the dead. He is
the stone despised by you builders,
which has become head of the corner.
12 There is no salvation by anyone else, nor even a second
Name under heaven appointed for us men and our salvation." They were astonished to notice how outspoken Peter
and John were, and to discover that they were uncultured
persons and mere outsiders; they recognized them as having been companions of Jesus, but as they saw the man
who had been healed standing beside them, they could say
nothing. Ordering them to withdraw from the Sanhedrin,
they proceeded to hold a consultation. "What are we to
do with these men?" they said. "It is plain to all the inhabitants of Jerusalem that a miracle has admittedly been
worked by them. That we cannot deny. However, to keep
things from going any further with the people, we had
better threaten them that they are not to tell anyone in
future about this Name." So they called the men in and
ordered them not to speak or teach a single sentence about
the Name of Jesus. But Peter and John replied, "Decide
for yourselves whether it is right before God to obey you
rather than God. Certainly we cannot give up speaking of
what we have seen and heard." Then they threatened
them still further and let them go; on account of the
people they found themselves unable to find any means of
punishing them, for everybody was glorifying God over
what had happened (the man on whom this miracle of healing had been performed, being more than forty years old).
23 On being released they went to their friends and related

* With a touch of superciliousness ('men like you!'), which is perhaps better expressed in reading aloud than by any verbal periphrasis.

24 what the high priests and elders had said; and on hearing this the entire company raised their cry to God, "O Sovereign Lord, thou art he * who made *heaven, earth, and*
25 *sea, and all that in them is,* who said to our fathers † by the holy Spirit through the lips of thy servant David,
    Why did the Gentiles rage,
    and the peoples vainly conspire?
26 *The kings of the earth stood ready,*
    the rulers mustered together against the Lord and his Christ.
27 In this very city they actually mustered against thy holy Servant Jesus, whom thou didst consecrate—Herod and Pontius Pilate, together with the Gentiles and the peoples
28 of Israel, mustering to carry out what thy hand had traced,
29 thy purpose had decreed. So now, O Lord, consider the threats of these men, and grant that thy servants may be
30 perfectly fearless in speaking thy word, when thy hand is stretched out to heal and to perform miracles and wonders
31 by the name of thy holy Servant Jesus." At their prayer the place of meeting was shaken, and they were all filled
33 with the holy Spirit, speaking God's word fearlessly; the apostles gave their testimony to the resurrection of the Lord Jesus with great power, and great grace was upon them all.‡
32 Now there was but one heart and soul among the multitude of the believers; not one of them considered anything his personal property, they shared all they had with one
34 another. There was not a needy person among them, for those who owned land or houses would sell them and bring
35 the proceeds of the sale, laying the money before the feet of the apostles; it was then distributed according to each
36 individual's need. Thus Joseph, who was surnamed Barnabas or (as it may be translated) 'Son of Encouragement'
37 by the apostles, a Levite of Cypriote birth, sold a farm belonging to him and brought the money, which he placed before the feet of the apostles.

5 But a man called Ananias, who with his wife Sapphira
2 had sold some property, appropriated some of the purchase-money with the connivance of his wife; he only brought part of it to lay before the feet of the apostles.
3 "Ananias," said Peter, "why has Satan filled your heart and made you cheat the holy Spirit by appropriating some
4 of the money paid for the land? When it remained unsold,

---

* Omitting [ὁ θεὸς].
† Accepting Hort's suggestion that τοῦ πατρός is a corruption of τοῖς πατράσιν, though the text even then seems to include a gloss somewhere.
‡ Transposing ver. 33 to its original position after ver. 31.

did it not remain your own? And even after the sale,
was the money not yours to do as you pleased about it?
How could you think of doing a thing like this? You
5 have not defrauded men but God." When Ananias heard
this, he fell down and expired. (Great awe came over all
6 who heard of it.) And the younger men rose, wrapped
7 the body up and carried it away to be buried. After an
interval of about three hours his wife happened to come
8 in, quite unconscious of what had occurred. "Tell me,"
said Peter, "did you only sell the land for such and such a
9 sum?" "Yes," she said, "that was all we sold it for." Peter
said to her, "How could you arrange to put the Lord's
Spirit to the proof? Listen, there are the footsteps of
the men who have buried your husband! They are at the
10 door, and they will carry you out as well." Instantly she
fell down at their feet and expired. The younger men
came in to find her dead; they carried her out and buried
11 her beside her husband. Great awe came over the whole
church and over all who heard about this.
12 Now they all without exception met in the portico of
13 Solomon. Though the people extolled them, not a soul
14 from the outside dared to join them. On the other hand,
crowds of men and women who believed in the Lord were
12 brought in. Many miracles and wonders were performed
15 among the people by the apostles.* In fact, invalids were
actually carried into the streets and laid on beds and
mattresses, so that, when Peter passed, his shadow at any-
16 rate might fall on one or other of them. Crowds gathered
even from the towns round Jerusalem, bringing invalids
and people troubled with unclean spirits, all of whom were
healed.
17 This filled the high priest Annas † and his allies, the
18 Sudducean party, with bitter jealousy; they laid hands on
19 the apostles and put them into the public prison, but an
angel of the Lord opened the prison-doors during the night
20 and brought them out, saying, "Go and stand in the temple,
21 telling the people all about this Life." With these orders
they went into the temple about dawn and proceeded to
teach. Meantime the high priest and his allies met, called
the Sanhedrin together and the council of seniors belonging
to the sons of Israel, and then sent to prison for the men.
22 But as the attendants did not find them when they got to
23 the prison, they came back to report, "We found the prison
safely locked up, with the sentries posted at the doors,

* Transposing the first clause of ver. 12 to the beginning of ver. 15.
† Blass's brilliant conjecture for the ἀναστάς of the ordinary text.
It is not entirely without manuscript evidence.

24 but on opening the doors we found no one inside!" On hearing this the commander of the temple and the high priests were quite at a loss to know what to make of it.
25 However, someone came and reported to them, "Here are the very men you put in prison, standing in the temple and
26 teaching the people!" At this the commander went off with the attendants and fetched them—but without using violence, for fear that the people would pelt them with stones.
27 They conducted them before the Sanhedrin, and the high
28 priest asked them, "We strictly forbade you to teach about this Name, did we not? And here you have filled Jerusalem with your doctrine! You want to make us respon-
29 sible for this man's death!" Peter and the apostles an-
30 swered, "One must obey God rather than men. The God of our fathers raised Jesus whom you murdered by *hang-*
31 *ing him on a gibbet.* God lifted him up to his right hand as our pioneer and saviour, in order to grant repentance
32 and remission of sins to Israel. To these facts we bear witness, with the holy Spirit which God has given to those
33 who obey him." When they heard this, they were so furious
34 that they determined to make away with the apostles. But a Pharisee in the Sanhedrin called Gamaliel, a doctor of the Law who was highly respected by all the people, got up and ordered the apostles to be removed for a few
35 moments. Then he said, "Men of Israel, take care what you
36 do about these men. In days gone by Theudas started up, claiming to be a person of importance; a number of men, about four hundred of them, rallied to him, but he was slain, and all his followers were dispersed and wiped out.
37 After him Judas the Galilean started up at the time of the census, and got people to deser. to him; but he perished
38 too, and all his followers were scattered. So I advise you to-day to leave these men to themselves. Let them alone. If this project or enterprise springs from men, it will
39 collapse; whereas, if it really springs from God, you will be unable to put them down. You may even find yourselves
40 fighting God!" They gave in to him, and after summoning the apostles and giving them a flogging, they released them with instructions that they were not to speak about
41 the name of Jesus. The apostles left the Sanhedrin, rejoicing that they had been considered worthy of suffering
42 dishonour for the sake of the Name; not for a single day did they cease to teach and preach the gospel of Jesus the Christ in the temple and at home.

6 DURING these days, when the disciples were increasing in number, the Hellenists began to complain against the Hebrews, on the ground that their widows were being over-

2 looked in the daily distribution of food. So the twelve summoned the main body of the disciples and said: "It is not desirable that we should drop preaching the word of
3 God and attend to meals. Brothers, look out seven of your own number, men of good reputation who are full of the Spirit and of wisdom. We will appoint them to this duty,
4 but we will continue to devote ourselves to prayer and
5 the ministry of the word." This plan commended itself to the whole body, and they chose Stephen, a man full of faith and the holy Spirit, Philip, Prochorus, Nikanor, Timon, Parmenas and Nikolaos a proselyte from Antioch;
6 these men they presented to the apostles, who, after prayer, laid their hands upon them.
7 And the word of God spread; the number of the disciples in Jerusalem greatly increased, and a host of priests became obedient to the faith.
8 Now Stephen, who was full of grace and power, performed great wonders and miracles among the people.
9 Some of those who belonged to the so-called synagogue of the Libyans,* the Cyrenians, and the Alexandrians, as well as to that of the Cilicians and Asiatics, started a dispute
10 with Stephen, but they could not meet the wisdom and the
11 Spirit with which he spoke. They then instigated people to say, "We have heard him talking blasphemy against
12 Moses and God." In this way they excited the people, the elders, and the scribes, who rushed on him, dragged him
13 away, and took him before the Sanhedrin. They also brought forward false witnesses to say, "This fellow is never done talking against this holy Place and the Law!
14 Why, we have heard him say that Jesus the Nazarene will destroy this Place and change the customs handed down to us by Moses!"
15 Then all who were seated in the Sanhedrin fixed their eyes on him, and saw that his face shone like the face of an angel.

2 7 SAID the high priest, "Is this true?" "Listen, brothers and fathers," said Stephen. "The *God of glory* appeared to our father Abraham when he was still in Mesopotamia,
3 before ever he stayed in Haran, *and said to him, 'Leave your land and your countrymen and come to whatever* †
4 *land I show you.*' Then he left the land of the Chaldeans

---

* Reading Λιβυστίνων instead of the Λιβερτίνων of the text. This, as Blass points out, gives "the African Jews in the geographical order of their original dwelling-places."

† Omitting [τὴν].

THE ACTS VII 185

and stayed in Haran. From Haran God shifted him, after
5 his father's death, to this land which you now inhabit. But
he did not give him any inheritance in it, not *even a foot
of the land*. All he did was to promise he would *give it
as a possession to him and to his offspring after him* (he
6 at the time being childless). What God said was this:
'*His offspring will sojourn in a foreign land, where they
will be enslaved and oppressed for four hundred years.
7 But,*' said God, '*I* * *will pass sentence on the nation that
has made them slaves, and then they will get away to
8 worship me in this* Place.' God also gave him *the covenant
of circumcision*. So Abraham became the father of Isaac,
whom he circumcised on the eighth day, Isaac was the
9 father of Jacob, and Jacob of the twelve patriarchs. *Out
of jealousy* the patriarchs *sold Joseph into Egypt;* but *God
10 was with him*, rescuing him from all his troubles and
allowing him to find favour for his wisdom *with Pharaoh
king of Egypt, who appointed him viceroy over Egypt and
11 over all his own household*. Now *a famine came over
the whole of Egypt* and Canaan, attended with great
misery, so that our ancestors could not find provender.
12 *But, hearing there was food in Egypt,* Jacob sent our an-
13 cestors on their first visit to that country; at their second
visit *Joseph made himself known to his brothers*, and
14 Pharaoh was informed of Joseph's lineage. Then Joseph
sent for his father Jacob and all his kinsfolk, *amounting
15 to seventy-five souls;* and Jacob *went south to Egypt.
16 When he* and our ancestors *died, they were carried across
to Shechem and laid in the tomb which Abraham had
bought* for a sum of money *from the sons of Hamor in
17 Shechem.* As the time approached for the promise God
18 had made to Abraham, the people *grew and multiplied
in Egypt, till another king arose to rule Egypt who knew
19 nothing of Joseph. He took a cunning method with* our
race; *he oppressed* our ancestors by forcing them to expose
20 their infants, to prevent them *from surviving.* It was at
this period that Moses was born, a divinely *beautiful* child.
For three months he was brought up in his father's house;
21 then he was exposed, but *Pharaoh's daughter adopted* him
22 and brought him up *as her own son.* So Moses was educated in all the culture of the Egyptians; he was a strong
23 man in speech and action. When he had completed his
fortieth year, it occurred to him to visit *his brothers, the
24 sons of Israel.* He saw one of them being badly treated,

* The 'I' is emphatic. When the New Testament is read aloud,
as it was originally meant to be, such stresses can be brought out. They
often interpret the inner meaning of the text.

so he defended him, *struck down the Egyptian*, and thus
25 avenged the man who had been wronged. (He thought
his brothers would understand God was going to bring
them deliverance by means of him, but they did not under-
26 stand.) Next day he came upon two of them fighting and
tried to pacify them. "You are brothers!" he said, "why
27 injure one another?" But *the man who was injuring his
neighbour* pushed him aside. "*Who made you ruler and
28 umpire over us?*" he asked. "*Do you want to kill me, as
29 you killed the Egyptian yesterday?*" At that *Moses fled;
he became a sojourner in the land of Midian*, where he had
30 two sons born to him. At the close of forty years *an angel
[of the Lord] appeared to him in the flames of a burning
31 thorn-bush, in the desert of mount* Sinai. When Moses
saw this, he marvelled at the sight; and as he went up
32 to look at it, the voice of the Lord said, '*I am the God of
your fathers, the God of Abraham and Isaac and Jacob.*'
Moses was so terrified that he did not dare to look at the
33 bush. But the Lord said to him, '*Take the sandals off your
feet, for the place where you are standing is sacred ground.
34 I have indeed seen the oppression of my people in Egypt,
I have heard their groans, and I have come down to rescue
35 them. Come now, I will send you back to Egypt.*' The
Moses they refused, when they said, '*Who made you ruler
and umpire?*'—that was the very man whom God sent to
rule and to redeem them, by aid of the angel who had
36 appeared to him in the bush. He it was who led them
forth, performing *wonders and signs in the land of Egypt*,
37 at the Red Sea, and *in the desert during forty years*. (This
was the Moses who told the sons of Israel, '*God will raise
up a prophet for you from among your brotherhood, as he
38 raised me.*') This was the man who at the assembly in
the desert intervened between the angel who spoke to him
on mount Sinai and our fathers; he received living Words
39 to be given to us. But our fathers would not submit to
him; they pushed him aside and *hankered* secretly *after
40 Egypt*. They told Aaron, '*Make gods that will march in
front of us! As for this Moses who led us out of Egypt,
41 we don't know what has happened to him!*' They actually
made a calf in those days, *offered sacrifice* to this idol, and
grew festive over what their own hands had manufactured.
42 So God turned from them, abandoning them to the worship
of *the starry Host*—as it is written in the book of the
prophets, *Did you offer me victims and sacrifices during
43 the forty years in the desert, O house of Israel? No, it was
the tent of Moloch and the star-symbol of Rephan your
god that you carried, figures that you manufactured for
worship. So now I will transport you beyond Babylon!*

44 In the desert our fathers had the tent of witness as arranged by Him *who told Moses to make it after the pat-*
45 *tern he had seen.* It was passed on and borne in by our fathers as with Joshua they *took possession of* the territory of the nations whom God drove out before our fathers. So it remained down to the days of David.
46 He found favour with God and asked permission *to devise*
47 *a dwelling for the God of Jacob.* It was Solomon, how-
48 ever, who *built him a house.* And yet the most High does not dwell in houses made by hands. As the prophet says,
49 *Heaven is my throne,*
   the earth is a footstool for my feet!
   What house would you build me? saith the Lord.
   On what spot could I settle?
50 *Did not my hand make all this?*
51 *Stiff-necked, uncircumcised in heart and ear,* you are always *resisting the holy Spirit!* As with your fathers,
52 so with you! Which of the prophets did your fathers fail to persecute? They killed those who announced beforehand the coming of the Just One. And here you have
53 betrayed him, murdered him!—you who got the Law that angels transmitted, and have not obeyed it!"
54 When they heard this, they were furious and gnashed
55 their teeth at him. He, full of the holy Spirit, gazed up at heaven and saw the glory of God and Jesus standing
56 at God's right hand. "Look," he said, "I see heaven open
57 and the Son of man standing at God's right hand!" With a loud shriek they shut their ears and rushed at him like one
58 man. Putting him outside the city, they proceeded to stone him (the witnesses laid their clothes at the feet of a youth
59 called Saul). So they stoned Stephen, who called on the Lord, saying, "Lord Jesus, receive my spirit!" Then he
60 knelt down and cried aloud, "Lord, let not this sin stand against them!" With these words he slept the sleep of death. (Saul quite approved of his murder.)

8 That day a severe persecution broke out against the church in Jerusalem, and everyone, with the exception of the apostles, was scattered over Judaea and Samaria.
2 Devout men buried Stephen and made loud lamentation
3 over him, but Saul made havoc of the church by entering one house after another, dragging off men and women, and consigning them to prison.
4 Now those who were scattered went through the land
5 preaching the gospel. Philip travelled down to a town in
6 Samaria, where he preached Christ to the people. And the crowds attended like one man to what was said by Philip, listening to him and watching the miracles he performed.

7 For unclean spirits came screaming and shrieking out of many who had been possessed, and many paralytics and
8 lame people were healed. So there was great rejoicing in that
9 town. Now for some time previous a man called Simon had been practising magic arts in the town, to the utter astonishment of the Samaritan nation; he made himself
10 out to be a great person, and all sorts and conditions of people attached themselves to him, declaring he was that
11 Power of God which is known as 'the Great Power.' They attached themselves to him because he had dazzled them
12 with his skill in magic for a considerable time. But when they believed Philip, who preached the gospel of the Reign of God and the name of Jesus, they had themselves bap-
13 tized, both men and women; indeed Simon himself believed, and after his baptism kept close to Philip, utterly astonished to see the signs and striking miracles which were taking place.
14 When the apostles at Jerusalem heard that Samaria had accepted the word of God, they despatched Peter and John,
15 who came down and prayed that the Samaritans might
16 receive the holy Spirit. (As yet it had not fallen upon any of them; they had simply been baptized in the name
17 of the Lord Jesus.) Then they laid their hands on them,
18 and they received the holy Spirit. Now Simon noticed that the holy Spirit was conferred by the laying on of the
19 apostles' hands; so he brought them money, saying, "Let me share this power too, so that anyone on whom I lay
20 my hands may receive the holy Spirit." Peter said to him, "Death to you and your money, for dreaming you
21 could buy the gift of God! You come in for no share or lot in this religion. *Your heart is all wrong in the sight of*
22 *God*. So repent of this wickedness of yours, and ask God whether you cannot be forgiven for your heart's purpose.
23 For I see you are *a bitter poison* and *a pack of evil*."
24 Simon replied, "Beseech the Lord for me! Pray that nothing you have said may befall me!"
25 After bearing their testimony to the word of the Lord and preaching it, the apostles went back to Jerusalem, preaching the gospel to a number of the Samaritan
26 villages; but an angel of the Lord said to Philip, "Get up and go south, along the road from Jerusalem to Gaza" (the
27 desert-route). So he got up and went on his way. Now there was an Ethiopian eunuch, a high official of Candace the queen of the Ethiopians (he was her chief treasurer),
28 who had come to Jerusalem for worship and was on his way home. He was sitting in his chariot, reading the
29 prophet Isaiah. The Spirit said to Philip, "Go up and join
30 that chariot." When Philip ran up, he heard him reading

the prophet Isaiah. "Do you really understand * what you
31 are reading?" he asked. "Why, how can I possibly understand it," said the eunuch, "unless some one puts me on the right track?" And he begged Philip to get up and sit
32 beside him. Now the passage of scripture which he was reading was as follows:—

he was led like a sheep to be slaughtered,
and as a lamb is dumb before the shearer,
so he opens not his lips.
33 *By humbling himself he had his doom removed.*
Who can tell his family?
For his life is cut off from the earth.

34 So the eunuch said to Philip, "Pray, who is the prophet
35 speaking about? Is it himself or someone else?" Then Philip opened his lips, and starting from this scripture
36 preached the gospel of Jesus to him. As they travelled on, they came to some water, and the eunuch said, "Here is
38 water! What is to prevent me being baptized?" So he ordered the chariot to stop. Both of them stepped into the
39 water, and Philip baptized the eunuch. When they came up from the water, the Spirit of the Lord caught Philip away, and the eunuch lost sight of him. He went on his
40 way rejoicing, while Philip found himself at Azotus, where he passed on, preaching the gospel in every town, till he reached Caesarea.

9 MEANWHILE Saul still breathed threats of murder against the disciples of the Lord. He went to the high
2 priest and asked him for letters to the synagogues at Damascus empowering him to put any man or woman in chains whom he could find belonging to the Way, and
3 bring them to Jerusalem. As he neared Damascus in the course of his journey, suddenly a light from heaven flashed
4 round him; he dropped to the ground and heard a voice saying to him, "Saul, Saul, why do you persecute me?"
5 "Who are you?" † he asked. "I am Jesus," he said, "and
6 you persecute me. Get up and go into the city. There
7 you will be told what you have to do." His fellow-travellers stood speechless, for they heard the voice but they
8 could not see anyone. Saul got up from the ground, but though his eyes were open he could see nothing; so they

---

* The Vulgate preserves the play on words in the Greek. *Intellegis quae legis* brings out, as English cannot, the force of γινώσκεις ἃ ἀναγινώσκεις.

† I have deliberately left κύριε untranslated here, as in xxii. 8 and xxvi. 14, no less than in x. 4. Any English rendering would imply either too much or too little.

9 took his hand and led him to Damascus. For three days he remained sightless, he neither ate nor drank.
10 Now there was a disciple called Ananias in Damascus.
11 The Lord said to him in a vision, "Ananias." He said, "I am here, Lord." And the Lord said to him, "Go away to the street called 'The Straight Street,' and ask at the house of Judas for a man of Tarsus called Saul. He is
12 praying at this very moment, and he has seen a man called Ananias enter and lay his hands upon him to bring back
13 his sight." "But, Lord," Ananias answered, "many people have told me about all the mischief this man has done to
14 thy saints at Jerusalem! And in this city too he has authority from the high priests to put anyone in chains
15 who invokes thy Name!" But the Lord said to him, "Go; I have chosen him to be the means of bringing my Name before the Gentiles and their kings as well as before the
16 sons of Israel. I will show him all he has to suffer for the
17 sake of my Name." So Ananias went off and entered the house, laying his hands on him with these words, "Saul, my brother, I have been sent by the Lord, by Jesus who appeared to you on the road, to let you regain your sight
18 and be filled with the holy Spirit." In a moment something like scales fell from his eyes, he regained his sight,
19 got up and was baptized. Then he took some food and felt strong again. For several days he stayed at Damascus
20 with the disciples. He lost no time in preaching through-
21 out the synagogues that Jesus was the Son of God—to the amazement of all his hearers, who said, "Is this not the man who in Jerusalem harried those who invoke this Name, the man who came here for the express purpose of carrying them all in chains to the high priests?"
22 Saul became more and more vigorous. He put the Jewish residents in Damascus to confusion by his proof that
23 Jesus was the Christ; and the Jews, after a number of
24 days had elapsed, conspired to make away with him. But their plot came to the ears of Saul, and, although they kept watch on the gates day and night in order to make away
25 with him, his disciples managed one night to let him down
26 over the wall by lowering him in a basket. He got to Jerusalem and tried to join the disciples, but they were all afraid of him, unable to believe he was really a disciple.
27 Barnabas, however, got hold of him and brought him to the apostles. To them he related how he had seen the Lord upon the road, how He had spoken to him, and how he
28 had spoken freely in the name of Jesus at Damascus. He then went in and out among them at Jerusalem, speaking
29 freely in the name of the Lord; he also held conversations and debates with the Hellenists. But when the brothers

learned that the Hellenists were attempting to make
30 away with him, they took him down to Caesarea and sent
him off to Tarsus.

31 Now, all over Judaea, Galilee, and Samaria, the church
enjoyed peace; it was consolidated, inspired by reverence
for the Lord and by its invocation of the holy Spirit, and
32 so increased in numbers. Peter moved here and there
among them all, and it happened that in the course of his
tours he came down to visit the saints who stayed at
33 Lydda. There he found a man called Æneas who had
34 been bed-ridden for eight years with paralysis. "Æneas,"
said Peter, "Jesus the Christ cures you! Get up and make
35 your bed!" He got up at once. And all the inhabitants
of Lydda and Saron saw him, and they turned to the Lord.
36 At Joppa there was a disciple called Tabitha (which may
be translated Dorcas, or 'Gazelle'), a woman whose life
37 was full of good actions and of charitable practices. She
happened to take ill and die at this time, and after wash-
38 ing her body they laid it in an upper room. When the
disciples heard that Peter was at Lydda (for Joppa is not
far from Lydda), they sent two men to beg him to "Come
39 on to us without delay." So Peter got up and went with
them. When he arrived, they took him up to the room,
where all the widows stood beside him crying as they
showed him the garments and dresses that Dorcas used to
40 make when she was with them. Peter put them all outside; then he knelt down and prayed, and turning to the
body said, "Tabitha, rise." She opened her eyes, and on
41 seeing Peter she sat up. Then he gave her his hand, raised
her, and, after calling the saints and the widows he pre-
42 sented her to them alive. This became known all over
Joppa, and many believed in the Lord.
43 In Joppa Peter stayed for some time, at the house of
10 Simon a tanner. Now in Caesarea there was a man
called Cornelius, a captain in the Italian regiment,
2 a religious man, who reverenced God with all his household, who was liberal in his alms to the People, and who
3 constantly prayed to God. About three o'clock in the afternoon he distinctly saw in a vision an angel of God entering
4 and saying to him, "Cornelius." He stared at the angel in
terror, saying, "What is it?" He replied, "Your prayers
and your alms have risen before God as a sacrifice to be
5 remembered. You must now send some men to Joppa for
6 a certain Simon who is surnamed Peter; he is staying with
7 Simon a tanner, whose house stands by the sea." When
the angel who spoke to him had left, he called two of his
menservants and a religiously minded soldier who be-

8 longed to his personal retinue, and after describing all the
9 vision to them, he sent them to Joppa. Next day they
were still on the road and not far from the town, when
Peter went up to the roof of the house about noon to pray.
10 He became very hungry and longed for some food. But
as they were getting the meal ready, a trance came over
11 him. He saw heaven open and a vessel coming down, like
a huge sheet lowered by the four corners to the earth,
12 which contained all quadrupeds and creeping things of the
13 earth and wild birds. A voice came to him, "Rise, Peter,
14 kill and eat." But Peter said, "No, no, my Lord; I have
15 never eaten anything common or unclean." A second time
the voice came back to him, "What God has cleansed, you
16 must not regard as common." This happened three times;
17 then the vessel was at once raised to heaven. Peter was
quite at a loss to know the meaning of the vision he had
seen; but just then, the messengers of Cornelius, who had
made inquiries for the house of Simon, stood at the door
18 and called out to ask if Simon, surnamed Peter, was stay-
19 ing there. So the Spirit said to Peter, who was pondering
over the vision, "There are three men looking for you!
20 Come, get up and go down, and have no hesitation about
accompanying them, for it is I who have sent them."
21 Then Peter went down to the men, saying, "I am the man
you are looking for. What is your reason for coming?"
22 They said, "Cornelius, a captain, a good man who reverences God and enjoys a good reputation among the whole
Jewish nation, was instructed by a holy angel to send for
you to his house and to listen to what you had to say."
23 So he invited them in and entertained them. Next day
he was up and off with them, accompanied by some of the
24 brothers from Joppa; and on the next day he reached
25 Caesarea. Peter was just going into the house when Cornelius met him, fell at his feet, and worshipped him;
26 but Peter raised him, saying, "Get up, I am only a man
27 myself." Then talking to him he entered the house, to
24 find a large company assembled. (For Cornelius had been
expecting him and had called his kinsfolk and intimate
28 friends together.)* To them Peter said, "You know yourselves it is illegal for a Jew to join or accost anyone belonging to another nation; but God has shown me that I must
29 not call any man common or unclean, and so I have come
without any demur when I was sent for. Now I want to
30 know why you sent for me?" "Three days ago," said Cornelius, "at this very hour I was praying in my house at
three o'clock in the afternoon, when a man stood before

* Transposing ver. 24b to its right position between ver. 27 and ver. 28.

THE ACTS XI 193

31 me in shining dress, saying, 'Cornelius, your prayer has
32 been heard, your alms are remembered by God. You must
send to Joppa and summon Simon who is surnamed Peter;
he is staying in the house of Simon a tanner beside the
33 sea.' So I sent for you at once, and you have been kind
enough to come. Well now, here we are all present before
God to listen to what the Lord has commanded you to
34 say." Then Peter opened his lips and said, "I see quite
35 plainly that *God has no favourites*, but that he who reverences Him and lives a good life in any nation is wel-
36 comed by Him. You know *the message he sent to* the sons
of *Israel when he preached the gospel of peace* by Jesus
37 Christ (who is Lord of all); you know how it spread over
the whole of Judaea, starting from Galilee after the bap-
38 tism preached by John—how *God consecrated* Jesus of
Nazaret *with the* holy *Spirit* and power, and how he went
about doing good and curing all who were harassed by the
39 devil; for God was with him. As for what he did in the
land of the Jews and of Jerusalem, we can testify to that.
40 They slew him *by hanging him on a gibbet*, but God raised
41 him on the third day, and allowed him to be seen not by
all the People but by witnesses whom God had previously
selected, by us who ate and drank with him after his
42 resurrection from the dead, when he enjoined us to preach
to the People, testifying that this was he whom God has
43 appointed to be judge of the living and of the dead. All
the prophets testify that everyone who believes in him is
44 to receive remission of sins through his Name." While
Peter was still speaking, the holy Spirit fell upon all who
45 listened to what he said. Now the Jewish believers who
had accompanied Peter were amazed that the gift of the
holy Spirit had actually been poured out on the Gentiles—
46 for they heard them speak with 'tongues' and magnify God.
47 At this Peter asked, "Can any one refuse water for the
baptism of these people—people who have received the
48 holy Spirit just as we ourselves have?" And he ordered
them to be baptized in the name of Jesus Christ. Then
they begged him to remain for some days.

11 Now the apostles and the brothers in Judaea heard
that the Gentiles also had received the word of God.
2 So when Peter came up to Jerusalem, the circumcision
3 party fell foul of him. "You went into the houses of the
uncircumcised," they said, "and you ate with them!"
4 Then Peter proceeded to put the facts before them.
5 "I was in the town of Joppa at prayer," he said, "and in a
trance I saw a vision—a vessel coming down like a huge
sheet lowered from heaven by the four corners. It came

6 down to me, and when I looked steadily at it, I noted the
quadrupeds of the earth, the wild beasts, the creeping
7 things and the wild birds. Also I heard a voice saying to
8 me, 'Rise, Peter, kill and eat.' I said, 'No, no, my Lord;*
nothing common or unclean has ever passed my lips.'
9 But a voice answered me for the second time out of
heaven, 'What God has cleansed, you must not regard as
10 common.' This happened three times, and then the whole
11 thing was drawn back into heaven. At that very moment
three men reached the house where I was living, sent to me
12 from Caesarea. The Spirit told me to have no hesitation in
accompanying them; these six brothers went with me as
13 well, and we entered the man's house. He related to us
how he had seen the angel standing in his house and saying, 'Send to Joppa for Simon who is surnamed Peter;
14 he will tell you how you and all your household are to be
15 saved.' Now just as I began to speak, the holy Spirit fell
16 upon them as upon us at the beginning; and I remembered the saying of the Lord, that 'John baptized with
water, but you shall be baptized with the holy Spirit.'
17 Well then, if God has given them exactly the same gift as
he gave us when we believed in the Lord Jesus Christ, who
18 was I—how could I try—to thwart God?" On hearing this
they desisted and glorified God, saying, "So God has actually allowed the Gentiles to repent and live!"
19   Now those who had been scattered by the trouble which
arose over Stephen made their way as far as Phœnicia and
Cyprus and Antioch, but they preached the word to none
20 except Jews. Some of them, however, were Cypriotes and
Cyrenians, who on reaching Antioch told the Greeks † also
21 the gospel of the Lord Jesus; the strong hand of the
Lord was with them, and a large number believed and
22 turned to the Lord. The news of this reached the church
in Jerusalem, and they despatched Barnabas to Antioch.
23 When he came and saw the grace of God he rejoiced, and
encouraged them all to hold by the Lord with heartfelt
24 purpose (for he was a good man, full of the holy Spirit and
faith). Considerable numbers of people were brought in
25 for the Lord. So Barnabas went off to Tarsus to look for
26 Saul, and on finding him he brought him to Antioch, where
for a whole year they were guests of the church and taught
considerable numbers. It was at Antioch too that the
disciples were originally called "Christians."
27   During these days some prophets came down from Jeru-

* Here, as in x. 14, κύριε is translated. Peter was a Christian, and
the connexion of the Voice with the Spirit is evident from the context.
  † Reading Ἕλληνας with ℵc A D*, for which Ἑλληνιστὰς seems to
have been substituted under the influence of ix. 29.

THE ACTS XII   195

28 salem to Antioch, one of whom, named Agabus, showed by the Spirit that a severe famine was about to visit the whole world (the famine which occurred in the reign of
29 Claudius). So the disciples put aside money, as each of them was able to afford it, for a contribution to be sent to
30 the brothers in Judaea. This they carried out, sending their contribution to the presbyters by Barnabas and Saul.

2 **12** It was about that time that king Herod laid hands of violence on some members of the church. James
3 the brother of John he slew with the sword, and when he saw this pleased the Jews, he went on to seize Peter.
4 (This was during the days of unleavened bread.) After arresting him he put him in prison, handing him over to a guard of sixteen soldiers, with the intention of producing
5 him to the People after the passover. So Peter was closely guarded in prison, while earnest prayer for him was offered
6 to God by the church. The very night before Herod meant to have him produced, Peter lay asleep between two soldiers; he was fastened by two chains, and sentries in
7 front of the door guarded the prison. But an angel of the Lord flashed on him, and a light shone in the cell; striking Peter on the side he woke him, saying, "Quick, get up!"
8 The fetters dropped from his hands, and the angel said to him, "Gird yourself and put on your sandals." He did so. Then said the angel, "Put on your coat and follow me."
9 And he followed him out, not realizing that what the angel did was real, but imagining that he saw a vision.
10 When they had passed the first guard and the second they came to the iron gate leading into the city, which opened to them of its own accord; they passed out, and after they had gone through one street, the angel immediately left
11 him. Then Peter came to his senses and said, "Now I know for certain that the Lord has sent his angel and rescued me from the hand of Herod and from all that the
12 Jewish people were anticipating." When he grasped the situation, he went to the house of Mary, the mother of John who was surnamed Mark, where a number had met
13 for prayer. When he knocked at the door of the porch,
14 a maidservant called Rhoda came to answer it; but as soon as she recognized Peter's voice, instead of opening the door she ran inside from sheer joy and announced that
15 Peter was standing in front of the porch. "You are mad," they said. But she insisted it was true. "It is his angel,"
16 they said. But Peter kept on knocking, and when they
17 opened the door they were amazed to see him. He beckoned to them to keep quiet and then described to them how the Lord had brought him out of prison. "Report this

to James," he said, "and to the brothers." And off he
18 went to another place. Now when day broke there was a
great commotion among the soldiers over what could have
19 become of Peter. Herod made inquiries for him but could
not find him; so, after cross-examining the guards, he
ordered them off to death. He then went down from
20 Judaea to Caesarea, where he spent some time. As there
was a bitter feud between him and the inhabitants of Tyre
and Sidon, they waited on him unanimously and after conciliating the royal chamberlain Blastus they made overtures for peace, as their country depended for its food-
21 supply upon the royal territory. On a stated day Herod
arrayed himself in royal robes, took his seat on the dais,
22 and proceeded to harangue them. The populace shouted,
23 "It is a god's voice, not a man's!" and in a moment an
angel of the Lord struck him, because he had not given due
glory to God; he was eaten up by worms and so expired.
24 The word of God spread and multiplied.
25 After fulfilling their commission, Barnabas and Saul
returned from Jerusalem, bringing with them John who is
surnamed Mark.

13 Now in the local church at Antioch there were
prophets and teachers, Barnabas, Symeon (called
Niger) and Lucius the Cyrenian, besides Manaen (a foster-
2 brother of Herod the tetrarch) and Saul. As they were
worshipping the Lord and fasting, the holy Spirit said,
"Come! set me apart Barnabas and Saul for the work to
3 which I have called them." Then after fasting and praying they laid their hands on them and let them go.
4 Sent out thus by the holy Spirit, they went down to
5 Seleucia and from there they sailed to Cyprus. On reaching Salamis they proclaimed the word of God in the Jewish
6 synagogues, with John as their assistant. They covered
the whole island as far as Paphos, where they fell in with
a Jewish sorcerer and false prophet called Bar-Jesus;
7 he belonged to the suite of the proconsul Sergius Paulus,
an intelligent man who called for Barnabas and Saul, and
8 demanded to hear the word of God. But the sorcerer
Elymas (for that is the translation of his name) tried to
9 divert the proconsul from the faith. So Saul (who is also
called Paul), filled with the holy Spirit, looked steadily
10 at him and said, "You son of the devil, you enemy of all
good, full of all craft and all cunning, will you never stop
11 diverting *the straight paths of the Lord?* See here, the
Lord's hand will fall on you, and you will be blind, unable
for a time to see the sun." In a moment a dark mist fell
upon him, and he groped about for someone to take him
12 by the hand. Then the proconsul believed, when he saw

what had happened; he was astounded at the doctrine of the Lord.

13 Setting sail from Paphos, Paul and his companions reached Perga in Pamphylia; John left them and went
14 back to Jerusalem, but they passed on from Perga and arrived at Pisidian Antioch. On the sabbath they went
15 into the synagogue and sat down; and, after the reading of the Law and the prophets, the presidents of the synagogue sent to tell them, "Brothers, if you have any word
16 of counsel for the people, say it." So Paul stood up and motioning with his hand said, "Listen, men of Israel and
17 you who reverence God. The God of this People Israel chose our fathers; he multiplied the people as they sojourned in the land of Egypt and *with arm uplifted led*
18 *them out of it.* For about forty years *he bore with them*
19 *in the desert, and after destroying seven nations in the land of Canaan he gave* them *their land as an inheritance*
20 for about four hundred and fifty years. After that he gave
21 them judges, down to the prophet Samuel. Then it was that they begged for a king, and God gave them forty years of Saul, the son of Kish, who belonged to the tribe
22 of Benjamin. After deposing him, he raised up David to be their king, to whom he bore this testimony that *'In David, the son of Jessai, I have found a man after my*
23 *own heart, who will obey all my will.'* From his offspring God brought to Israel, as he had promised, a saviour in
24 Jesus, before whose coming John had already preached a
25 baptism of repentance for all the people of Israel. And as John was closing his career he said, 'What do you take me for? I am not He; no, he is coming after me, and I am not
26 fit to untie the sandals on his feet!' Brothers, sons of Abraham's race and all among you who reverence God,
27 *the message* of this salvation *has been sent* to us. The inhabitants of Jerusalem and their rulers, by condemning him * in their ignorance, fulfilled the words of the prophets
28 which are read every sabbath; though they could find him guilty of no crime that deserved death they begged Pilate
29 to have him put to death, and, after carrying out all that had been predicted of him in scripture, they lowered him
30 from the gibbet and laid him in a tomb. But God raised
31 him from the dead. For many days he was seen by those who had come up with him from Galilee to Jerusalem;
32 they are now his witnesses to the People. So we now preach to you the glad news that the promise made to the

---

* The Greek text is difficult. I prefer, as the least radical treatment, Lachmann's proposal to read κρίναντες immediately after ἀγνοήσαντες καί, which at anyrate yields a fair sense.

33 fathers has been fulfilled by God for us their children, when he raised Jesus. As it is written in the second psalm,
> *thou art my son,*
> *to-day have I become thy father.*

34 And as a proof that he has raised him from the dead, never to return to decay, he has said this: *I will give you the*
35 *holiness of David that fails not.* Hence in another psalm he says,
> *thou wilt not let thy holy One suffer decay.*

36 Of course *David*, after serving God's purpose in his own generation, died and was laid *beside his fathers;* he suf-
37 fered decay, but He whom God raised did not suffer decay.
38 So you must understand, my brothers, that remission of
39 sins is proclaimed to you through him, and that by him everyone who believes is absolved from all that the law of
40 Moses never could absolve you from. Beware then in case the prophetic saying applies to you:
41 *Look, you disdainful folk, wonder at this and perish—*
    for in your days I do a deed,
    a deed you will never believe, not though one were to explain it to you."

42 As Paul and Barnabas went out, the people begged to have
43 all this repeated to them on the following sabbath. After the synagogue broke up, a number of the Jews and the devout proselytes followed them; Paul and Barnabas talked to them and encouraged them to hold by the grace of God.
44 And on the next sabbath nearly all the town gathered to
45 hear the word of the Lord. But when the Jews saw the crowds they were filled with jealousy; they began to con-
46 tradict what Paul said and to abuse him. So Paul and Barnabas spoke out fearlessly. "The word of God," they said, "had to be spoken to you in the first instance; but as you push it aside and judge yourselves unworthy of eter-
47 nal life, well, here we turn to the Gentiles! For these are the Lord's orders to us:
> *I have set you to be a light for the Gentiles,*
> *to bring salvation to the end of the earth."*

48 When the Gentiles heard this they rejoiced and glorified the word of the Lord and believed, that is, all who had
49 been ordained to eternal life; and the word of the Lord
50 went far and wide over the whole country. But the Jews incited the devout women of high rank and the leading men in the town, who stirred up persecution against Paul
51 and Barnabas and drove them out of their territory. They shook the dust off their feet as a protest and went to
52 Iconium. As for the disciples, they were filled with joy and the holy Spirit.

THE ACTS XIV 199

14 At Iconium the same thing happened. They went into the synagogue of the Jews and spoke in such a way that a great body both of Jews and Greeks believed.
3 Here they spent a considerable time, speaking fearlessly about the Lord, who attested the word of his grace by allow-
2 ing signs and wonders to be performed by them.* But the refractory Jews stirred up and exasperated the feeling of the
4 Gentiles against the brothers. The populace of the town was divided; some sided with the Jews, some with the apostles.
5 But, when the Gentiles and Jews along with their rulers
6 made a hostile movement to insult and stone them, the apostles grasped the situation and escaped to the Lycaonian towns of Lystra and Derbe and to the surrounding
7 country; there they continued to preach the gospel.
8 At Lystra there was a man sitting, who was powerless in his feet, a lame man unable to walk ever since he was
9 born. He heard Paul speaking, and Paul, gazing steadily at him and noticing that he had faith enough to make him
10 better, said in a loud voice, "Stand erect on your feet."
11 Up he jumped and began to walk. Now when the crowds saw what Paul had done, they shouted in the Lycaonian language, "The gods have come down to us in human
12 form!" Barnabas they called Zeus, and Paul Hermes,
13 since he was the chief spokesman. Indeed the priest of the temple of Zeus in front of the town brought oxen and garlands to the gates, intending to offer sacrifice along
14 with the crowds. But when the apostles, Paul and Barnabas, heard this they rent their clothes and sprang out
15 among the crowd, shouting, "Men, what is this you are doing? We are but human, with natures like your own! The gospel we are preaching to you is to turn from such futile ways to the living God *who made the heaven, the*
16 *earth, the sea, and all that in them is.* In bygone ages
17 he allowed all nations to go their own ways, though as the bountiful Giver he did not leave himself without a witness, giving you rain from heaven and fruitful seasons, giving
18 you food and joy to your heart's content." Even by saying this it was all they could do to keep the crowds from sacrificing to them.
19 But Jews from Antioch and Iconium arrived, who won over the crowds, and after pelting Paul with stones they dragged him outside the town, thinking he was dead.
20 However, as the disciples gathered round him, he got up and went into the town.
21 Next day he went off with Barnabas to Derbe, and after

* Restoring ver. 3 to what appears to have been its original position between vers. 1 and 2.

preaching the gospel to that town and making a number of disciples, they turned back to Lystra, Iconium and An-
22 tioch, strengthening the souls of the disciples, encouraging them to hold by the faith, and telling them that "we have to get into the Realm of God through many a trouble."
23 They chose presbyters for them in every church, and with prayer and fasting entrusted them to the Lord in whom
24 they had believed. Then they came through Pisidia to
25 Pamphylia, and after speaking the word of the Lord in
26 Perga they went down to Attaleia; thence they sailed for Antioch, where they had been commended to the grace of God for the work they had now completed. On their
27 arrival they gathered the church together and reported how God had been with them, what he had done, and how he had opened a door into faith for the Gentiles.
28 They spent a considerable time with the disciples there.
15 But certain individuals came down from Jerusalem and taught the brothers that "unless you get circumcised
2 after the custom of Moses you cannot be saved." As a sharp dispute and controversy sprang up between them and Paul and Barnabas, it was arranged that Paul and Barnabas, along with some others of their number, should go up to Jerusalem to see the apostles and presbyters at Jerusalem
3 about this question. The church sped them on their journey, and they passed through both Phœnicia and Syria informing the brothers, to the great joy of all, that the
4 Gentiles were turning to God. On arriving at Jerusalem they were received by the church, the apostles and the presbyters, and they reported how God had been with them
5 and what he had done. But some of the believers who belonged to the Pharisaic party got up and said, "Gentiles must be circumcised and told to observe the law of Moses."
6 The apostles and the presbyters met to investigate this
7 question, and a keen controversy sprang up; but Peter rose and said to them, "Brothers, you are well aware that from the earliest days God chose that of you all I should be the one by whom the Gentiles were to hear the word
8 of the gospel and believe it. The God who reads the hearts of all attested this by giving them the holy Spirit
9 just as he gave it to us; in cleansing their hearts by faith he made not the slightest distinction between us and them.
10 Well now, why are you trying * to impose a yoke on the neck of the disciples which neither our fathers nor we
11 ourselves could bear? No, it is by the grace of the Lord Jesus that we believe and are saved, in the same way as
12 they are." So the whole meeting was quieted and listened

* Omitting τὸν θεόν.

to Barnabas and Paul recounting the signs and wonders
13 God had performed by them among the Gentiles. When
they had finished speaking, James spoke. "Brothers," he
14 said, "listen to me. Symeon has explained how it was
God's original concern to secure a People from among the
15 Gentiles to bear his Name. This agrees with the words of
the prophets; as it is written,
16   *After this I will return and rebuild David's fallen tent,
      its ruins I will rebuild and erect it anew,*
17   *that the rest of men may seek for the Lord,
      even all the Gentiles who are called by my name,*
18
19 *saith the Lord, who makes this known from of old.* Hence,
in my opinion, we ought not to put fresh difficulties in the
way of those who are turning to God from among the
20 Gentiles, but write them injunctions to abstain from whatever is contaminated by idols, from sexual vice, from the
flesh of animals that have been strangled, and from tasting
21 blood; for Moses has had his preachers from the earliest
ages in every town, where he is read aloud in the syna-
22 gogues every sabbath." Then the apostles and the presbyters, together with the whole church, decided to select
some of their number and send them with Paul and Barnabas to Antioch. The men selected were Judas (called
Bar-Sabbas) and Silas, prominent members of the brother-
23 hood. They conveyed the following letter. "The apostles
and the presbyters of the brotherhood to the brothers who
belong to the Gentiles throughout Antioch and Syria and
24 Cilicia: greeting. Having learned that some of our
number,* quite unauthorized by us, have unsettled you
25 with their teaching and upset your souls, we have decided
unanimously to select some of our number and send them
26 to you along with our beloved Paul and Barnabas who
have risked their lives for the sake of our Lord Jesus
27 Christ. We therefore send Judas and Silas with the
following message, which they will also give to you orally.
28 The holy Spirit and we have decided not to impose any
extra burden on you, apart from these essential require-
29 ments: abstain from food that has been offered to idols,
from tasting blood, from the flesh of animals that have
been strangled, and from sexual vice. Keep clear of all
30 this and you will prosper. Goodbye." When the messengers were despatched, they went down to Antioch and
after gathering the whole body they handed them the
31 letter. On reading it the people rejoiced at the encourage-
32 ment it brought; and as Judas and Silas were themselves
prophets, they encouraged and strengthened the brothers

* Omitting ἐξελθόντες.

33 with many a counsel. Then after some time had passed the brothers let them go with a greeting of peace to those who
35 had sent them. Paul and Barnabas, however, stayed on in Antioch, teaching and preaching the word of the Lord along with a number of others.
36 Some days later, Paul said to Barnabas, "Come and let us go back to visit the brothers in every town where we have proclaimed the word of the Lord. Let us see how
37 they are doing." But while Barnabas wanted to take
38 John (who was called Mark) along with them, Paul held they should not take a man with them who had deserted them in Pamphylia, instead of accompanying them on
39 active service. So in irritation they parted company, Bar-
40 nabas taking Mark with him and sailing for Cyprus, while Paul selected Silas and went off, commended by the
41 brothers to the grace of the Lord. He made his way through Syria and Cilicia, strengthening the churches.

16 He also came down to Derbe and Lystra, where there was a disciple called Timotheus, the son of a believ-
2 ing Jewess and a Greek father. He had a good reputation
3 among the brothers at Lystra and Iconium; so, as Paul wished him to go abroad with him, he took and circumcised him on account of the local Jews, all of whom knew his
4 father had been a Greek. As they travelled on from town to town, they handed over to the people the resolutions which the apostles and the presbyters in Jerusalem had
5 decided were to be obeyed; and the churches were strengthened in the faith and increased in numbers day
6 by day. They crossed Phrygia and the country of Galatia, the holy Spirit having stopped them from preaching the
7 word in Asia; when they got as far as Mysia, they tried to enter Bithynia, but the Spirit of Jesus would not allow
8 them, and so they passed Mysia by and went down to
9 Troas. A vision appeared to Paul by night, the vision of a Macedonian standing and appealing to him with the
10 words, "Cross to Macedonia and help us." As soon as he saw the vision, we made efforts to start for Macedonia, inferring that God had called us to preach the gospel to
11 them. Setting sail then from Troas we ran straight to
12 Samothrace and on the following day to Neapolis. We then came to the Roman colony of Philippi, which is the foremost town of the district of Macedonia. In this town
13 we spent some days. On the sabbath we went outside the gate to the bank of the river, where as usual there was a place of prayer; we sat down and talked to the women who
14 had gathered. Among the listeners there was a woman called Lydia, a dealer in purple who belonged to the town of Thyatira. She reverenced God, and the Lord opened

15 her heart to attend to what Paul said. When she was baptized, along with her household, she begged us, saying, "If you are convinced I am a believer in the Lord, come and stay at my house." She compelled us to come.
16 Now it happened as we went to the place of prayer that a slave-girl met us, possessed by a spirit of ventriloquism, and a source of great profit to her owners by her power
17 of fortune-telling. She followed Paul and the rest of us, shrieking, "These men are servants of the Most High God,
18 they proclaim to you the way of salvation!" She did this for a number of days. Then Paul turned in annoyance and told the spirit, "In the name of Jesus Christ I order you
19 out of her!" And it left her that very moment. But when her owners saw their chance of profit was gone, they caught hold of Paul and Silas and dragged them before the mag-
20 istrates in the forum. Bringing them before the praetors they declared, "These fellows are Jews who are making
21 an agitation in our town; they are proclaiming customs which as Romans we are not allowed to accept or observe!"
22 The crowd also joined in the attack upon them, while the praetors, after having them stripped and after ordering
23 them to be flogged with rods, had many lashes inflicted on them and put them into prison, charging the jailer to
24 keep them safe. On receiving so strict a charge, he put them into the inner prison and secured their feet in the
25 stocks. But about midnight, as Paul and Silas were praying and singing to God, while the prisoners listened,
26 all of a sudden there was a great earthquake which shook the very foundations of the prison; the doors all flew open in an instant and the fetters of all the prisoners were un-
27 fastened. When the jailer started from his sleep and saw the prison-doors open, he drew his sword and was on the point of killing himself, supposing the prisoners had made
28 their escape; but Paul shouted aloud, "Do not harm yqur-
29 self, we are all here!" So calling for lights he rushed in,
30 fell in terror before Paul and Silas, and brought them out (after securing the other prisoners).* "Sirs," he said,
31 "what must I do to be saved?" "Believe in the Lord Jesus Christ," they said, "and then you will be saved, you and
32 your household as well." And they spoke the word of the
33 Lord to him and to all in his house. Then he took them at that very hour of the night and washed their wounds
34 and got baptized instantly, he and all his family. He took them up to his house and put food before them, overjoyed
35 like all his household at having believed in God. When

* Adding τοὺς λοιποὺς ἀσφαλισάμενος with D and the (Harklean) Syriac version.

day broke, the praetors sent the lictors with the message,
36 "Release these men." The jailer repeated this to Paul.
"The praetors," he said, "have sent to release you. So
37 come out and go in peace?" But Paul replied, "They flogged
us in public and without a trial, flogged Roman citizens!
They put us in prison, and now they are going to get rid
of us secretly! No indeed! Let them come here them-
38 selves and take us out!" The lictors reported this to the
praetors, who, on hearing the men were Roman citizens,
39 became alarmed; they went to appease them and after taking them out of prison begged them to leave the town.
40 So they left the prison and went to Lydia's house, where
they saw the brothers and encouraged them; then they
departed.

17 Travelling on through Amphipolis and Apollonia
they reached Thessalonica. Here there was a Jewish
2 synagogue, and Paul as usual went in; for three sabbaths
3 he argued with them on the scriptures, explaining and
quoting passages to prove that the messiah had to suffer
and rise from the dead, and that "the Jesus I proclaim to
4 you is the messiah." Some were persuaded and threw in
their lot with Paul and Silas, including a host of devout
5 Greeks and a large number of the leading women. But the
Jews were aroused to jealousy; they got hold of some idle
rascals to form a mob and set the town in an uproar; they
attacked Jason's house in the endeavour to bring them
6 out before the populace, but as they failed to find Paul
and Silas they haled Jason and some of the brothers before
the politarchs, yelling, "These upsetters of the whole world
7 have come here too! Jason has welcomed them! They
all violate the decrees of Caesar by declaring someone else
8 called Jesus is king." Both the crowd and the politarchs
9 were disturbed when they heard this; however, they let
Jason and the others go, after binding them over to keep
10 the peace. Then the brothers at once sent off Paul and
Silas by night to Berœa. When they arrived there, they
11 betook themselves to the Jewish synagogue, where the people were more amenable than at Thessalonica; they were
perfectly ready to receive the Word and made a daily
study of the scriptures to see if it was really as Paul said.
12 Many of them believed, together with a large number of
13 prominent Greeks, both women and men. But when the
Jews of Thessalonica heard that Paul was proclaiming the
word of God at Berœa as well, they came to create a dis-
14 turbance and a riot among the crowds at Berœa too. The
brothers then sent off Paul at once on his way to the sea,
while Silas and Timotheus remained where they were.
15 Paul's escort brought him as far as Athens and left with

THE ACTS XVII 205

instructions that Silas and Timotheus were to join him as soon as possible.
16 While Paul was waiting for them at Athens, his soul was irritated at the sight of the idols that filled the city.
17 He argued in the synagogue with the Jews and the devout proselytes and also in the marketplace daily with those
18 who chanced to be present. Some of the Epicurean and Stoic philosophers also came across him. Some said, "Whatever does the fellow mean with his scraps of learning?" Others said, "He looks like a herald of foreign deities" (this was because he preached 'Jesus' and 'the
19 Resurrection'). Then taking him to the Areopagus they asked, "May we know what is this novel teaching of yours?
20 You talk of some things that sound strange to us; so we
21 want to know what they mean." (For all the Athenians and the foreign visitors to Athens occupied themselves with nothing else than repeating or listening to the latest
22 novelty.) So Paul stood in the middle of the Areopagus and said, "Men of Athens, I observe at every turn that you
23 are a most religious people. Why, as I passed along and scanned your objects of worship, I actually came upon an altar with the inscription

TO AN UNKNOWN GOD.

Well, I proclaim to you what you worship in your ignorance.
24 *The God who made* the world *and* all *things in it*, he, as Lord *of heaven and earth*, does not dwell in shrines that
25 are made by human hands; he is not served by human hands as if he needed anything, for it is he who *gives* life
26 and *breath* and all things to all men. All nations he has created from a common origin, to dwell all over the earth, fixing their allotted periods and the boundaries of their
27 abodes, meaning them to seek for God on the chance of finding him in their groping for him. Though indeed he
28 is close to each one of us, for it is in him that we live and move and exist—as some of your own poets have said,
'We too belong to His race.'
29 Well, as the race of God, we ought not to imagine that the divine nature resembles gold or silver or stone, the product
30 of human art and invention. Such ages of ignorance God overlooked, but he now charges men that they are all
31 everywhere to repent, inasmuch as he has fixed a day on which *he will judge the world justly* by a man whom he has destined for this. And he has given proof of this to
32 all by raising him from the dead." But on hearing of a 'resurrection of dead men,' some sneered, while others said,
33 "We will hear you again on that subject." So Paul with-
34 drew from them. Some men, however, did join him and

believe, including Dionysius the Areopagite, a woman called Damaris, and some others.

18 After this Paul left Athens and went to Corinth.
2 There he came across a Jew called Aquila, a native of Pontus, who had recently arrived from Italy with his wife Priscilla, as Claudius had ordered all Jews to leave
3 Rome. Paul accosted them, and as he belonged to the same trade he stayed with them and they all worked
4 together. (They were workers in leather by trade.) Every sabbath he argued in the synagogue, persuading both Jews
5 and Greeks. By the time Silas and Timotheus came south from Macedonia, Paul was engrossed in this preaching of the word, arguing to the Jews that the messiah was Jesus.
6 But as they opposed and abused him, he shook out his garments in protest, saying, "Your blood be on your own heads! I am not responsible! After this I will go to the
7 Gentiles." Then he removed to the house of a devout proselyte called Titus Justus, which adjoined the syna-
8 gogue. But Crispus the president of the synagogue believed in the Lord, as did all his household, and many of the
9 Corinthians listened, believed, and were baptized. And the Lord said to Paul in a vision by night, *"Have no fear,* speak
10 on and never stop, *for I am with you,* and no one shall attack and injure you; I have many people in this city."
11 So he settled there for a year and six months, teaching them the word of God.
12 But when Gallio was proconsul of Achaia the Jews without exception rose against Paul and brought him up be-
13 fore the tribunal, crying, "This fellow incites men to
14 worship God contrary to the Law." Paul was just on the point of opening his lips to reply, when Gallio said to the Jews, "If it had been a misdemeanour or wicked crime, there would be some reason in me listening to you, O Jews
15 But as these are merely questions of words and persons and your own Law, you can attend to them for yourselves. I decline to adjudicate upon matters like that."
16
17 And he drove them from the tribunal. Then all [the Greeks] caught hold of Sosthenes the president of the synagogue and beat him in front of the tribunal; but Gallio took no notice.
18 After waiting on for a number of days Paul said goodbye to the brothers and sailed for Syria, accompanied by Priscilla and Aquila. (As the latter was under a vow,
19 he had his head shaved at Cenchreæ.) When they reached Ephesus, Paul left them there. He went to the synagogue
20 and argued with the Jews, who asked him to stay for a
21 while. But he would not consent; he said goodbye to them,

telling them, "I will come back to you, if it is the will of
22 God." Then, sailing from Ephesus, he reached Caesarea,
went up to the capital to salute the church, and travelled
23 down to Antioch. After spending some time there he went
off on a journey right through the country of Galatia and
Phrygia, strengthening the disciples.
24 There came to Ephesus a Jew called Apollos, who was
a native of Alexandria, a man of culture, strong in his
25 knowledge of the scriptures. He had been instructed in
the Way of the Lord and he preached and taught about
Jesus with ardour and accuracy, though all the baptism he
26 knew was that of John. In the synagogue he was very
outspoken at first; but when Aquila and Priscilla listened
to him, they took him home and explained more accurately
27 to him what the Way of God really meant. As he wished
to cross to Achaia, the brothers wrote and urged the disciples there to give him a welcome. And on his arrival he
proved of great service to those who by God's grace had
28 believed, for he publicly refuted the Jews with might and
main, showing from the scriptures that the messiah was
Jesus.

19 It was when Apollos was in Corinth that Paul, after
passing through the inland districts, came down to
2 Ephesus. There he found some disciples, whom he asked,
"Did you receive the holy Spirit when you believed?"
"No," they said, "we never even heard of its existence."
3 "Then," said he, "what were you baptized in?" "In John's
4 baptism," they replied. "John," said Paul, "baptized with
a baptism of repentance, telling the people to believe in
Him who was to come after him, that is, in Jesus."
5 When they heard this, they had themselves baptized in
6 the name of the Lord Jesus, and after Paul laid his hands
on them the holy Spirit came upon them, they spoke with
7 'tongues' and prophesied. They numbered all together
about twelve men.
8 Then Paul entered the synagogue and for three months
spoke out fearlessly, arguing and persuading people about
9 the Reign of God. But as some grew stubborn and disobedient, decrying the Way in presence of the multitude,
he left them, withdrew the disciples, and continued his
argument every day from eleven to four* in the lecture-
10 room of Tyrannus. This went on for two years, so that
all the inhabitants of Asia, Jews as well as Greeks, heard
the word of the Lord.
11 God also worked no ordinary miracles by means of Paul;

* The words ἀπὸ ὥρας πέμπτης ἕως δεκάτης (D, etc.) are probably original.

12 people even carried away towels or aprons he had used, and at their touch sick folk were freed from their diseases
13 and evil spirits came out of them. Some strolling Jewish exorcists also undertook to pronounce the name of the Lord Jesus over those who had evil spirits, saying, "I adjure
14 you by the Jesus whom Paul preaches!" The seven sons
15 of Sceuas, a Jewish high priest, used to do this. But the evil spirit retorted, "Jesus I know and Paul I know, but
16 you—who are you?" And the man in whom the evil spirit resided leapt at them, overpowered them all, and belaboured them, till they rushed out of the house stripped
17 and wounded. This came to the ears of all the inhabitants of Ephesus, Jews as well as Greeks; awe fell on them all,
18 and the name of the Lord Jesus was magnified. Many believers would also come to confess and disclose their magic
19 spells; and numbers who had practised magic arts collected their books and burned them in the presence of all. On adding up the value of them, it was found that they were worth two thousand pounds.
20   Thus did the word of the Lord increase and prevail mightily.
21   After these events Paul resolved in the Spirit to travel through Macedonia and Achaia on his way to Jerusalem. "After I get there," he said, "I must also visit Rome."
22 So he despatched two of his assistants to Macedonia, Timotheus and Erastus, while he himself stayed on awhile
23 in Asia. It was about that time that a great commotion
24 arose over the Way. This was how it happened. By making silver shrines of Artemis a silversmith called Demetrius
25 was the means of bringing rich profit to his workmen. So he got them together, along with the workmen who belonged to similar trades, and said to them: "My men, you
26 know this trade is the source of our wealth. You also see and hear that not only at Ephesus but almost all over Asia this fellow Paul has drawn off a considerable number of people by his persuasions. He declares that hand-made
27 gods are not gods at all. Now the danger is not only that we will have our trade discredited but that the temple of the great goddess Artemis will fall into contempt and that she will be degraded from her majestic glory, she
28 whom all Asia and the wide world worship." When they heard this they were filled with rage and raised the cry,
29 "Great is Artemis of Ephesus!" So the city was filled with confusion. They rushed like one man into the amphitheatre, dragging along Gaius and Aristarchus, Macedo-
30 nians who were travelling with Paul. (Paul wanted to enter the popular assembly, but the disciples would not allow
31 him. Some of the Asiarchs, who were friends of his, also

sent to beg him not to venture into the amphitheatre.)
32 Some were shouting one thing, some another; for the assembly was in confusion, and the majority had no idea
33 why they had met. Some of the mob concluded it must be Alexander, as the Jews pushed him to the front. So Alexander, motioning with his hand, wanted to defend himself
34 before the people; but when they discovered he was a Jew, a roar broke from them all, and for about two hours they shouted, "Great is Artemis of Ephesus! Great is Artemis
35 of Ephesus!" The secretary of state then got the mob calmed down, and said to them, "Men of Ephesus, who on earth does not know that the city of Ephesus is Warden of the temple of the great Artemis and of the statue that
36 fell from heaven? All this is beyond question. So you
37 should keep calm and do nothing reckless. Instead of that, you have brought these men here who are guilty neither of
38 sacrilege nor of blasphemy against our goddess. If Demetrius and his fellow tradesmen have a grievance against anybody, let both parties state their charges; assizes are
39 held and there are always the proconsuls. Any wider claim must be settled in the legal assembly of the citizens.
40 Indeed there is a danger of our being charged with riot over to-day's meeting; there is not a single reason we can
41 give for this disorderly gathering." With these words he dismissed the assembly.

20 WHEN the tumult had ceased, Paul sent for the disciples and encouraged them; he then took leave of
2 them and went his way to Macedonia. After passing through the districts of Macedonia and encouraging the
3 people at length, he came to Greece, where he spent three months. Just as he was on the point of sailing for Syria, the Jews laid a plot against him. He therefore resolved to
4 return through Macedonia. His company as far as Asia consisted of Sopater of Berœa (the son of Pyrrhus), Aristarchus and Secundus from Thessalonica, Gaius of Derbe, Timotheus, and Tychicus and Trophimus from Asia.
5 They went on to wait for us at Troas, while we sailed
6 from Philippi, after the days of unleavened bread, and joined them five days later at Troas. There we spent
7 seven days. On the first day of the week we met for the breaking of bread; Paul addressed them, as he was to leave
8 next day, and he prolonged his address till midnight (there were plenty of lamps in the upper room where we met).
9 In the window sat a young man called Eutychus, and as Paul's address went on and on, he got overcome with drowsiness, went fast asleep, and fell from the third
10 storey. He was picked up a corpse, but Paul went down-

stairs, threw himself upon him, and embraced him. "Do
11 not lament," he said, "the life is still in him." Then he
went upstairs, broke bread, and ate; finally, after convers-
12 ing awhile with them till the dawn, he went away. As for
the lad, they took him away alive, much to their relief.
13 Now we had gone on beforehand to the ship and set sail
for Assos, intending to take Paul on board there. This was
his own arrangement, for he intended to travel by land.
14 So when he met us at Assos, we took him on board and
15 got to Mitylene. Sailing thence on the following day we
arrived off Chios; next day we crossed over to Samos, and
[after stopping at Trogyllium] we went on next day to
16 Miletus. This was because Paul had decided to sail past
Ephesus, to avoid any loss of time in Asia; he wanted to
reach Jerusalem, if possible, by the day of Pentecost.
17 From Miletus he sent to Ephesus for the presbyters of
18 the church. When they came to him, he said, "You know
quite well how I lived among you all the time ever since
19 I set foot in Asia, how I served the Lord in all humility,
with many a tear and many a trial which I encountered
20 owing to the plots of the Jews, how I never shrank from
letting you know anything for your good, or from teaching
21 you alike in public and from house to house, bearing my
testimony, both to Jews and Greeks, of repentance before
22 God and faith in our Lord Jesus Christ. Now here I go to
Jerusalem under the binding force of the Spirit. What
23 will befall me there, I do not know. Only, I know this, that
in town after town the holy Spirit testifies to me that
24 bonds and troubles are awaiting me. But then, I set no
value on my own life as compared with the joy of finishing my course and fulfilling the commission I received
from the Lord Jesus to attest the gospel of the grace of
25 God. I know to-day that not one of you will ever see my
face again—not one of you among whom I moved as I
26 preached the Reign. Therefore do I protest before you
this day that I am not responsible for the blood of any
27 of you; I never shrank from letting you know the entire
28 purpose of God. Take heed to yourselves and to all the
flock of which the holy Spirit has appointed you guardians;
shepherd *the church of the Lord* which *he has purchased*
29 *with his own blood.* I know that when I am gone, fierce
wolves will get in among you, and they will not spare the
30 flock; yes, and men of your own number will arise with
perversions of the truth to draw the disciples after them.
31 So be on the alert, remember how for three whole years
I never ceased night and day to watch over each one of
32 you with tears. And now I entrust you to God and the
word of his grace; he is able to upbuild you and give you

33 your *inheritance* among *all the consecrated.* Silver, gold,
34 or apparel I never coveted; you know yourselves how these
   hands of mine provided everything for my own needs and
35 for my companions. I showed you how this was the way
   to work hard and succour the needy, remembering the
   words of the Lord Jesus, who said, 'To give is happier than
36 to get.'" With these words he knelt down and prayed be-
37 side them all. They all broke into loud lamentation and
38 falling upon the neck of Paul kissed him fondly, sorrowing
   chiefly because he told them they would never see his face
   again. Then they escorted him to the ship.

21 WHEN we had torn ourselves away from them and
   set sail, we made a straight run to Cos, next day to
2 Rhodes, and thence to Patara; as we found a ship there
3 bound for Phœnicia, we went on board and set sail. After
   sighting Cyprus and leaving it on our left, we sailed for
   Syria, landing at Tyre, where the ship was to unload her
4 cargo. We found out the local disciples and stayed there
   for seven days. These disciples told Paul by the Spirit
5 not to set foot in Jerusalem; but, when our time was up,
   we started on our journey, escorted by them, women and
   children and all, till we got outside the town. Then,
6 kneeling on the beach, we prayed and said goodbye to one
7 another. We went on board and they went home. By
   sailing from Tyre to Ptolemais we completed our voyage;
8 we saluted the brothers, spent a day with them, and started
   next morning for Caesarea, where we entered the house of
9 Philip the evangelist (he belonged to the Seven, and had
   four unmarried daughters who prophesied). We stayed
10 with him. While we remained there for a number of days,
11 a prophet called Agabus came down from Judaea. He
   came to us, took Paul's girdle and bound his own feet and
   hands, saying, "Here is the word of the holy Spirit: 'So
   shall the Jews bind the owner of this girdle at Jerusalem
12 and hand him over to the Gentiles'." Now when we heard
   this, we and the local disciples besought Paul not to go up
13 to Jerusalem. Then Paul replied, "What do you mean by
   weeping and disheartening me? I am ready not only to
   be bound but also to die at Jerusalem for the sake of the
14 Lord Jesus." As he would not be persuaded, we ac-
   quiesced, saying, "The will of the Lord be done."
15 After these days we packed up and started for Jerusalem,
16 accompanied by some of the disciples from Caesarea, who
   conducted us to the house of Mnason, a Cypriote, with
   whom we were to lodge. He was a disciple of old standing.
17 The brothers welcomed us gladly on our arrival at Jeru-
18 salem. Next day we accompanied Paul to James; all the

19 presbyters were present, and after saluting them Paul described in detail what God had done by means of his
20 ministry among the Gentiles. They glorified God when they heard it. Then they said to him, "Brother, you see how many thousands of believers there are among the
21 Jews, all of them ardent upholders of the law. Now, they have heard that you teach all Jews who live among Gentiles to break away from Moses and not to circumcise their
22 children, nor to follow the old customs. What is to be done? They will be sure to hear you have arrived.* So do as we
23
24 tell you. We have four men here under a vow; associate yourself with them, purify yourself with them, pay their expenses so that they may be free to have their heads shaved, and then everybody will understand there is nothing in these stories about you, but that, on the contrary,
25 you are guided by obedience to the Law. As for Gentile believers, we have issued our decision that they must avoid food that has been offered to idols, the taste of blood, flesh of animals that have been strangled, and sexual vice."
26 Then Paul associated himself with the men next day; he had himself purified along with them and went into the temple to give notice of the time when *the days of purification* would be completed—the time, that is to say, when the sacrifice could be offered for each one of them.
27 The seven days were almost over when the Asiatic Jews, catching sight of him in the temple, stirred up all the crowd
28 and laid hands on him, shouting, "To the rescue, men of Israel! Here is the man who teaches everyone everywhere against the People and the Law and this Place! And he has actually brought Greeks inside the temple and defiled
29 this holy Place!" (They had previously seen Trophimus the Ephesian along with him in the city, and they sup-
30 posed Paul had taken him inside the temple.) The whole city was thrown into turmoil. The people rushed together, seized Paul and dragged him outside the temple; where-
31 upon the doors were immediately shut. They were attempting to kill him, when word reached the commander of the garrison that the whole of Jerusalem was in confusion.
32 Taking some soldiers and officers, he at once rushed down to them, and when they saw the commander and the
33 soldiers they stopped beating Paul. Then the commander came up and seized him; he ordered him to be bound with a couple of chains, and asked "Who is he?" and "What has
34 he done?" Some of the crowd roared one thing, some another, and as he could not learn the facts owing to the
35 uproar, he ordered Paul to be taken to the barracks. By

* Omitting [δεῖ πλῆθος συνελθεῖν] and [γάρ].

the time he reached the steps, he had actually to be carried by the soldiers on account of the violence of the crowd,
36 for the whole mass of the people followed shouting, "Away
37 with him!" Just as he was being taken into the barracks, Paul said to the commander, "May I say a word to you?"
38 "You know Greek!" said the commander. "Then you are not the Egyptian who in days gone by raised the four thou-
39 sand assassins and led them out into the desert?" Paul said, "I am a Jew, a native of Tarsus in Cilicia, the citizen
40 of a famous town. Pray let me speak to the people." As he gave permission, Paul stood on the steps and motioned to the people. A great hush came over them, and he addressed them as follows in Hebrew.

22 "BROTHERS and fathers, listen to the defence I now
2 make before you." When they heard him addressing them in Hebrew they were all the more quiet. So he went
3 on. "I am a Jew, born at Tarsus in Cilicia, but brought up in this city, educated at the feet of Gamaliel in all the strictness of our ancestral Law, ardent for God as you all
4 are to-day. I persecuted this Way of religion to the death,
5 chaining and imprisoning both men and women, as the high priest and all the council of elders can testify. It was from them that I got letters to the brotherhood at Damascus and then journeyed thither to bind those who had gathered there and bring them back to Jerusalem for
6 punishment. Now as I neared Damascus on my journey, suddenly about noon a brilliant light from heaven flashed
7 round me. I dropped to the earth and heard a voice saying
8 to me, 'Saul, Saul, why do you persecute me?' 'Who are you?' I asked. He said to me, 'I am Jesus the Nazarene,
9 and you are persecuting me.' (My companions saw the light, but they did not hear the voice of him who talked
10 to me.) I said, 'What am I to do?' And the Lord said to me, 'Get up and make your way into Damascus; there
11 you shall be told about all you are destined to do.' As I could not see owing to the dazzling glare of that light, my companions took my hand and so I reached Damascus.
12 Then a certain Ananias, a devout man in the Law, who had
13 a good reputation among all the Jewish inhabitants, came to me and standing beside me said, 'Saul, my brother, regain your sight!' The same moment I regained my sight
14 and looked up at him. Then he said, 'The God of our fathers has appointed you to know his will, to see the Just
15 One, and to hear him speak with his own lips. For you are to be a witness for him before all men, a witness of
16 what you have seen and heard. And now, why do you wait?

Get up and be baptized and wash away your sins, invoking his name.'
17 When I returned to Jerusalem, it happened that while I
18 was praying in the temple I fell into a trance and saw Him saying to me, 'Make haste, leave Jerusalem quickly,
19 for they will not accept your evidence about me.' 'But, Lord,' I said, 'they surely know it was I who imprisoned and flogged those who believed in you throughout the syna-
20 gogues, and that I stood and approved when the blood of your martyr Stephen was being shed, taking charge of
21 the clothes of his murderers!' But he said to me, 'Go;
22 I will send you afar to the Gentiles——'" Till he said that, they had listened to him. But at that they shouted, "Away with such a creature from the earth! He is not fit to live!"
23 They yelled and threw their clothes into the air and flung
24 dust about, till the commander ordered him to be taken inside the barracks and examined under the lash, so as to find out why the people shouted at him in this way.
25 They had strapped him up, when Paul said to the officer who was standing by, "Are you allowed to scourge a Roman
26 citizen—and to scourge him without a trial?" When the officer heard this, he went to the commander and said to him, "What are you going to do? This man is a Roman
27 citizen." So the commander went to him and said, "Tell
28 me, are you a Roman citizen?" "Yes," he said. The commander replied, "I had to pay a large sum for this
29 citizenship." "But I was born a citizen," said Paul. Then those who were to have examined him left him at once alone; even the commander was alarmed to find that Paul was a Roman citizen and that he had bound him.
30 Next day, as he was anxious to find out the real reason why the Jews accused him, he unbound him, ordered the high priests and all the Sanhedrin to meet, and brought

23 Paul down, placing him in front of them. With a steady look at the Sanhedrin Paul said, "Brothers, I have lived with a perfectly good conscience before God
2 down to the present day." Then the high priest Ananias ordered those who were standing next Paul to strike him
3 on the mouth. At this Paul said to him, "You white-washed wall, God will strike you! You sit there to judge me by the Law, do you? And you break the Law by
4 ordering me to be struck!" The bystanders said, "What!
5 would you rail at God's high priest?" "Brothers," said Paul, "I did not know he was high priest" (for it is written, *You must not speak evil of any ruler of your people*).
6 Then, finding half the Sanhedrin were Sadducees and the other half Pharisees, Paul shouted to them, "I am a Pharisee, brothers, the son of Pharisees! It is for the hope of

7 the resurrection from the dead that I am on trial!" When
he said this, a quarrel broke out between the Pharisees and
8 the Sadducees; the meeting was divided. For while the
Sadducees declare there is no such thing as resurrection,
9 angels, or spirits, the Pharisees affirm them all. Thus a
loud clamour broke out. Some of the scribes who belonged
to the Pharisaic party got up and contended, "We find
nothing wrong about this man. What if some spirit or
10 angel has spoken to him?" The quarrel then became so
violent that the commander was afraid they would tear
Paul in pieces; he therefore ordered the troops to march
down and take him from them by force, bringing him
11 inside the barracks. On the following night the Lord stood
by Paul and said, "Courage! As you have testified to me
at Jerusalem, so you must testify at Rome."
12 When day broke, the Jews formed a conspiracy, taking
a solemn oath neither to eat nor to drink till they had
13 killed Paul. There were more than forty of them in this
14 plot. They then went to the high priests and elders, saying, "We have taken a solemn oath to taste no food till we
15 have killed Paul. Now you and the Sanhedrin must inform the commander that you propose to investigate this
case in detail, so that he may have Paul brought down to
you. We will be all ready to kill him on the way down."
16 Now Paul's nephew heard about their treacherous ambush;
17 so he got admission to the barracks and told Paul. Paul
summoned one of the officers and said, "Take this young
man to the commander, for he has some news to give him."
18 So the officer took him to the commander, saying, "The
prisoner Paul has summoned me to ask if I would bring
this young man to you, as he has something to tell you."
19 The commander then took him by the hand aside and asked
20 him in private, "What is the news you have for me?" He
answered, "The Jews have agreed to ask you to bring Paul
down to-morrow to the Sanhedrin, on the plea that they*
21 propose to examine his case in detail. Now do not let them
persuade you. More than forty of them are lying in ambush for him, and they have taken a solemn oath neither
to eat nor to drink till they have murdered him. They are
22 all ready at this moment, awaiting your consent." Then
the commander dismissed the youth, bidding him "Tell
23 nobody that you have informed me of this." He summoned
two of the officers and said, "Get ready by nine o'clock tonight two hundred infantry to march as far as Caesarea,
24 also seventy troopers, and two hundred spearmen." Horses

* Reading either μέλλοντες with the Latin, Syriac, Sahidic, and
Ethiopic versions, or μελλόντων (אc, Chrysostom, and some minuscules).

were also to be provided, on which they were to mount
25 Paul and carry him safe to Felix the governor. He then
26 wrote a letter in the following terms. "Claudius Lysias,
27 to his excellency the governor Felix: greeting. This man
had been seized by the Jews and was on the point of being
murdered by them, when I came on them with the troops
and rescued him, as I had ascertained that he was a Roman
28 citizen. Anxious to find out why they accused him, I took
29 him down to their Sanhedrin, where I found he was accused
of matters relating to their Law but not impeached for
30 any crime that deserved death or imprisonment. I am
informed a plot is to be laid against him, so I am sending
him to you at once,* telling his accusers that they must
31 impeach him before you. Farewell." The soldiers, according to their instructions, took Paul and brought him by
32 night to Antipatris. Next day the infantry returned to
33 their barracks, leaving the troopers to ride on with him.
They reached Caesarea, presented the letter to the governor,
34 and also handed Paul over to him. On reading the
letter he asked what province he belonged to, and finding
35 it was Cilicia he said, "I will go into your case whenever
your accusers arrive," giving orders that he was to be
kept in the praetorium of Herod.

24 Five days later down came the high priest Ananias
with some elders and a barrister called Tertullus.
They laid information before the governor against Paul.
2 So Paul was summoned, and then Tertullus proceeded to
accuse him. "Your excellency," he said to Felix, "as it is
owing to you that we enjoy unbroken peace, and as it is
owing to your wise care that the state of this nation has
3 been improved in every way and everywhere, we acknowl-
4 edge all this with profound gratitude. I have no wish
to weary you, but I beg of you to grant us in your courtesy
5 a brief hearing. The fact is, we have found this man is a
perfect pest; he stirs up sedition among the Jews all over
the world and he is a ringleader of the Nazarene sect.
6 He actually tried to desecrate the temple, but we got hold
8 of him. Examine him for yourself and you will be able
to find out about all these charges of ours against him."
9 The Jews joined in the attack, declaring that such were
10 the facts of the case. Then at a nod from the governor
Paul made his reply. "As I know you have administered
justice in this nation for a number of years," he said, "I
11 feel encouraged to make my defence, because it is not more
than twelve days, as you can easily ascertain, since I went

* Reading ἐξαυτῆς instead of ἐξ αὐτῶν.

12 up to worship at Jerusalem. They never found me arguing
with anyone in the temple or causing a riot either in the
13 synagogues or in the city; they cannot furnish you with
14 any proof of their present charges against me. I certainly
admit to you that I worship our fathers' God according to
the methods of what they call a 'sect'; but I believe all
15 that is written in the Law and in the prophets, and I
cherish the same hope in God as they accept, namely that
there is to be a resurrection of the just and the unjust.
16 Hence I too endeavour to have a clear conscience before
17 God and men all the time. After a lapse of several years
18 I came up with alms and offerings for my nation,* and it
was in presenting these that I was found within the temple.
I was ceremonially pure, I was not mixed up in any mob
or riot; no, the trouble was caused by some Jews from
19 Asia, who ought to have been here before you with any
20 charge they may have against me. Failing them, let these
men yonder tell what fault they found with my appear-
21 ance before the Sanhedrin!—unless it was with the single
sentence I uttered, when I stood and said, 'It is for the
resurrection of the dead that I am on my trial to-day
·22 before you.'" As Felix had a pretty accurate knowledge
of the Way, he remanded Paul, telling the Jews, "When
Lysias the commander comes down, I will decide your
23 case." He gave orders to the officer to have Paul kept in
custody but to allow him some freedom and not to prevent
any of his own people from rendering him any service.
24 Some days later Felix arrived with his wife Drusilla,
who was a Jewess. He sent for Paul and heard what he
25 had to say about faith in Christ Jesus; but when he argued
about morality, self-mastery, and the future judgment,
Felix grew uneasy. "You may go for the present," he
said; "when I can find a moment, I will send for you"
26 (though at the same time he hoped Paul would give him
a bribe). So he did send for him pretty frequently
27 and conversed with him. But when two years had
elapsed, Felix was succeeded by Porcius Festus, and as
Felix wanted to ingratiate himself with the Jews, he
left Paul still in custody.

25 Three days after Festus entered his province, he went
2   up from Caesarea to Jerusalem. The high priests and
the Jewish leaders laid information before him against

---

* It is hardly possible to make sense of the following Greek text, and none of the various readings or of the emendations that have been proposed is entirely satisfactory. All one can do is to reproduce the general drift of the passage.

3 Paul, and begged him, as a special favour, to send for him
to Jerusalem, meaning to lay an ambush for him and
4 murder him on the road. Festus replied that Paul would
be kept in custody at Caesarea, but that he himself meant
5 to leave for Caesarea before long—"when," he added, "your
competent authorities can come down with me and charge
6 the man with whatever crime he has committed." After
staying not more than eight or ten days with them, he
went down to Caesarea. Next day he took his seat on the
7 tribunal and ordered Paul to be brought before him. When
he arrived, the Jews who had come down from Jerusalem
surrounded him and brought a number of serious charges
8 against him, none of which they were able to prove. Paul's
defence was, "I have committed no offence against the Law
9 of the Jews, against the temple, or against Caesar." As
Festus wanted to ingratiate himself with the Jews, he
asked Paul, "Will you go up to Jerusalem and be tried
10 there by me upon these charges?" Paul said, "I am
standing before Caesar's tribunal; that is where I ought to
be tried. I have done no wrong whatever to the Jews—
11 you know that perfectly well. If I am a criminal, if I have
done anything that deserves death, I do not object to die;
but if there is nothing in any of their charges against me,
then no one can give me up to them. I appeal to Caesar!"
12 Then, after conferring with the council, Festus answered,
"You have appealed to Caesar? Very well, you must go to
Caesar!"

13 Some days had passed, when king Agrippa and Bernice
14 came to Caesarea to pay their respects to Festus. As they
were spending several days there, Festus laid Paul's case
before the king. "There is a man," he said, "who was
15 left in prison by Felix. When I was at Jerusalem, the
high priests and elders of the Jews informed me about
16 him and demanded his condemnation. I told them Romans
were not in the habit of giving up any man until the
accused met the accusers face to face and had a chance of
17 defending himself against the impeachment. Well, the day
after they came here along with me, I took my seat on the
tribunal without any loss of time. I ordered the man to
18 be brought in, but when his accusers stood up they did
not charge him with any of the crimes that I had expected.
19 The questions at issue referred to their own religion and to
20 a certain Jesus who had died. Paul said he was alive. As
I felt at a loss about the method of inquiry into such topics,
I asked if he would go to Jerusalem and be tried there on
21 these charges. But Paul entered an appeal for his case
to be reserved for the decision of the emperor; so I ordered
him to be detained till I could remit him to Caesar."

22 "I should like to hear the man myself," said Agrippa to Festus. "You shall hear him to-morrow," said Festus.
23 So next day Agrippa and Bernice proceeded with great pomp to the hall of audience, accompanied by the military commanders and the prominent civilians of the town.
24 Festus then ordered Paul to be brought in. "King Agrippa and all here present," said Festus, "you see before you a man of whom the entire body of the Jews at Jerusalem and also here have complained to me. They loudly insist
25 he ought not to live any longer. I could not find he had done anything that deserved death, so I decided to send
26 him, on his own appeal, to the emperor. Only, I have nothing definite to write to the sovereign about him. So I have brought him up before you all, and especially before you, O king Agrippa, in order that I may have something
27 to write as the result of your cross-examination. For it seems absurd to me to forward a prisoner without notifying the particulars of his charge." Then Agrippa

26 said to Paul, "You have our permission to speak upon your own behalf." At this Paul stretched out his hand
2 and began his defence. "I consider myself fortunate, king Agrippa, in being able to defend myself to-day before you
3 against all that the Jews charge me with; for you are well acquainted with all Jewish customs and questions. Pray
4 listen to me then with patience. How I lived from my youth up among my own nation and at Jerusalem, all that
5 early career of mine, is known to all the Jews. They know me of old. They know, if they chose to admit it, that as a Pharisee I lived by the principles of the strictest party in
6 our religion. To-day I am standing my trial for hoping
7 in the promise made by God to our fathers, a promise which our twelve tribes hope to gain by serving God earnestly both night and day. And I am actually impeached by
9 Jews for this hope, O king! I once believed it my duty in-
10 deed actively to oppose the name of Jesus the Nazarene. I did so in Jerusalem. I shut up many of the saints in prison, armed with authority from the high priests; when they
11 were put to death, I voted against them; there was not a synagogue where I did not often punish them and force them to blaspheme; and in my frantic fury I persecuted
12 them even to foreign towns. I was travelling to Damascus on this business, with authority and a commission from
13 the high priests, when at mid-day on the road, O king, I saw a light from heaven, more dazzling than the sun,
14 flash round me and my fellow-travellers. We all fell to the ground, and I heard a voice saying to me in Hebrew, 'Saul, Saul, why do you persecute me? You hurt yourself by
15 kicking at the goad.' 'Who are you?' I asked. And the

16 Lord said, 'I am Jesus, and you are persecuting me. Now get up and *stand on your feet,* for I have appeared to you in order to appoint you to my service as a witness to what you have seen and to the visions you shall have of me.
17 *I will rescue you* from the People and also *from the*
18 *Gentiles—to whom I send you, that* their *eyes may be opened* and that they may turn *from darkness to light,* from the power of Satan to God, to get remission of their sins and an inheritance among those who are consecrated
19 by faith in me.' Upon this, O king Agrippa, I did not dis-
20 obey the heavenly vision; I announced to those at Damascus and at Jerusalem in the first instance, then all over the land of Judaea, and also to the Gentiles, that they were to repent and turn to God by acting up to their repentance.
21 This is why the Jews seized me in the temple and tried to
22 assassinate me. To this day I have had the help of God in standing, as I now do, to testify alike to low and high, never uttering a single syllable beyond what the prophets
8 and Moses predicted was to take place. Why should you
23 consider it incredible that God raises the dead,* that the Christ is capable of suffering, and that he should be the first to rise from the dead and bring the message of light
24 to the People and to the Gentiles?" When he brought this forward in his defence, Festus called out, "Paul, you are quite mad! Your great learning is driving you insane."
25 "Your excellency," said Paul to Festus, "I am not mad, I
26 am speaking the sober truth. Why, the king is well aware of this! To the king I can speak without the slightest hesitation. I do not believe any of it has escaped his
27 notice, for this was not done in a corner. King Agrippa, you
28 believe the prophets? I know you do." "At this rate," Agrippa remarked, "it won't be long before you believe you
29 have made a Christian of me!" "Long or short," said Paul, "I would to God that not only you but all my hearers
30 to-day could be what I am—barring these chains! Then the king rose, with the governor and Bernice and those who had
31 been seated beside them. They retired to discuss the affair, and agreed that "this man has done nothing to deserve
32 death or imprisonment." "He might have been released," said Agrippa to Festus, "if he had not appealed to Caesar."

27 WHEN it was decided we were to sail for Italy, Paul and some other prisoners were handed over to an
2 officer of the Imperial regiment called Julius. Embarking in an Andramyttian ship which was bound for the Asiatic seaports, we set sail, accompanied by a Macedonian from

* Restoring ver. 8 to its original position at the beginning of ver. 23.

THE ACTS XXVII 221

3 Thessalonica called Aristarchus. Next day we put in at
Sidon, where Julius very kindly allowed Paul to visit his
4 friends and be looked after. Putting to sea from there,
we had to sail under the lee of Cyprus, as the wind was
5 against us; then, sailing over the Cilician and Pamphylian
6 waters, we came to Myra in Lycia. There the officer found
an Alexandrian ship bound for Italy, and put us on board
7 of her. For a number of days we made a slow passage
and had great difficulty in arriving off Cnidus; then, as the
wind checked our progress, we sailed under the lee of
8 Crete off Cape Salmonê, and coasting along it with great
difficulty we reached a place called Fair Havens, not far
9 from the town of Lasea. By this time it was far on in
the season and sailing had become dangerous (for the
10 autumn Fast was past), so Paul warned them thus: "Men,"
said he, "I see this voyage is going to be attended with
hardship and serious loss not only to the cargo and the
11 ship but also to our own lives." However the officer let
himself be persuaded by the captain and the owner rather
12 than by anything Paul could say, and, as the harbour was
badly placed for wintering in, the majority proposed to
set sail and try if they could reach Phœnix and winter
there (Phœnix is a Cretan harbour facing S.W. and N.W.).
13 When a moderate southerly breeze sprang up, they thought
they had secured their object, and after weighing anchor
they sailed along the coast of Crete, close inshore.
14 Presently down rushed a hurricane of a wind called Euro-
15 clydon; the ship was caught and unable to face the wind,
16 so we gave up and let her drive along. Running under
the lee of a small island called Clauda, we managed with
17 great difficulty to get the boat hauled in; once it was
hoisted aboard, they used ropes* to undergird the ship, and
in fear of being stranded on the Syrtis they lowered
18 the sail and lay to. As we were being terribly battered by
19 the storm, they had to jettison the cargo next day, while
two days later they threw the ship's gear overboard with
20 their own hands; for many days neither sun nor stars
could be seen, the storm raged heavily, and at last we
21 had to give up all hope of being saved. When they had
gone without food for a long time, Paul stood up among
them and said, "Men, you should have listened to me and
spared yourselves this hardship and loss by refusing to set
22 sail from Crete. I now bid you cheer up. There will be
23 no loss of life, only of the ship. For last night an angel of
24 the God I belong to and serve, stood before me, saying,
'Have no fear, Paul; you must stand before Caesar. And

* Naber's conjecture βοείαις for the βοηθείαις of the MSS. yields this
excellent sense.

God has granted you the lives of all your fellow-voyagers.'
25 Cheer up, men! I believe God, I believe it will turn out
26 just as I have been told. However, we are to be stranded
on an island."
27 When the fourteenth night arrived, we were drifting
about in the sea of Adria, when the sailors about midnight
28 suspected land was near. On taking soundings they found
twenty fathoms, and a little further on, when they sounded
29 again, they found fifteen. Then, afraid of being stranded
on the rocks, they let go four anchors from the stern and
30 longed for daylight. The sailors tried to escape from the
ship. They had even lowered the boat into the sea, pretending they were going to lay out anchors from the bow,
31 when Paul said to the officer and the soldiers, "You cannot
32 be saved unless these men stay by the ship." Then the
soldiers cut away the ropes of the boat and let her fall
33 off. Just before daybreak Paul begged them all to take
some food. "For fourteen days," he said, "you have been
34 on the watch all the time, without a proper meal. Take
some food then, I beg of you; it will keep you alive. You
are going to be saved! Not a hair of your heads will
35 perish." With these words he took a loaf and after thanking God, in presence of them all, broke it and began to eat.
36 Then they all cheered up and took food for themselves
37 (there were about* seventy-six souls of us on board, all
38 told); and when they had eaten their fill, they lightened
39 the ship by throwing the wheat into the sea. When day
broke, they could not recognize what land it was; however,
they noticed a creek with a sandy beach, and resolved to
40 see if they could run the ship ashore there. So the anchors
were cut away and left in the sea, while the crew unlashed
the ropes that tied the rudders, hoisted the foresail to
41 the breeze, and headed for the beach. Striking a reef,
they drove the ship aground; the prow jammed fast, but
the stern began to break up under the beating of the waves.
42 Now the soldiers resolved to kill the prisoners, in case
43 any of them swam off and escaped; but as the officer
wanted to save Paul, he put a stop to their plan, ordering
those who could swim to jump overboard first and get to
44 land, while the rest were to manage with planks or pieces
of wreckage. In this way it turned out that the whole
company got safe to land.

28 It was only after our escape that we found out the
2 island was called Malta. The natives showed us uncommon kindness, for they lit a fire and welcomed us all

---
* Reading ὡς (B and Sahidic version) for διακόσιαι.

3 to it, as the rain had come on and it was chilly. Now
Paul had gathered a bundle of sticks and laid them on the
fire, when a viper crawled out with the heat and fastened
4 on his hand. When the natives saw the creature hanging
from his hand, they said to each other, "This man must
be a murderer! He has escaped the sea, but Justice will
5 not let him live." However, he shook off the creature into
6 the fire and was not a whit the worse. The natives waited
for him to swell up or drop down dead in a moment, but
after waiting a long while and observing that no harm had
befallen him, they changed their minds and declared he
was a god.
7 There was an estate in the neighbourhood which
belonged to a man called Publius, the governor of the
island; he welcomed us and entertained us hospitably for
8 three days. His father, it so happened, was laid up with
fever and dysentery, but Paul went in to see him and after
9 prayer laid his hands on him and cured him. When this
had happened, the rest of the sick folk in the island also
10 came and got cured; they made us rich presents and furnished us, when we set sail, with all we needed.
11 We set sail, after three months, in an Alexandrian ship,
with the Dioscuri on her figure-head, which had wintered at
12 the island. We put in at Syracuse and stayed for three
13 days. Then tacking round we reached Rhegium; next day
a south wind sprang up which brought us in a day to
14 Puteoli, where we came across some of the brotherhood,
who invited us to stay a week with them.
15 In this way we reached Rome. As the local brothers had
heard about us, they came out to meet us as far as Appii
Forum and Tres Tabernae, and when Paul saw them he
16 thanked God and took courage. When we did reach Rome,
Paul got permission* to live by himself, with a soldier to
17 guard him. Three days later, he called the leading Jews
together, and when they met he said to them, "Brothers,
although I have done nothing against the People or our
ancestral customs, I was handed over to the Romans as
18 a prisoner from Jerusalem. They meant to release me
after examination, as I was innocent of any crime that
19 deserved death. But the Jews objected, and so I was
obliged to appeal to Caesar—not that I had any charge to
20 bring against my own nation. This is my reason for asking
to see you and have a word with you. I am wearing this
21 chain because I share Israel's hope." They replied, "We
have had no letters about you from Judaea, and no brother

---

* Omitting [ὁ ἑκατόνταρχος παρέδωκεν τοὺς δεσμίους τῷ στρατοπεδάρχῳ] and [δέ].

has come here with any bad report or story about you.
22 We think it only right to let you tell your own story; but as regards this sect, we are well aware that there are
23 objections to it on all hands." So they fixed a day and came to him at his quarters in large numbers. From morning to evening he explained the Reign of God to them from personal testimony, and tried to convince them about Jesus
24 from the law of Moses and the prophets. Some were convinced by what he said, but the others would not believe.
25 As they could not agree among themselves, they were turning to go away, when Paul added this one word: "It was an apt word that the holy Spirit spoke by the prophet
26 Isaiah to your fathers, when he said,
Go and tell this people,
'You will hear and hear but never understand,
you will see and see but never perceive.'
27 For the heart of this people is obtuse,
their ears are heavy of hearing,
their eyes they have closed,
lest they see with their eyes and hear with their ears,
lest they understand with their heart and turn again,
and I cure them.
28 Be sure of this, then, that this *salvation of God* has been
30 sent *to the Gentiles;* they will listen to it." For two full years he remained in his private lodging, welcoming any-
31 one who came to visit him; he preached the Reign of God and taught about the Lord Jesus Christ quite openly and unmolested.

THE EPISTLE OF PAUL THE APOSTLE TO THE

ROMANS

1 PAUL, a servant of Jesus Christ, called to be an apostle,
2 set apart for the gospel of God (which he promised of
3 old by his prophets in the holy scriptures) concerning his Son, who was born of David's offspring by natural
4 descent and installed as Son of God with power by the Spirit of holiness when he was raised from the dead—con-
5 cerning Jesus Christ our Lord, through whom I have received the favour of my commission to promote obedience
6 to the faith for his sake among all the Gentiles, including
7 yourselves who are called to belong to Jesus Christ: to all in Rome who are beloved by God, called to be saints, grace and peace to you from God our Father and the Lord Jesus Christ.
8 First of all, I thank my God through Jesus Christ for you all, because the report of your faith is over all the
9 world. God is my witness, the God whom I serve with
10 my spirit in the gospel of his Son, how unceasingly I always mention you in my prayers, asking if I may at last
11 be sped upon my way to you by God's will. For I do yearn to see you, that I may impart to you some spiritual gift
12 for your strengthening—or, in other words, that I may be encouraged by meeting you, I by your faith and you by
13 mine. Brothers, I would like you to understand that I have often purposed to come to you (though up till now I have been prevented) so as to have some results among
14 you as well as among the rest of the Gentiles. To Greeks and to barbarians, to wise and to foolish alike, I owe a duty.
15 Hence my eagerness to preach the gospel to you in Rome
16 as well. For I am proud of the gospel; it is God's saving power for everyone who has faith, for the Jew first and for
17 the Greek as well. God's righteousness is revealed in it by faith and for faith—as it is written, *Now by faith shall the*
18 *righteous live.* But God's anger is revealed from heaven against all the impiety and wickedness of those who hinder
19 the Truth by their wickedness. For whatever is to be known of God is plain to them; God himself has made it
20 plain—for ever since the world was created, his invisible nature, his everlasting power and divine being, have been

quite perceptible in what he has made. So they have no
21 excuse. Though they knew God, they have not glorified
him as God nor given thanks to him; they have turned
to futile speculations till their ignorant minds grew dark.
22 They claimed to be wise, but they have become fools;
23 they have *exchanged the glory of* the immortal *God for the
semblance* of the likeness of mortal man, of birds, of
24 quadrupeds, and of reptiles. So God has given them up,
in their heart's lust, to sexual vice, to the dishonouring of
25 their own bodies,—since they have exchanged the truth
of God for an untruth, worshipping and serving the creature rather than the Creator who is blessed for ever: Amen.
26 That is why God has given them up to vile passions; their
women have exchanged the natural function of sex for
27 what is unnatural, and in the same way the males have
abandoned the natural use of women and flamed out in lust
for one another, men perpetrating shameless acts with their
own sex and getting in their own persons the due recom-
28 pense of their perversity. Yes, as they disdained to
acknowledge God any longer, God has given them up to a
reprobate instinct for the perpetration of what is im-
29 proper, till they are filled with all manner of wickedness,
depravity, lust, and viciousness, filled to the brim with
30 envy, murder, quarrels, intrigues, and malignity—slanderers,
defamers, loathed by God, outrageous, haughty, boastful,
inventive in evil, disobedient to parents, devoid of con-
31 science, false to their word, callous, merciless; though they
32 know God's decree that people who practise such vice
deserve death, they not only do it themselves but applaud
those who practise it.

2 Therefore you are inexcusable, whoever you are, if
you pose as a judge, for in judging another you condemn yourself; you, the judge, do the very same things
2 yourself. 'We know the doom of God falls justly upon
3 those who practise such vices.' Very well; and do you
imagine you will escape God's doom, O man, you who judge
those who practise such vices and do the same yourself?
4 Or are you slighting all his wealth of kindness, forbearance, and patience? Do you not know his kindness is
5 meant to make you repent? In your stubbornness and
impenitence of heart you are simply storing up anger for
yourself on the Day of anger, when the just doom of God
6 is revealed. For *he will render to everyone according to
7 what he has done*, eternal life to those who by patiently
8 doing good aim at glory, honour, and immortality, but anger
and wrath to those who are wilful, who disobey the Truth
9 and obey wickedness—anguish and calamity for every

human soul that perpetrates evil, for the Jew first and for
10 the Greek as well, but glory, honour, and peace for everyone who does good, for the Jew first and for the Greek as
11 well. There is no partiality about God.
12 All who sin outside the Law will perish outside the Law, and all who sin under the Law will be condemned by the Law.
13 For it is not the hearers of the Law who are just in the eyes of God, it is those who obey the Law who will be
16 acquitted, on the day when God judges the secret things of
14 men, as my gospel holds, by Jesus Christ. (When Gentiles who have no law obey instinctively the Law's requirements, they are a law to themselves, even though they have
15 no law; they exhibit the effect of the Law written on their hearts, their conscience bears them witness, as their moral convictions accuse or it may be defend them.)*
17 If you bear the name of 'Jew,' relying on the Law, prid-
18 ing yourself on God, understanding his will, and with a sense of what is vital in religion; if you are instructed by
19 the Law and are persuaded you are a guide to the blind, a
20 light to darkened souls, a tutor for the foolish, a teacher of the simple, because in the Law you have the embodi-
21 ment of knowledge and truth—well then, do you ever teach yourself, you teacher of other people? You preach
22 against stealing; do you steal? You forbid adultery; do you commit adultery? You detest idols; do you rob
23 temples? You pride yourself on the Law; do you dis-
24 honour God by your breaches of the Law? Why, it is *owing to you that the name of God is maligned among the*
25 *Gentiles*, as scripture says! Circumcision is certainly of use, provided you keep the Law; but if you are a breaker of the Law, then your circumcision is turned into uncir-
26 cumcision. (If then the uncircumcised observe the requirements of the Law, shall not their uncircumcision be
27 reckoned equivalent to circumcision? And shall not those who are physically uncircumcised and who fulfil the Law, judge you who are a breaker of the Law for all your written code and circumcision?)
28 He is no Jew who is merely a Jew outwardly,
 nor is circumcision something outward in the flesh;
29 he is a Jew who is one inwardly,
 and circumcision is a
 matter of the heart, spiritual not literal—
 praised by God, not by man.

* Ver. 16 is the sequel to the first clause of ver. 14. The rest of ver. 14 and the whole of ver. 15 form a short paragraph which is either a marginal note or an awkward insertion. To preserve the sequence of thought I have re-arranged the verses as above.

3 Then what is the Jew's superiority? What is the good
2 of circumcision? Much in every way. This to begin
with—Jews were entrusted with the scriptures of God.
3 Even supposing some of them have proved untrustworthy,
is their faithlessness to cancel the faithfulness of God?
4 Never! Let God be true to his word, though *every man be
perfidious*—as it is written,
*That thou mayest be vindicated in thy pleadings,
and triumph in thy trial.*
5 But if our iniquity thus serves to bring out the justice
of God, what are we to infer? That it is unfair of God to
inflict his anger on us? (I speak in a merely human way.)
6 Never! In that case, how could he judge the world? You
7 say, "If my perfidy serves to make the truthfulness of God
redound to his glory, why am I to be judged as a sinner?
8 Why should we not do evil that good may come out of it?"
(which is the calumny attributed to me—the very thing
some people declare I say). Such arguments are rightly
condemned.
9 Well now, are we Jews in a better position? Not at all.
I have already charged all, Jews as well as Greeks, with
10 being under sin—as it is written,
None is righteous, no, not one;
11 *no one understands, no one seeks for God.*
12 *All have swerved, one and all have gone wrong,
no one does good, not a single one.*
13 *Their throat is an open grave,
they are treacherous with their tongues,
the venom of an asp lies under their lips.*
14 *Their mouth is full of cursing and bitterness.*
15 *their feet are swift for bloodshed,*
16 *their ways bring destruction and calamity,*
17 *they know nothing of the way of peace;*
18 *there is no reverence for God before their eyes.*
19 Whatever the Law says, we know, it says to those who
are inside the Law, that every mouth may be shut and
20 all the world made answerable to God; for *no person will
be acquitted in his sight* on the score of obedience to law.
21 What the Law imparts is the consciousness of sin. But
now we have a righteousness of God disclosed apart from
law altogether; it is attested by the Law and the prophets,
22 but it is a righteousness of God which comes by believing
in Jesus Christ. And it is meant for all who have faith.
23 No distinctions are drawn. All have sinned, all come short
24 of the glory of God, but they are justified for nothing by
his grace through the ransom provided in Christ Jesus,
25 whom God put forward as the means of propitiation by his
blood, to be received by faith. This was to demonstrate

the justice of God in view of the fact that sins previously committed during the time of God's forbearance had been
26 passed over; it was to demonstrate his justice at the present epoch, showing that God is just himself and that he justifies man on the score of faith in Jesus.
27 Then what becomes of our boasting? It is ruled out absolutely. On what principle? On the principle of doing
28 deeds? No, on the principle of faith. We hold a man is justified by faith apart from deeds of the Law altogether.
29 Or is God only the God of Jews? Is he not the God of the
30 Gentiles as well? Surely he is. Well then, there is one God, a God who will justify the circumcised as they believe
31 and the uncircumcised on the score of faith. Then 'by this faith' we 'cancel the Law'? Not for one moment! We uphold the Law.

4 But if so, what can we say about Abraham,* our fore-
2 father by natural descent? This, that if 'Abraham was justified on the score of what he did,' he has something to be proud of. But not to be proud of before God.
3 For what does scripture say? *Abraham believed God and*
4 *this was counted to him as righteousness.* Now a worker has his wage counted to him as a due, not as a favour;
5 but a man who instead of 'working' believes in Him who justifies the ungodly, has his faith counted as righteous-
6 ness. Just as David himself describes the bliss of the man who has righteousness counted to him by God apart from what he does—
7   *Blessed are they whose breaches of the Law are forgiven, whose sins are covered!*
8   *Blessed is the man whose sin the Lord will not count to him.*
9 Now is that description of bliss meant for the circumcised, or for the uncircumcised as well? *Abraham's faith,*
10 I repeat, *was counted to him as righteousness.* In what way? When he was a circumcised man or an uncircumcised man? Not when he was circumcised, but when he
11 was uncircumcised. He only got circumcision as a sign or seal of the righteousness which belonged to his faith as an uncircumcised man. The object of this was to make him the father of all who believe as uncircumcised persons
12 and thus have righteousness counted to them, as well as a father of those circumcised persons who not only share circumcision but walk in the steps of the faith which our father Abraham had as an uncircumcised man.
13   The promise made to Abraham and his offspring that

* Omitting, with B, 1908* and Origen, εὑρηκέναι.

he should inherit the world, did not reach him through
14 the Law, but through the righteousness of faith. For if
it is adherents of the Law who are heirs, then faith is
15 empty of all meaning and the promise is void. (What
the Law produces is the Wrath, not the promise of God;
where there is no law, there is no transgression either.)
16 That is why all turns upon faith; it is to make the promise
a matter of favour, to make it secure for all the offspring,
not simply for those who are adherents of the Law but also
for those who share the faith of Abraham—of Abraham
17 who is the father of us all (as it is written, *I have made
you a father of many nations*). Such a faith implies the
presence of the God in whom he believed, a God who makes
the dead live and calls into being what does not exist.
18 For Abraham, when hope was gone, hoped on in faith, and
thus became *the father of many nations*—even as he was
19 told, *So numberless shall your offspring be*. His faith
never quailed even when he noted the utter impotence of his
own body (for he was about a hundred years old) or the
20 impotence of Sara's womb; no unbelief made him waver
about God's promise; his faith won strength as he gave
21 glory to God and felt convinced that He was able to do
22 what He had promised. Hence his faith *was counted to*
23 *him as righteousness*. And these words *counted to him*
24 have not been written for him alone but for our sakes as
well; faith will be *counted to* us as we believe in Him who
25 raised Jesus our Lord from the dead, Jesus who was *delivered up for our trespasses* and raised that we might be justified.

5 As we are justified by faith, then, let us enjoy the peace we have with God through our Lord Jesus Christ.
2 Through him we have got access * to this grace where we have our standing, and triumph in the hope of God's glory.
3 Not only so, but we triumph even in our troubles, knowing
4 that trouble produces endurance, endurance produces char-
5 acter, and character produces hope—a *hope* which *never disappoints* us, since God's love floods our hearts through
6 the holy Spirit which has been given to us. For when we were still in weakness, Christ died in due time for the
7 ungodly. For the ungodly! Why, a man will hardly die for the just—though one might bring oneself to die, if need
8 be, for a good man. But God proves his love for us by this, that Christ died for us when we were still sinners.
9 Much more then, now that we are justified by his blood,
10 shall we be saved by him from Wrath. If we were recon-

* Omitting τῇ πίστει with B D G, the Old Latin, and Origen.

ciled to God by the death of his Son when we were enemies, much more, now that we are reconciled, shall we be saved
11 by his life. Not only so, but we triumph in God through our Lord Jesus Christ, by whom we now enjoy our reconciliation.
12 Thus, then, sin came into the world by one man, and death came in by sin; and so death spread to all men, inas-
13 much as all men sinned. Sin was indeed in the world before the Law, but sin is never counted in the absence
14 of law. Nevertheless, from Adam to Moses death reigned even over those whose sins were not like Adam's trans-
15 gression. Adam prefigured Him who was to come, but the gift is very different from the trespass. For while the rest of men died by the trespass of one man, the grace of God and the free gift which comes by the grace of the one man Jesus Christ overflowed far more richly upon the rest
16 of men. Nor is the free gift like the effect of the one man's sin; for while the sentence ensuing on a single sin resulted in doom, the free gift ensuing on many trespasses issues
17 in acquittal. For if the trespass of one man allowed death to reign through that one man, much more shall those who receive the overflowing grace and free gift of righteousness
18 reign in life through One, through Jesus Christ. Well then,
as one man's trespass issued in doom for all,
so one man's act of redress issues in acquittal and life for all.
19 Just as one man's disobedience made all the rest sinners, so one man's obedience will make all the rest righteous.
20 Law slipped in to aggravate the trespass; sin increased,
21 but grace surpassed it far, so that, while sin had reigned the reign of death, grace might also reign with a righteousness that ends in life eternal through Jesus Christ our Lord.

6 Now what are we to infer from this? That we are to 'remain on in sin, so that there may be all the more
2 grace'? Never! How can we live in sin any longer when
3 we died to sin? Surely you know that all of us who have been baptized into Christ Jesus have been baptized into his
4 death! Our baptism in his death made us share his burial, so that, as Christ was raised from the dead by the glory of the Father, we too might live and move in the new sphere of Life.
5 For if we have grown into him by a death like his, we shall
6 grow into him by a resurrection like his, knowing as we do that our old self has been crucified with him in order to crush the sinful body and free us from any further
7 slavery to sin (for once dead, a man is absolved from the
8 claims of sin). We believe that as we have died with

9 Christ we shall also live with him; for we know that
Christ never dies after his resurrection from the dead—
10 death has no more hold over him; the death he died was
11 for sin, once for all, but the life he lives is for God. So you
must consider yourselves dead to sin and alive to God in
12 Christ Jesus our Lord. Sin is not to reign, then, over your
13 mortal bodies and make you obey their passions; you must
not let sin have your members for the service of vice, you
must dedicate yourselves to God as men who have been
brought from death to life, dedicating your members to
14 God for the service of righteousness. Sin must have no
hold over you, for you live under grace, not under law.
15 What follows, then? Are we 'to sin, because we live
16 under grace, not under law'? Never! Do you not know
you are the servants of the master you obey, of the master
to whom you yield yourselves obedient, whether it is Sin,
whose service ends in death, or Obedience, whose service
17 ends in righteousness? Thank God, though you did serve
sin, you have rendered whole-hearted obedience to what
18 you were taught under the rule of faith; set free from sin,
19 you have passed into the service of righteousness. (I use
this human analogy to bring the truth home to your weak
nature.) As you once dedicated your members to the
service of vice and lawlessness,* so now dedicate them to
the service of righteousness that means consecration.
20 When you served sin, you were free of righteousness.
21 Well, what did you gain then by it all? Nothing but what
you are now ashamed of! The end of all that is death;
22 but now that you are set free from sin, now that you have
passed into the service of God, your gain is consecration,
23 and the end of that is life eternal. Sin's wage is death, but
God's gift is life eternal in Christ Jesus our Lord.

7 Surely you know, my brothers—for I am speaking to
men who know what law means—that the law has hold
2 over a person only during his lifetime! Thus a married
woman is bound by law to her husband while he is alive;
but if the husband dies, she is done with the law of 'the
3 husband.' Accordingly, she will be termed an adulteress
if she becomes another man's while her husband is alive;
but if her husband dies, she is freed from the law
of 'the husband,' so that she is no adulteress if she becomes
4 another man's. It is the same in your case, my brothers.
The crucified body of Christ made you dead to the Law,

* Omitting εἰς τὴν ἀνομίαν, which Hort brackets, as a gloss introduced
to complete the parallel of εἰς ἁγιασμόν.

so that you might belong to another, to him who was raised
5 from the dead that we might be fruitful to God. For when
we were unspiritual, the sinful cravings excited by the Law
were active in our members and made us fruitful to Death;
6 but now we are done with the Law, we have died to what
once held us, so that we can serve in a new way, not under
the written code as of old but in the Spirit.
7 What follows, then? That 'the Law is equivalent to sin'?
Never! Why, had it not been for the Law, I would never
have known what sin meant! Thus I would never have
known what it is to covet, unless the Law had said, *You*
8 *must not covet*. The command gave an impulse to sin, and
sin resulted for me in all manner of covetous desire—for
9 sin, apart from law, is lifeless. I lived at one time without law myself, but when the command came home to me,
10 sin sprang to life and I died; the command that meant life
11 proved death for me. The command gave an impulse to
sin, sin beguiled me and used the command to kill me.
12 So the Law at any rate is holy, the command is holy, just,
13 and for our good. Then did what was meant for my good
prove fatal to me? Never! It was sin; sin resulted in
death for me by making use of this good thing. This was
how sin was to be revealed in its true nature; it was to use
14 the command to become sinful in the extreme. The Law is
spiritual; we know that. But then I am a creature of the
15 flesh, in the thraldom of sin. I cannot understand my own
actions; I do not act as I want to act; on the contrary,
16 I do what I detest. Now, when I act against my wishes,
17 that means I agree that the Law is right. That being so,
it is not I who do the deed but sin that dwells within me.
18 For in me (that is, in my flesh) no good dwells, I know;
the wish is there, but not the power of doing what is right.
19 I cannot be good as I want to be, and I do wrong against
20 my wishes. Well, if I act against my wishes, it is not I
21 who do the deed but sin that dwells within me. So this
is my experience of the Law: I want to do what is right,
22 but wrong is all I can manage; I cordially agree with God's
23 law, so far as my inner self is concerned, but then I find
quite another law in my members which conflicts with the
law of my mind and makes me a prisoner to sin's law that
25 resides in my members. (Thus, left to myself, I serve the
law of God with my mind, but with my flesh I serve the
24 law of sin.)* Miserable wretch that I am! Who will
25 rescue me from this body of death? God will! Thanks be
to him through Jesus Christ our Lord!

* Restoring the second part of ver. 25 to what seems its original and logical position before the climax of ver. 24.

ROMANS VIII

8 Thus there is no doom now for those who are in Christ
2 Jesus; the law of the Spirit brings the life which is in
Christ Jesus, and that law has set me free from the law of
3 sin and death. For God has done what the Law, weakened
here by the flesh, could not do; by sending his own Son in
the guise of sinful flesh, to deal with sin, he condemned
4 sin in the flesh, in order to secure the fulfilment of the
Law's requirements in our lives, as we live and move not
by the flesh but by the Spirit.
5 For those who follow the flesh have their interests in
the flesh,
and those who follow the Spirit have their interests in
the Spirit.
6 The interests of the flesh mean death,
the interests of the Spirit mean life and peace.
7 For the interests of the flesh are hostile to God; they do
8 not yield to the law of God (indeed they cannot). Those
9 who are in the flesh cannot satisfy God. But you are not
in the flesh, you are in the Spirit, since the Spirit of God
dwells within you. Anyone who does not possess the Spirit
10 of Christ does not belong to Him. On the other hand,
if Christ is within you, though the body is a dead thing
owing to Adam's sin, the spirit is living as the result of
11 righteousness. And if the Spirit of Him who raised Jesus
from the dead dwells within you, then He who raised Christ
from the dead will also make your mortal bodies live by
his indwelling Spirit in your lives.
12 Well then, my brothers, we owe a duty—but it is not to
the flesh! It is not to live by the flesh! If you live by
13 the flesh, you are on the road to death; but if by the Spirit
you put the actions of the body to death, you will live.
14 For the sons of God are those who are guided by the Spirit
15 of God. You have received no slavish spirit that would
make you relapse into fear; you have received the Spirit
16 of sonship. And when we cry, "Abba! Father!", it is this
Spirit testifying along with our own spirit that we are
17 children of God; and if children, heirs as well, heirs of
God, heirs along with Christ—for we share his sufferings
in order to share his glory.
18 Present suffering, I hold, is a mere nothing compared
19 to the glory that we are to have revealed. Even the creation waits with eager longing for the sons of God to be
20 revealed. For creation was not rendered futile by its own
choice, but by the will of Him who thus made it subject,
21 the hope being that creation as well as man would one
day be freed from its thraldom to decay and gain the
22 glorious freedom of the children of God. To this day, we
23 know, the entire creation sighs and throbs with pain; and

not only so, but even we ourselves, who have the Spirit as a foretaste of the future, even we sigh to ourselves as we wait for the redemption of the body that means our full
24 sonship. We were saved with this hope in view. Now when an object of hope is seen, there is no further need to
25 hope. Who ever hopes for what he sees already? But if we hope for something that we do not see, we wait for it patiently.
26 So too the Spirit assists us in our weakness; for we do not know how to pray aright, but the Spirit pleads for
27 us with sighs that are beyond words, and He who searches the human heart knows what is in the mind of the Spirit, since the Spirit pleads before God for the saints.
28 We know also that those who love God, those who have been called in terms of his purpose, have his aid and
29 interest in everything. For he decreed of old that those whom he predestined should share the likeness of his Son —that he might be the firstborn of a great brotherhood.
30 Then he calls those whom he has thus decreed; then he justifies those whom he has called; then he glorifies those whom he has justified.
31 Now what follows from all this? If God is for us, who
32 can be against us? The God who did not spare his own Son but gave him up for us all, surely He will give us
33 everything besides! Who is to accuse the elect of God?
34 When God *acquits, who shall condemn?* Will Christ?— the Christ who died, yes and rose from the dead! the Christ who is at God's right hand, who actually pleads for us!
35 What can ever part us from Christ's love? Can anguish or calamity or persecution or famine or nakedness or
36 danger or the sword? (*Because*, as it is written,
For thy sake we are being killed all the day long,
we are counted as sheep to be slaughtered.)
37 No, in all this we are more than conquerors through him
38 who loved us. For I am certain neither death nor life, neither angels nor principalities, neither the present nor
39 the future, no powers of the Height or of the Depth, nor anything else in all creation will be able to part us from God's love in Christ Jesus our Lord.

9 I AM telling the truth in Christ—it is no lie, my con-
2 science bears me out in the holy Spirit when I say that I am in sore pain. I suffer endless anguish of heart.
3 I could have wished myself accursed and banished from Christ for the sake of my brothers, my natural kinsmen;
4 for they are Israelites, theirs is the Sonship, the Glory, the covenants, the divine legislation, the Worship, and the
5 promises; the patriarchs are theirs, and theirs too (so far

as natural descent goes) is the Christ. (Blessed for evermore be the God who is over all! Amen.)
6 It is not, of course, as if God's word had failed! Far from it! 'Israel' does not mean everyone who belongs to
7 Israel; they are not all children of Abraham because they are descended from Abraham. No, *it is through Isaac*
8 *that your offspring shall be reckoned*—meaning that instead of God's children being the children born to him by natural descent, it is the children of the Promise who are
9 reckoned as his true offspring. For when God said, *I will come about this time and Sara shall have a son*, that was
10 a word of promise. And further, when Rebecca became pregnant by our father Isaac, though one man was the
11 father of both children, and though the children were still unborn and had done nothing either good or bad (to con-firm the divine purpose in election which depends upon
12 the call of God, not on anything man does), she was told
13 that *the elder will serve the younger*. As it is written, *Jacob I loved but Esau I hated*.
14 Then are we to infer that there is injustice in God?
15 Never! God says to Moses,
I will have mercy on whom I choose to have mercy,
I will have compassion on whom I choose to have compassion.
16 You see, it is not a question of human will or effort but
17 of the divine mercy. Why, scripture says to Pharaoh,
It was for this that I raised you up,
to display my power in you,
and to spread news of my name over all the earth.
18 Thus God has mercy on anyone just as he pleases, and *he makes* anyone *stubborn* just as he pleases.
19 "Then," you will retort, "why does He go on finding
20 fault? Who can oppose his will?" But who are you, my man, to speak back to God? *Is something a man has moulded to ask him who has moulded it*, "Why did you
21 make me like this?" What! has *the potter no right over the clay?* Has he no right to make out of the same lump one vessel for a noble purpose and another for a menial?
22 What if God, though desirous to display his anger and show his might, has tolerated most patiently the objects
23 of his anger, ripe and ready to be destroyed? What if he means to show the wealth that lies in his glory for the objects of his mercy, whom he has made ready before-
24 hand to receive glory—that is, for us whom he has called
25 from among the Gentiles as well as the Jews? As indeed he says in Hosea,
Those who were no people of mine, I will call 'my People,'

and her 'beloved' who was not beloved;
26 on the very spot where they were told, 'You are no people of mine,'
there shall they be called 'sons of the living God.'
27 And Isaiah exclaims, with regard to Israel, *Though the number of the sons of Israel be like the sand of the sea,*
28 *only a remnant of them shall be saved; for the Lord will carry out his sentence on earth with rigour and despatch.*
29 Indeed, as Isaiah foretold,
Had not the Lord of hosts left us with some descendants, we would have fared like Sodom, we would have been like Gomorra.
30 What are we to conclude, then? That Gentiles who never aimed at righteousness have attained righteousness, that
31 is, righteousness by faith; whereas Israel who did aim at the law of righteousness have failed to reach that law.
32 And why? Simply because Israel has relied not on faith but on what they could do. They have stumbled over *the*
33 *stone that makes men stumble*—as it is written,
Here I lay a stone in Sion that will make men stumble, even a rock to trip them up; but he who believes in Him will never be disappointed.

10 Oh for their salvation, brothers! That is my heart's
2 desire and prayer to God! I can vouch for their zeal
3 for God; only, it is not zeal with knowledge. They would not surrender to the righteousness of God, because they were ignorant of his righteousness and therefore essayed
4 to set up a righteousness of their own. Now Christ is an end to law, so as to let every believer have righteousness.
5 Moses writes of law-righteousness, *Anyone who can per-*
6 *form it, shall live by it.* But here is what faith-righteousness says:—*Say not in your heart, 'Who will go up to*
7 *heaven?'* (that is, to bring Christ down). Or, *'who will go down to the abyss?'* (that is, to bring Christ from the
8 dead). No, what it does say is this:—*The word is close to you, in your very mouth and in your heart* (that is, the
9 word of faith which we preach). Confess *with your mouth* that 'Jesus is Lord,' believe *in your heart* that God raised
10 him from the dead, and you will be saved; for
with his heart man believes and is justified,
with his mouth he confesses and is saved.
11 *No one who believes in him,* the scripture says, *will ever*
12 *be disappointed.* No one—for there is no distinction of Jew and Greek, the same Lord is Lord of them all, with
13 ample for all who invoke him. *Everyone who invokes the*
14 *name of the Lord shall be saved.* But how are they to invoke One in whom they do not believe? And how are

they to believe in One of whom they have never heard?
15 And how are they ever to hear, without a preacher? And how can men preach unless they are sent?—as it is written,
How pleasant is the coming of men with glad, good news!
16 But they have not all given in to the gospel of glad news? No, Isaiah says, *Lord, who has believed what they*
17 *heard from us?* (You see, faith must come from what is heard, and what is heard comes from word of Christ.)
18 But, I ask, "Have they never heard?" Indeed they have.
Their voice carried over all the earth,
and their words to the end of the world.
19 Then, I ask, "Did Israel not understand?" Why, first of all Moses declares,
I will make you jealous of a nation that is no nation,
I will provoke you to anger over a nation devoid of understanding.
20 And then Isaiah dares to say,
I have been found by those who never sought me,
I have shown myself to those who never inquired of me.
21 He also says of Israel, *All the day long I have held out my hands to a disobedient and contrary people.*

11 Then, I ask, has God repudiated his People? Never! Why, I am an Israelite myself, a descendant of Abra-
2 ham, a member of the tribe of Benjamin! God has not repudiated his People, his predestined People! Surely you know what scripture says in the passage called 'Elijah'?
3 You know how he pleads with God against Israel: *Lord, they have killed thy prophets, they have demolished thine*
4 *altars; I alone am left, and they seek my life.* Yet what is the divine answer? *I have left myself seven thousand*
5 *men who have not knelt to Baal.* Well, at the present
6 day there is also a remnant, selected by grace. Selected by grace, and therefore not for anything they have done; otherwise grace would cease to be grace.*
7 Now what are we to infer from this? That Israel has failed to secure the object of its quest; the elect have secured it, and the rest of men have been rendered insen-
8 sible to it—as it is written,
God has given them a spirit of torpor,
eyes that see not, ears that hear not—
9 *down to this very day.* And David says,
Let their table prove a snare and a trap,
a pitfall and a retribution for them;
10 *let their eyes be darkened, that they cannot see,*
bow down their backs for ever.

* Omitting [εἰ δὲ ἐξ ἔργων, οὐκέτι ἐστὶν χάρις, ἐπεὶ τὸ ἔργον οὐκέτι ἐστὶν ἔργον] with the Latin version and most MSS.

11 Now I ask, have they stumbled to their ruin? Never! The truth is, that by their lapse salvation has passed to
12 the Gentiles, so as to make them jealous. Well, if their lapse has enriched the world, if their defection is the gain of the Gentiles, what will it mean when they all come in?
13 I tell you this, you Gentiles, that as an apostle to the
14 Gentiles I lay great stress on my office, in the hope of being able to make my fellow-Jews jealous and of manag-
15 ing thus to save some of them. For if their exclusion means that the world is reconciled to God, what will their admission mean? Why, it will be life from the dead!
16 If the first handful of dough is consecrated, so is the rest of the lump;
  if the root is consecrated, so are the branches.
17 Supposing some of the branches have been broken off, while you have been grafted in like a shoot of wild olive
18 to share the rich growth of the olive-stem, do not pride yourself at the expense of these branches. Remember, in
19 your pride, the stem supports you, not you the stem. You will say, "But branches were broken off to let me be
20 grafted in!" Granted. They were broken off—for their lack of faith. And you owe your position to your faith.
21 You should feel awed instead of being uplifted. For if God did not spare the natural branches, he will not spare
22 you either. Consider both the kindness and the severity of God; those who fall come under his severity, but you come under the divine kindness, provided you adhere to that kindness. Otherwise, you will be cut away too.
23 And even the others will be grafted in, if they do not adhere to their unbelief; God can graft them in again.
24 For if you have been cut from an olive which is naturally wild, and grafted, contrary to nature, upon a garden olive, how much more will the natural branches be grafted into their proper olive?
25 To prevent you from being self-conceited, brothers, I would like you to understand this secret: it is only a partial insensibility that has come over Israel, until the full
26 number of the Gentiles come in. This done, all Israel will be saved—as it is written,
  The deliverer will come from Sion,
  he will banish all godlessness from Jacob:
27 *this is my covenant with them,*
  when I take their sins away.
28 So far as the gospel goes, they are enemies of God—which is to your advantage; but so far as election goes, they are
29 beloved for their father's sake. For God never goes back upon his gifts and call.
30 Once you disobeyed God,

ROMANS XII

and now you enjoy his mercy thanks to their disobedience;
in the same way they at present are disobedient,
31 so that they in turn may enjoy the same mercy as yourselves.
32 For God has consigned all men to disobedience,
that he may have mercy upon all.
33 What a fathomless wealth lies in the wisdom and knowledge of God! How inscrutable his judgments! How mysterious his methods!
34 *Whoever understood the thoughts of the Lord?*
Who has ever been his counsellor?
35 *Who has first given to him and has to be repaid?* All comes from him, all lives by him, all ends in him. Glory to him for ever, Amen!

12 WELL then, my brothers, I appeal to you by all the mercy of God to dedicate your bodies as a living sacrifice, consecrated and acceptable to God; that is your
2 cult, a spiritual rite. Instead of being moulded to this world, have your mind renewed, and so be transformed in nature, able to make out what the will of God is, namely, what is good and acceptable to him and perfect.
3 In virtue of my office, I tell everyone of your number who is self-important,* that he is not to think more of himself than he ought to think; he must take a sane view of himself, corresponding to the degree of faith which
4 God has assigned to each. In our one body we have a number of members, and the members have not all the
5 same function; so too, for all our numbers, we form one Body in Christ and we are severally members one of
6 another. Our talents differ with the grace that is given us; if the talent is that of prophecy, let us employ it in
7 proportion to our faith; if it is practical service, let us mind our service; the teacher must mind his teaching,
8 the speaker his words of counsel; the contributor must be liberal, the superintendent must be in earnest, the sick
9 visitor must be cheerful. Let your love be a real thing, with a loathing for evil and a bent for what is good.
10 Put affection into your love for the brotherhood; be for-
11 ward to honour one another; never let your zeal flag;
12 maintain the spiritual glow; serve the Lord; let your hope
13 be a joy to you; be stedfast in trouble, attend to prayer, contribute to needy saints, make a practice of hospitality.
14 Bless those who make a practice of persecuting you; bless
15 them instead of cursing them. Rejoice with those who

* I accept the ingenious conjecture that τι has fallen out after ὄντι.

16 rejoice, and weep with those who weep. Keep in harmony with one another; instead of being ambitious, associate
17 with humble folk; *never be self-conceited.* Never pay back evil for evil to anyone; *aim to be above reproach in the*
18 *eyes of all;* be at peace with all men, if possible, so far
19 as that depends on you. Never revenge yourselves, beloved, but let the Wrath of God have its way; for it is written, *Vengeance is mine, I will exact a requital*—the Lord has said it. No,
20 *if your enemy is hungry, feed him,*
if he is thirsty, give him drink;
for in this way you will make him
feel a burning sense of shame.
21 Do not let evil get the better of you; get the better of evil by doing good.

13 Every subject must obey the government-authorities, for no authority exists apart from God; the existing
2 authorities have been constituted by God. Hence anyone who resists authority is opposing the divine order, and
3 the opposition will bring judgment on themselves. Magistrates are no terror to an honest man,* though they are to a bad man. If you want to avoid being alarmed at the government-authorities, lead an honest life and you will be
4 commended for it; the magistrate is God's servant for your benefit. But if you do wrong, you may well be alarmed; a magistrate does not wield the power of the sword for nothing, he is God's servant for the infliction of
5 divine vengeance upon evil-doers. You must be obedient, therefore, not only to avoid the divine vengeance but as
6 a matter of conscience, for the same reason as you pay taxes—since magistrates are God's officers, bent upon the
7 maintenance of order and authority. Pay them all their respective dues, tribute to one, taxes to another, respect
8 to this man, honour to that. Be in debt to no man—apart from the debt of love one to another. He who loves his
9 fellow-man has fulfilled the law. *You must not commit adultery, you must not kill, you must not steal, you must not covet*—these and any other command are summed up in a single word, *You must love your neighbour as yourself.*
10 Love never wrongs a neighbour; that is why love is the fulfilment of the law.
11 And then you know what this Crisis means, you know it is high time to waken up; for Salvation is nearer to us

---

* Reading ἀγαθοεργῷ, Patrick Young's attractive conjecture (confirmed by the Ethiopic version). As Hort points out, " the apparent antithesis to τῷ κακῷ could hardly fail to introduce τῷ ἀγαθῷ."

12 now than when we first believed. It is far on in the night, the day is almost here; so let us drop the deeds of dark-
13 ness and put on the armour of the light; let us live decorously as in the open light of day—no revelry or bouts of drinking, no debauchery or sensuality, no quarrelling or
14 jealousy. No, put on the character of the Lord Jesus Christ, and never think how to gratify the cravings of the flesh.

14 Welcome a man of weak faith, but not for the purpose
2 of passing judgment on his scruples. While one man has enough confidence to eat any food, the man of
3 weak faith only eats vegetables. The eater must not look down upon the non-eater, and the non-eater must not
4 criticize the eater, for God has welcomed him. Who are you to criticize the servant of Another? It is for his Master to say whether he stands or falls; and stand he
5 will, for the Master has power to make him stand. Then again, this man rates one day above another, while that man rates all days alike. Well, everyone must be convinced
6 in his own mind; the man who values a particular day does so to the Lord.*
  The eater eats to the Lord,
    since he thanks God for his food;
  the non-eater abstains to the Lord,
    and he too thanks God.
7 For none of us lives to himself,
    and none of us dies to himself;
8 if we live, we live to the Lord,
    and if we die, we die to the Lord.
9 Thus we are the Lord's whether we live or die; it was for this that Christ died and rose and came to life, to be Lord
10 both of the dead and of the living. So why do you criticize your brother? And you, why do you look down upon your brother? All of us have to stand before the tribunal of
11 God—for it is written,
  As I live, saith the Lord, every knee shall bend before me,
    every tongue shall offer praise to God.
12 Each of us then will have to answer for himself to God.
13 So let us stop criticizing one another; rather make up your mind never to put any stumbling-block or hindrance
14 in your brother's way. I know, I am certain in the Lord Jesus, that nothing is in itself unclean; only, anything is
15 unclean for a man who considers it unclean. If your brother is being injured because you eat a certain food,

* Omitting [καὶ ὁ μὴ φρονῶν τὴν ἡμέραν κυρίῳ οὐ φρονεῖ] with the Latin version and most manuscripts.

then you are no longer living by the rule of love. Do not
let that food of yours ruin the man for whom Christ died.
16 Your rights must not get a bad name. The Reign of God
17 is not a matter of eating and drinking, it means right-
18 eousness, joy, and peace in the holy Spirit; he who serves
Christ on these lines, is acceptable to God and esteemed
19 by men. Peace, then, and the building up of each other,
20 these are what we must aim at. You must not break down
God's work for the mere sake of food! Everything may
be clean, but it is wrong for a man to prove a stumbling-
21 block by what he eats; the right course is to abstain from
flesh or wine or indeed anything that your brother feels
22 to be a stumbling-block.* Certainly keep your own conviction on the matter, as between yourself and God; he
is a fortunate man who has no misgivings about what he
23 allows himself to eat. But if anyone has doubts about
eating and then eats, that condemns him at once; it was
not faith that induced him to eat, and any action that is
not based on faith is a sin.

15 We who are strong ought to bear the burdens that the
weak make for themselves and us. We are not to
2 please ourselves. Each of us must please his neighbour,
3 doing him good by building up his faith. Christ certainly
did not please himself, but, as it is written, *The reproaches
of those who denounced Thee have fallen upon me.—*
4 All such words were written of old for our instruction,
that by remaining stedfast and drawing encouragement
5 from the scriptures we may cherish hope. May the God
who inspires stedfastness and encouragement grant you
6 such harmony with one another, after Christ Jesus, that
you may unite in a chorus of praise and glory to the God
7 and Father of our Lord Jesus Christ! Welcome one another, then, as Christ has welcomed yourselves, for the
8 glory of God. Christ, I mean, became a servant to the
circumcised in order to prove God's honesty by fulfilling
9 His promises to the fathers, and also in order that the
Gentiles should glorify God for His mercy—as it is written,
*Therefore will I offer praise to Thee among the Gentiles,
and sing to thy name;*
10 or again,
Rejoice, O Gentiles, with his People;
11 or again,
*Extol the Lord, all Gentiles,
let all the peoples praise him;*
12 or again, as Isaiah says,

* Omitting [ἢ σκανδαλίζεται ἢ ἀσθενεῖ] with ℵ* A C, Origen, the Peshitto, etc., as a homiletic gloss.

> Then shall the Scion of Jessai live,
> he who rises to rule the Gentiles;
> on him shall the Gentiles set their hope.

13 May the God of your hope so fill you with all joy and peace in your faith, that you may be overflowing with hope by the power of the holy Spirit!

14 Personally I am quite certain, my brothers, that even as it is you have ample goodness of heart, you are filled with knowledge of every kind, and you are well able to give
15 advice to one another. Still, by way of refreshing your memory, I have written you with a certain freedom, in
16 virtue of my divine commission as a priest of Christ Jesus to the Gentiles in the service of God's gospel. My aim is to make the Gentiles an acceptable offering, consecrated
17 by the holy Spirit. Now in Christ Jesus I can be proud
18 of my work for God. I will not make free to speak of anything except what Christ has accomplished by me in the way of securing the obedience of the Gentiles, by my words
19 and by my deeds, by the force of miracles and marvels, by the power of the Spirit of God. Thus from Jerusalem right round to Illyricum, I have been able to complete the
20 preaching of the gospel of Christ—my ambition always being to preach it only in places where there had been no mention of Christ's name, that I might not build on founda-
21 tions laid by others, but that (as it is written)
> They should see who never had learned about him,
> and they who had never heard of him should understand.

22 This is why I have been so often prevented from visiting
23 you. But now, as I have no further scope for work in these parts, and as for a number of years I have had a longing
24 to visit you whenever I went to Spain, I am hoping to see you on my way there, and to be sped forward by you
25 after I have enjoyed your company for a while. At the moment I am off to Jerusalem on an errand to the saints.
26 For Macedonia and Achaia have decided to make a con-
27 tribution for the poor among the saints at Jerusalem. Such was their decision; and yet this is a debt they owe to these people, for if the Gentiles have shared their spiritual blessings, they owe them a debt of aid in material blessings.
28 Well, once I finish this business by putting the proceeds of the collection safely in their hands, I will start for
29 Spain and take you on the way. When I do come to you, I know I will bring a full blessing from Christ.
30 Brothers, I beg of you, by our Lord Jesus Christ and by the love that the Spirit inspires, rally round me by pray-
31 ing to God for me; pray that I may be delivered from the unbelievers in Judaea, and also that my mission to Jeru-

32 salem may prove acceptable to the saints. Then, by God's
will, I shall gladly come to you and rest beside you.
33 The God of peace be with you all! Amen.

16 LET me introduce our sister Phoebe, a deaconess of
2 the church at Cenchreae; receive her in the Lord
as saints should receive one another, and give her any help
she may require. She has been a help herself to many
people, including myself.
3 Salute Prisca and Aquila, my fellow-workers in Christ
4 Jesus, who have risked their lives for me; I thank them,
5 and not only I but all the Gentile churches as well. Also,
salute the church that meets in their house. Salute my
beloved Epaenetus, the first in Asia to be reaped for
6 Christ. Salute Mary, who has worked hard for you.
7 Salute Andronicus and Junias, fellow-countrymen and fellow-prisoners of mine; they are men of note among the
apostles, and they have been in Christ longer than I have.
8 Salute Amplias, my beloved in the Lord. Salute Urbanus,
9 our fellow-worker in Christ, and my beloved Stachys.
10 Salute that tried Christian, Apelles. Salute those who
11 belong to the household of Aristobulus. Salute my fellow-countryman Herodion. Salute such members of the
12 household of Narcissus as are in the Lord. Salute Tryphaena and Tryphosa, who work hard in the Lord. Salute
the beloved Persis; she has worked very hard in the Lord.
13 Salute that choice Christian, Rufus; also his mother, who
14 has been a mother to me. Salute Asyncritus, Phlegon,
Hermes, Patrobas, Hermas, and the brothers of their com-
15 pany. Salute Philologus and Julia, Nereus and his sister,
16 Olympas too, and all the saints in their company. Salute
one another with a holy kiss. All the churches of Christ
salute you.
17 Brothers, I beg of you to keep your eye on those who
stir up dissensions and put hindrances in your way, contrary to the doctrine which you have been taught. Avoid
18 them. Such creatures are no servants of Christ our Lord,
they are slaves of their own base desires; with their plausible and pious talk they beguile the hearts of unsuspecting
19 people. But surely not of you! Everyone has heard of
your loyalty to the gospel; it makes me rejoice over you.
Still, I want you to be experts in good and innocents in
20 evil. The God of peace will soon crush Satan under your
feet!
The grace of our Lord Jesus Christ be with you.
21 Timotheus my fellow-worker salutes you; so do my fellow-countrymen Lucius, Jason, and Sosipater.
22 I Tertius, who write the letter, salute you in the Lord,

23 Gaius, my host and the host of the church at large, salutes you. Erastus the city-treasurer salutes you; so does brother Quartus.
25 [Now to Him who can strengthen you by my gospel, by the preaching of Jesus Christ, by revealing the secret
26 purpose which after the silence of long ages has now been disclosed and made known on the basis of the prophetic scriptures (by command of the eternal God) to all the
27 Gentiles for their obedience to the faith—to the only wise God be glory through Jesus Christ for ever and ever: Amen.]

THE FIRST EPISTLE OF PAUL THE APOSTLE TO THE

CORINTHIANS

1 PAUL, called to be an apostle of Jesus Christ by the will
2 of God, with brother Sosthenes, to the church of God
at Corinth, to those who are consecrated in Christ Jesus,
called to be saints, as well as to all who, wherever they
may be, invoke the name of our Lord Jesus Christ, their
3 Lord no less than ours: grace and peace to you from God
our Father and the Lord Jesus Christ.
4 I always thank my God for the grace of God that has
5 been bestowed on you in Christ Jesus; in him you have
received a wealth of all blessing, full power to speak of
6 your faith and full insight into its meaning, all of which
verifies the testimony we bore to Christ when we were
7 with you. Thus you lack no spiritual endowment during
these days of waiting till our Lord Jesus Christ is revealed;
8 and to the very end he will guarantee that you are vin-
9 dicated on the day of our Lord Jesus Christ. Faithful is
the God who called you to this fellowship with his Son
Jesus Christ our Lord.
10 Brothers, for the sake of our Lord Jesus Christ I beg
of you all to drop these party-cries. There must be no
cliques among you; you must regain your common temper
11 and attitude. For Chloe's people inform me that you are
12 quarrelling. By 'quarrelling' I mean that each of you has
his party-cry, "I belong to Paul," "And I to Apollos," "And
13 I to Cephas," "And I to Christ." Has Christ been parcelled
out? Was it Paul who was crucified for you? Was it in
14 Paul's name that you were baptized? I am thankful now
that I baptized none of you, except Crispus and Gaius,
15 so that no one can say you were baptized in my name.
16 (Well, I did baptize the household of Stephanas, but no one
17 else, as far as I remember.) Christ did not send me to
baptize but to preach the gospel.
   And to preach it with no fine rhetoric, lest the cross of
18 Christ should lose its power! Those who are doomed
to perish find the story of the cross 'sheer folly,' but it
19 means the power of God for those whom he saves. It is
written,
   I will destroy the wisdom of the sages,
20 *I will confound the insight of the wise.* Sage, scribe,

critic of this world, *where are they* all? Has not God
21 stultified the wisdom of the world? For when the world
with all its wisdom failed to know God in his wisdom, God
resolved to save believers by the 'sheer folly' of the Chris-
22 tian message. Jews demand miracles and Greeks want
23 wisdom, but our message is Christ the crucified—a stum-
24 bling-block to the Jews, 'sheer folly' to the Gentiles, but for
those who are called, whether Jews or Greeks, a Christ who
is the power of God and the wisdom of God.
25 For the 'foolishness' of God is wiser than men,
   and the 'weakness' of God is stronger than men.
26 Why, look at your own ranks, my brothers; not many
wise men (that is, judged by human standards), not many
leading men, not many of good birth, have been called!
27 No,
   God has chosen what is foolish in the world
      to shame the wise;
28 God has chosen what is weak in the world
      to shame what is strong;
   God has chosen what is mean and despised in the world—
      things which are not, to put down things that are;
29
30 that no person may boast in the sight of God. This is the
God to whom you owe your being in Christ Jesus, whom
God has made our 'Wisdom,' that is, our righteousness
31 and consecration and redemption; so that, as it is written,
let him who boasts boast of the Lord.

2 Thus when I came to you, my brothers, I did not come
  to proclaim to you God's secret purpose* with any elab-
2 orate words or wisdom. I determined among you to be
ignorant of everything except Jesus Christ, and Jesus
3 Christ the crucified. It was in weakness and fear and
4 with great trembling that I visited you; what I said, what
I preached, did not rest on the plausible arguments of
'wisdom' but on the proof supplied by the Spirit and its
5 power, so that your faith might not rest on any human
'wisdom' but on the power of God.
6 We do discuss 'wisdom' with those who are mature;
only it is not the wisdom of this world or of the dethroned
7 Powers who rule this world, it is the mysterious Wisdom
of God that we discuss, that hidden wisdom which God
8 decreed from all eternity for our glory. None of the Powers
of this world understands it (if they had, they would never
9 have crucified the Lord of glory). No, as it is written,

* The textual evidence for μαρτύριον is slightly stronger, but I incline
upon the whole to regard it as a secondary reading, due to i. 6, and to
adopt μυστήριον.

what no eye has ever seen,
what no ear has ever heard,
what never entered the mind of man,
God has prepared all that for those who love him.
10 And God has revealed it to us by the Spirit, for the Spirit fathoms everything, even the depths of God.
11 What human being can understand the thoughts of a man,
except the man's own inner spirit?
So too no one understands the thoughts of God,
except the Spirit of God.
12 Now we have received the Spirit—not the spirit of the world but the Spirit that comes from God, that we may
13 understand what God bestows upon us. And this is what we discuss, using language taught by no human wisdom but by the Spirit. We interpret what is spiritual in spirit-
14 ual language. The unspiritual man rejects these truths of the Spirit of God; to him they are 'sheer folly,' he cannot understand them. And the reason is, that they
15 must be read with the spiritual eye. The spiritual man, again, can read the meaning of everything; and yet no one
16 can read what he is. For *who ever understood the thoughts of the Lord, so as to give him instruction?* No one. Well, our thoughts are Christ's thoughts.

3 BUT I could not discuss things with you, my brothers, as spiritual persons; I had to address you as worldlings,
2 as mere babes in Christ. I fed you with milk, not with solid food. You were not able for solid food, and you are
3 not able even now; you are still worldly. For with jealousy and quarrels in your midst, are you not worldly,
4 are you not behaving like ordinary men? When one cries, "I belong to Paul," and another, "I belong to Apollos,"
5 what are you but men of the world? Who is Apollos? Who is Paul? They are simply used by God to give you faith, each as the Lord assigns his task.
6 I did the planting, Apollos did the watering,
but it was God who made the seed grow.
7 So neither planter nor waterer counts,
but God alone who makes the seed grow.
8 Still, though planter and waterer are on the same level, each will get his own wage for the special work that he has done.
9 We work together in God's service; you are God's
10 field to be planted, God's house to be built. In virtue of my commission from God, I laid the foundation of the house like an expert master-builder. It remains for another to build on this foundation. Whoever he is, let him be

11 careful how he builds. The foundation is laid, namely
12 Jesus Christ, and no one can lay any other. On that
foundation anyone may build gold, silver, precious stones,
13 wood, hay, or straw, but in every case the nature of his
work will come out; the Day will show what it is, for the
Day breaks in fire, and the fire will test the work of each,
no matter what that work may be.
14   If the structure raised by any man survives,
     he will be rewarded;
15   if a man's work is burnt up,
     he will be a loser—
        and though he will be saved himself, he will be
          snatched from the very flames.
16   Do you not know you are God's temple and that God's
17 Spirit dwells within you? God will destroy anyone who
would destroy God's temple, for God's temple is sacred—
and that is what you are.
18   Let no one deceive himself about this; whoever of you
imagines he is wise with this world's wisdom must become
19 a 'fool,' if he is really to be wise. For God ranks this
world's wisdom as 'sheer folly.' It is written, *He seizes*
20 *the wise in their craftiness*, and again, *The Lord knows
the reasoning of the wise is futile*.
21   So you must not boast about men. For all belongs to
22 you; Paul, Apollos, Cephas, the world, life, death, the
23 present and the future—all belongs to you; and you belong
to Christ, and Christ to God.

4 This is how you are to look upon us, as servants of
2 Christ and stewards of God's secret truths. Now in
this matter of stewards your first requirement is that they
3 must be trustworthy. It matters very little to me that you
or any human court should cross-question me on this point.
4 I do not even cross-question myself; for, although I am
not conscious of having anything against me, that does not
clear me. It is the Lord who cross-questions me on the
5 matter. So do not criticize at all; the hour of reckoning has still to come, when the Lord will come to bring
dark secrets to the light and to reveal life's inner aims and
motives. Then each of us will get his meed of praise
from God.
6   Now I have applied what has been said above to myself
and Apollos, to teach you . . . *that you are not to be
puffed up with rivalry over one teacher as against another.

* The text and the meaning of the phrase between μάθητε and ἵνα μή are beyond recovery.

I. CORINTHIANS V 251

7 Who singles you out, my brother? What do you possess
that has not been given you? And if it was given you,
why do you boast as if it had been gained, not given?
8 You Corinthians have your heart's desire already, have
you? You have heaven's rich bliss already! You have
come into your kingdom without us! I wish indeed you
had come into your kingdom, so that we could share it
9 with you! For it seems to me that God means us apostles
to come in at the very end, like the doomed gladiators
in the arena! We are made a spectacle to the world, to
10 angels and to men! We, for Christ's sake, are 'fools';
you in Christ are sensible. We are weak, you are strong;
11 you are honoured, we are in disrepute. To this very hour
we hunger and thirst, we are ill-clad and knocked about,
12 we are waifs, we work hard for our living; when reviled,
13 we bless; when persecuted, we put up with it; when
defamed, we try to conciliate. To this hour we are treated
as the scum of the earth, the very refuse of the world!
14 I do not write this to make you feel ashamed, but to
15 instruct you as beloved children of mine. You may have
thousands to superintend you in Christ, but you have not
more than one father. It was I who in Christ Jesus became
16 your father by means of the gospel. Then imitate me,
17 I beg of you. To ensure this, I am sending you Timotheus,
my beloved and trustworthy son in the Lord; he will
remind you of those methods in Christ Jesus which I
18 teach everywhere in every church. Certain individuals
have got puffed up, have they, as if I were not coming my-
19 self? I will come to you before long, if the Lord wills, and
then I will find out from these puffed up creatures not
20 what their talk but what their power amounts to. For God's
21 Reign does not show itself in talk but in power. Which is
it to be? Am I to come to you with a rod of discipline
or with love and a spirit of gentleness?

5 IT is actually reported that there is immorality among
you, and immorality such as is unknown even among
2 pagans—that a man has taken his father's wife! And yet
you are puffed up! You ought much rather to be mourning the loss of a member! Expel the perpetrator of such a
3 crime! For my part, present with you in spirit though
absent in body, I have already, as in your presence, passed
4 sentence on such an offender as this, by the authority of
our Lord Jesus Christ; I have met with you in spirit and
5 by the power of our Lord Jesus I have consigned that
individual to Satan for the destruction of his flesh, in order
that his spirit may be saved on the Day of the Lord Jesus.

I. CORINTHIANS VI

6 Your boasting is no credit to you. Do you not know that
7 a morsel of dough will leaven the whole lump? Clean out the old dough that you may be a fresh lump. For you are free from the old leaven; *Christ our paschal lamb has been*
8 *sacrificed.* So let us celebrate our festival, not with any old leaven, not with vice and evil, but with the unleavened bread of innocence and integrity.
9 In my letter I wrote that you were not to associate with
10 the immoral. I did not mean you were literally to avoid contact with the immoral in this world, with the lustful and the thievish, or with idolaters; in that case you would
11 have to leave the world altogether. What I now write is that you are not to associate with any so-called brother who is immoral or lustful or idolatrous or given to abuse or drink or robbery. Associate with him! Do not even
12 eat with him! Outsiders it is no business of mine to judge. No, you must judge those who are inside the church, for
13 yourselves; as for outsiders, God will judge them. *Expel the wicked from your company.*

6 When any of you has a grievance against his neighbour, do you dare to go to law in a sinful pagan court,
2 instead of laying the case before the saints? Do you not know the saints are to manage the world? If the world is to come under your jurisdiction, are you incompetent to
3 adjudicate upon trifles? Do you not know we are to manage
4 angels, let alone mundane issues? And yet, when you have mundane issues to settle, you refer them to the judgment of men who from the point of view of the church are
5 of no account! I say this to put you to shame. Has it come to this, that there is not a single wise man among you who could decide a dispute between members of the
6 brotherhood, instead of one brother going to law with
7 another—and before unbelievers too! Even to have lawsuits with one another is in itself evidence of defeat. Why not rather let yourselves be wronged? Why not
8 rather let yourselves be defrauded? But instead of that you inflict wrong and practise frauds—and that upon
9 members of the brotherhood! What! do you not know that the wicked will not inherit the Realm of God? Make no mistake about it; neither the immoral nor idolaters nor
10 adulterers nor catamites nor sodomites nor thieves nor the lustful nor the drunken nor the abusive nor robbers
11 will inherit the Realm of God. Some of you were once like that; but you washed yourselves clean, you were consecrated, you were justified in the name of our Lord Jesus Christ and in the Spirit of our God.

I. CORINTHIANS VII 253

12 'All things are lawful for me'?
Yes, but not all are good for me.
'All things are lawful for me'?
Yes, but I am not going to let anything master me.
13 'Food is meant for the stomach, and the stomach for food'?
Yes, and God will do away with the one and the other. The body is not meant for immorality but for the Lord,
14 and the Lord is for the body; and the God who raised the
15 Lord will also raise us by his power. Do you not know your bodies are members of Christ? Am I to take Christ's
16 members and devote them to a harlot? Never! Do you not know that
he who joins himself to a harlot
is one with her in body
(for *the pair*, it is said, *shall become one flesh*),
17 while he who joins himself to the Lord
is one with him in spirit.
18 Shun immorality! Any other sin that a man commits is outside the body, but the immoral man sins against his
19 body. Do you not know your body is the temple of the holy Spirit within you—the Spirit you have received from
20 God? You are not your own, you were bought for a price; then glorify God with your body.

7 Now about the questions in your letter.
It is an excellent thing for a man to have no intercourse
2 with a woman; but there is so much immorality that every man had better have a wife of his own and every woman a husband of her own.
3 The husband must give the wife her conjugal dues,
and the wife in the same way must give her husband his;
4 the wife cannot do as she pleases with her body—her husband has power,
and in the same way the husband cannot do as he pleases with his body—his wife has power.
5 Do not withhold sexual intercourse from one another, unless you agree to do so for a time in order to devote yourselves to prayer. Then come together again. You
6 must not let Satan tempt you through incontinence. But what I have just said is by way of concession, not com-
7 mand. I would like all men to be as I am. However, everyone is endowed by God in his own way; he has a gift for the one life or the other.
8 To the unmarried and to widows I would say this: it is an excellent thing if like me they remain as they are.

I. CORINTHIANS VII

9 Still, if they cannot restrain themselves, let them marry. Better marry than be aflame with passion!
10 For married people these are my instructions (and they are the Lord's, not mine). A wife is not to separate from
11 her husband—if she has separated, she must either remain single or be reconciled to him—and a husband must not put away his wife.
12 To other people I would say (not the Lord):—
if any brother has a wife who is not a believer,
and if she consents to live with him,
he must not put her away;
13 and if any wife has a husband who is not a believer,
and if he consents to live with her,
she must not put her husband away.
14 For the unbelieving husband is consecrated in the person of his wife,
and the unbelieving wife is consecrated in the person of the Christian brother she has married;
otherwise, of course, your children would be unholy instead
15 of being consecrated to God. (Should the unbelieving partner be determined to separate, however, separation let it be; in such cases the Christian brother or sister is not tied to marriage.) It is to a life of peace that God has
16 called us.* O wife, how do you know you may not save your husband? O husband, how do you know you may not save your wife?
17 Only, everyone must lead the lot assigned him by the Lord; he must go on living the life in which God's call came to him. (Such is the rule I lay down for all the churches).
18 Was a man circumcised at the time he was called?
Then he is not to efface the marks of it.
Has any man been called when he was uncircumcised?
Then he is not to get circumcised.
19 Circumcision counts for nothing, uncircumcision counts for nothing; obedience to God's commands is everything.
20 Everyone must remain in the condition of life where he
21 was called. You were a slave when you were called? Never mind. Of course, if you do find it possible to get
22 free, you had better avail yourself of the opportunity. But a slave who is called to be in the Lord is a freedman of the Lord. Just as a free man who is called is a slave of
23 Christ (for you were bought for a price; you must not
24 turn slaves to any man). Brothers, everyone must remain with God in the condition of life where he was called.

* Reading ἡμᾶς with B D G, the Latin version, Origen, Chrysostom, etc., instead of ὑμᾶς.

I. CORINTHIANS VII   255

25 I have no orders from the Lord for unmarried women, but I will give you the opinion of one whom you can trust,
26 after all the Lord's mercy to him. Well, what I think is this: that, considering the imminent distress in these days, it would be an excellent plan for you to remain just as you are.
27 Are you tied to a wife? Never try to untie the knot. Are you free? Never try to get married.
28 Of course, if you are actually married, there is no sin in that;
   and if a maid marries, there is no sin in that. (At the same time those who marry will have outward
29 trouble—and I would spare you that.) I mean, brothers,— the interval has been shortened;
   so let those who have wives live as if they had none,
30 let mourners live as if they were not mourning, let the joyful live as if they had no joy,
   let buyers live as if they had no hold on their goods,
31 let those who mix in the world live as if they were not engrossed in it,
   for the present phase of things is passing away.
32 I want you to be free from all anxieties. The unmarried man is anxious about the Lord's affairs, how best to satisfy the Lord;
33 the married man is anxious about worldly affairs,
34 how best to satisfy his wife—so he is torn in two directions.
   The unmarried woman or the maid * is also anxious about the Lord's affairs,
   how to be consecrated, body and spirit;
   once married, she is anxious about worldly affairs, how best to satisfy her husband.
35 I am saying this in your own interests. Not that I want to restrict your freedom. It is only to secure decorum and concentration upon a life of devotion to the Lord.
36 At the same time, if any man considers he is not behaving properly to the maid who is his spiritual bride, if his passions are strong and if it must be so, then let him do what he wants—let them be married; it is no sin for him.
37 But the man of firm purpose who has made up his mind, who, instead of being forced against his will, has determined to himself to keep his maid a spiritual bride—that
38 man will be doing the right thing. Thus both are right alike in marrying and in refraining from marriage, but he who does not marry will be found to have done better.
39 A woman is bound to her husband during his lifetime;

* Reading ἡ γυνὴ ἡ ἄγαμος καὶ ἡ παρθένος with p15 B P, the Vulgate, etc.

but if he dies, she is free to marry anyone she pleases—
40 only, it must be a Christian. However, she is happier if she remains as she is; that is my opinion—and I suppose I have the Spirit of God as well as other people!

8 WITH regard to food that has been offered to idols. Here, of course, 'we all possess knowledge'! Knowledge
2 puffs up, love builds up. Whoever imagines he has attained to some degree of knowledge, does not possess the true
3 knowledge yet; but if anyone loves God, he is known by
4 Him. Well then, with regard to food that has been offered to idols, I am quite aware that 'there is no such thing as an idol in the world' and that 'there is only the one
5 God,' (So-called gods there may be, in heaven or on earth— as indeed there are plenty of them, both gods and 'lords'—
6 but for us
there is one God, the Father,
from whom all comes,
and for whom we exist;
one Lord, Jesus Christ,
by whom all exists,
and by whom we exist.)
7 But remember, it is not everyone who has this 'knowledge.' Some who have hitherto been accustomed to idols eat the food as food which has been really offered to an idol, and
8 so their weaker conscience is contaminated. Now mere food will not bring us any nearer to God;
if we abstain we do not lose anything,
and if we eat we do not gain anything.
9 But see that the exercise of your right does not prove any
10 stumbling-block to the weak. Suppose anyone sees you, a person of enlightened mind, reclining at meat inside an idol's temple; will that really 'fortify his weak conscience'? Will it not embolden him to violate his scruples of con- science by eating food that has been offered to idols?
11 He is ruined, this weak man, ruined by your 'enlightened
12 mind,' this brother for whose sake Christ died! By sin- ning against the brotherhood in this way and wounding their weaker consciences, you are sinning against Christ.
13 Therefore if food is any hindrance to my brother's welfare, sooner than injure him I will never eat flesh as long as I live, never!

9 AM I not free? Am I not an apostle? Have I not seen Jesus our Lord? Are you not the work I have accom-
2 plished in the Lord? To other people I may be no apostle, but to you I am, for you are the seal set upon my apostle-

I. CORINTHIANS IX

3 ship in the Lord. Here is my reply to my inquisitors.
4 Have we no right to eat and drink at the expense of the
5 churches? Have we no right to travel with a Christian
wife, like the rest of the apostles, like the brothers of the
6 Lord, like Cephas himself? What! are we the only ones,
myself and Barnabas, who are denied the right of abstain-
7 ing from work for our living? Does a soldier provide his
own supplies? Does a man plant a vineyard without eating
its produce? Does a shepherd get no drink from the milk
8 of the flock? Human arguments, you say? But does not
9 Scripture urge the very same? It is written in the law
of Moses, *You must not muzzle an ox when he is treading*
10 *the grain.* Is God thinking here about cattle? Or is he
speaking purely for our sakes? Assuredly for our sakes.
This word was written for us, because the ploughman needs
to plough in hope, and the thresher to thresh in the hope of
11 getting a share in the crop. If we sowed you the seeds
of spiritual good, is it a great matter if we reap your
12 worldly goods? If others share this right over you, why
not we all the more? We did not avail ourselves of it,
you say? No, we do not mind any privations if we can
only avoid putting any obstacle in the way of the gospel
13 of Christ. Do you not know that as men who perform
temple-rites get their food from the temple, and as attend-
14 ants at the altar get their share of the sacrifices, so the
Lord's instructions were that those who proclaim the
15 gospel are to get their living by the gospel? Only, I have
not availed myself of any of these rights, and I am not
writing in order to secure any such provision for myself.
I would die sooner than let anyone deprive me of this, my
16 source of pride. What I am proud of is not the mere
preaching of the gospel; that I am constrained to do.
17 Woe to me if I do not preach the gospel! I get a reward
if I do it of my own accord, whereas to do it otherwise
is no more than for a steward to discharge his trust.
18 And my reward? This, that I can preach the gospel free
of charge, that I can refrain from insisting on all my rights
19 as a preacher of the gospel. Why,
 free as I am from all, I have made myself the slave of all,
  to win over as many as I could.
20 To Jews I have become like a Jew,
  to win over Jews;
 to those under the Law I have become as one of themselves—
 though I am not under the Law myself—
  to win over those under the Law;
21 to those outside the Law I have become like one of themselves—

I. CORINTHIANS X

though I am under Christ's law, not outside God's Law—
to win over those outside the Law;
22 to the weak I have become as weak myself,
to win over the weak.
To all men I have become all things,
to save some by all and every means.
23 And I do it all for the sake of the gospel, to secure my
24 own share in it. Do you not know that in a race, though
all run, only one man gains the prize? Run so as to win
25 the prize. Every athlete practices self-restraint all round;
but while they do it to win a fading wreath, we do it for
26 an unfading. Well, I run without swerving; I do not plant
27 my blows upon the empty air—no, I maul and master my
body, in case, after preaching to other people, I am disqualified myself.

10 For I would have you know this, my brothers, that
while our fathers all lived under the cloud, all crossed
2 through the sea, all were baptized into Moses by the cloud
3 and by the sea, all ate the same supernatural food, and all
4 drank the same supernatural drink (drinking from the
5 supernatural Rock which accompanied them—and that
Rock was Christ), still with most of them God was not
6 satisfied; *they were laid low in the desert.* Now this took
place as a warning for us, to keep us from *craving* for evil
7 as *they craved.* And you must not be idolaters, like some
of them; as it is written,
the people sat down to eat and drink,
and they rose up to make sport.
8 Nor must we commit immorality, as some of them did—
and in a single day twenty-three thousand of them fell.
9 Nor must we presume upon the Lord as some of them did
10 —only to be destroyed by serpents. And you must not
murmur, as some of them did—only to be destroyed by the
11 Destroying angel. It all happened to them by way of warning for others, and it was written down for the purpose
of instructing us whose lot has been cast in the closing
12 hours of the world. So let anyone who thinks he stands
13 secure, take care in case he falls. No temptation has waylaid you that is beyond man's power; trust God, he will
never let you be tempted beyond what you can stand, but
when temptation comes, he will provide the way out of it,
so that you can bear up under it.
14 Shun idolatry, then, my beloved. I am speaking to sen-
15 sible people; weigh my words for yourselves.
16 The cup of blessing, which we bless,
is that not participating in the blood of Christ?

I. CORINTHIANS XI

The bread we break,
is that not participating in the body of Christ?
17 (for many as we are, we are one Bread, one Body, since
18 we all partake of the one Bread). Look at the rites of
Israel. Do not those who eat the sacrifices participate in
19 the altar? Do I imply, you ask, that 'food offered to an
idol has any meaning, or that an idol itself means any-
20 thing'? No, what I imply is that anything people sacrifice
is sacrificed to daemons, not to God. And I do not want
21 you to participate in daemons! You cannot drink the cup
of the Lord and also the cup of daemons; you cannot partake of the table of the Lord and also of the table of
22 daemons. What! *do we intend to rouse the Lord's jealousy?* Are we stronger than he is?
23 'All things are lawful'?
Yes, but not all are good for us.
'All things are lawful'?
Yes, but not all are edifying.
24 Each of us must consult his neighbour's interests, not his
25 own. Eat any food that has been sold in the market,
instead of letting scruples of conscience oblige you to
26 ask any questions about it; *the earth and all its contents
27 belong to the Lord.* When an unbeliever invites you to
dinner and you agree to go, eat whatever is put before
you, instead of letting scruples of conscience induce you
28 to ask any questions about it. But if someone tells you,
'This was sacrificial meat,' then do not eat it; you must
consider the man who told you, and also take conscience
29 into account—his conscience, I mean, not your own; for
why should one's own freedom be called in question by
30 someone else's conscience? If one partakes of food after
saying a blessing over it, why should one be denounced
31 for eating what one has given thanks to God for? So
whether you eat or drink, or whatever you do, let it be all
32 done for the glory of God. Put no stumbling-block in the
33 way of Jews or Greeks or the church of God. Such is my
own rule, to satisfy all men in all points, aiming not at my
own advantage but at the advantage of the greater number—at their salvation. Copy me, as I copy Christ.
2 **11** I commend you for always bearing me in mind
and for maintaining the traditions I passed on to you.
3 But I would like you to understand this: Christ is
the head of every man, man is the head of woman, and
4 God is the head of Christ. Any man who prays or proph-
5 esies with a veil on his head dishonours his head, while
any woman who prays or prophesies without a veil on her
head dishonours her head; she is no better than a shaven
6 woman. If a woman will not veil herself, she should cut

off her hair as well. But she ought to veil herself; for it
is disgraceful that a woman should have her hair cut off
7 or be shaven. Man does not require to have a veil on his
head, for he represents *the likeness and supremacy of God;*
8 but woman represents the supremacy of man. (Man was
9 not made from woman, woman was made from man; and
man was not created for woman, but woman for man.)
10 Therefore, in view of the angels, woman must wear a
11 symbol of subjection on her head. (Of course, in the Lord,
woman does not exist apart from man, any more than
12 man apart from woman; for as woman was made from
man, so man is now made from woman, while both, like
13 all things, come from God.) Judge for yourselves; is it
14 proper for an unveiled woman to pray to God? Surely
nature herself teaches you that while long hair is disgrace-
15 ful for a man, for a woman long hair is a glory? Her hair
16 is given her as a covering. If anyone presumes to raise
objections on this point—well, I acknowledge no other
mode of worship, and neither do the churches of God.
17 But in giving you the following injunction I cannot
commend you; for you are the worse, not the better, for
18 assembling together. First of all, in your church-meet-
ings I am told that cliques prevail. And I partly believe
19 it. There must be parties among you, if genuine Chris-
20 tians are to be recognized. But this makes it impossible
for you to eat the 'Lord's' supper when you hold your
21 gatherings. As you eat, everyone takes his own supper;
22 one goes hungry while another gets drunk. What! have
you no houses to eat and drink in? Do you think you can
show disrespect to the church of God and put the poor
to shame? What can I say to you? Commend you? Not
23 for this. I passed on to you what I received from the
Lord himself, namely, that on the night he was betrayed
24 the Lord Jesus took a loaf, and after thanking God he
broke it, saying, 'This means my body broken* for you;
25 do this in memory of me.' In the same way he took the
cup after supper, saying, 'This cup means the new *covenant*
ratified *by* my *blood;* as often as you drink it, do it in
26 memory of me.' For as often as you eat this loaf and
drink this cup, you proclaim the Lord's death until he
27 comes. Hence anyone who eats the loaf or drinks the cup
of the Lord carelessly, will have to answer for a sin against
28 the body and the blood of the Lord. Let a man test him-

---

* Von Soden brackets κλώμενον, but it must be read with אc C³, two
correctors of D (which originally read θρυπτόμενον), G, the Old Latin and
Syriac Vulgate, Chrysostom, etc. If it is a gloss, it is a correct one,
unless the Lucan διδόμενον be preferred.

I. CORINTHIANS XII

self; then he can eat from the loaf and drink from the cup.
29 For he who eats and drinks without a proper sense of the
30 Body, eats and drinks to his own condemnation. That is why many of you are ill and infirm, and a number even
31 dead. If we only judged our own lives truly, we would
32 not come under the Lord's judgment. As it is, we are chastened when we are judged by him, so that we may not be condemned along with the world.
33 Well then, my brothers, when you gather for a meal, wait
34 for one another; and if anyone is hungry let him eat at home. You must not gather, only to incur condemnation.
   I will give you my instructions upon the other matters when I come.

12 But I want you to understand about spiritual gifts,
2   brothers. You know when you were pagans, how
3 your impulses led you to dumb idols; so I tell you now, that no one is speaking in the Spirit of God when he cries, 'Cursed be Jesus,' and that no one can say, 'Jesus is Lord,' except in the holy Spirit.
4   There are varieties of talents,
      but the same Spirit;
5   varieties of service,
      but the same Lord;
6   varieties of effects,
      but the same God who effects everything in everyone.
7 Each receives his manifestation of the Spirit for the
8 common good. One man is granted words of wisdom by the Spirit, another words of knowledge by the same Spirit;
9 one man in the same Spirit has the gift of faith, another
10 in the one Spirit has gifts of healing; one has prophecy, another the gift of distinguishing spirits, another the gift of 'tongues' in their variety, another the gift of interpreting
11 'tongues.' But all these effects are produced by one and the same Spirit, apportioning them severally to each individual as he pleases.
12 As the human body is one and has many members, all the members of the body forming one body for all their
13 number, so is it with Christ. For by one Spirit we have all been baptized into one Body, Jews or Greeks, slaves or
14 freemen; we have all been imbued with one Spirit. Why, even the body consists not of one member but of many.
15 If the foot were to say, 'Because I am not the hand, I do not belong to the body,' that does not make it no part of
16 the body. If the ear were to say, 'Because I am not the eye, I do not belong to the body,' that does not make it
17 no part of the body. If the body were all eye, where would hearing be? If the body were all ear, where would

18 smell be? As it is, God has set the members in the body,
19 each as it pleased him. If they all made up one member,
20 what would become of the body? As it is, there are many
21 members and one body. The eye cannot say to the hand,
'I have no need of you,' nor again the head to the feet, 'I
22 have no need of you.' Quite the contrary. We cannot do
without those very members of the body which are con-
23 sidered rather delicate, just as the parts we consider rather
dishonourable are the very parts we invest with special
honour; our indecorous parts get a special care and atten-
24 tion which does not need to be paid to our more decorous
parts. Yes, God has tempered the body together, with a
25 special dignity for the inferior parts, so that there may
be no disunion in the body, but that the various members
26 should have a common concern for one another. Thus
   if one member suffers,
      all the members share its suffering;
   if one member is honoured,
      all the members share its honour.
27 Now you are Christ's Body, and severally members of it.
28 That is to say, God has set people within the church to
be first of all apostles, secondly prophets, thirdly teachers,
then workers of miracles, then healers, helpers, administra-
29 tors, and speakers in 'tongues' of various kinds. Are all
apostles? Are all prophets? Are all teachers? Are all
30 workers of miracles? Are all endowed with the gifts of
healing? Are all able to speak in 'tongues'? Are all able
to interpret?
31   Set your hearts on the higher talents. And yet I will
go on to show you a still higher path. Thus,

13 I may speak with the tongues of men and of angels,
     but if I have no love,
        I am a noisy gong or a clanging cymbal;
2 I may prophesy, fathom all mysteries and secret lore,
   I may have such absolute faith that I can move hills
      from their place,
   but if I have no love,
      I count for nothing;
3 I may distribute all I possess in charity,
   I may give up my body to be burnt,
     but if I have no love,
       I make nothing of it.
4 Love is very patient, very kind. Love knows no jealousy;
5 love makes no parade, gives itself no airs, is never rude,
6 never selfish, never irritated, *never resentful;* love is never
glad when others go wrong, love is gladdened by good-
7 ness, always slow to expose, always eager to believe the
8 best, always hopeful, always patient. Love never dis-

I. CORINTHIANS XIV

appears. As for prophesying, it will be superseded; as for 'tongues,' they will cease; as for knowledge, it will be
9 superseded. For we only know bit by bit, and we only
10 prophesy bit by bit; but when the perfect comes, the im-
11 perfect will be superseded. When I was a child, I talked like a child, I thought like a child, I argued like a child; now that I am a man, I am done with childish ways.
12 At present we only see the baffling reflections in a mirror,
but then it will be face to face;
at present I am learning bit by bit,
but then I shall understand, as all along I have myself been understood.
13 Thus 'faith and hope and love last on, these three,' but the greatest of all is love. Make love your aim, and
14 then set your heart on the spiritual gifts—especially
2 upon prophecy. For he who speaks in a 'tongue' addresses God not men; no one understands him; he is talking of
3 divine secrets in the Spirit. On the other hand, he who prophesies addresses men in words that edify, encourage,
4 and console them. He who speaks in a 'tongue' edifies him-
5 self, whereas he who prophesies edifies the church. Now I would like you all to speak with 'tongues,' but I would prefer you to prophesy. The man who prophesies is higher than the man who speaks with 'tongues'—unless indeed the latter interprets, so that the church may get edifica-
6 tion. Suppose now I were to come to you speaking with 'tongues,' my brothers; what good could I do you, unless I had some revelation or knowledge or prophecy or teach-
7 ing to lay before you? Inanimate instruments, such as the flute or the harp, may give a sound, but if no intervals occur in their music, how can one make out the air that
8 is being played either on flute or on harp? If the trumpet
9 sounds indistinct, who will get ready for the fray? Well, it is the same with yourselves. Unless your tongue utters language that is readily understood, how can people make out what you say? You will be pouring words into the
10 empty air! There are ever so many kinds of language in
11 the world, every one of them meaning something. Well, unless I understand the meaning of what is said to me, I shall appear to the speaker to be talking gibberish, and
12 to my mind he will be talking gibberish himself. So with yourselves; since your heart is set on possessing 'spirits,' make the edification of the church your aim in this desire
13 to excel. Thus a man who speaks in a 'tongue' must pray
14 for the gift of interpreting it. For if I pray with a 'tongue,' my spirit prays, no doubt, but my mind is no use
15 to anyone. Very well then, I will pray in the Spirit, but I will also pray with my mind; I will sing praise in the

I. CORINTHIANS XIV

16 Spirit, but I will also sing praise with my mind. Otherwise, suppose you are blessing God in the Spirit, how is the outsider to say 'Amen' to your thanksgiving? The man
17 does not understand what you are saying! Your thanksgiving may be all right, but then—the other man is not
18 edified! Thank God, I speak in 'tongues' more than any
19 of you; but in church I would rather say five words with my own mind for the instruction of other people than ten thousand words in a 'tongue.'
20 Brothers, do not be children in the sphere of intelligence; in evil be mere infants, but be mature in your intelligence.
21 It is written in the Law, *By men of alien tongues and by the lips of aliens I will speak to this People; but even so,*
22 *they will not listen* to me, saith the Lord. Thus 'tongues' are intended as a sign, not for believers but for unbelievers; whereas prophesying is meant for believers, not for unbe-
23 lievers. Hence if at a gathering of the whole church everybody speaks with 'tongues,' and if outsiders or unbelievers come in, will they not say you are insane?
24 Whereas, if everybody prophesies, and some unbeliever or outsider comes in, he is exposed by all, brought to book by
25 all; the secrets of his heart are brought to light, and so, falling on his face, *he will worship God, declaring, 'God is really among you.'*
26 Very well then, brothers; when you meet together, each contributes something—a song of praise, a lesson, a revelation, a 'tongue,' an interpretation? Good; but let every-
27 thing be for edification. As for speaking in a 'tongue,' let only two or at most three speak at one meeting, and that
28 in turn. Also, let someone interpret; if there is no interpreter, let the speaker keep quiet in church and address
29 himself and God. Let only two or three prophets speak, while the rest exercise their judgment upon what is said.
30 Should a revelation come to one who is seated, the first
31 speaker must be quiet. You can all prophesy quite well, one after another, so as to let all learn and all be en-
32 couraged. Prophets can control their own prophetic spirits,
33 for God is a God not of disorder but of harmony.*
37 If anyone considers himself a prophet or gifted with the Spirit, let him understand that what I write to you is a
38 command of the Lord. Anyone who disregards this will be himself disregarded.
39 To sum up, my brothers. Set your heart on the prophetic gift, and do not put any check upon speaking in

---

* Transposing vers. 33b–36 to the end of the chapter, in order to preserve the sequence of thought. There is some early textual evidence for reading 34–35 after 40.

I. CORINTHIANS XV 265

40 'tongues'; but let everything be done decorously and in order.
33 34 As is the rule in all churches of the saints, women must keep quiet at gatherings of the church. They are not allowed to speak; they must take a subordinate place, as
35 the Law enjoins. If they want any information, let them ask their husbands at home; it is disgraceful for a woman
36 to speak in church. You challenge this rule? Pray, did God's word start from you? Are you the only people it has reached?

15 Now, brothers, I would have you know the gospel I once preached to you, the gospel you received, the
2 gospel in which you have your footing, the gospel by which you are saved—provided you adhere to my statement of it—unless indeed your faith was all haphazard.
3 First and foremost, I passed on to you what I had myself received, namely, that Christ died for our sins as the
4 scriptures had said, that he was buried, that he rose on the
5 third day as the scriptures had said, and that he was seen
6 by Cephas, then by the twelve; after that, he was seen by over five hundred brothers all at once, the majority
7 of whom survive to this day, though some have died; after
8 that, he was seen by James, then by all the apostles, and finally he was seen by myself, by this so-called 'abortion'
9 of an apostle. For I am the very least of the apostles, unfit to bear the name of apostle, since I persecuted the church
10 of God. But by God's grace I am what I am. The grace he showed me did not go for nothing; no, I have done far more work than all of them—though it was not I but God's
11 grace at my side. At any rate, whether I or they have done most, such is what we preach, such is what you believed.
12 Now if we preach that Christ rose from the dead, how can certain individuals among you assert that 'there is no such
13 thing as a resurrection of the dead'? If 'there is no such thing as a resurrection from the dead,' then even Christ
14 did not rise; and if Christ did not rise, then our preaching has gone for nothing, and your faith has gone for nothing
15 too. Besides, we are detected bearing false witness to God by affirming of him that he raised Christ—whom he did not
16 raise, if after all dead men never rise. For if dead men
17 never rise, Christ did not rise either; and if Christ did not
18 rise, your faith is futile, you are still in your sins. More than that: those who have slept the sleep of death in
19 Christ have perished after all. Ah, if in this life we have nothing but a mere hope in Christ, we are of all men to be pitied most!

I. CORINTHIANS XV

20 But it is not so! Christ did rise from the dead, he was the first to be reaped of those who sleep in death.
21 For since death came by man,
   by man came also resurrection from the dead;
22 as all die in Adam,
   so shall all be made alive in Christ.
23 But each in his own division:—Christ the first to be reaped; after that, all who belong to Christ, at his arrival.
24 Then comes the end, when he hands over his royal power to God the Father, after putting down all other rulers, all other authorities and powers.
25 For he must reign until all his foes are put under his feet.
26 (Death is the last foe to be put down.)
27 For *God has put everything under his feet.* When it is said that *everything* has been put under him, plainly that excludes Him who put everything under him;
28 and when everything is put under him, then the Son himself will be put under Him who put everything under him, so that God may be everything to everyone.
29 Otherwise, if there is no such thing as a resurrection, what is the meaning of people getting baptized on behalf of their dead? If dead men do not rise at all, why do people get baptized on their behalf?
30 Yes, and why am I myself in danger every hour?
31 (Not a day but I am at death's door! I swear it by my pride in you, brothers,
32 through Christ Jesus our Lord.) What would it avail me that, humanly speaking, I 'fought with wild beasts' at Ephesus? · If dead men do not rise, *let us eat and drink, for we will be dead to-morrow!*
33 Make no mistake about this: 'bad company is the ruin of good character.'
34 Get back to your sober senses and avoid sin, for some of you—and I say this to your shame —some of you are insensible to God.
35 But, someone will ask, 'how do the dead rise? What kind of body have they when they come?'
36 Foolish man! What you sow never comes to life unless it dies.
37 And what you sow is not the body that is to be; it is a mere grain of wheat, for example, or some other seed.
38 God gives it a body as he pleases, gives each kind of seed a body of its own.
39 Flesh is not all the same; there is human flesh, there is flesh of beasts, flesh of birds, and flesh of fish.
40 There are heavenly bodies and also earthly bodies, but the splendour of the heavenly is one thing and the splendour of the earthly is another.
41 There is a splendour of the sun and a splendour of the moon and a splendour of the stars—for one star differs from another in splendour.
42 So with the resurrection of the dead:
   what is sown is mortal,
   what rises is immortal;

43 sown inglorious,
it rises in glory;
sown in weakness,
it rises in power;
44 sown an animate body,
it rises a spiritual body.
As there is an animate body, so there is a spiritual body.
45 Thus it is written,
'*The first man, Adam, became an animate being,
the last Adam a life-giving Spirit*';
46 but the animate, not the spiritual, comes first,
and only then the spiritual.
47 *Man the first is from the earth, material;*
Man the second is from heaven.
48 As Man the material is, so are the material;
as Man the heavenly is, so are the heavenly.
49 Thus, as we have borne the likeness of material Man,
so we are to bear * the likeness of the heavenly Man.
50 I tell you this, my brothers, flesh and blood cannot inherit
the Realm of God, nor can the perishing inherit the im-
51 perishable. Here is a secret truth for you: not all of us
52 are to die, but all of us are to be changed—changed in a
moment, in the twinkling of an eye, at the last trumpet-
call. The trumpet will sound, the dead will rise imperish-
53 able, and we shall be changed. For this perishing body
must be invested with the imperishable, and this mortal
54 body invested with immortality; and when this mortal
body has been invested with immortality,† then the saying
of Scripture will be realized,
Death is swallowed up in victory.
55 *O Death, where is your victory?*
O Death, where is your sting? ‡
57 The victory is ours, thank God! He makes it ours by our
58 Lord Jesus Christ. Well then, my beloved brothers, hold
your ground, immovable; abound in work for the Lord
at all times, for you may be sure that in the Lord your
labour is never thrown away.

16 With regard to the collection for the saints, you must
carry out the same arrangements as I made for the
2 churches of Galatia. On the first day of the week let each

* Reading φορέσομεν with B 181 arm aeth, etc., instead of the strongly
supported φορέσωμεν.
† Omitting τὸ φθαρτὸν τοῦτο ἐνδύσηται ἀφθαρσίαν, καὶ with ℵ* C* and
most of the versions. The phrase was probably inserted for the sake of
completing the parallel.
‡ After this verse, the words " The sting of sin is death, and the
strength of sin is the Law " have been added either as a gloss by some
editor or perhaps as a marginal note by Paul himself.

of you put aside a sum from his weekly gains, so that the
3 money may not have to be collected when I come. On my
arrival I will furnish credentials for those whom you
select, and send them to convey your bounty to Jerusalem;
4 if the sum makes it worth my while to go too, they shall
accompany me.
5 I mean to visit you after my tour in Macedonia, for I am
6 going to make a tour through Macedonia. The chances are,
I shall spend some time with you, possibly even pass the
winter with you, so that you may speed me forward on
7 any journey that lies before me. I do not care about seeing
you at this moment merely in the by-going; my hope is
to stay among you for some time, with the Lord's permis-
8 sion. I am staying on for the present at Ephesus till
9 Pentecost, for I have wide opportunities here for active
service—and there are many to thwart me.
10 If Timotheus arrives, see that you make him feel quite at
home with you; he carries on the work of the Lord as I
11 do. So let no one disparage him. When he leaves to re-
join me, speed him cordially on his journey, for I am expecting him along with the other brothers.
12 As for our brother Apollos, I urged him to accompany the
other brothers on a visit to you; he will come as soon as
he has time, but for the present it is not the will of God
that he should visit you.
13 Watch, stand firm in the faith, play the man, be strong!
14 Let all you do be done in love.
15 I ask this favour of you, my brothers. The household of
Stephanas, you know, was the first to be reaped in Achaia,
and they have laid themselves out to serve the saints.
16 Well, I want you to put yourselves under people like that,
under everyone who sets his hand to the work.
17 I am glad that Stephanas and Fortunatus and Achaicus
have arrived, for they have made up for your absence.
18 They refresh my spirit as they do your own. You should
appreciate men like that.
19 The churches of Asia salute you. Aquila and Prisca,
with the church that meets in their house, salute you
20 warmly in the Lord. All the brotherhood salutes you.
Salute one another with a holy kiss.
21
22 I Paul write this salutation with my own hand. 'If anyone has no love for the Lord, God's curse be on him! Maran
23 atha!* The grace of the Lord Jesus be with you. My
24 love be with you all in Christ Jesus.' [Amen.]

* An Aramaic phrase, probably meaning " Lord, come " (see Rev.
xxii. 20).

THE SECOND EPISTLE OF PAUL THE APOSTLE TO THE

CORINTHIANS

1 PAUL an apostle of Christ Jesus by the will of God, and brother Timotheus, to the church of God at Corinth as well as to all the saints throughout the whole of Achaia:
2 grace and peace to you from God our Father and the Lord Jesus Christ.
3 Blessed be the God and Father of our Lord Jesus Christ, the Father of tender mercies and the God of all comfort,
4 who comforts me in all my distress, so that I am able to comfort people who are in any distress by the comfort with
5 which I myself am comforted by God. For as the sufferings of Christ are abundant in my case, so my comfort is
6 also abundant through Christ. If I am in distress, it is in the interests of your comfort and salvation; if I am comforted, it is in the interests of your comfort, which is effective as it nerves you to endure the same sufferings as I
7 suffer myself. Hence my hope for you is well-founded, since I know that as you share the sufferings you share the comfort also.
8 Now I would like you to know about the distress which befell me in Asia, brothers. I was crushed, crushed far more than I could stand, so much so that I despaired even
9 of life; in fact I told myself it was the sentence of death. But that was to make me rely not on myself but on the
10 God who raises the dead; he rescued me from so terrible a death, he rescues still, and I rely upon him for the hope
11 that he will continue to rescue me. Let me have your co-operation in prayer, so that many a soul may render thanks to him on my behalf for the boon which many have been the means of him bestowing on myself.
12 My proud boast is the testimony of my conscience that holiness and godly sincerity, not worldly cunning but the grace of God, have marked my conduct in the outside world
13 and in particular my relations with you. You don't have to read between the lines of my letters; you can understand them. Yes, I trust you will understand the full
14 meaning of my letters as you have partly understood the meaning of my life, namely that I am your source of pride (as you are mine) on the Day of our Lord Jesus.

15 Relying on this I meant to visit you first, to let you have
16 a double delight; I intended to take you on my way to Macedonia, and to visit you again on my way back from Macedonia, so as to be sped by you on my journey to
17 Judaea. Such was my intention. Now, have I shown myself 'fickle'? When I propose some plan, do I propose it in a worldly way, ready to mean 'no' as well as 'yes'?
18 By the good faith of God, my word to you was not 'yes
19 and no'; for the Son of God, Jesus Christ, who was proclaimed among you by us (by myself and Silvanus and Timotheus) was not 'yes and no'—the divine 'yes' has at
20 last sounded in him, for in him is the 'yes' that affirms all the promises of God. Hence it is through him that we
21 affirm our 'amen' in worship, to the glory of God. And it is God who confirms me along with you in Christ, who con-
22 secrated me, who stamped me with his seal and gave me
23 the Spirit as a pledge in my heart. I call God to witness against my soul, it was to spare you that I refrained from
24 revisiting Corinth. (Not that we lord it over your faith—no, we co-operate for your joy: you have a standing of your own in the faith.) I decided I would not pay you
2 2 another painful visit. For if I pain you, then who is to give me pleasure? None but the very people I am
3 paining! So the very reason I wrote was that I might not come only to be pained by those who ought to give me joy; I relied on you all, I felt sure that my joy would be
4 a joy for every one of you. For I wrote you in sore distress and misery of heart, with many a tear—not to pain you but to convince you of my love, my special love for you.
5 If a certain individual has been causing pain, he has been causing pain not so much to me as to all of you—at anyrate (for I am not going to overstate the case) to a section
6 of you. This censure from the majority is severe enough
7 for the individual in question, so that instead of censuring you should now forgive him and comfort him, in case the
8 man is overwhelmed by excessive remorse. So I beg you
9 to reinstate him in your love. For my aim in writing was simply to test you, to see if you were absolutely obedient.
10 If you forgive the man, I forgive him too; anything I had to forgive him has been forgiven in the presence of Christ
11 for your sakes, in case Satan should take advantage of our position—for I know his manœuvres!
12 Well, when I reached Troas to preach the gospel of Christ, though I had a wide opportunity in the Lord,
13 my spirit could not rest, because I did not find Titus my brother there; so I said goodbye and went off to Mace-
14 donia. Wherever I go, thank God, he makes my life a constant pageant of triumph in Christ, diffusing the perfume

II. CORINTHIANS III

15 of his knowledge everywhere by me. I live for God as the fragrance of Christ breathed alike on those who are being
16 saved and on those who are perishing, to the one a deadly fragrance that makes for death, to the other a vital fragrance that makes for life. And who is qualified for this
17 career? I am, for I am not like most, adulterating the word of God; like a man of sincerity, like a man of God, I speak the word in Christ before the very presence of God.

3 AM I beginning again to 'commend' myself? Do I need, like some people, to be commended by written certifi-
2 cates either to you or from you? Why, you are my certificate yourselves, written on my heart, recognized and read
3 by all men; you make it obvious that you are a letter of Christ which I have been employed to inscribe, *written* not with ink but with the Spirit of the living God, not *on*
4 *tablets of stone* but *on tablets of the human heart*. Such is the confidence I possess through Christ in my service of
5 God. It is not that I am personally qualified to form any judgment by myself; my qualifications come from God,
6 and he has further qualified me to be the minister of a new covenant—a covenant not of written law but of spirit;
7 for the written law kills but the Spirit makes alive. Now if the administration of death which was engraved in letters of stone, was invested with glory—so much so, that the children of Israel could not gaze at the face of *Moses* on account of *the dazzling glory* that was fading from *his*
8 *face;* surely the administration of the Spirit must be in-
9 vested with still greater glory. If there was glory in the administration that condemned, then the administration
10 that acquits abounds far more in glory (indeed, in view of the transcendent glory, *what was glorious has thus* no
11 *glory* at all); if what faded had its glory, then what lasts
12 will be invested with far greater glory. Such being my
13 hope then, I am quite frank and open—not like *Moses*, who *used to hang a veil over his face* to keep the children of Israel from gazing at the last rays of a fading glory.
14 Besides, their minds were dulled, for to this very day, when the Old Testament is read aloud, the same veil hangs. Veiled from them the fact that the glory fades in Christ!
15 Yes, down to this day, whenever Moses is read aloud, the
16 veil rests on their heart; though *whenever they turn to*
17 *the Lord, the veil is removed.* (The Lord means the Spirit, and wherever the Spirit of the Lord is, there is open
18 freedom.) But we all mirror *the glory of the Lord* with face unveiled, and so we are being transformed into the same likeness as himself, passing from one glory to

4 another—for this comes of the Lord the Spirit. Hence, as I hold this ministry by God's mercy to me, I never
2 lose heart in it; I disown those practices which very shame conceals from view; I do not go about it craftily; I do not falsify the word of God; I state the truth openly and so commend myself to every man's conscience before God.
3 Even if my gospel is veiled, it is only veiled in the case
4 of the perishing; there the god of this world has blinded the minds of unbelievers, to prevent them seeing the light thrown by the gospel of the glory of Christ, who is the
5 likeness of God. (It is Christ Jesus as Lord, not myself, that I proclaim; I am simply a servant of yours for Jesus'
6 sake.) For God who said, "Light shall shine out of darkness," has shone within my heart to illuminate men with the knowledge of God's glory in the face of Christ.
7 But I possess this treasure in a frail vessel of earth, to show that the transcending power belongs to God, not to
8 myself; on every side I am harried but not hemmed in,
9 perplexed but not despairing, persecuted but not abandoned, struck down but not destroyed—
10 wherever I go, I am being killed in the body as Jesus was,
so that the life of Jesus may come out in my body:
11 every day of my life I am being given over to death for Jesus' sake,
so that the life of Jesus may come out within my mortal flesh.
12
13 In me then death is active, in you life. But since our spirit of faith is the same, therefore—as it is written *I*
14 *believed and so I spoke*—I too believe and so I speak, sure that He who raised the Lord Jesus will raise me too with
15 Jesus and set me at your side in his presence. It is all in your interests, so that the more grace abounds, the more thanksgiving may rise and redound to the glory of God.
16 Hence I never lose heart; though my outward man decays,
17 my inner man is renewed day after day. The slight trouble of the passing hour * results in a solid glory past all com-
18 parison, for those of us whose eyes are on the unseen, not on the seen; for the seen is transient, the unseen eternal.

5 I know that if this earthly tent of mine is taken down, I get a home from God, made by no human hands,
2 eternal in the heavens. It makes me sigh indeed, this yearning to be under the cover of my heavenly habitation,
3 since I am sure that once so covered I shall not be 'naked'
4 at the hour of death. I do sigh within this tent of mine with heavy anxiety—not that I want to be stripped, no,

* Omitting ἡμῶν.

II. CORINTHIANS VI

but to be under the cover of the other, to have my mortal
5 element absorbed by life. I am prepared for this change
by God, who has given me the Spirit as its pledge and
6 instalment. Come what may, then, I am confident; I know
that while I reside in the body I am away from the Lord
7 (for I have to lead my life in faith, without seeing him):
8 and in this confidence I would fain get away from the body
9 and reside with the Lord. Hence also I am eager to
10 satisfy him, whether in the body or away from it; for we
have all to appear without disguise before the tribunal
of Christ, each to be requited for what he has done with
his body, well or ill.
11 If I 'appeal to the interests of men,' then, it is with the
fear of the Lord before my mind. What I am is plain to
God without disguise, plain also, I trust, to your own con-
12 science. This is not 'recommending myself to you again';
it is giving you an incentive to be proud of me, which you
can use against men who are proud of externals instead
13 of the inward reality. 'I am beside myself,' am I? Well,
that is between myself and God. I am 'sane,' am I?
14 Well, that is in your interests; for I am controlled by the
love of Christ, convinced that as One has died for all,
15 then all have died, and that he died for all in order to have
the living live no longer for themselves but for him who
16 died and rose for them. Once convinced of this, then, I
estimate no one by what is external; even though I once
estimated Christ by what is external, I no longer estimate
17 him thus. There is a new creation whenever a man comes
to be in Christ; what is old is gone, the new has come.
18 It is all the doing of the God who has reconciled me to
himself through Christ and has permitted me to be a
19 minister of his reconciliation. For in Christ God reconciled
the world to himself instead of counting men's trespasses
against them; and he entrusted me with the message of
20 his reconciliation. So I am an envoy for Christ, God
appealing by me, as it were—be reconciled to God, I entreat
21 you on behalf of Christ. For our sakes He made him to be
sin who himself knew nothing of sin, so that in him we
might become the righteousness of God.   I appeal to
6 you too, as a worker with God, do not receive the grace
2 of God in vain. (He saith,

I have heard you in the time of favour,
and helped you on the day of salvation.

Well, here is *the time of favour*, here is *the day of salva-*
3 *tion.*) I put no obstacle in the path of any, so that my
4 ministry may not be discredited; I prove myself at all
points a true minister of God, by great endurance, by suf-
5 fering, by troubles, by calamities, by lashes, by imprison-

6 ment; mobbed, toiling, sleepless, starving; with innocence,
insight, patience, kindness, the holy Spirit, unaffected love,
7 true words, the power of God; with the weapons of integ-
8 rity for attack or for defence, amid honour and dishonour,
amid evil report and good report, an 'impostor' but honest,
9 'unknown' but well-known, *dying* but here I am *alive*,
10 *chastened but not killed*, grieved but always glad, a
'pauper', but the means of wealth to many, without a penny
but possessed of all.
11 O Corinthians, I am keeping nothing back from you;
12 my *heart is wide open* for you. 'Restraint'?—that lies
13 with you, not me. A fair exchange now, as the children
say! Open your hearts wide to me.
14 [Keep out of all incongruous ties with unbelievers.
What have righteousness and iniquity in common,
or how can light associate with darkness?
15 What harmony can there be between Christ and Beliar,
or what business has a believer with an unbeliever?
16 What compact can there be between God's temple and
idols?
For we are the temple of the living God—as God has
said,
I will dwell and move among them,
I will be their God and they shall be my people.
17 Therefore *come away from them,*
separate, saith the Lord,
touch not what is unclean;
then I will receive you,
18 *I will be a Father to you,*
and you shall be *my sons and daughters,*
saith the Lord almighty.

7 As these great promises are ours, beloved, let us cleanse
ourselves from everything that contaminates either flesh
or spirit; let us be fully consecrated by reverence for God].*
2 Make a place for me in your hearts; I have wronged no
one, ruined no one, taken advantage of no one.
3 I am not saying this to condemn you. Condemn you?
Why, I repeat, you are in my very heart, and you will be
4 there in death and life alike. I have absolute confidence
in you, I am indeed proud of you, you are a perfect comfort to me, I am overflowing with delight, for all the
5 trouble I have to bear. For I got no relief from the strain
of things, even when I reached Macedonia; it was trouble
at every turn, wrangling all round me, fears in my own
6 mind. But the God who comforts the dejected comforted

---

* This bracketed paragraph (vi. 14–vii. 1) belongs to some other part of Paul's correspondence with the Corinthian church.

II. CORINTHIANS VIII

7 me by the arrival of Titus. Yes, and by more than his arrival, by the comfort which you had been to him; for he gave me súch a report of how you longed for me, how sorry you were, and how eagerly you took my part, that
8 it added to my delight. In fact, if I did pain you by that letter, I do not regret it. I did regret it when I discovered * that my letter had pained you even for the time
9 being, but I am glad now—not glad that you were pained but glad that your pain induced you to repent. For you were pained as God meant you to be pained, and so you got
10 no harm from what I did; the pain God is allowed to guide ends in a saving repentance never to be regretted, whereas
11 the world's pain ends in death. See what this pain divine has done for you, how serious it has made you, how keen to clear yourselves, how indignant, how alarmed, how eager for me, how determined, how relentless! You have shown
12 in every way that you were honest in the business. So my letter was written to you, not on account of the offender nor for the sake of the injured party, but in order to let you realize before God how seriously you do care for me.
13 That is what comforts me.
And over and above my personal comfort, I was specially delighted at the delight of Titus. You have all set his
14 mind at rest. I told him of my pride in you, and I have not been disappointed. No, just as all I have had to say to you has been true, so all I said about you to Titus, all
15 my pride in you, has also proved true. His own heart goes out to you all the more when he remembers how you all obeyed him, and how you received him with reverence
16 and trembling. I am glad to have full confidence in you.

8 Now, brothers, I have to tell you about the grace God
2 has given to the churches of Macedonia. Amid a severe ordeal of trouble, their overflowing joy and their deep poverty together have poured out a flood of rich generosity;
3 I can testify that up to their means, aye and beyond their
4 means, they have given—begging me of their own accord, most urgently, for the favour of contributing to the sup-
5 port of the saints. They have done more than I expected; they gave themselves to the Lord, to begin with, and then (for so God willed it) they put themselves at my disposal.
6 This has led me to ask Titus to complete the arrangements for the same gracious contribution among yourselves, as it
7 was he who started it. Now then, you are to the front in

---

* Reading βλέπων with the Vulgate, which " alone has preserved the true reading, ὣ being read as ω" (Hort).

II. CORINTHIANS IX

everything, in faith, in utterance, in knowledge, in all zeal, and in love for us*—do come to the front in this gracious
8 enterprise as well. I am not issuing any orders, only using the zeal of others to prove how sterling your own love is.
9 (You know how gracious our Lord Jesus Christ was; rich though he was, he became poor for the sake of you, that
10 by his poverty you might be rich.) But I will tell you what I think about it; it is to your interest to go on with this enterprise, for you started it last year, you were the first not merely to do anything but to want to do anything.
11 Now, carry it through, so that your readiness to take it up may be equalled by the way you carry it through—so
12 far as your means allow. If only one is ready to give, according to his means, it is acceptable; he is not asked
13 to give what he has not got. This does not mean that
14 other people are to be relieved and you to suffer: it is a matter of give and take; at the present moment your surplus goes to make up what they lack, in order that their
15 surplus may go to make up what you lack. Thus it is to give and take—as it is written,
He who got much had nothing over,
and he who got little had not too little.

16 Thanks be to God who has inspired Titus with an
17 interest in you equal to my own; he has indeed responded to my request, but he is off to you by his own choice, so
18 keen is his interest in you. Along with him I am sending that brother whose services to the gospel are praised by all
19 the churches; besides, he has been appointed by the churches to travel with me on the business of administering this fund to the glory of the Lord. His appointment
20 has my full consent, for I want to take precautions against any risk of suspicion in connection with the administration
21 of this charity; I aim at being above reproach not only
22 from God but also from men. Along with them I am also sending our brother: I have had ample proof of his keen interest on many occasions, and it is specially keen on this
23 occasion, as he has absolute confidence in you. Titus is my colleague, he shares my work for you, and these brothers of mine are apostles of the church, a credit to
24 Christ. So let them have proof of how you can love, and of my reasons for being proud of you; it will be a proof read by the churches. Indeed it is quite super-
9 fluous for me to be writing to you about this chari-
2 table service to the saints; I know how willing you are, I am proud of it, I have boasted of you to the Macedonians:

* Reading ἐξ ὑμῶν ἐν ἡμῖν with ℵ C D G, almost all the evidence of the Latin and Syriac versions, etc.

II. CORINTHIANS X

"Achaia," I tell them, "was all ready last year." And your
3 zeal has been a stimulus to the majority of them. At the
same time I am sending these brothers just in case my
pride in you should prove an empty boast in this particular
instance; I want you to be "all ready," as I have been tell-
4 ing them that you would be, in case any Macedonians
accompany me and find you are not ready—which would
make me (not to speak of yourselves) ashamed of having
5 been so sure. That is why I have thought it necessary to
ask these brothers to go on in advance and get your
promised contribution ready in good time. I want it to be
forthcoming as a generous gift, not as money wrung out
6 of you. Mark this: he who sows sparingly will reap sparingly, and he who sows generously will reap a generous
7 harvest. Everyone is to give what he has made up his
mind to give; there is to be no grudging or compulsion
about it, for God loves the giver who gives cheerfully.
8 God is able to bless you with ample means, so that you
may always have quite enough for any emergency of your
9 own and ample besides for any kind act to others; as it is
written,

He scatters his gifts to the poor broadcast,
his charity lasts for ever.

10 He who furnishes the sower with seed and with bread to
eat will supply seed for you and multiply it; he will
11 increase the crop of your charities—you will be enriched
on all hands, so that you can be generous on all occasions,
and your generosity, of which I am the agent, will make
12 men give thanks to God; for the service rendered by this
fund does more than supply the wants of the saints, it
13 overflows with many a cry of thanks to God. This service
shows what you are, it makes men praise God for the way
you have come under the gospel of Christ which you confess, and for the generosity of your contributions to them-
14 selves and to all; they are drawn to you and pray for you,
on account of the surpassing grace which God has shown
15 to you. Thanks be to God for his unspeakable gift!

10 I APPEAL to you myself by the gentleness and consid-
eration of Christ—the Paul who is 'humble enough to
your face when he is with you, but outspoken enough when
2 he gets away from you.' I beg of you that when I do come
I may not have to speak out and be peremptory; but my
mind is made up to tackle certain people who have made
up their minds that I move on the low level of the flesh.
3 I do live in the flesh, but I do not make war as the flesh
4 does; the weapons of my warfare are not weapons of the
5 flesh, but divinely strong to demolish fortresses—I demol-

ish theories and any rampart thrown up to resist the knowledge of God, I take every project prisoner to make it
6 obey Christ, I am prepared to court-martial anyone who remains insubordinate, once your submission is complete.
7 Look at this obvious fact. So-and-so is perfectly sure he 'belongs to Christ'? Well then, let him understand, on second thoughts, that I 'belong to Christ' as much as he
8 does. Even supposing I were to boast somewhat freely of my authority (and the Lord gave it to me for building you up, not for demolishing you), I would feel quite justified.
9 But I am not going to seem as if I were 'overawing you
10 with a letter,' so to speak. My opponent says, 'Paul's letters are weighty and telling, but his personality is weak
11 and his delivery is beneath contempt.' Let him understand that I will act when I arrive, as forcibly as I express
12 myself by letter when I am absent. I do not venture to class myself or to compare myself with certain exalted individuals! They belong to the class of self-praisers; while I limit myself to my own sphere,* I compare myself
13 with my own standard, and so my boasting never goes beyond the limit—it is determined by the limits of the sphere marked out for me by God. That sphere stretches
14 to include yourselves; I am not overstepping the limit, as if you lay beyond my sphere; I was the very first to reach
15 you with the gospel of Christ. I do not boast beyond my limits in a sphere where other men have done the work; my hope rather is that the growth of your faith will allow
16 me to enlarge the range of my appointed sphere and preach the gospel in the lands that lie beyond you, instead of boasting within another's province over work that is
17 already done. However, *let him who boasts boast of the*
18 *Lord;* for it is not the self-praiser with his own recommendations who is accepted, it is the man whom the Lord recommends.

11 I WISH you would put up with a little 'folly' from me.
2 Do put up with me, for I feel a divine jealousy on your behalf; I betrothed you as a chaste maiden to pre-
3 sent you to your one husband Christ, but I am afraid of your thoughts getting seduced from a single devotion to Christ, just as *the serpent beguiled* Eve with his cunning.
4 You put up with it all right, when some interloper preaches a second Jesus (not the Jesus I preached), or when you are treated to a Spirit different from the Spirit you once received, and to a different gospel from what I gave you!
5 Why not put up with me? I hold I am not one whit in-

* Omitting οὐ συνιοῦσιν · ἡμεῖς δὲ with D*, etc.

6 ferior to these precious 'apostles'! I am no speaker, perhaps, but knowledge I do possess; I never failed to make myself intelligible to you.
7 But perhaps I did wrong in taking a humble place that you might have a high one—I mean, in preaching the gos-
8 pel of God to you for nothing! I made a levy on other churches, I took pay from them so as to minister to you;
9 even when I ran short, during my stay with you, I was no encumbrance to anybody, for the brothers who came from Macedonia supplied my wants. Thus I kept myself, as I intend to keep myself, from being a burden to you in any
10 way. By the truth of Christ within me, I am going to make this my pride and boast unchecked throughout the
11 regions of Achaia! Why? Because I do not love you?
12 God knows I do. No, I intend to go on as I am doing, in order to checkmate those who would fain make out that in the apostolate of which they boast they work on the same
13 terms as I do. 'Apostles'? They are spurious apostles, false workmen—they are masquerading as 'apostles of
14 Christ.' No wonder they do, for Satan himself masquerades
15 as an angel of light. So it is no surprise if his ministers also masquerade as ministers of righteousness. Their doom will answer to their deeds.
16 I repeat, no one is to think me a fool; but even so, pray bear with me, fool as I am, that I may have my little boast
17 as well as others! (What I am now going to say is not inspired by the Lord: I am in the rôle of a 'fool,' now, on
18 this business of boasting. Since many boast on the score
19 of the flesh, I will do the same.) You put up with fools so
20 readily, you who know so much! You put up with a man who assumes control of your souls, with a man who spends your money, with a man who dupes you, with a man who
21 gives himself airs, with a man who flies in your face. I am quite ashamed to say I was not equal to that sort of thing! But let them vaunt as they please, I am equal to them
22 (mind, this is the rôle of a fool!). Are they Hebrews? so am I. Israelites? so am I. Descended from Abraham? so am
23 I. Ministers of Christ? yes perhaps, but not as much as I am (I am mad to talk like this!), with all my labours, with all my lashes, with all my time in prison—a record longer far
24 than theirs. I have been often at the point of death; five times have I got forty lashes (all but one) from the Jews,
25 three times I have been beaten by the Romans, once pelted with stones, three times shipwrecked, adrift at sea for a
26 whole night and day; I have been often on my travels, I have been in danger from rivers and robbers, in danger from Jews and Gentiles, through dangers of town and of desert, through dangers on the sea, through dangers among false

27 brothers—through labour and hardship, through many a sleepless night, through hunger and thirst, starving many a
28 time, cold and ill-clad, and all the rest of it. And then there is the pressing business of each day, the care of all the
29 churches. Who is weak, and I do not feel his weakness? Whose faith is hurt, and I am not aglow with indignation?
30 If there is to be any boasting, I will boast of what I am
31 weak enough to suffer! The God and Father of the Lord Jesus, He who is blessed for ever, He knows I am telling the
32 truth! (At Damascus the ethnarch of king Aretas had patrols out in the city of the Damascenes to arrest me, but I was lowered in a basket from a loophole in the wall,

12 and so managed to escape his clutches.) There is nothing to be gained by this sort of thing, but as I am obliged to boast, I will go on to visions and revelations of
2 the Lord. I know a man in Christ who fourteen years ago was caught up to the third heaven. In the body or out of
3 the body? That I do not know: God knows. I simply know
4 that in the body or out of the body (God knows which) this man was caught up to paradise and heard sacred secrets
5 which no human lips can repeat. Of an experience like that I am prepared to boast, but not of myself personally
6 —not except as regards my weaknesses. (If I did care to boast of other things, I would be no 'fool,' for I would have a true tale to tell; however, I abstain from that—I want no one to take me for more than he can see in me or make
7 out from me.) My wealth of visions might have puffed me up, so I was given a thorn in the flesh, an angel of Satan to rack me and keep me from being puffed up;
8 three times over I prayed the Lord to make it leave me,
9 but he told me, "It is enough for you to have my grace: it is in weakness that [my] power is fully felt." So I am proud to boast of all my weaknesses, and thus to have the
10 power of Christ resting on my life. It makes me satisfied, for Christ's sake, with weakness, insults, trouble, persecution, and calamity; for I am strong just when I am weak.
11 Now this is playing the fool! But you forced me to it, instead of coming forward yourselves and vouching for me. That was what I deserved; for, 'nobody' as I am, I am not
12 one whit inferior to these precious 'apostles.' You had all the miracles that mark an apostle done for you fully and
13 patiently—miracles, wonders, and deeds of power. Where were you inferior to the rest of the churches?—unless in this, that your apostle did not choose to make himself a burden to you. Pray pardon me this terrible wrong!
14 Here am I all ready to pay you my third visit. And I will not be a burden to you; I want yourselves and not your money. Children have not to put money by for their

II. CORINTHIANS XIII

15 parents; that is what parents do for their children. And for your souls I will gladly spend my all and be spent myself. Am I to be loved the less because I love you more than others?
16 But let that pass, you say; I was not a burden to you, no, but I was clever enough to dupe you with my tricks?
17 Was I? Did I make something out of you by any of my
18 messengers? I asked Titus to go, and with him I sent our brother. Titus did not make anything out of you, did he? And did not I act in the same spirit as he did? Did I not take the very same steps?
19 You think all this time I am defending myself to you? No, I am speaking in Christ before the presence of God, and speaking every word, beloved, in order to build you up.
20 For I am afraid I may perhaps come and find you are not what I could wish, while you may find I am not what you could wish; I am afraid of finding quarrels, jealousy, temper, rivalry, slanders, gossiping, arrogance, and dis-
21 order—afraid that when I come back to you, my God may humiliate me before you, and I may have to mourn for many who sinned some time ago and yet have never repented of the impurity, the sexual vice, and the sensuality which they have practised.

13 This will be my third visit to you: *every case is to be decided on the evidence of two or of three witnesses.*
2 I warned you already, on my second visit, and I warn you now before I come, both you who sinned some time ago and the rest of you as well, that I will spare no one if I
3 come back. That will prove to you that I am indeed a spokesman of Christ. It is no weak Christ you have to do
4 with, but a Christ of power. For though he was crucified in his weakness, he lives by the power of God; and though I am weak as he was weak, you will find I am alive as he
5 is alive by the power of God. Put yourselves to the proof, not me; test yourselves, to see if you are in the faith. Do you not understand that Christ Jesus is within you?
6 Otherwise you must be failures. But I trust you will find
7 I am no failure, and I pray to God that you may not go wrong—not to prove I am a success, that is not the point, but that you should come right, even if I seemed to be a
8 failure. (Fail or succeed, I cannot work against the truth
9 but for it!) I am glad to be weak if you are strong;
10 mend your ways, that is all I ask. I am writing thus to you in absence, so that when I do come I may not have to deal sharply with you; I have the Lord's authority for that, but he gave it to me for building you up, not for demolishing you.
11 Now brothers, goodbye; mend your ways, listen to what

I have told you, live in harmony, keep the peace; then the God of love and peace will be with you.
12   Salute one another with a holy kiss. All the saints salute you.
13   The grace of the Lord Jesus Christ and the love of God and the fellowship of the holy Spirit be with you all.

THE EPISTLE OF PAUL TO THE

GALATIANS

1 PAUL an apostle—not appointed by men nor commissioned by any man but by Jesus Christ and God the
2 Father who raised him from the dead,—with all the brothers who are beside me, to the churches of Galatia;
3 grace and peace to you from God our Father and the Lord
4 Jesus Christ who gave himself for our sins to rescue us from the present evil world—by the will of our God and
5 Father, to whom be glory for ever and ever: Amen.
6 I am astonished you are hastily shifting like this, deserting Him who called you by Christ's grace and going over
7 to another gospel. It simply means that certain individuals are unsettling you; they want to distort the gospel of
8 Christ. Now even though it were myself or some angel from heaven, whoever preaches a gospel that contradicts
9 the gospel I preached to you, God's curse be on him! I have said it before and I now repeat it: whoever preaches a gospel to you that contradicts the gospel you have already received, God's curse be on him!
10 Now is that 'appealing to the interests of men' or of God? Trying to 'satisfy men'? Why, if I still tried to give satisfaction to human masters, I would be no servant of
11 Christ. No, brothers, I tell you the gospel that I preach
12 is not a human affair; no man put it into my hands, no man taught me what it meant, I had it by a revelation
13 of Jesus Christ. You know the story of my past career in Judaism; you know how furiously I persecuted the
14 church of God and harried it, and how I outstripped many of my own age and race in my special ardour for the
15 ancestral traditions of my house. But the God who had set me apart *from my very birth called* me by his grace,
16 and when he chose to reveal his Son to me, that I might preach him to the Gentiles, instead of consulting with any
17 human being, instead of going up to Jerusalem to see those who had been apostles before me, I went off at once to
18 Arabia, and on my return I came back to Damascus. Then, after three years, I went up to Jerusalem to make the ac-
19 quaintance of Cephas. I stayed a fortnight with him. I saw no other apostle, only James the brother of the Lord.

20 (I am writing you the sheer truth, I swear it before God!)
21 Then I went to the districts of Syria and of Cilicia. Per-
22 sonally I was quite unknown to the Christian churches of
23 Judaea; they merely heard that 'our former persecutor is
24 now preaching the faith he once harried,' which made them
2 praise God for me.   Then, fourteen years later, I went
up to Jerusalem again, accompanied by Barnabas; I
2 took Titus with me also. (It was in consequence of a
revelation that I went up at all.) I submitted the gospel
I am in the habit of preaching to the Gentiles, submitting
it privately to the authorities, to make sure that my course
3 of action would be and had been sound. But even my companion Titus, Greek though he was, was not obliged to be
4 circumcised. There were traitors of false brothers, who
had crept in to spy out the freedom we enjoy in Christ
5 Jesus; they did aim at enslaving us again. But we refused
to yield for a single instant to their claims; we were determined that the truth of the gospel should hold good for
6 you. Besides, the so-called 'authorities' (it makes no difference to me what their status used to be—God pays no
regard to the externals of men); these 'authorities' had no
7 additions to make to my gospel. On the contrary, when
they saw I had been entrusted with the gospel for the
benefit of the uncircumcised, just as Peter had been for the
8 circumcised (for He who equipped Peter to be an apostle
of the circumcised equipped me as well for the uncircumcised), and when they recognized the grace I had
9 been given, then the so-called 'pillars' of the church,
James and Cephas and John, gave myself and Barnabas
the right hand of fellowship. Our sphere was to be the
10 Gentiles, theirs the circumcised. Only, we were to 'remember the poor.' I was quite eager to do that myself.
11 But when Cephas came to Antioch, I opposed him to his
12 face. The man stood self-condemned. Before certain
emissaries of James arrived, he ate along with the Gentile
Christians; but when they arrived, he began to draw back
and hold aloof, because he was afraid of the circumcision
13 party. The rest of the Jewish Christians also played false
along with him, so much so that even Barnabas was carried
14 away by their false play. But I saw they were swerving
from the true line of the gospel; so I said to Cephas in
presence of them all, "If you live like the Gentiles and not
like the Jews, though you are a Jew yourself, why do you
15 oblige the Gentiles to become Jews?"—We may be Jews
16 by birth and not 'Gentile sinners,' but since we know a
man is justified simply by faith in Jesus Christ and not by
doing what the Law commands, we ourselves have believed
in Christ Jesus so as to get justified by faith in Christ and

not by doing what the Law commands—for by doing what
17 the law commands *no person shall be justified.* If it is
discovered that in our quest for justification in Christ we
are 'sinners' as well as the Gentiles, does that make Christ
18 an agent of sin? Never! I really convict myself of trans-
19 gression when I rebuild what I destroyed. For through the
20 Law I died to the Law that I might live for God; I have
been crucified with Christ, and it is no longer I who live,
Christ lives in me; the life I now live in the flesh I live by
faith in the Son of God who loved me and gave himself up
21 for me. I do not annul God's grace; but if righteousness
comes by way of the Law, then indeed Christ's death was
useless.

3 O SENSELESS Galatians, who has bewitched you—you who
had Jesus Christ the crucified placarded before your very
2 eyes? I simply want to ask you one thing: did you receive
the Spirit by doing what the Law commands or by believ-
3 ing the gospel message? Are you such fools? Did you begin
4 with the spirit only to end now with the flesh? Have you
had all that experience for nothing (if it has really gone for
5 nothing)? When He supplies you with the Spirit and works
miracles among you, is it because you do what the Law
6 commands or because you believe the gospel message? Why,
it is as with Abraham, *he had faith in God and that was*
7 *counted to him as righteousness.* Well then, you see that the
8 real sons of Abraham are those who rely on faith. Besides,
Scripture anticipated God's justification of the Gentiles
by faith when it announced the gospel beforehand to
Abraham in these terms: *All nations shall be blessed in*
9 *thee.* So that those who rely on faith are blessed along
10 with believing Abraham. Whereas a curse rests on all
who rely upon obedience to the Law; for it is written,
Cursed is everyone who does not hold by all that is written
11 *in the book of the law, to perform it.* And because no one
is justified on the score of the Law before God (plainly,
12 *the just shall live by faith,*—and the Law is not based on
faith: no, *he who performs these things shall live by them*),
13 Christ ransomed us from the curse of the Law by becom-
ing accursed for us (for it is written, *Cursed is everyone*
14 *who hangs on a gibbet*), that the blessing of Abraham
might reach the Gentiles in Christ Jesus, so that by faith
we might receive the promised Spirit.
15 To take an illustration from human life, my brothers.
Once a man's will is ratified, no one else annuls it or adds
16 a codicil to it. Now the Promises were made to Abraham
and to his offspring; it is not said, 'and to your offsprings'
in the plural, but in the singular *and to your offspring—*

17 which is Christ. My point is this: the Law which arose
four hundred and thirty years later does not repeal a will
18 previously ratified by God, so as to cancel the Promise. If
the Inheritance is due to law, it ceases to be due to
promise. Now it was by a promise that God bestowed it
19 on Abraham. Then what about the Law? Well, it was
interpolated for the purpose of producing transgressions
till such time as the Offspring arrived to whom the Promise
was made; also, it was transmitted by means of angels
20 through the agency of an intermediary (an intermediary
21 implies more than one party, but God is one). Then the
Law is contrary to God's Promises? Never! Had there
been any law which had the power of producing life,
22 righteousness would really have been due to law, but
Scripture has consigned all without exception to the custody of sin, in order that the promise due to faith in
Jesus Christ might be given to those who have faith.
23 Before this faith came, we were confined by the Law and
kept in custody, with the prospect of the faith that was to
24 be revealed; the Law thus held us as wards in discipline,
till such time as Christ came, that we might be justified
25 by faith. But faith has come, and we are wards no longer;
26 you are all sons of God by your faith in Christ Jesus
27 (for all of you who had yourselves baptised into Christ have
28 taken on the character of Christ). There is no room for
Jew or Greek, there is no room for slave or freeman, there
is no room for male and female; you are all one in Christ
29 Jesus. Now if you are Christ's, then you are Abraham's

4 offspring; in virtue of the Promise, you are heirs. What
I mean is this. As long as an heir is under age, there
is no difference between him and a servant, though he is
2 lord of all the property; he is under guardians and trustees
3 till the time fixed by his father. So with us. When we
were under age, we lived under the thraldom of the
4 Elemental spirits of the world; but when the time had
fully expired, God sent forth his Son, born of a woman,
5 born under the Law, to ransom those who were under the
6 Law, that we might get our sonship. It is because you are
sons that God has sent forth the Spirit of his Son into
7 your hearts crying 'Abba! Father!' So you are servant
no longer but son, and as son you are also heir, all owing
to God.
8 In those days, when you were ignorant of God, you were
9 in servitude to gods who are really no gods at all; but now
that you know God—or rather, are known by God—how
is it you are turning back again to the weakness and
poverty of the Elemental spirits? Why do you want to be
10 enslaved all over again by them? You observe days and

11 months and festal seasons and years! Why, you make me
   afraid I may have spent my labour on you for nothing!
12 Do take my line, brothers, I beg of you—just as I once
13 took yours. I have no complaint against you; no, although
   it was because of an illness (you know) that I preached
14 the gospel to you on my former visit, and though my flesh
   was a trial to you, you did not scoff at me nor spurn me,
   you welcomed me like an angel of God, like Christ Jesus.
15 You congratulated yourselves. Now, what has become of
   all that? (I can bear witness that you would have torn
   out your very eyes, if you could, and given me them.)
16 Am I your enemy to-day, because I have been honest with
17 you? These men make much of you—yes, but for dishonest ends; they want to debar you from us, so that you
18 may make much of them. Now it is fine for you to be made
   much of honestly and all the time—not simply when I can
19 be with you. O my dear children, you with whom I am
   in travail over again till Christ be formed within you,
20 would that I could be with you at this moment, and alter
21 my tone, for I am at my wits' end about you! Tell me, you
   who are keen to be under the Law, will you not listen to
22 the Law? Surely it is written in the Law that Abraham
   had two sons, one by the slave-woman and one by the free-
23 woman; but while the son of the slave-woman was born by
   the flesh, the son of the free-woman was born by the
24 promise. Now this is an allegory. The women are two
   covenants. One comes from mount Sinai, bearing children
25 for servitude; that is Hagar, for mount Sinai * is away in
   Arabia. She corresponds to the present Jerusalem, for the
26 latter is in servitude with her children. But the Jeru-
27 salem on high is free, and she is 'our' mother. For it is
   written,
   Rejoice, O thou barren who bearest not,
   break into joy, thou who travailest not;
   for the children of the desolate woman are far more than
   of the married.
28 Now you are the children of the Promise, brothers, like
29 Isaac; but just as in the old days the son born by the flesh
   persecuted the son born by the Spirit, so it is still to-day.
30 However, what does the scripture say? *Put away the slave-*
   woman and her son, for the son of the slave-woman shall
31 *not be heir along with the son of the free-woman.* Hence
5 we are children of no slave-woman, my brothers, but of
   the free-woman.† with the freedom for which Christ

* Omitting Ἀγαρ as a gloss, with the Latin, Sahidic, and Ethiopic
versions, ℵ C G, Origen, and many others.

† Whether $\hat{\eta}$ is read after $τ\hat{\eta}$ ἐλευθερίᾳ or instead of $τ\hat{\eta}$, the opening
words of 5^1 must be connected with the closing words of 4^{31}. I think

set us free. Make a firm stand then, do not slip into any yoke of servitude.
2 Here, listen to Paul! I tell you, if you get circumcised,
3 Christ will be no use to you. I insist on this again to everyone who gets circumcised, that he is obliged to carry
4 out the whole of the Law. You are for justification by the Law? Then you are done with Christ, you have deserted
5 grace, for it is by faith that 'we' wait in the Spirit for the
6 righteousness we hope for; in Christ Jesus circumcision is not valid, neither is uncircumcision, but only faith active
7 in love. You were doing splendidly. Who was it that
8 prevented you from obeying the Truth? That sort of
9 suasion does not come from Him who called you! (A
10 morsel of dough will leaven the whole lump.) I feel persuaded in the Lord that you will not go wrong. But he who unsettles you will have to meet his doom, no matter who
11 he is. I am 'still preaching circumcision myself,' am I? Then, brothers, why am I still being persecuted? And so the stumbling-block of the cross has lost its force, for-
12 sooth! O that those who are upsetting you would get themselves castrated!
13 Brothers, you were called to be free; only, do not make your freedom an opening for the flesh, but serve one an-
14 other in love. For the entire Law is summed up in one word,
15 in *You must love your neighbour as yourself* (whereas, if you snap at each other and prey upon each other, take care
16 in case you destroy one another). I mean, lead the life of the Spirit; then you will never satisfy the passions of the
17 flesh. For the passion of the flesh is against the Spirit, and the passion of the Spirit against the flesh—the two are at
18 issue, so that you are not free to do as you please. If you are under the sway of the Spirit, you are not under the Law.
19 Now the deeds of the flesh are quite obvious, such as sexual
20 vice, impurity, sensuality, idolatry, magic, quarrels, dissen-
21 sion, jealousy, temper, rivalry, factions, party-spirit, envy, [murder], drinking bouts, revelry, and the like; I tell you beforehand as I have told you already, that people who indulge in such practices will never inherit the Realm of
22 God. But the harvest of the Spirit is love, joy, peace, good
23 temper, kindliness, generosity, fidelity, gentleness, self-control:—there is no law against those who practice such
24 things. Now those who belong to Christ * have crucified

on the whole that this interpretation of the text, which is advocated by modern editors like Lightfoot and Zahn, has the best claim to be regarded as authentic; it goes back to Marcion and has the powerful support of the Latin version, of G, of Origen, Ambrosiaster, Jerome, and others.

* Omitting Ἰησοῦ with D G, the Latin, Gothic, and Armenian versions, Marcion, Chrysostom, and others.

25 the flesh with its emotions and passions. As we live by the
26 Spirit, let us be guided by the Spirit; let us have no vanity,
6 no provoking, no envy of one another. Even if anyone
is detected in some trespass, brothers, you are spiritual,
you must set the offender right in a spirit of gentleness;
let each of you look to himself, in case he too is tempted.
2 Bear one another's burdens, and so fulfil the law of Christ
3 If anyone imagines he is somebody, he is deceiving him-
4 self, for he is nobody; let everyone bring his own work to
the test—then he will have something to boast about on
his own account, and not in comparison with his fellows.
5 For everyone will have to bear his own load of responsi-
bility.
6 Those who are taught must share all the blessings of
7 life with those who teach them the Word. Make no mistake—God is not to be mocked—a man will reap just what
8 he sows; he who sows for his flesh will reap destruction
from the flesh, and he who sows for the Spirit will reap
9 life eternal from the Spirit. Never let us grow tired of
doing what is right, for if we do not faint we shall reap
10 our harvest at the opportune season. So then, as we have
opportunity, let us do good to all men and in particular
to the household of the faith.
11 See what big letters I make, when I write you in my own
hand!
12 These men who are keen upon you getting circumcised
are just men who want to make a grand display in the
flesh—it is simply to avoid being persecuted for the cross
13 of Christ. Why, even the circumcision party do not observe
the Law themselves! They merely want you to get cir-
14 cumcised, so as to boast over your flesh! But no boasting
for me, none except in the cross of our Lord Jesus Christ,
by which the world has been crucified to me and I crucified
15 to the world. For what counts is neither circumcision nor
16 uncircumcision, it is the new creation. On all who will be
guided by this rule, may *peace* and mercy rest, even *upon
the Israel* of God.
17 Let no one interfere with me after this, for I bear
branded on my body the owner's stamp of Jesus.
18 The grace of our Lord Jesus Christ be with your spirit,
brothers. Amen.

THE EPISTLE OF PAUL THE APOSTLE TO THE
EPHESIANS

1 Paul, by the will of God an apostle of Jesus Christ, to
2 the saints who are faithful* in Jesus Christ: grace and
peace to you from God our Father and the Lord Jesus
Christ.
3 Blessed be the God and Father of our Lord Jesus Christ
who in Christ has blessed us with every spiritual blessing!
4 He chose us in him ere the world was founded, to be con-
5 secrated and unblemished in his sight, destining us in love
6 to be his sons through Jesus Christ. Such was the purpose
of his will, redounding to the praise of his glorious grace
7 bestowed on us in the Beloved, in whom we enjoy our
redemption, the forgiveness of our trespasses, by the blood
8 he shed. So richly has God lavished his grace upon us!
9 He has granted us complete insight and understanding of
the open secret of his will, showing us how it was the
10 purpose of his design so to order it in the fulness of the
ages that all things in heaven and earth alike should be
11 gathered up in Christ—in the Christ in whom we have
had our heritage allotted us (as was decreed in the design
of him who carries out everything according to the counsel
12 of his will), to make us redound to the praise of his glory
13 by being the first to put our hope in Christ. You also
have heard the message of the truth, the gospel of your
salvation, and in him you also by your faith have been
stamped with the seal of the long-promised holy Spirit
14 which is the pledge and instalment of our common heritage,
that we may obtain our divine possession and so redound
to the praise of his glory.
15 Hence, as I have heard of your faith in the Lord Jesus
16 and your love for all the saints, I never cease to give
17 thanks for you, when I mention you in my prayers. May
the God of our Lord Jesus Christ, the glorious Father, grant
you the Spirit of wisdom and revelation for the knowl-
18 edge of himself, illuminating the eyes of your heart so that
you can understand the hope to which He calls us, the
19 wealth of his glorious heritage in the saints, and the

* Omitting [ἐν Ἐφέσῳ].

surpassing greatness of his power over us believers—a
20 power which operates with the strength of the might which
he exerted in raising Christ from the dead and *seating him*
21 *at his right hand* in the heavenly sphere, above all the
angelic Rulers, Authorities, Powers, and Lords, above every
Name that is to be named not only in this age but in the
22 age to come—*he has put everything under his feet* and set
him as head over everything for the church, the church
23 which is his Body, filled by him who fills the universe
entirely. And as with us so with you. You were dead
2 2 in the trespasses and sins in which you moved as you
followed the course of this world, under the sway of the
prince of the air—the spirit which is at present active
3 within those sons of disobedience among whom all of us
lived, we as well as you, when we obeyed the passions of
our flesh, carrying out the dictates of the flesh and its
impulses, when we were objects of God's anger by nature,
4 like the rest of men. But, dead in trespasses as we were,
5 God was so rich in mercy that for his great love to us he
made us live together with Christ (it is by grace you have
6 been saved); together with Christ he raised and seated
7 us within the heavenly sphere in Christ Jesus, to display
throughout ages to come his surpassing wealth of grace
8 and goodness toward us in Christ Jesus. For it is by grace
you have been saved, as you had faith; it is not your doing
9 but God's gift, not the outcome of what you have done—lest
10 anyone should pride himself on that; God has made us
what we are, creating us in Christ Jesus for the good deeds
which are prepared beforehand by God as our sphere
of action.
11 Remember, then, that once upon a time you Gentiles in
the flesh, who are called 'the Uncircumcision' by that so-
called 'Circumcision' which is itself the product of human
12 hands in the flesh—remember you were in those days outside Christ, aliens to the commonwealth of Israel, and
strangers to the covenants of the Promise, devoid of hope
13 and God within the world. Whereas now, within Christ
Jesus, you who once were *far away* have been brought *near*
14 by the blood of Christ. For he is our *peace*, he who has
made both of us a unity and destroyed the barrier which
15 kept us apart; in his own flesh he put an end to the feud
of the Law with its code of commands, so as to make
peace by the creation of a new Man in himself out of both
16 parties, so as himself to give the death-blow to that feud
by reconciling them both to God in one Body through the
17 cross; he came *with a gospel of peace for those far away*
18 (that is, for you) *and for those who were near*, for it is
through him that we both enjoy our access to the Father

19 in one Spirit. Thus you are strangers and foreigners no longer, you share the membership of the saints, you be-
20 long to God's own household, you are a building that rests on the apostles and prophets as its foundation, with Christ
21 Jesus as the cornerstone; in him the whole structure is welded together and rises into a sacred temple in the Lord, and in him you are yourselves built into this to form a habitation for God in the Spirit.

3 For this reason I Paul, I whom Jesus has made a
2 prisoner for the sake of you Gentiles—for surely you have heard how the grace of God which was vouchsafed
3 me in your interests has ordered it, how the divine secret was disclosed to me by a revelation (if you read what I
4 have already written briefly about this, you can understand
5 my insight into that secret of Christ which was not disclosed to the sons of men in other generations as it has now been revealed to his sacred apostles and prophets by
6 the Spirit), namely, that in Christ Jesus the Gentiles are co-heirs, companions, and co-partners in the * Promise. Such
7 is the gospel which I was called to serve by the endowment of God's grace which was vouchsafed me, by the energy
8 of his power; less than the least of all saints as I am, this grace was vouchsafed me, that I should bring the Gentiles
9 the gospel of the fathomless wealth of Christ and enlighten all men upon the new order of that divine secret which
10 God the Creator of all concealed from eternity—intending to let the full sweep of the divine wisdom be disclosed now by the church to the angelic Rulers and Authorities in the
11 heavenly sphere, in terms of the eternal purpose which he
12 has realized in Christ Jesus our Lord, through whom, as we have faith in him, we enjoy our confidence of free access.
13 So I beg of you not to lose heart over what I am suffering on your behalf; my sufferings are an honour to you.
14 For this reason, then, I kneel before the Father from
15 whom every family in heaven and on earth derives its
16 name and nature, praying Him out of the wealth of his glory to grant you a mighty increase of strength by his
17 Spirit in the inner man. May Christ dwell in your hearts
18 as you have faith! May you be so fixed and founded in love that you can grasp with all the saints what is the meaning of 'the Breadth,' 'the Length,' 'the Depth' and
19 'the Height,' by knowing the love of Christ which surpasses all knowledge! May you be filled with the entire fulness
20 of God! Now to him who by the action of his power within

* Omitting [αὐτοῦ].

us can do all things, aye far more than we ever ask or
21 imagine, to him be glory in the church and in Christ
Jesus throughout all generations for ever and ever: Amen.

2 **4** As the Lord's prisoner, then, I beg of you to live a
life worthy of your calling, with perfect modesty and
gentleness, showing forbearance to one another patiently,
3 zealous in love to preserve the unity of the Spirit by bind-
4 ing peace upon yourselves. For there is one Body and one
Spirit—as you were called for the one hope that belongs
5 to your call—one Lord, one faith, one baptism, one God
6 and Father of all, who is over us all, who pervades us all,
7 who is within us all. But each one of us is granted his
own grace, as determined by the full measure of Christ's
8 gift. Thus it is said,
*When he ascended on high he led a host captive
and granted gifts to men.*
9 What does *he ascended* mean, except that he first de-
10 scended to the nether regions of the earth? He who
descended is he who ascended above all the heavens to fill
11 the universe; he *granted* some men to be apostles, some to
be prophets, some to be evangelists, some to shepherd and
12 teach, for the equipment of the saints, for the business
of the ministry, for the upbuilding of the Body of Christ,
13 till we should all attain the unity of the faith and knowledge of God's Son, reaching maturity, reaching the full
measure of development which belongs to the fulness of
14 Christ—instead of remaining immature, blown from our
course and swayed by every passing wind of doctrine, by
the adroitness of men who are dexterous in devising error;
15 we are to hold by the truth, and by our love to grow up
16 wholly into Him. For He, Christ, is the head and under
him, as the entire Body is welded together and compacted by every joint with which it is supplied, the due
activity of each part enables the Body to grow and build
itself up in love.
17 Now in the Lord I insist and protest that you must give
18 up living like pagans; for their purposes are futile, their
intelligence is darkened, they are estranged from the life
of God by the ignorance which their dulness of heart has
19 produced in them—men who have recklessly * abandoned
themselves to sensuality, with a lust for the business of
20 impurity in every shape and form. That is not how you
21 have understood the meaning of Christ (for it is Christ
whom you have been taught, it is in Christ that you have

---

* Reading ἀπηλπικότες with D G, the Latin version, the Syriac Vulgate, Irenaeus, Victorinus, etc.

22 been instructed—the real Christ who is in Jesus); you must lay aside the old nature which belonged to your former course of life, that nature which crumbles to ruin
23 under the passions of moral deceit, and be renewed in the
24 spirit of your mind, putting on the new nature, that divine pattern which has been created in the upright and pious
25 character of the Truth. Lay aside falsehood, then, *let each tell his neighbour the truth,* for we are members one
26 of another. *Be angry but do not sin;* never let the sun
27 set upon your exasperation, give the devil no chance.
28 Let the thief steal no more; rather let him work and put his hands to an honest task, so as to have something to con-
29 tribute to the needy. Let no bad word pass your lips, but only such speech as is good for edification, as occasion may require, words that are gracious and a means of grace
30 to those who hear them. And do not vex God's holy Spirit, by whom you have been sealed for the day of redemption.
31 Drop all bitter feeling and passion and anger and clamour-
32 ing and insults, together with all malice; be kind to each other, be tender-hearted, be generous to each other as God has been generous to you in Christ. Copy God, then,
5
2 as his beloved children, and lead lives of love, just as Christ loved you and gave himself up for you to be *a fragrant offering and sacrifice* to God.
3 Never let any sexual vice or impurity or lust be so much as mentioned by you—that is the proper course for saints
4 to take; no, nor indecent, silly, or scurrilous talk—all that
5 is improper. Rather, voice your thanks to God. Be sure of this, that no one guilty of sexual vice or impurity or lust (that is, an idolater) possesses any inheritance in the
6 realm of Christ and God. Let no one deceive you with specious arguments; these are the vices that bring down
7 God's anger on the sons of disobedience. So avoid the com-
8 pany of such men. For while once upon a time you were darkness, now in the Lord you are light; lead the life of
9 those who are children of the light (for the fruit of light
10 consists in all that is good and right and true), verifying
11 what pleases the Lord. Have nothing to do with the fruit-
12 less enterprises of the darkness; rather expose them. One is indeed ashamed even to speak about what such men do
13 in secret; still, whatever the light exposes becomes illuminated—for anything that is illuminated turns into light.
14 Thus it is said,

'Wake up, O sleeper, and rise from the dead;
   so Christ will shine upon you.'

15 Be strictly * careful then about the life you lead; act

---

* Reading ἀκριβῶς πῶς with ℵ*, B, Origen, etc.

EPHESIANS VI 295

16 like sensible men, not like thoughtless; make the very
17 most of your time, for these are evil days. So do not be
18 senseless, but understand what is the Lord's will; and do
not get drunk with wine—that means profligacy—but be
19 filled with the Spirit, converse with one another in the music
of psalms, in hymns, and in songs of the spiritual life,
20 praise the Lord heartily with words and music, and render
thanks to God the Father in the name of our Lord Jesus
Christ at all times and for all things.
21 Be subject to one another out of reverence for Christ.
22 Wives, be subject to your husbands as to the Lord, for the
23 husband is the head of the wife as Christ also (though he
24 is the saviour of the Body) is the head of the church; as
the church is subject to Christ, so wives are to be subject
25 to their husbands in every respect. Husbands, love your
wives, just as Christ loved the church and gave himself up
26 for her to consecrate her by cleansing her in the bath of
27 baptism as she utters her confession, in order to have the
church as his very own, standing before him in all her
glory, with never a spot or wrinkle or any such flaw, but
28 consecrated and unblemished. So ought husbands to love
their wives—to love them as their own bodies (he who loves
29 his wife loves himself). For no one ever hates his flesh;
no, he nourishes and cherishes it (just as Christ does the
30 church for we are members of his Body).* *Therefore shall*
31 *a man leave father and mother and cleave to his wife, and*
32 *the pair shall be one flesh.* This is a profound symbol, I
33 mean as regards Christ and the church. However, let every
man of you love his wife as himself, and let the wife rever-
6 ence her husband. Children, obey your parents in the
2 Lord, for this is right; *honour your father and mother*
3 (it is the first command with a promise), *that it may be*
4 *well with you and that you may live long on earth.* As
for you fathers, do not exasperate your children, but bring
them up in *the discipline* and on *the admonitions of the*
Lord.
5 Servants, be obedient to those who are your masters here
below with reverence and trembling, with singleness of
6 heart as to Christ himself; instead of merely working when
their eye is on you, like those who court human favour,
7 do God's will from the heart like servants of Christ, by
rendering service with goodwill as to the Lord and Master,
8 not to men. Be sure that everyone, slave or free, will be
paid back by the Lord and Master for the good he has done.
9 And as for you masters, act by your servants in the same

---

* Omitting [ἐκ τῆς σαρκὸς αὐτοῦ καὶ ἐκ τῶν ὀστέων αὐτοῦ] with ℵ*, A B,
Origen, etc.

way, and stop threatening them; be sure that they and you have a Lord and Master in heaven, and there is no partiality about him.

10 To conclude. Be strong in the Lord and in the strength
11 of his might; put on God's armour so as to be able to stand
12 against the stratagems of the devil. For we have to struggle, not with blood and flesh but with the angelic Rulers, the angelic Authorities, the potentates of the dark present,
13 the spirit-forces of evil in the heavenly sphere. So take God's armour, that you may be able to make a stand upon the evil day and hold your ground by overcoming all the
14 foe. Hold your ground, *tighten the belt of truth about*
15 *your loins, wear integrity as your coat of mail*, and have your *feet shod with the stability of the gospel of peace;*
16 above all, take faith as your shield, to enable you to quench
17 all the fire-tipped darts flung by the evil one, put on *salvation as your helmet*, and take *the Spirit as* your *sword*
18 (that is, *the word of God*), praying at all times in the Spirit with all manner of prayer and entreaty—be alive to that, attend to it unceasingly, interceding on behalf of all
19 the saints and on my behalf also, that I may be allowed to speak and open my lips in order to expound fully and
20 freely that open secret of the gospel for the sake of which I am in custody as its envoy. Pray that I may have freedom to declare it as I should.

21 Our beloved brother Tychicus, a faithful minister in the Lord, will give you all information about me, so that you
22 may know how I am; that is why I am sending him to you, to let you know how I am and to encourage your hearts.

23 Peace and love with faith be to the brothers from God
24 the Father and the Lord Jesus Christ. Grace be with all who have an undying love for our Lord Jesus Christ.

THE EPISTLE OF PAUL THE APOSTLE TO THE
PHILIPPIANS

1 PAUL and Timotheus, servants of Christ Jesus, to all the saints in Christ Jesus who are at Philippi, as well
2 as to the bishops and deacons: grace and peace to you from God our Father and the Lord Jesus Christ.
3 I thank my God for all your remembrance of me;
4 in all my prayers for you all I always pray with a sense of
5 joy for what you have contributed to the gospel from the
6 very first day down to this moment; of this I am confident, that he who has begun the good work in you will go on
7 completing it until the day of Jesus Christ. It is only natural for me to be thinking of you all in this way, for alike in my prison and as I defend and vindicate the gospel, I bear in mind how you all share with me in the
8 grace divine. God is my witness that I yearn for you all
9 with the affection of Christ Jesus himself! And it is my prayer that your love may be more and more rich in knowledge and all manner of insight, enabling you to have a
10 sense of what is vital, so that you may be transparent and
11 no harm to anyone in view of the day of Christ, your life covered with that harvest of righteousness which Jesus Christ produces to the glory and the praise of God.
12 I would have you understand, my brothers, that my
13 affairs have really tended to advance the gospel; throughout the whole of the praetorian guard and everywhere else it is recognized that I am imprisoned on account of my con-
14 nexion with Christ, and my imprisonment has given the majority of the brotherhood greater confidence in the Lord to venture on speaking the word of God without being
15 afraid. Some of them, it is true, are actually preaching
16 Christ from envy and rivalry, others from goodwill; the latter do it from love to me, knowing that I am set here
17 to defend the gospel, but the former proclaim Christ for their own ends, with mixed motives, intending to annoy
18 me as I lie in prison. What does it matter? Anyhow, for ulterior ends or honestly, Christ is being proclaimed, and I rejoice over that; yes and I will rejoice over it.
19 *The outcome of all this*, I know, *will be my release*, as you continue to pray for me, and as I am provided with

20 the Spirit of Jesus Christ—my eager desire and hope being that I may never feel ashamed but that now as ever I may do honour to Christ in my own person by fearless courage. Whether that means life or death, no matter!
21 As life means Christ to me, so death means gain. But then,
22 if it is to be life here below, that means fruitful work.
23 So—well, I cannot tell which to choose; I am in a dilemma between the two. My strong desire is to depart and be
24 with Christ, for that is far the best. But for your sakes
25 it is necessary I should live on here below. I am sure it is, and so I know I shall remain alive and serve you all by forwarding your progress and fostering the joy of your
26 faith. Thus you will have ample cause to glory in Christ Jesus over me—over my return to you.
27 Only, do lead a life that is worthy of the gospel of Christ. Whether I come and see you or only hear of you in absence, let me know you are standing firm in a common spirit, fighting side by side like one man for the faith of
28 the gospel. Never be scared for a second by your opponents: your fearlessness is a clear omen of ruin for them
29 and of your own salvation—at the hands of God. For on behalf of Christ you have the favour of suffering no less
30 than of believing in him, by waging the same conflict that,
2 as once you saw and now you hear, I wage myself. So by all the stimulus of Christ, by every incentive of love, by all your participation in the Spirit, by all your affec-
2 tionate tenderness, I pray you to give me the utter joy of knowing you are living in harmony, with the same feel-
3 ings of love, with one heart and soul, never acting for private ends or from vanity, but humbly considering each
4 other the better man, and each with an eye to the inter-
5 ests of others as well as to his own. Treat one another with the same spirit as you experience in Christ Jesus.
6 Though he was divine by nature, he did not snatch at
7 equality with God but emptied himself by taking the
8 nature of a servant; born in human guise and appearing in human form, he humbly stooped in his obedience even
9 to die, and to die upon the cross. Therefore God raised him high and conferred on him a Name above all names,
10 so that before the Name of Jesus *every knee should bend*
11 in heaven, on earth, and underneath the earth, *and every tongue confess* that 'Jesus Christ is Lord,' to the glory of God the Father.
12 Therefore, my beloved, as you have been obedient always and not simply when I was present, so, now that I am absent, work all the more strenuously at your salvation
13 with reverence and trembling, for it is God who in his
14 goodwill enables you to will this and to achieve it. In all

15 that you do, avoid grumbling and disputing, so as to be blameless and innocent, *faultless children of God* in *a*
16 *crooked and perverse generation* where you shine like stars' in a dark world; hold fast the word of life, so that I can be proud of you on the Day of Christ, because I have not
17 run or *worked for nothing*. Even if my life-blood has to be poured as a libation on the sacred sacrifice of faith you
18 are offering to God, I rejoice, I congratulate you all—and you in turn must rejoice and congratulate me.
19 I hope in the Lord Jesus to send you Timotheus before
20 long, that I may be heartened by news of you. I have no
21 one like him, for genuine interest in your welfare. Every-
22 body is selfish, instead of caring for Jesus Christ. But you know how he has stood the test, how he has served
23 with me in the gospel, like a son helping his father. I hope to send him then, as soon as ever I see how it will go
24 with me—though I am confident in the Lord that I shall
25 be coming myself before long. As for Epaphroditus, however, my brother, my fellow-worker, my fellow-soldier, and your messenger to meet my wants, I think it necessary
26 to send you him at once, for he has been yearning for you all. He has been greatly concerned because you heard he
27 was ill. And he was ill, nearly dead with illness. But God had mercy on him, and not only on him but on me,
28 to save me from having one sorrow upon another. So I am specially eager to send him, that you may be glad when you see him again, and thus my own anxiety may be
29 lightened. Give him a welcome in the Lord, then, with
30 your hearts full of joy. Value men like that, for he nearly died in the service of Christ by risking his life to make up for the services you were not here to render me.

3 WELL then, my brothers, rejoice in the Lord. I am repeating this word 'rejoice' in my letter, but that does
2 not tire me and it is the safe course for you.—Beware of these dogs, these wicked workmen, the incision-party!
3 We are the true Circumcision, we who worship God in spirit, we who pride ourselves on Christ Jesus, we who rely
4 upon no outward privilege. Though I could rely on outward privilege, if I chose. Whoever thinks he can rely on
5 that, I can outdo him. I was circumcised on the eighth day after birth; I belonged to the race of Israel, to the tribe of Benjamin; I was the Hebrew son of Hebrew
6 parents, a Pharisee as regards the Law, in point of ardour a persecutor of the church, immaculate by the standard
7 of legal righteousness. But for Christ's sake I have
8 learned to count my former gains a loss; indeed I count anything a loss, compared to the supreme value of know-

ing Christ Jesus my Lord. For his sake I have lost everything (I count it all the veriest refuse in order to gain
9 Christ and be found at death in him, possessing no legal righteousness of my own but the righteousness of faith in Christ, the divine righteousness that rests on
10 faith. I would know him in the power of his resurrection and the fellowship of his sufferings, with my
11 nature transformed to die as he died, to see if I too can
12 attain the resurrection from the dead. Not that I have already attained this or am already perfect, but I press forward to appropriate it, because I have been appropriated
13 myself by Christ Jesus. Brothers, I for one do not consider myself to have appropriated this; my one thought is, by forgetting what lies behind me and straining to what
14 lies before me, to press on to the goal for the prize of God's
15 high call in Christ Jesus. For all those of our number who are mature, this must be the point of view; God will reveal that to any of you who look at things differently.
16 Only, we must let our steps be guided by such truth as we have attained.
17 Copy me, brothers, one and all of you, and notice those
18 who live by the example you get from me. For many—as I have often told you and tell you now with tears—many
19 live as enemies of the cross of Christ. Destruction is their fate, the belly is their god, they glory in their shame, these
20 men of earthly mind! But we are a colony of heaven, and we wait for the Saviour who comes from heaven, the
21 Lord Jesus Christ, who will transform the body that belongs to our low estate till it resembles the body of his Glory, by the same power that enables him to make everything subject to himself. So then, my brothers, for
4 whom I cherish love and longing, my joy and crown, this is how you must stand firm in the Lord, O my beloved.
2 I entreat Euodia and I entreat Syntyche to agree in the
3 Lord. And you, my true comrade, lend a hand to these women, I beg of you; they have fought at my side in the active service of the gospel, along with Clement and the rest of my fellow-workers, whose names are in *the book of life.*
4 Rejoice in the Lord always. I will say it again, 'rejoice.'
5 Let your forbearance be known to everyone; the Lord is
6 at hand. Never be anxious, but always make your requests known to God in prayer and supplication with thanks-
7 giving; so shall God's peace, that surpasses all our dreams, keep guard over your hearts and minds in Christ Jesus.
8 Finally, brothers, keep in mind whatever is true, whatever is worthy, whatever is just, whatever is pure, whatever is attractive, whatever is high-toned, all excellence,

9 all merit. Practise also what you have learned and received from me, what you heard me say and what you saw me do; then the God of peace will be with you.
10 It was a great joy to me in the Lord that your care for me could revive again; for what you lacked was never
11 the care but the chance of showing it. Not that I complain of want, for I have learned how to be content
12 wherever I am. I know how to live humbly; I also know how to live in prosperity. I have been initiated into the secret for all sorts and conditions of life, for plenty and
13 for hunger, for prosperity and for privations. In him who
14 strengthens me I am able for anything. But you were
15 kind enough to take your share in my trouble. You Philippians are well aware that in the early days of the gospel, when I had left Macedonia, no church but your-
16 selves had any financial dealings with me; even when 1 was in Thessalonica, you sent money more than once for
17 my needs. It is not the money I am anxious for; what I am anxious for is the interest that accumulates in this
18 way to your divine credit! Your debt to me is fully paid and more than paid! I am amply supplied with what you have sent by Epaphroditus, *a fragrant perfume*, the sort
19 of sacrifice that God approves and welcomes. My God will supply all your own needs from his wealth in Glory in
20 Christ Jesus. Glory to God our Father for ever and ever: Amen.
21 Salute every saint in Christ Jesus. The brothers beside
22 me salute you. All the saints salute you, especially the Imperial slaves.
23 The grace of the Lord Jesus Christ be with your spirit. Amen.

THE EPISTLE OF PAUL THE APOSTLE TO THE
COLOSSIANS

1 PAUL, by God's will an apostle of Christ Jesus, and
2 brother Timotheus, to the consecrated and faithful
brothers in Christ at Colossae: grace and peace to you from
God our Father.
3 We always thank the God and Father of our Lord Jesus
4 Christ when we pray for you, since we have heard of your
faith in Christ Jesus and your love for all the saints,
5 due to the hope which is laid up for you in heaven. You
heard of this hope originally in the message of the Truth,
6 in that gospel which has reached you as it spreads over all
the world with fruit and increase. Such has been your
life from the day you learned to know what God's grace
7 really is. You got that lesson from our beloved fellow-
servant Epaphras, a minister of Christ who is faithful to
8 your interests; and it is he who has informed us of your
9 love in the Spirit. Hence, from the day we heard of it,
we have never ceased to pray for you, asking God to fill
you with the knowledge of his will in all spiritual wisdom
10 and insight, so that you may lead a life that is worthy
of the Lord and give him entire satisfaction. May you be
fruitful and increase in the doing of all good, as you thus
11 know God! May his glorious might nerve you with full
power to endure and to be patient cheerfully, whatever
12 comes, thanking the Father who has qualified us to share
13 the lot of the saints in the Light, rescuing us from the
power of the Darkness and transferring us to the realm of
14 his beloved Son! In him we enjoy our redemption, that
15 is, the forgiveness of sins. He is the likeness of the un-
16 seen God, born first before all the creation—for it was by
him that all things were created both in heaven and on
earth, both the seen and the unseen, including Thrones,
angelic Lords, celestial Powers and Rulers; all things have
17 been created by him and for him; he is prior to all, and
18 all coheres in him. Also, he is the head of the Body, that
is, of the church, in virtue of his primacy as the first to
be born from the dead—that gives him preeminence over
19 all. For it was in him that the divine Fulness willed to
20 settle without limit, and by him it willed to reconcile in

his own person all on earth and in heaven alike, in a peace
21 made by the blood of his cross. Once you were estranged
yourselves, your hearts hostile to him in evildoing; but
now he has reconciled you by dying in his mortal body,
22 so as to set you consecrated and unblemished and irre-
23 proachable in his presence—that is, if you adhere to the
foundations and stability of the faith, instead of moving
away from the hope you have learned in the gospel, that
gospel which has been preached to every creature under
heaven, and of which I Paul was made a minister.
24 I am suffering now on your behalf, but I rejoice in that;
I would make up the full sum of all that Christ has to
suffer in my person on behalf of the church, his Body;
25 for I am a minister of the church by the divine commission
which has been granted me in your interests, to make
26 a full presentation of God's message—of that open secret
which, though concealed from ages and generations of old,
27 has now been disclosed to the saints of God. It is His
will that they should understand the glorious wealth which
this secret holds for the Gentiles, in the fact of Christ's
28 presence among you as your hope of glory. This is the
Christ we proclaim; we train everyone and teach everyone
the full scope of this knowledge, in order to set everyone
29 before God mature in Christ; I labour for that end, striving
for it with the divine energy which is a power within me.

2 Striving? Yes, I want you to understand my deep
concern for you and for those at Laodicea, for all who
2 have never seen my face. May their hearts be encouraged!
May they learn the meaning of love! May they have all the
wealth of conviction that comes from insight! May they
learn to know that open secret of God, the Father of
3 Christ, in whom all *the treasures of wisdom and knowledge*
4 lie *hidden!* I say this to prevent you from being deluded
5 by plausible arguments from anybody; for although I am
absent in body I am with you in spirit, and it is a joy to
note your steadiness and the solid front of your faith in
Christ.
6 Since you have had the messiah, even Jesus the Lord,
7 brought to you, lead your life in him, fixed and founded
in him, confirmed in the faith as you have been taught it,
8 and overflowing with thankfulness to God. Beware of anyone getting hold of you by means of a theosophy which is
specious make-believe, on the lines of human tradition, corresponding to the Elemental spirits of the world and not
9 to Christ. It is in Christ that the entire Fulness of deity
10 has settled bodily, it is in him that you reach your full
life, and he is the Head of every angelic Ruler and Power;
11 in him you have been circumcised with no material circum-

cision that cuts flesh from the body, but with Christ's own circumcision, when you were buried with him in your baptism and thereby raised with him as you believed in the power of the God who raised him from the dead. For though you were dead in your trespasses, your flesh uncircumcised, He made you live with Christ, He forgave us all our trespasses, He cancelled the regulations that stood against us—all these obligations he set aside when he nailed them to the cross, when he cut away the angelic Rulers and Powers from us, exposing them to all the world and triumphing over them in the cross. So let no one take you to task on questions of eating and drinking or in connexion with the observance of festivals or new moons or sabbaths. All that is the mere shadow of what is to be; the substance belongs to Christ. Let no one lay down rules for you as he pleases, with regard to fasting and the cult of angels, presuming on his visions and inflated by his sensuous notions, instead of keeping in touch with that Head under whom the entire Body, supplied with joints and sinews and thus compacted, grows with growth divine. As you died with Christ to the Elemental spirits of the world, why live as if you still belonged to the world? Why submit to rules and regulations like "Hands off this!" "Taste not that!" "Touch not this!"—referring to things that perish by being used? These rules are determined by *human precepts and tenets;* they get the name of 'wisdom' with their self-imposed devotions, with their fasting, with their rigorous discipline of the body, but they are of no value, they simply pamper the flesh!

3 Since then you have been raised with Christ, aim at what is above, where Christ is, *seated at the right hand of God;* mind what is above, not what is on earth, for you died and your life is hidden with Christ in God. When Christ, who is our life, appears, then you will appear with him in glory. So put to death those members that are on earth: sexual vice, impurity, appetite, evil desire, and lust (which is idolatry), things that bring down the anger of God on the sons of disobedience. Once you moved among them, when you lived in them; but off with them all now, off with anger, rage, malice, slander, foul talk! Tell no lies to one another; you have stripped off the old nature with its practices, and put on the new nature which is renewed *in the likeness of its Creator* for the knowledge of him. In it there is no room for Greek and Jew, circumcised and uncircumcised, barbarian, Scythian, slave, or free man; Christ is everything and everywhere.

As God's own chosen, then, as consecrated and beloved, be clothed with compassion, kindliness, humility, gentle-

COLOSSIANS IV 305

13 ness, and good temper—forbear and forgive each other in any case of complaint; as Christ forgave you, so must you
14 forgive. And above all you must be loving, for love is the
15 link of the perfect life. Also, let the peace of Christ be supreme within your hearts—that is why you have been called as members of the one Body. And you must be
16 thankful. Let the inspiration of Christ dwell in your midst with all its wealth of wisdom; teach and train one another with the music of psalms, with hymns, and songs of the spiritual life; praise God with thankful hearts.
17 Indeed, whatever you say or do, let everything be done in dependence on the Lord Jesus, giving thanks in his name to God the Father.
18 Wives, be subject to your husbands; that is your proper
19 duty in the Lord. Husbands, love your wives, do not be
20 harsh to them. Children, obey your parents at every
21 point, for this pleases the Lord right well. Fathers, avoid
22 irritating your children, in case they get dispirited. Servants, obey your masters here below at every point; do not work simply when their eye is on you, like those who court human favour, but serve them with a single heart
23 out of reverence for your Lord and Master. Whatever be your task, work at it heartily, as servants of the Lord and
24 not of men; remember, you will receive from the Lord the inheritance which is your due; serve Christ your Lord and
25 Master, for the wrongdoer will be paid back for his wrongdoing—there will be no favour shown. Masters, treat
4 your servants justly and fairly; remember you have a Master of your own in heaven.
2 Attend to your prayers, maintain your zest for prayer
3 by thanksgiving; and pray for me as well, that God may give me an opening for the word, to speak of the open
4 secret of Christ for which I am in custody. Pray that I
5 may unfold it as I should. Let Christian wisdom rule your behaviour to the outside world; make the very most
6 of your time; let your talk always have a saving salt of grace about it, and learn how to answer any question put to you.
7 Tychicus, that beloved brother and faithful minister and fellow-servant in the Lord, will give you all information
8 about me. The reason why I am sending him to you is that he may ascertain how you are, and encourage your
9 hearts. He is accompanied by that faithful and beloved brother Onesimus, who is one of yourselves. They will inform you of all that goes on here.
10 Aristarchus my fellow-prisoner salutes you; so does Mark, the cousin of Barnabas, about whom you have got in-
11 structions (if he comes to you, give him a welcome); and

so does Jesus who is called Justus. These are the only comrades in the work of God's realm, belonging to the cir-
12 cumcised, who have been any comfort to me. Epaphras, who is one of yourselves, salutes you—a servant of Christ Jesus who is always earnest in prayer for you, that you may stand firm like mature and convinced Christians, what-
13 ever be the will of God for you. I can testify to his exertions on your behalf and on behalf of those at Laodicea
14 and Hierapolis. Our beloved Luke, the doctor, salutes you;
15 so does Demas. Salute the brothers at Laodicea, also
16 Nympha and the church which meets at her house. And when this letter has been read to you, see that it is also read in the church of the Laodiceans; also, see that you
17 read the letter that reaches you from Laodicea. And tell Archippus, 'Attend to the ministry you have received in the Lord; see that you fulfil it.'
18 This salutation is in my own hand, from Paul. 'Remember I am in prison. Grace be with you.'

THE FIRST EPISTLE OF PAUL THE APOSTLE TO THE

THESSALONIANS

1 PAUL and Silvanus and Timotheus, to the church of the Thessalonians in God the Father and the Lord Jesus Christ: grace and peace to you.
2 We always thank God for you all when we mention you
3 constantly in our prayers, as we recall your active faith and labour of love and patient hope in our Lord Jesus
4 Christ, before our God and Father. O brothers beloved by
5 God, we know he has chosen you; for our gospel came to you not with mere words but also with power and with the holy Spirit, with ample conviction on our part (you
6 know what we were to you, for your own good), and you started to copy us and the Lord, welcoming the word, though it brought you heavy trouble, with a joy inspired
7 by the holy Spirit. Thus you became a pattern to all the
8 believers in Macedonia and in Achaia; for the word of the Lord has resounded from you not only through Macedonia and Achaia—no, your faith in God has reached every place.
9 We never need to speak about it. People tell us of their own accord about the visit we paid to you, and how you turned to God from idols, to serve a living and a real God
10 and to wait for the coming of his Son from heaven—the Son whom he raised from the dead, Jesus who rescues us from the Wrath to come.

2 BUT you remember yourselves, brothers, that our visit
2 to you was no failure. At Philippi, as you know, we had been ill-treated and insulted, but we took courage and confidence in our God to tell you the gospel of God in spite
3 of all the strain. For the appeal we make does not spring from any delusion or from impure motives—it does not
4 work by cunning; no, God has attested our fitness to be entrusted with the gospel, and so we tell the gospel not to satisfy men but to satisfy the God who tests our hearts.
5 We never resorted to flattery (you know that), nor to any
6 pretext for self-seeking (God is witness to that); we never sought honour from men, from you or from anybody else, though as apostles of Christ we had the power of claiming
7 to be men of weight; no, we behaved gently when we were

among you, like a nursing mother cherishing her own
8 children, fain, in our yearning affection for you, to impart
not only the gospel of God to you but our very souls as well
9 —you had so won our love. Brothers, you recollect our
hard labour and toil, how we worked at our trade night
and day, when we preached the gospel to you, so as not
10 to be a burden to any of you. You are witnesses, and so is
God, to our behaviour among you believers, how pious and
11 upright and blameless it was, how (as you know) we
treated each of you as a father treats his children, beseech-
12 ing you, encouraging you, and charging you to lead a life
worthy of the God who called you to his own realm and
glory.
13 We thank God constantly for this too, that when you received the word of the divine message from us, you took
it not as a human word but for what it really is, the word
14 of God. It proves effective in you believers, for you have
started, my brothers, to copy the churches of God in Christ
Jesus throughout Judaea; you have suffered from your
15 compatriots just as they have suffered from the Jews, who
killed the Lord Jesus and the prophets, who harassed our-
16 selves, who offend God and oppose all men by hindering
us from speaking words of salvation to the Gentiles. So
they would fill up the measure of their sins to the last
drop! But the Wrath is on them to the bitter end!
17 Brothers, when we were bereft of you for a little while
(out of sight, not out of mind), we were the more eager
18 to see you. We had a keen longing for you. (We did
want to reach you—I did, I Paul, more than once—but
19 Satan stopped us.) For who is our hope, our joy, our
crown of pride (who but you?) in the presence of our Lord
20 Jesus on his arrival? Why, you, you are our glory and
joy! So, unable to bear it any longer, I made up my
3 mind to be left behind at Athens all alone; I sent
Timotheus our brother, a minister of God in the gospel of
Christ, for your strengthening and encouragement in the
3 faith, to prevent anyone being disturbed by these troubles.
4 (Troubles are our lot, you know that well; for we told
you beforehand, when we were with you, that "we Christians are to have trouble"—and, as you know, it has been
5 so.) Well then, unable to bear it any longer, I sent to find
out about your faith, in case the Tempter had tempted you
6 and our labour had been thrown away. But when Timotheus reached me a moment ago on his return from you,
bringing me the good news of your faith and love and of
how you always remember me kindly, longing to see me as
7 I long to see you, then, amid all my own distress and
trouble, I was cheered—this faith of yours encouraged me.

I. THESSALONIANS IV

8 It is life to me now, if you stand firm in the Lord. How can
9 I render thanks enough to God for you, for all the joy
10 you make me feel in the presence of our God? Night and
day I pray specially that I may see your faces and sup-
11 ply what is defective in your faith. May our God and
12 Father and our Lord Jesus direct my way to you! And
may the Lord make you increase and excel in love to one
13 another and to all men (as is my love for you), so as to
strengthen your hearts and make them blameless in holiness before our God and Father when our Lord Jesus
comes with all his holy ones. [Amen.]

4 FINALLY, brothers, we beg and beseech you in the Lord
Jesus to follow our instructions about the way you are
to live so as to satisfy God; you are leading that life, but
2 you are to excel in it still further. You remember the instructions we gave you on the authority of the Lord Jesus.
3 It is God's will that you should be consecrated, that you
4 abstain from sexual vice, that each of you should learn to
5 take a wife for himself chastely and honourably, not to
gratify sensual passion like *the Gentiles in their ignorance*
6 *of God*—no one is to defraud or overreach his brother
in this matter, for *the Lord avenges* all *these sins*, as we
7 told you already in our solemn protest against them. God
8 did not call us to be impure but to be consecrated; hence,
he who disregards this, disregards not man but the God
9 who gave you his holy Spirit. You need no one to write
you upon brotherly love, for you are yourselves taught by
10 God to love one another, as indeed is your practice towards
all the brothers throughout all Macedonia. We beseech
11 you, brothers, to excel in this more and more; also, endeavour to live quietly, attend to your own business, and
12 —as we charged you—work with your hands, so that
your life may be correct in the eyes of the outside world
and self-supporting.
13 We would like you, brothers, to understand about those
who are asleep in death. You must not grieve for them,
14 like the rest of men who have no hope. Since we believe
that Jesus died and rose again, then it follows that by
means of Jesus God will bring with him those who have
15 fallen asleep. For we tell you, as the Lord has told us,
that we the living, who survive till the Lord comes, are by
no means to take precedence of those who have fallen
16 asleep. The Lord himself will descend from heaven with
a loud summons, when the archangel calls and the trumpet
17 of God sounds; the dead in Christ will rise first; then we
the living, who survive, will be caught up along with them
in the clouds to meet the Lord in the air, and so we shall

18 be with the Lord for ever. Now then, encourage one another with these words.

5 As regards the course and periods of time, brothers, you
2 have no need of being written to. You know perfectly well that the day of the Lord comes like a thief in the
3 night; when 'all's well' and 'all is safe' are on the lips of men, then all of a sudden Destruction is upon them, like
4 pangs on a pregnant woman—escape there is none. But, brothers, you are not in the darkness for the Day to sur-
5 prise you like thieves;* you are all sons of the Light and sons of the day. We do not belong to the night or the
6 darkness. Well then, we must not sleep like the rest of
7 men, but be wakeful and sober; for sleepers sleep by night
8 and drunkards are drunk by night, but we must be sober—we who belong to the day, clad in faith and love as *our coat of*
9 *mail*, with the hope of *salvation as our helmet*—for God destined us not for Wrath but to gain salvation through
10 our Lord Jesus Christ, who died for us that waking in life or sleeping in death we should live together with him.
11 Encourage one another, therefore, and let each edify the other—as indeed you are doing.
12 Brothers, we beg you to respect those who are working among you, presiding over you in the Lord and maintain-
13 ing discipline; hold them in special esteem and affection, for the sake of their work. Be at peace among yourselves.
14 We beseech you, brothers, keep a check upon loafers, encourage the faint-hearted, sustain weak souls, never lose
15 your temper with anyone; see that none of you pays back
16 evil for evil, but always aim at what is kind to one another
17 and to all the world; rejoice at all times, never give up
18 prayer, thank God for everything—such is his will for you
19 in Christ Jesus; never quench the fire of the Spirit,
20 never disdain prophetic revelations but test them all,
21 retaining what is good and *abstaining from whatever* kind
22 *is evil*.
23 May the God of peace consecrate you through and through! Spirit, soul, and body, may you be kept without break or blame till the arrival of our Lord Jesus Christ!
24 He who calls you is faithful, he will do this.
25 Pray for us too, brothers.
26 Salute every one of the brothers with a holy kiss.
27 I adjure you by the Lord to have this letter read aloud to all the [holy] brothers.
28 The grace of our Lord Jesus Christ be with you. [Amen.]

* Reading κλέπτας with A B and the Bohairic version.

THE SECOND EPISTLE OF PAUL THE APOSTLE TO THE
THESSALONIANS

1 PAUL and Silvanus and Timotheus, to the church of the Thessalonians in God our Father and the Lord Jesus
2 Christ: grace and peace to you from God the Father and the Lord Jesus Christ.
3 We are bound always to thank God for you, brothers—it is proper that we should, because your faith grows apace
4 and your mutual love, one and all, is increasing. So much so, that throughout the churches of God we are proud of you, proud of the stedfastness and faith you display through all the persecutions and the troubles in which you
5 are involved. They are proof positive of God's equity; you are suffering for the realm of God, and he means to make
6 you worthy of it—since God considers it but just
    to repay with trouble those who trouble you,
7   and repay you who are troubled (as well as us) with rest and relief,
    when the Lord Jesus is revealed from heaven
8   together with the angels of his power *in flaming fire*,
    to inflict punishment on those who ignore God,
    even on *those who refuse obedience* to the gospel of our Lord Jesus,
9   men who will pay the penalty of being destroyed eternally
    from the presence of the Lord
    and from the glory of his might,
10   *when he comes to be glorified in his saints*
    and *marvelled at* in all believers
    on that day (for our testimony has found confirmation * in
11 your lives). In view of this we always pray for you, asking our God to make you worthy of his calling and by his power to fulfil every good resolve and every effort of faith,
12 so that the name of our Lord Jesus *may be glorified in you* (and you glorified in him), by the grace of our God and the Lord Jesus Christ.

* Reading with Markland and Hort ἐπιστώθη (104 469 Ambrosiaster) for the ἐπιστεύθη of most manuscripts and all versions.

II. THESSALONIANS II, III

2 **2** With regard to the arrival of the * Lord Jesus Christ and our muster before him, I beg you, brothers, not to let your minds get easily unsettled or excited by any spirit of prophecy or any declaration or any letter· purporting to come from me, to the effect that the Day of the Lord
3 is already here. Let nobody delude you into this belief, whatever he may say. It will not come till the Rebellion takes place first of all, with the revealing of the Lawless †
4 One, the doomed One, the adversary *who vaunts himself above and against every so-called god or object of worship, actually seating himself in the temple of God* with the proc-
5 lamation that he himself is God. Do you not remember
6 I used to tell you this when I was with you? Well, you can recall now what it is that restrains him from being
7 revealed before his appointed time. For the secret force of lawlessness is at work already; only, it cannot be revealed till he who at present restrains it is removed.
8 Then shall the Lawless One be revealed,
 whom the Lord Jesus *will destroy with the breath of his lips*
 and quell by his appearing and arrival—
9 that One whose arrival is due to Satan's activity,
 with the full power, the miracles and portents, of falsehood,
10 and with the full deceitfulness of evil for those who are doomed to perish,
 since they refuse to love the Truth that would save them.
11 Therefore God visits them with an active delusion,
 till they put faith in falsehood,
12 so that all may be doomed who refuse faith in the Truth but delight in evil.
13 Now we are bound always to thank God for you, brothers *beloved by the Lord*, because God has chosen you as the first to be reaped for salvation, by the consecration of your
14 spirit and by faith in the Truth; it was for this that he called you by our gospel, to gain the glory of our Lord
15 Jesus Christ. Well, then, brothers, stand firm and hold to the rules which you have learned from us orally or by
16 letter. And may our Lord Jesus Christ himself and God our Father who has loved us and given us eternal encour-
17 agement and good hope, graciously encourage your hearts and strengthen them for all good in deed and word.

3 **3** FINALLY, brothers, pray for us, that the word of the Lord may speed on and triumph, as in your own case,
2 and that we may be delivered from perverse and evil men

* Omitting ἡμῶν with B Syrhkl.
† Reading ἀνομίας with ℵ B, etc., for the Western paraphrastic ἁμαρτίας.

II. THESSALONIANS III

3 —for the faith is not held by all. However, the Lord is
faithful; he will be sure to strengthen you and protect you
4 from the Evil one. Now, we rely on you in the Lord, con-
5 fident that you do and will do what we enjoin. May the
Lord direct your hearts towards God's love and towards
Christ's patience!
6 Brothers, we charge you in the name of the Lord Jesus
Christ to shun any brother who is loafing, instead of fol-
7 lowing the rule you got * from us. For you know quite
8 well how to copy us; we did not loaf in your midst, we did
not take free meals from anyone; no, toiling hard at our
trade, we worked night and day, so as not to be a burden
9 to any of you. Not that we have no right to such support;
10 it was simply to give you a pattern to copy. We used to
charge you even when we were with you, 'If a man will not
11 work, he shall not eat.' But we are informed that some
of your number are loafing, busybodies instead of busy.
12 Now in the Lord Jesus Christ we charge and exhort such
persons to keep quiet, to do their work and earn their
13 own living. As for yourselves, brothers, never grow tired
14 of doing what is right. Only, if anyone will not obey
our orders in this letter, mark that man, do not associate
15 with him—that will make him feel ashamed! You are not
to treat him as an enemy, but to put him under discipline
as a brother.
16 May the Lord of peace himself grant you peace con-
tinually, whatever comes.
The Lord be with you all.
17 The salutation is in my own hand, Paul's; that is a
mark in every letter of mine. This is how I write.
18 'The grace of our Lord Jesus Christ be with you all.'

* Reading παρελάβετε with B G, etc., for παρελάβοσαν.

THE FIRST EPISTLE OF PAUL THE APOSTLE TO
TIMOTHEUS

1 Paul an apostle of Christ Jesus by command of God our
2 Saviour and Christ Jesus our Hope, to Timotheus his lawful son in the faith: grace, mercy, peace from God the Father and Christ Jesus our Lord.
3 As I asked you when I was on my way to Macedonia, stay where you are at Ephesus and warn certain individ-
4 uals against teaching novelties and studying myths and interminable genealogies; such studies bear upon speculations rather than on the divine order which belongs
5 to faith. Whereas the aim of the Christian discipline is the love that springs from a pure heart, from a good con-
6 science, and from a sincere faith. Certain individuals have
7 failed here by turning to empty argument; doctors of the Law is what they want to be, but they have no idea either of the meaning of the words they use or of the themes
8 on which they harp. I am quite aware that 'the Law is admirable'—provided that one makes a lawful use of it;
9 he must keep in mind that no law is ever made for honest people but for the lawless and the insubordinate, for the impious and the sinful, for the irreverent and the profane,
10 for parricides and matricides, murderers, immoral persons, sodomites, kidnappers, liars, perjurers, and whatever else
11 is contrary to sound doctrine as laid down by that glorious gospel of the blessed God with which I have been entrusted.
12 I render thanks to Christ Jesus our Lord, who has made me able for this; he considered me trustworthy and
13 appointed me to the ministry, though I had formerly been a blasphemer and a persecutor and a wanton aggressor. I obtained mercy because in my unbelief I had acted out
14 of ignorance; and the grace of our Lord flooded my life along with the faith and love that Christ Jesus inspires.
15 It is a sure word, it deserves all praise, that "Christ Jesus came into the world to save sinners"; and though I am the
16 foremost of sinners, I obtained mercy, for the purpose of furnishing Christ Jesus with the chief illustration of his utter patience; I was to be the typical instance of all who
17 were to believe in him and gain eternal life. To the King

of eternity, immortal, invisible, the only God, be honour and glory for ever and ever: Amen.

18 I transmit these instructions to you, Timotheus my son, in accordance with what the prophets said who first directed me to you; fight the good fight on these lines, 19 keeping hold of faith and a good conscience. Certain individuals have scouted the good conscience and thus come 20 to grief over their faith—including Hymenaeus and Alexander, whom I have made over to Satan. That will teach them to stop their blasphemous ongoings!

2 WELL, my very first counsel is that supplications, prayers, petitions, and thanksgiving, are to be offered 2 for all men—for kings and all in authority, that we may 3 lead a tranquil life in all piety and gravity; it is good to 4 pray thus, it is acceptable to our Saviour, to the God who desires all men to be saved and to attain the knowledge 5 of the Truth. For "there is one God" and "one interme- 6 diary between God and men, the man Christ Jesus who gave himself as a ransom for all":—in due time this was 7 attested, and I was appointed to be its herald and apostle (I am not telling a lie, it is quite true), to teach the Gentiles faith and truth.

8 Now I want the men to offer prayer at any meeting of the church; and let the hands they lift to heaven be holy— 9 they must be free from anger and dissension. Women in turn are to dress modestly and quietly in seemly garb; they are not to adorn themselves with plaits of hair, with 10 gold or pearls or expensive finery, but with good deeds 11 (as befits women who make a religious profession. A woman must listen quietly in church and be perfectly 12 submissive; I allow no woman to teach or dictate to men, 13 she must keep quiet. For Adam was created first, then 14 Eve; and Adam was not deceived, it was Eve who was 15 deceived and who fell into sin. However, women will get safely through childbirth if they continue to be faithful and loving and holy as well as unassuming.

3 It is a popular * saying that "whoever aspires to office is 2 set upon an excellent occupation." Well, for the office of a bishop a man must be above reproach; he must be only married once, he must be temperate, master of him- 3 self, unruffled, hospitable, a skilled teacher, not a drunkard or violent, but lenient and conciliatory, not a lover of

---

* Reading ἀνθρώπινος with D, the Old Latin, Ambrosiaster, and Western codices known to Jerome. It is much more easy to understand how it was altered to πιστός for the sake of uniformity with i. 15, etc., than vice versa.

I. TIMOTHEUS IV

4 money, able to manage his own household properly and
5 keep his children submissive and perfectly respectful (if
a man does not know how to manage his own household,
6 how is he to look after the church of God?); he must not
be a new convert, in case he gets conceited and incurs the
7 doom passed on the devil; also, he must have a good reputation among outsiders, in case he incurs slander and is trapped by the devil.
8 Deacons in turn are to be serious men; they are not to
9 be tale-bearers or addicted to drink or pilfering; they must maintain the divine truth of the faith with a pure
10 conscience. They too must be put on probation; after that, if they are above reproach, they can serve as deacons.
11 Their wives must be serious too; they must not be slanderers but temperate and absolutely trustworthy.
12 Deacons are only to be married once, and they must manage
13 their children and households properly. For those who do good service as deacons win a good position for themselves as well as great freedom in the faith of Christ Jesus.
14 Though I hope to come to you before long, I am writing
15 to you in this way, in case I am detained, to let you see how people ought to behave within the household of God; it is the church of the living God, the pillar and bulwark
16 of the Truth. And who does not admit how profound is the divine truth of our religion?—it is He who was

"manifest in the flesh,
vindicated by the Spirit,
seen by the angels,
preached among the nations,
believed on throughout the world,
taken up to glory."

4 But in later days, the Spirit distinctly declares, certain
2 people will rebel against the faith; they will listen to spirits of error and to the doctrines that daemons teach
2 through plausible sophists who are seared in conscience—
3 men who prohibit marriage and insist on abstinence from foods which God created for believing men, who under-
4 stand the Truth, to partake of with thanksgiving. Anything God has created is good, and nothing is to be tabooed—
5 provided it is eaten with thanksgiving, for then it is consecrated by the prayer said over it.
6 Lay this before the brotherhood, and you will be an excellent minister of Christ Jesus, brought up on the truths of the faith and on the lessons of the good doctrine
7 you have already followed. Shut your mind against these profane, drivelling myths; train for the religious life.
8 The training of the body is of small service, but religion is of service in all directions; it contains the promise of

I. TIMOTHEUS V 317

9 life both for the present and for the future. It is a sure
10 word, it deserves all praise, that "we toil and strive *
because our hope is fixed upon the living God, the Saviour
of all men"—of believers in particular.
11 Give these orders and teach these lessons. Let no one
12 slight you because you are a youth, but set the believers
an example of speech, behaviour, love, faith, and purity.
13 Attend to your Scripture-reading, your preaching, and your
14 teaching, till I come. You have a gift that came to you
transmitted by the prophets, when the presbytery laid
15 their hands upon you; do not neglect that gift. Attend to
these duties, let them absorb you, so that all men may note
16 your progress. Watch yourself and watch your teaching;
stick to your work; if you do that, you will save your
hearers as well as yourself.

5 Never censure an older man harshly; appeal to him as
2 a father. Treat younger men like brothers, older
women like mothers, younger women like sisters—with perfect propriety.
3 Widows who really need it must be supported from the
4 funds. (When a widow has children or grandchildren,
they must learn that the first duty of religion is to their
own household, and that they should make some return to
those who have brought them up. In God's sight this is
5 an acceptable thing.) The really forlorn widow has her
hope fixed on God, night and day she is at her prayers and
6 supplications; whereas the widow who plunges into dissi-
7 pation is dead before ever she dies. So lay down the
following rules, to prevent any reproach being incurred.
8 Whoever does not provide for his own relatives and particularly for his own family, has repudiated the faith; he
9 is worse than an infidel. No one under sixty is to be put
on the church's list of widows; and she must have been
10 only once married, she must have a reputation for good
service, as a woman who has brought up children, shown
hospitality, washed the feet of the saints, relieved distress,
11 and interested herself in all good works. Refuse to put
young widows on the list; for when their wanton desires
12 alienate them from Christ, they want to marry and thus are
13 guilty of breaking their first troth to Him. Besides, they
become idle unconsciously † by gadding about from one
house to another—and not merely idle but gossips and
busybodies, repeating things they have no right to men-

* Reading ἀγωνιζόμεθα with ℵ* A C G K, etc. The context requires
an aggressive, active verb. The "sure words" all have a more or less
eschatological outlook.

† I accept the conjecture λανθάνουσι for the μανθάνουσι of the canonical
text, which makes the grammatical construction very awkward.

14 tion. So I prefer young widows to marry again, to bear
children, to look after their households, and not to afford
15 our opponents any chance of reviling us. As it is, some
16 widows have already turned after Satan.—Any believer,
man or woman, who has widowed relatives, must give them
relief; the church is not to be burdened with them; she
has to relieve the widows who really need relief.
17 Presbyters who are efficient presidents are to be considered worthy of ample remuneration, particularly those
18 who have the task of preaching and teaching: Scripture
says, *You must not muzzle an ox when he is treading the
grain*, and *A workman deserves his wages*.
19 Never let any charge be brought against a presbyter,
20 unless it is certified by two or three witnesses. Those
who are guilty of sin you must expose in public, to overawe the others.
21 In the presence of God and the Lord Jesus Christ and
the elect angels, I adjure you to be unprejudiced in carrying out these orders; be absolutely impartial.
22 Never be in a hurry to ordain a presbyter; do not make
yourself responsible for the sins of another man—keep
24 your own life pure.* Some people's sins are notorious and call for judgment, but in some cases sin only comes
25 out afterwards. Good works are equally conspicuous; and
even when they are not, they cannot escape notice for ever.

6 Let all servants who are under the yoke of slavery
remember that their masters are entitled to perfect
respect—otherwise it will be a scandal to the Name of God
2 and to our doctrine. Those who have Christian believers
as their masters must not take liberties with them because
they are brothers; they must be all the better servants
because those who get the good of their service are
believers and beloved.

3 This is what you are to teach and preach. Anyone who
teaches novelties and refuses to fall in with the sound
words of our Lord Jesus Christ and the doctrine that
4 tallies with piety, is a conceited, ignorant creature, with a
morbid passion for controversy and argument which only
5 leads to envy, dissension, insults, insinuations, and constant friction between people who are depraved in mind
and deprived of the Truth. They imagine religion is a
6 paying concern. And so it is—provided it goes with a
7 contented spirit; for we bring nothing into the world,

---

* The words, " Give up being a total abstainer; take a little wine for
the sake of your stomach and your frequent attacks of illness," which
follow, are either a marginal gloss or misplaced.

I. TIMOTHEUS VI 319

8 and we can take nothing out of it. If we have food and
9 clothes, we must be content with that. Those who are
eager to be rich get tempted and trapped in many senseless
and pernicious propensities that drag men down to ruin
10 and destruction. For love of money is the root of all mischief; it is by aspiring to be rich that certain individuals
have gone astray from the faith and found themselves
11 pierced with many a pang of remorse. Shun that, O man
of God, aim at integrity, piety, faith, love, stedfastness, and
12 suavity; fight in the good fight of the faith, secure that life
eternal to which you were called when you voiced the good
13 confession in the presence of many witnesses. In the presence of God who is the Life of all, and of Christ Jesus who
testified to the good confession before Pontius Pilate, I
14 charge you to keep your commission free from stain,
free from reproach, till the appearance of our Lord Jesus
15 Christ—which will be brought about in due time by that
blessed and only Sovereign, King of kings and Lord of
16 lords, who alone has immortality, who dwells in light that
none can approach, whom no man has ever seen or can
see. To him be honour and eternal dominion: Amen.
17 Charge the rich of this world not to be supercilious, and
not to fix their hopes on so uncertain a thing as riches
but on the living God who richly provides us with all the
18 enjoyments of life; tell them to be bountiful, rich in good
19 works, open-handed and generous, amassing right good *
treasure for themselves in the world to come, in order to
secure the life which is life indeed.
20 O Timotheus, keep the securities of the faith intact:
avoid the profane jargon and contradictions of what is
21 falsely called 'Knowledge.' Certain individuals have failed
in the faith by professing that.
Grace be with you. [Amen.]

* For θεμέλιον I accept the attractive conjecture θέμα λίαν, in view of the close parallel in Tobit iv. 9–10 (θέμα γὰρ ἀγαθὸν θησαυρίζεις σεαυτῷ εἰς ἡμέραν ἀνάγκης · διότι ἐλεημοσύνη ἐκ θανάτου ῥύεται).

THE SECOND EPISTLE OF PAUL THE APOSTLE TO
TIMOTHEUS

1 Paul an apostle of Christ Jesus by the will of God in the service of the Life he has promised in Christ Jesus
2 —to his beloved son Timotheus: grace, mercy, peace, from God the Father and Christ Jesus our Lord.
3 I render thanks to God, the God of my fathers whom I worship with a pure conscience, as I mention you con-
4 stantly in my prayers. When I recall the tears you shed when we parted, I long by night and day to see you again.
5 That would fill me with joy, for I am reminded of your sincere faith, a faith which dwelt first in your grandmother Lois and your mother Eunice, as it dwells (I feel sure)
6 in yourself. Hence I would remind you to rekindle the divine gift which you received when my hands were laid
7 upon you; for God has not given us a timid spirit but a
8 spirit of power and love and discipline. So do not be ashamed to testify to our Lord, and do not be ashamed of a prisoner of the Lord like me; join me in bearing suffer-
9 ing for the gospel by the power of the God who has saved us and called us to a life of consecration—not for anything we have done but because he chose to do it himself, by the
10 grace which he gave us ages ago in Christ Jesus and has now revealed in the appearance of our Saviour Jesus Christ, who has put down death and brought life and immortality
11 to light by the gospel. Of that gospel I have been ap-
12 pointed a herald and an apostle and a teacher, and this is why I am suffering. Still, I am not ashamed of it; I know whom I have trusted and I am certain he is able to keep what I have put into his hands till the great Day.
13 Model yourself on the sound instruction you have had
14 from me in the faith and love of Christ Jesus. Keep the great securities of your faith intact, by aid of the holy
15 Spirit that dwells within us. You are aware that all the Asiatics have discarded me, including Phygelus and
16 Hermogenes. May the Lord show favour to the household of Onesiphorus, for many a time he braced me up; he was
17 not ashamed of my imprisonment—no, he made eager search for me when he reached Rome, and he found me
18 (may he find favour with the Lord on the great Day!

II. TIMOTHEUS II

The Lord grant it!). And you know very well what a help he was to me in Ephesus.

2 Now, my son, be strong in the grace of Christ Jesus, and transmit the instructions I gave you in presence of many witnesses to trustworthy men, that they may be
3 competent to teach others. Join the ranks of those who
4 bear suffering, like a loyal soldier of Christ Jesus. No soldier gets entangled in civil pursuits; his aim is to satisfy
5 his commander. Again, a competitor in the games is not
6 crowned unless he observes the rules. The farmer who has done the work must have the first share of the fruit.
7 Think what I mean! The Lord will help you to understand perfectly.
8 Never forget "Jesus Christ risen from the dead, descended
9 from David"—that is my gospel, for which I have to suffer imprisonment as if I were a criminal. (But there is
10 no prison for the word of God.) All I endure is for the sake of the elect, to let them obtain their share of the
11 salvation of Christ Jesus and also of eternal glory. It is a sure word, that

"If we have died with him, we shall live with him,
12 if we endure, then we shall reign with him,
if we disown him, then he shall disown us,
13 if we are faithless, he remains faithful"—
for he cannot be untrue to himself.

14 Remind men of this: adjure them before the Lord not to bandy arguments—no good comes out of that, it only
15 means the undoing of your audience. Do your utmost to let God see that you at least are a sound workman, with no need to be ashamed of the way you handle the word of
16 the Truth. Avoid all that profane jargon, for it leads
17 people still further into irreligion, and their doctrine spreads like a gangrene. So it is with Hymenaeus and
18 Philetus; they have failed in the Truth by arguing that the resurrection has taken place already, and they are
19 undermining some people's faith. But the solid foundation laid by God remains, and this is its inscription:

the Lord knows who are his,

and

'let everyone who names the name of the Lord give up evil.'

20 In any great house there are indeed vessels not only of gold and silver but also of wood and clay, some for noble,
21 some for menial service. If one will only keep clear of the latter, he will be put to noble use, he will be consecrated and useful to the Owner of the House, he will be set apart
22 for good work of all kinds. So shun the lusts of youth and aim at integrity, faith, love and peace, in the company

II. TIMOTHEUS III, IV

23 of those who invoke the Lord out of a pure heart. Shut your mind against foolish, popular controversy; be sure
24 that only breeds strife. And the Lord's servant must not be a man of strife; he must be kind to everybody, a skilled
25 teacher, a man who will not resent injuries; he must be gentle in his admonitions to the opposition—God may per-
26 haps let them change their mind and admit the Truth; they may come to their senses again and escape the snare of the devil, as they are brought back to life by God to do his will.

3 Mark this, there are hard times coming in the last days.
2 For men will be selfish, fond of money, boastful, haughty, abusive, disobedient to their parents, ungrateful,
3 irreverent, callous, relentless, scurrilous, dissolute, and
4 savage; they will hate goodness, they will be treacherous,
5 reckless and conceited, preferring pleasure to God—for though they keep up a form of religion, they will have
6 nothing to do with it as a force. Avoid all such. Some of them worm their way into families and get hold of the women-folk who feel crushed by the burden of their sins—
7 wayward creatures of impulse, who are always curious to learn and never able to attain the knowledge of the Truth.
8 For these guides of theirs are hostile to the Truth, just as Jannes and Jambres were hostile to Moses; they are de-
9 praved in mind and useless for all purposes of faith. However, they will get no further, for their aberration will be detected by everyone, as was the case with these magicians.
10 Now you have followed my teaching, my practice, my
11 aims, my faith, my patience, my love, my stedfastness, my persecutions, my sufferings—all that befell me at Antioch, Iconium and Lystra, all the persecutions I had to undergo,
12 from which the Lord rescued me. Yes, and all who want to live the religious life in Christ Jesus will be persecuted.
13 Bad characters and impostors will go from bad to worse,
14 deceiving others and deceived themselves; but hold you to what you have been taught, hold to your convictions, remem-
15 ber who your teachers were, remember you have known from childhood the sacred writings that can impart sav-
16 ing wisdom by faith in Christ Jesus. All scripture is inspired by God and profitable for teaching, for reproof, for
17 amendment, and for moral discipline, to make the man of God proficient and equip him for good work of every kind.

4 In the presence of God and of Christ Jesus who will judge the living and the dead, in the light of his appear-
2 ance and his reign, I adjure you to preach the word; keep at it in season and out of season, refuting, checking, and exhorting men; never lose patience with them, and never

II. TIMOTHEUS IV

3 give up your teaching, for the time will come when people will decline to be taught sound doctrine and will accumulate teachers to suit themselves and tickle their own
4 fancies; they will give up listening to the Truth and turn to myths.
5 Whatever happens, be self-possessed, flinch from no suffering, do your work as an evangelist, and discharge all your duties as a minister.
6 The last drops of my own sacrifice are falling; my time
7 to go has come. I have fought in the good fight; I have
8 run my course; I have kept the faith. Now the crown of a good life awaits me, with which the Lord, that just Judge, will reward me on the great Day—and not only me but all who have loved and longed for his appearance.
9 Do your best to come soon to me, for Demas, in his love
10 for this world, has deserted me and gone to Thessalonica;
11 Crescens is off to Gaul, Titus to Dalmatia, Luke is the only one who is with me. Pick up Mark and bring him along
12 with you, for he is of great use in helping me. (I have had
13 to send Tychicus to Ephesus.) When you come, bring the mantle I left at Troas with Carpus, also my books, and particularly my paper.
14 Alexander the blacksmith has done me a lot of harm: *the Lord will pay him back for what he has done* (beware
15 of him), for he has been bitterly hostile to anything I
16 have said. The first time I had to defend myself, I had no supporters; everyone deserted me. God grant it may not be
17 brought up against them! But the Lord supported me and gave me strength to make a full statement of the gospel and let all the heathen hear it. I was rescued *from the jaws of*
18 *the lion.* The Lord will rescue me from every assault of evil, he will bring me safe to his own realm in heaven. To him be glory for ever and ever! Amen.
19 Salute Prisca and Aquila and the household of Onesiphorus.
20 Erastus stayed on at Corinth: I left Trophimus ill at
21 Miletus. Do your best to come before winter.
Eubulus salutes you; so do Pudens, Linus, Claudia, and all the brotherhood.
22 The Lord Jesus be with your spirit. Grace be with you all.

THE EPISTLE OF PAUL TO
TITUS

1 Paul a servant of God and an apostle of Jesus Christ
for the faith of God's elect and for their knowledge of
2 the Truth that goes with a religious life, serving in hope
of the life eternal which God, who never lies, promised
3 ages ago—he gave effect to his word in due time by a
proclamation with which I have been entrusted by command
4 of God our Saviour:—to Titus my lawful son in a faith
we hold in common; grace and peace from God the Father
and Christ Jesus our Saviour.

5 I left you behind in Crete in order to finish putting things
right and to appoint presbyters in every town as I told
6 you, men who are above reproach, only once married, with
children who believe and who are not liable to the charge
7 of being profligate or insubordinate. [For a bishop must
be above reproach—he is a steward of God's house—he must
not be presumptuous or hot-tempered or a drunkard or
8 violent or addicted to pilfering; he must be hospitable, a
lover of goodness, master of himself, a just man, a reli-
9 gious man, and abstemious; he must hold by the sure
truths of doctrine so as to be able to give instruction in
10 sound doctrine and refute objections raised by any.]* For
there are plenty of insubordinate creatures who impose on
people with their empty arguments, particularly those who
11 have come over from Judaism; they must be silenced, for
they are undermining whole families by teaching objec-
12 tionable doctrine for the base end of making money. It has
been said by one of themselves, by a prophet of their own,
that—

"Cretans are always liars, evil beasts, lazy gluttons."
13 That is a true statement. So deal sharply with them, to
14 have them sound in the faith instead of studying Jewish
myths and rules laid down by men who have discarded the
15 Truth. For the pure all things are pure, but nothing is
pure for the polluted and unbelieving; their very mind and
16 conscience are polluted. They profess to know God, but

* This passage seems to have been added, rather awkwardly, to the
original text.

they deny him by their deeds; they are detestable, disobedient, and useless for good work of any kind.

2 You must instruct people in what is due to sound doctrine. Tell the older men to be temperate, serious, masters of themselves, sound in faith, in love, and in sted-
3 fastness. Tell the older women also to be reverent in their demeanour and not to be slanderers or slaves to drink;
4 they must give good counsel, so that the young women may
5 be trained to love their husbands and children, to be mistress of themselves, chaste, domestic, kind, and submissive to their husbands—otherwise it will be a scandal
6 to the gospel. Tell the young men also to be masters
7 of themselves at all points; set them an example of good
8 conduct; be sincere and serious in your teaching, let your words be sound and such that no exception can be taken to them, so that the opposite side may be confounded by
9 finding nothing that they can say to our discredit. Tell servants to be submissive to their masters and to give
10 them satisfaction all round, not to be refractory, not to embezzle, but to prove themselves truly faithful at all points, so as to be an ornament to the doctrine of God our
11 Saviour in all respects. For the grace of God has appeared
12 to save all men, and it schools us to renounce irreligion and worldly passions and to live a life of self-mastery, of
13 integrity, and of piety in this present world, awaiting the blessed hope of the appearance of the Glory of the great
14 God and of our Saviour Christ Jesus, who gave himself up for us to redeem us from all iniquity and secure himself a clean people with a zest for good works. ·
15 Tell them all this, exhort and reprove, with full authority; let no one slight you.

3 Remind them to be submissive to their rulers and authorities; they must obey, they must be ready for any
2 good work, they must abuse no one, they must not quarrel, but be conciliatory and display perfect gentleness to all
3 men. For we ourselves were once senseless, disobedient, astray, enslaved to all manner of passions and pleasures; we spent our days in malice and envy, we were hateful,
4 and we hated one another. But "the goodness and affection
5 of God our Saviour appeared; and he saved us, not for anything we had done but from his own pity for us, by the water that means regeneration and renewal under the
6 holy Spirit which he poured upon us richly through Jesus
7 Christ our Saviour, that we might be justified by his grace
8 and become heirs to the hope of life eternal." It is a sure saying.

I want you to insist on this, that those who have faith

in God must profess honest occupations. Such counsels
9 are right and good for men. But avoid foolish controversy,
and let genealogies and dissensions and strife over the Law
alone, for these are fruitless and futile.
10 After a first and a second warning have no more to do
11 with a factious person; you may be sure a man like that is
perverted; he is sinning and he knows it.
12 Whenever I send Artemas or Tychicus to you, do your
best to come to me at Nicopolis, for I have decided to winter
13 there. Give a hearty send-off to Zenas the jurist and
14 Apollos; see that they want for nothing. Our people must
really learn to profess honest occupations, so as to be able
to meet such special occasions; they must not be idle.
15 All who are with me salute you.
Salute those who love us in the faith.
Grace be with you all.

THE EPISTLE OF PAUL TO
PHILEMON

1 PAUL a prisoner of Christ Jesus and brother Timotheus,
2 to our beloved fellow-worker Philemon, to our sister
Apphia, to our fellow-soldier Archippus, and to the church
3 that meets in your house: grace and peace to you from
God our Father and the Lord Jesus Christ.
4 I always thank my God when I mention you in my
5 prayers; for as I hear of your love and loyalty to the Lord
6 Jesus and to all the saints, I pray that by their participation in your loyal faith they may have a vivid sense of how much good we * Christians can attain.
7 I have had great joy and encouragement over your love,
my brother, over the way you have refreshed the hearts
8 of the saints. Hence, although in Christ I would feel quite
9 free to order you to do your duty, I prefer to appeal to you on the ground of love. Well then, as Paul the old man,
10 who now-a-days is a prisoner for Christ Jesus, I appeal to you on behalf of my spiritual son born while I was in
11 prison. It is Onesimus! Once you found him a worthless character, but now-a-days he is worth something to you and
12 me. I am sending him back to you, and parting with my
13 very heart. I would have liked to keep him beside me, that as your deputy he might serve me during my imprison-
14 ment for the gospel; but I did not want to do anything without your consent, so that your goodness to me might come of your own free will, without any appearance of constraint.
15 Perhaps this was why you and he were parted for a
16 while, that you might get him back for good, no longer a mere slave but something more than a slave—a beloved brother; especially dear to me but how much more to you
17 as a man and as a Christian! You count me a partner?
18 Then receive him as you would receive me, and if he has cheated you of any money or owes you any sum, put that
19 down to my account. This is in my own handwriting: 'I

* Reading ἡμῖν instead of ὑμῖν. As Lightfoot observes, " scribes would be strongly tempted to alter ἡμῖν into ὑμῖν from a misapprehension of the sense, and a wish to apply the words to Philemon and his household."

PHILEMON

Paul promise to refund it'—not to mention that you owe
20 me, over and above, your very soul. Come, brother, let me
have some return from you in the Lord! Refresh my heart
in Christ.
21 I send you this letter relying on your obedience; I know
22 you will do even more than I tell you. And get quarters
ready for me, for I am hoping that by your prayers I shall
be restored to you.
23 Epaphras my fellow-prisoner in Christ Jesus salutes you.
24 So do Mark, Aristarchus, Demas and Luke, my fellow-workers.
25 The grace of the Lord Jesus Christ be with your spirit.
Amen.

THE EPISTLE TO THE

HEBREWS

1 MANY were the forms and fashions in which God spoke
2 of old to our fathers by the prophets, but in these days at the end he has spoken to us by a Son—a Son whom he appointed heir of the universe, as it was by him that he
3 created the world. He, reflecting God's bright glory and stamped with God's own character, sustains the universe with his word of power; when he had secured our purification from sins, he sat down at the right hand of the
4 Majesty on high; and thus he is superior to the angels, as
5 he has inherited a Name superior to theirs. For to what angel did God ever say,
'Thou art my son,
to-day have I become thy father'?
Or again,
'I will be a father to him,
and he shall be a son to me'?
6 And further, when introducing the Firstborn into the world, he says,
'Let all God's angels worship him.'
7 While he says of angels,
'Who makes his angels into winds,
his servants into flames of fire,'
8 he says of the Son,
'God is thy throne for ever and ever,
thy royal sceptre is the sceptre of equity:
9 thou hast loved justice and hated lawlessness,*
therefore God, thy God, has consecrated thee
with the oil of rejoicing beyond thy comrades'—
10 and,
'Thou didst found the earth at the beginning, O Lord,
and the heavens are the work of thy hands;
11 they will perish, but thou remainest,
they will all be worn out like a garment,
12 thou wilt roll them up like a mantle and † they will be changed,

* Reading ἀνομίαν instead of ἀδικίαν.
† Omitting [ὡς ἱμάτιον], which has been repeated from the previous line.

      but thou art the same,
      and thy years will never fail.'
13 To what angel did he ever say,
      'Sit at my right hand,
      till I make your enemies a footstool for your feet'?
14 Are not all angels merely spirits in the divine service, commissioned for the benefit of those who are to inherit salvation?

2 We must therefore pay closer attention to what we have heard, in case we drift away. For if the divine word spoken by angels held good, if transgression and disobedi-
3 ence met with due punishment in every case, how shall we escape the penalty for neglecting a salvation which was originally proclaimed by the Lord himself and guaranteed
4 to us by those who heard him; while God corroborated their testimony with signs and wonders and a variety of miraculous powers, distributing the holy Spirit as it pleased him.
5 For the world to come, of which I am speaking, was not
6 put under the control of angels. One writer, as we know, has affirmed,
      What is man, that thou art mindful of him?
      or the son of man, that thou carest for him?
7   *For a little while thou hast put him lower than the angels,*
      crowning him with glory and honour,
8   *putting all things under his feet.**
Now by *putting all things under* him, the writer meant to leave nothing out of his control. But, as it is, we do not
9 yet see *all things controlled by man;* what we do see is Jesus *who was put lower than the angels for a little while* to suffer death, and *who has been crowned with glory and honour* that by God's grace he might taste death for every-
10 one. In bringing many sons to glory, it was befitting that He for whom and by whom the universe exists, should
11 perfect the Pioneer of their salvation by suffering. For sanctifier and sanctified have all one origin. That is why
12 he is not ashamed to call them brothers, saying,
      'I will proclaim thy name to my brothers,
      in the midst of the church I will sing of thee,'
13 and again,
      'I will put my trust in him,'
   and again,
      'Here am I and the children God has given me.'
14 Since the children then share blood and flesh, he himself participated in their nature, so that by dying he might crush him who wields the power of death (that is to say,

---

* Omitting καὶ κατεστησας αὐτὸν ἐπὶ τὰ ἔργα τῶν χειρῶν σου.

15 the devil) and release from thraldom those who lay under
16 a life-long fear of death. (For of course it is not angels
17 that *he succours, it is the offspring of Abraham.*) He had
to resemble his brothers in every respect, in order to prove
a merciful and faithful high priest in things divine, to
18 expiate the sins of the People. It is as he suffered by his
temptations that he is able to help the tempted.

3 Holy brothers, you who participate in a heavenly calling,
look at Jesus then, at the apostle and high priest of our
2 confession; he is faithful to Him who appointed him. For
while Moses also was *faithful in every department of God's
3 house,* Jesus has been adjudged greater glory than Moses,
inasmuch as the founder of a house enjoys greater honour
4 than the house itself. (Every house is founded by someone,
5 but God is the founder of all.) Besides, while Moses was
faithful in every department of God's house as an attendant
6 —by way of witness to the coming revelation—Christ is
faithful as a Son over God's house.

Now we are this house of God, if we will only keep confi-
7 dent and proud of our hope.* Therefore, as the holy Spirit
says,
  To-day, when you hear his voice,
8   *harden not your hearts as at the Provocation,*
  on the day of the Temptation in the desert,
9   *where your fathers put me to the proof,*
  and for forty years felt what I could do.
10 *Therefore I grew exasperated with that generation,*
  I said, 'They are always astray in their heart':
  They would not learn my ways;
11   *so I swore in my anger,*
  'they shall never enter my Rest.'
12 Brothers, take care in case there is a wicked, unbelieving
heart in any of you, moving you to apostatize from the liv-
13 ing God. Rather admonish one another daily, so long as
this word *To-day* is uttered, that none of you may be
14 deceived by sin and *hardened.* For we only participate in
Christ provided that we keep firm to the very end the
15 confidence with which we started, this word ever sounding
in our ears,
  To-day, when you hear his voice,
  harden not your hearts as at the Provocation.
16 Who heard and yet *provoked* him? Was it not all who left
17 Egypt under the leadership of Moses? And with whom
was he *exasperated for forty years?* Was it not with those
18 who sinned, whose *corpses fell in the desert?* And to whom

* Omitting μεχρὶ τέλους βεβαίαν, which has probably been inserted from ver. 14, where the same words occur in a similar connexion.

did he swear that they would never enter his Rest? To whom but those who disobeyed? Thus we see it was owing to unbelief that they could not enter. Well 4 then, as the promise of entrance is still left to us, let us be afraid of anyone being judged to have
2 missed it. For we have had the good news as well as they; only, the message they heard was of no use to them,
3 because it did not meet with * faith in the hearers. For we do *enter the Rest* by our faith: according to his word,
*As I swore in my anger,
they shall never enter my Rest*—
although his works were all over by the foundation of the
4 world. For he says this somewhere about the seventh day: *And God rested from all his works on the seventh day.*
5 And again in this passage, *they shall never enter my Rest.*
6 Since then it is reserved for some *to enter it*, and since those who formerly got the good news failed to enter owing
7 to their disobedience, he again fixes a day; *To-day*—as he says in 'David' after so long an interval, and as has been already quoted—
*To-day, when you hear his voice,
harden not your hearts.*
8 Thus if Joshua had given them Rest, God would not speak
9 later about another day. There is a sabbath-Rest, then,
10 reserved still for the People of God (for once *a man enters his rest*, he *rests from work* just as God did).
11 Let us be eager then to *enter that Rest*, in case anyone
12 falls into the same sort of disobedience. For the Logos of God is a living thing, active and more cutting than any sword with double edge, penetrating to the very division of soul and spirit, joints and marrow—scrutinizing the very
13 thoughts and conceptions of the heart. And no created thing is hidden from him; all things lie open and exposed before the eyes of him with whom we have to reckon.

14 As we have a great high priest, then, who has passed through the heavens, Jesus the Son of God, let us hold fast
15 to our confession; for ours is no high priest who is incapable of sympathizing with our weaknesses, but one who has been tempted in every respect like ourselves, yet with-
16 out sinning. So let us approach the throne of grace with confidence, that we may receive mercy and find grace to help us in the hour of need.

5 Every high priest who is selected from men and appointed to act on behalf of men in things divine, offer-

* Reading συγκεκερασμένος or συγκεκραμένος with ℵ, the Old Latin, the Peshitto, etc.

HEBREWS VI

2 ing gifts and sacrifices for sins, can deal gently with those who err through ignorance, since he himself is beset with
3 weakness—which obliges him to present offerings for his
4 own sins as well as for those of the People. Also, it is an office which no one elects to take for himself; he is
5 called to it by God, just as Aaron was. Similarly, Christ was not raised to the glory of the high priesthood by himself but by Him who declared to him,

Thou art my son,
to-day have I become thy father.

6 Just as elsewhere he says,

Thou art a priest for ever, with the rank of Melchizedek.

7 In the days of his flesh, with bitter cries and tears, he offered prayers and supplications to Him who was able to save him from death; and he was heard, because of his
8 godly fear. Thus, Son though he was, he learned by all
9 he suffered how to obey, and by being thus perfected he became the source of eternal salvation for all who obey
10 him, being designated by God high priest *with the rank of Melchizedek.*

11 On this point I have a great deal to say, which it is hard to make intelligible to you. For you have grown dull of
12 hearing. Though by this time you should be teaching other people, you still need someone to teach you once more the rudimentary principles of the divine revelation. You
13 are in need of milk, not of solid food. (For anyone who is fed on milk is unskilled in moral truth; he is a mere
14 babe. Whereas solid food is for the mature, for those who have their faculties trained by exercise to distinguish good and evil.)

6 Let us pass on then to what is mature, leaving elementary Christian doctrine behind, instead of laying the foundation over again with repentance from dead works,
2 with faith in God, with instruction about ablutions and the laying on of hands, about the resurrection of the dead, and
3 eternal punishment. With God's permission, we will take
4 this step.* For in the case of people who have been once enlightened, who tasted the heavenly Gift, who participated
5 in the holy Spirit, who tasted the goodness of God's word and the powers of the world to come, and then fell away
6 —it is impossible to make them repent afresh, since they crucify the Son of God in their own persons and hold him
7 up to obloquy. For *land* which absorbs the rain that often falls on it, and bears *plants* that are useful to those for

---

* Reading ποιήσομεν with ℵ B, the Latin version, etc., instead of ποιήσωμεν.

8 whom it is tilled, receives a blessing from God; whereas, if it *produces thorns and thistles*, it is reprobate and on the verge of being *cursed*—its fate is to be burned.

9 Though I say this, beloved, I feel sure you will take the
10 better course that means salvation. God is not unfair; he will not forget what you have done, or the love you have shown for his sake in ministering, as you still do, to the
11 saints. It is my heart's desire that each of you would prove equally keen upon realizing your full hope to the very end,
12 so that instead of being slack you may imitate those who inherit the promises by their stedfast faith.

13 For in making a promise to Abraham God *swore by him-*
14 *self* (since he could swear by none greater), *I will indeed*
15 *bless you and multiply you.* Thus it was that Abraham by his stedfastness obtained what he had been promised.
16 For as men swear by a greater than themselves, and as an
17 oath means to them a guarantee that ends any dispute, God, in his desire to afford the heirs of the Promise a special proof of the solid character of his purpose, interposed with
18 an oath; so that by these two solid facts (the Promise and the Oath), where it is impossible for God to be false, we refugees might have strong encouragement to seize the
19 hope set before us, anchoring the soul to it safe and sure, as *it enters the inner Presence behind the veil.*
20 There Jesus entered for us in advance, when he became
7 high priest *for ever with the rank of Melchizedek*. For Melchizedek, *the king of Salem, a priest of the Most High God*, who *met Abraham on his return from the*
2 *slaughter of the kings and blessed him*—who had *a tenth part of everything* assigned him by *Abraham*—this Melchizedek is primarily a *king of righteousness* (that is the meaning of his name); then, besides that, *king of Salem*
3 (which means, king of peace). He has neither father nor mother nor genealogy, neither a beginning to his days nor an end of his life, but, resembling the Son of God, continues
4 to be *priest* permanently. Now mark the dignity of this man. The patriarch *Abraham paid* him *a tenth* of the
5 spoils. Those sons of Levi who receive the priestly office are indeed ordered by law to tithe the people (that is, their brothers), although the latter are descended from Abra-
6 ham; but he who had no Levitical genealogy actually tithed
7 Abraham and *blessed* the possessor of the promises! (And there is no question that it is the inferior who is blessed by
8 the superior.) Again, it is mortal men in the one case who receive *tithes*, while in the other it is one of whom the
9 witness is that 'he lives.' In fact, we might almost say that even Levi the receiver of tithes paid tithes through
10 Abraham; for he was still in the loins of his father when

HEBREWS VIII

11 *Melchizedek met him.* Further, if the Levitical priesthood had been the means of reaching perfection (for it was on the basis of that priesthood that the Law was enacted for the People), why was it still necessary for another sort of priest to emerge *with the rank of Melchizedek,* instead of
12 simply *with the rank* of Aaron (for when the priesthood
13 is changed, a change of law necessarily follows)? He who
14 is thus described belongs to another tribe, no member of which ever devoted himself to the altar; for it is evident that our Lord sprang from Judah, and Moses never men-
15 tioned priesthood in connexion with that tribe. This becomes all the more plain when another *priest* emerges
16 resembling Melchizedek, one who has become a priest by the power of an indissoluble Life and not by the law of an
17 external command; for the witness to him is,

Thou art priest for ever, with the rank of Melchizedek.

18 A previous command is set aside on account of its weak-
19 ness and uselessness (for the Law made nothing perfect),
20 and there is introduced a better Hope, by means of which we can draw near to God. A better Hope, because it was
21 not promised apart from an oath. Previous priests became priests apart from any oath, but he has an oath from Him who said to him,

The Lord has sworn, and he will not change his mind, thou art a priest for ever.

22 And this makes Jesus surety for a superior covenant.
23 Also, while they became priests in large numbers, since
24 death prevents them from continuing to serve, he holds his priesthood without any successor, since he continues *for*
25 *ever.* Hence for all time he is able to save those who approach God through him, as he is always living to intercede on their behalf.
26 Such was the high priest for us, saintly, innocent, unstained, lifted high above the heavens, far from all contact
27 with the sinful, one who has no need, like yonder high priests, day by day to offer sacrifices first for their own sins and then for those of the People—he did that once for all
28 in offering up himself. For the Law appoints human beings in their weakness to the priesthood; but the word of the Oath appoints a Son who is made perfect *for ever.*

8 The point * of all this is, we do have such a high priest, one who is *seated at the right hand* of the throne
2 of Majesty in the heavens, and who officiates in *the* sanctuary or true *tabernacle set up by the Lord* and not by
3 man. Now, as every high priest is appointed to offer gifts

---

* Or, as Coverdale translates, "the pith." "All this" means "all the previous argument."

4 and sacrifices, he too must have something to offer. Were
he on earth, he would not be a priest at all, for there are
5 priests already to offer the gifts prescribed by Law (men
who serve a mere outline and shadow of the heavenly—
as Moses was instructed, when he was about to execute the
building of the tabernacle: *see*, God said, *that you make
everything on the pattern shown you upon the mountain*).
6 As it is, however, the divine service he has obtained is
superior, owing to the fact that he mediates a superior
7 covenant, enacted with superior promises. For if the first
covenant had been faultless, there would have been no occa-
8 sion for a second. Whereas God does find fault with the
people of that covenant, when he says:

The day is coming, saith the Lord,
when I will conclude a new covenant with the house of
Israel and with the house of Judah.
It will not be on the lines of the covenant I made with
their fathers,
9 *on the day I took them by the hand to lead out of Egypt's*
land;
for they would not hold to my covenant,
so I let them alone,* saith the Lord.
10 *This is the covenant I will make with the house of Israel*
when that day comes, saith the Lord;
I will set my laws within their mind,
inscribing them upon their hearts;
I will be a God to them,
and they shall be a People to me;
11 *one citizen will no longer teach his fellow,*
one man will no longer teach his brother,
saying, 'Know the Lord,'
for all will know me, low and high together.
12 *I will be merciful to their iniquities,*
and remember their sins no more.
13 By saying 'a new covenant,' he antiquates the first. And
whatever is antiquated and aged is on the verge of
vanishing.

9 The first covenant had indeed its regulations for worship and a material sanctuary. A tent was set up, the
outer tent, containing the lampstand, the table, and the
3 loaves of the Presence; this is called the Holy place. But
behind the second veil was the tent called the Holy of
4 Holies, containing the golden altar of incense, and also the
ark of the covenant covered all over with gold, which held
the golden pot of manna, the rod of Aaron that once

---

* The same Greek word as is translated " neglected " in ii. 3.

HEBREWS IX

5 blossomed, and the tablets of the covenant; above this were the cherubims of the Glory, overshadowing the mercy seat—matters which it is impossible for me to discuss at
6 present in detail. Such were the arrangements for worship. The priests constantly enter the first tent, in the discharge
7 of their ritual duties, but the second tent is entered only once a year by the high priest alone—and it must not be without blood, which he presents on behalf of himself and
8 the errors of the People. By this the holy Spirit means that the way into the Holiest Presence was not disclosed
9 so long as the first tent (which foreshadowed the present age) was still standing, with its offerings of gifts and sacrifices which cannot possibly make the conscience of the
10 worshipper perfect, since they relate merely to food and drink and a variety of ablutions—outward regulations for the body, that only hold till the period of the New Order.
11 But when Christ arrived as the high priest of the bliss that was to be, he passed through the greater and more perfect tent which no hands had made (no part, that is
12 to say, of the present order), not taking any blood of goats and oxen but his own blood, and entered once for all into the Holy place. He secured an eternal redemption.
13 For if the blood of goats and bulls and the ashes of a heifer, sprinkled on defiled persons, give them a holiness
14 that bears on bodily purity, how much more shall the blood of Christ, who in the spirit of the eternal offered himself as an unblemished sacrifice to God, cleanse your conscience
15 from dead works to serve a living God? He mediates a new covenant for this reason, that those who have been called may obtain the eternal inheritance they have been promised, now that a death has occurred which redeems them from the transgressions involved in the first covenant.
16 Thus in the case of a will, the death of the testator must be
17 announced. A will only holds in cases of death; it is never
18 valid so long as the testator is alive. Hence even the first covenant of God's will was not inaugurated apart from
19 blood; for after Moses had announced every command in the Law to all the people, he took the blood of calves and goats, together with water, scarlet wool and hyssop,
20 sprinkling the book and all the people, and saying, *This is the blood of that covenant which is God's command for you.*
21 He even sprinkled with blood the tent and all the utensils
22 of worship in the same way. In fact, one might almost say that by Law everything is cleansed with blood. No blood
23 shed, no remission of sins! Now, while the copies of the heavenly things had to be cleansed with sacrifices like these, the heavenly things themselves required nobler
24 sacrifices. For Christ has not entered a holy place which

human hands have made (a mere type of the reality!);
he has entered heaven itself, now to appear in the presence
25 of God on our behalf. Nor was it to offer himself repeatedly, like the high priest entering the holy place every
26 year with blood that was not his own:—for in that case
he would have had to suffer repeatedly, ever since the world
was founded. Nay, once for all, at the end of the world,
27 he has appeared with his self-sacrifice to abolish sin. And
just as it is appointed for men to die once and after that
28 to be judged, so Christ, after being once sacrificed to bear
the sins of many, will appear again, not to deal with
sin but for the saving of those who look out * for him.

10 For as the Law has a mere shadow of the bliss that
is to be, instead of representing the reality of that
bliss, it can never perfect those who draw near with the
2 same annual sacrifices that are perpetually offered. Otherwise, they would surely have ceased to be offered; for the
worshippers, once cleansed, would no longer be conscious
3 of sins! As it is, they are an annual reminder of sins
4 (for the blood of bulls and goats cannot possibly remove
5 sins!). Hence, on entering the world he says,
*Thou hast no desire for sacrifice or offering;
it is a body thou hast prepared for me—*
6 *in holocausts and sin-offerings thou takest no delight.*
7 *So I said, 'Here I come—in the roll of the book this is
written of me—
I come to do thy will, O God.'*
8 He begins by saying, *thou hast no desire for, thou takest
no delight in, sacrifices and offerings and holocausts and
sin-offerings* (and these are what are offered in terms of
9 the Law); he then adds, *Here I come to do thy will*. He
does away with the first in order to establish the second.
10 And it is by this *will* that we are consecrated, because Jesus
Christ once for all has *offered up his body*.
11 Again, while every priest † stands daily at his service,
offering the same sacrifices repeatedly, sacrifices which
12 never can take sins away—He offered a single sacrifice
for sins and then *seated himself for all time at the right
13 hand of God*, to wait *until his enemies are made a footstool
14 for his feet*. For by a single offering he has made the
15 sanctified perfect for all time. Besides, we have the testimony of the holy Spirit; for after saying,
16 *This is the covenant I will make with them when that day
comes, saith the Lord,*

---

* Paul's word in Phil. iii. 20; but I translate "look out" here, in order
to suggest the antithesis in x. 27.

† Reading ἱερεὺς instead of ἀρχιερεύς.

HEBREWS X

*I will set my laws upon their hearts,
inscribing them upon their minds,*
he adds,
17 *And their sins and breaches of the law I will remember
no more.*
18 Now where these are remitted, an offering for sin exists
no longer.

19 Brothers, since we have confidence to enter the holy
20 Presence in virtue of the blood of Jesus, by the fresh, living way which he has inaugurated for us through the veil
21 (that is, through his flesh), and since we have *a great Priest*
22 *over the house of God,* let us draw near with a true heart, in absolute assurance of faith, our hearts sprinkled clean from a bad conscience, and our bodies washed in pure
23 water; let us hold the hope we avow without wavering
24 (for we can rely on him who gave us the Promise); and let us consider how to stir up one another to love and good
25 deeds—not ceasing to meet together, as is the habit of some, but admonishing one another, all the more so, as you see
26 the Day coming near. For if we sin deliberately, after receiving the knowledge of the Truth, there is no longer
27 any sacrifice for sins left, nothing but an awful outlook of doom, of that *burning Wrath which will consume the*
28 *foes of God.* Anyone who has rejected the law of Moses *dies without mercy, on the evidence of two or of three*
29 *witnesses.* How much heavier, do you suppose, will be the punishment assigned to him who has spurned the Son of God, who has profaned *the covenant-blood* with which he was sanctified, who has insulted the Spirit of grace?
30 We know who said, *Vengeance is mine, I will exact a requital:* and again, *The Lord will pass sentence on his peo-*
31 *ple.* It is an awful thing to fall into the hands of the living God.
32 Recall the former days when, after you were enlightened,
33 you endured a hard struggle of suffering, partly by being held up yourselves to obloquy and anguish, partly by mak-
34 ing common cause with those who fared in this way; for you did sympathize with the prisoners, and you took the confiscation of your own belongings cheerfully, conscious that elsewhere you had higher, you had lasting, possessions.
35 Now do not drop that confidence of yours; it carries with
36 it a rich hope of reward. Steady patience is what you need, so that after doing the will of God you may get what you
37 have been promised. For *in a little, a very little* now, *The Coming One will arrive without delay.*
38 *Meantime my just man shall live on by his faith;
if he shrinks back, my soul takes no delight in him.*

39 We are not the men to shrink back and be lost, but to have faith and so to win our souls.

11 Now faith means we are confident of what we hope for, convinced of what we do not see. It was for
3 this that the men of old won their record. It is by faith we understand that the world was fashioned by the word of God, and thus the visible was made out of the invisible.
4 It was by faith that Abel offered God a richer sacrifice than Cain did, and thus won from God the record of being 'just,' on the score of what he gave; he died, but by his faith
5 he is speaking to us still. It was by faith that Enoch was taken to heaven, so that he never died (*he was not overtaken by death, for God had taken him away*). For before he was taken to heaven, his record was that *he*
6 *had satisfied* * *God;* and apart from faith it is impossible to satisfy him, for the man who draws near to God must believe that he exists and that he does reward those who
7 seek him. It was by faith that Noah, after being told by God what was still unseen, reverently constructed an ark to save his household; thus he condemned the world and
8 became heir of the righteousness that follows faith. It was by faith that Abraham obeyed his call to *go forth* to a place which he would receive as an inheritance; he went forth, although he did not know where he was to go.
9 It was by faith that he *sojourned* in the promised land, as in a foreign country, residing in tents, as did Isaac and Jacob who were co-heirs with him of the same promise;
10 he was waiting for the City with its fixed foundations,
11 whose builder and maker is God. It was by faith that even Sara got strength to conceive, bearing a son when she was past the age for it—because she considered she could rely
12 on Him who gave the promise. Thus a single man, though he was physically impotent, had issue in number *like the stars in heaven, countless as the sand on the seashore*.
13 (These all died in faith without obtaining the promises; they only saw them far away and hailed them, owning
14 they were '*strangers and exiles* upon earth.' Now people who speak in this way plainly show they are in search of
15 a fatherland. If they thought of the land they have left
16 behind, they would have time to go back, but they really aspire to the better land in heaven. That is why God is not ashamed to be called their God; he has prepared a
17 City for them.) It was by faith, *when Abraham was put to the test, that he sacrificed Isaac;* he was ready to sacrifice *his only son*, although he had received the prom-

---

* Here, as elsewhere, " satisfy " is used in the sense of a servant giving satisfaction to his master.

18 ises and had been told that *it is through Isaac that your*
19 *offspring shall be reckoned*—for he considered God was
able even to raise men from the dead. Hence he did get
him back, by what was a parable of the resurrection.
20 It was by faith that Isaac blessed Jacob and Esau in con-
21 nection with the future. It was by faith that, when Jacob
was dying, he blessed each of the sons of Joseph, *bending*
22 *in prayer over the head of his staff.* It was by faith that
Joseph at his end thought about the exodus of the sons of
23 Israel, and gave orders about his own bones. It was by
faith that Moses *was hidden for three months* after birth
by his parents, because *they saw the child was beautiful,*
24 and had no fear of the royal decree. It was by faith that
Moses refused, *when he had grown up*, to be called the son
25 of Pharaoh's daughter; ill-treatment with God's people he
26 preferred to the passing pleasures of sin, considering
obloquy with the messiah to be richer wealth than all
27 Egypt's treasures—for he had an eye to the Reward. It
was by faith that he left Egypt, not from any fear of the
king's wrath; like one who saw the King Invisible, he
28 never flinched. It was by faith that he celebrated *the
passover* and performed the sprinkling by blood, so that
29 *the destroying angel* might not touch Israel's first-born. It
was by faith that they crossed the Red Sea like dry land
—and when the Egyptians attempted it they were drowned.
30 It was by faith that the walls of Jericho collapsed, after
31 being surrounded for only seven days. It was by faith
that Rahab the harlot did not perish along with those who
were disobedient, as she had welcomed the scouts peace-
ably.
32 And what more shall I say? Time would fail me to tell
of Gideon, of Barak, and Samson and Jephthah, of David
33 and Samuel and the prophets—men who by faith conquered kingdoms, administered justice, obtained promises,
34 shut the mouth of lions, quenched the power of fire,
escaped the edge of the sword, from weakness won to
strength, proved valiant in warfare, and routed hosts of
35 foreigners. Some were given back to their womankind,
raised from the very dead; others were broken on the
wheel, refusing to accept release, that they might obtain
36 a better resurrection; others, again, had to experience
37 scoffs and scourging, aye chains and imprisonment—they
were stoned,* sawn in two, and cut to pieces; they had to
roam about in sheepskins and goatskins, forlorn, oppressed,

---

* The next word, ἐπειράσθησαν, is either due to dittography (with the following ἐπρίσθησαν) or a corruption of some word like ἐπυράσθησαν or ἐπειρώθησαν. I have left it untranslated.

38 ill-treated (men of whom the world was not worthy), wanderers in the desert and among the hills, in caves and
39 gullies. They all won their record for faith, but the
40 Promise they did not obtain. God had something better in store for us; he would not have them perfected apart from us.

12 Therefore, with all this host of witnesses * encircling us, we must strip off every handicap, strip off sin with its clinging folds, to run our appointed course steadily,
2 our eyes fixed upon Jesus as the pioneer and the perfection of faith—upon Jesus who, in order to reach his own appointed joy, steadily endured the cross, thinking nothing of its shame, and is now *seated at the right hand* of the
3 throne of God. Compare him who steadily endured all that hostility from sinful men, so as to keep your own hearts
4 from fainting and failing. You have not had to shed blood
5 yet in the struggle against sin. And have you forgotten the word of appeal that reasons with you as sons?—
My son, never make light of the Lord's discipline,
never faint under his reproofs;
6 *for the Lord disciplines the man he loves,*
and scourges every son he receives.
7 It is for discipline that you have to endure. God is treating you as sons; for where is the son who is not disciplined
8 by his father? Discipline is the portion of all; if you get
9 no discipline, then you are not sons but bastards. Why, we had fathers of our flesh to discipline us, and we yielded to them! Shall we not far more submit to the Father of
10 our spirits, and so live? For while their discipline was only for a time, and inflicted at their pleasure, he disciplines us for our good, that we may share in his own
11 holiness. Discipline always seems for the time to be a thing of pain, not of joy; but those who are trained by it reap the fruit of it afterwards in the peace of an upright
12 life. *So up with your listless hands! Strengthen your*
13 *weak knees! And make straight paths for your feet to walk in.* You must not let the lame get dislocated, but
14 rather make them whole. Aim at peace with all—and at that consecration without which no one will ever see the
15 Lord; see to it that no one misses the grace of God; that *no root of bitterness grows up to be a trouble* by contami-
16 nating all the rest of you; that no one turns to sexual vice or to a profane life as Esau did—Esau, who for a single
17 meal *parted with his birthright.* You know how later on, when he wanted to obtain his inheritance of blessing,

* The Greek word is beginning already to hover round the special sense of "martyrs"; but the broader sense is obviously required here.

HEBREWS XIII

he was set aside; he got no chance to repent, though he tried for it with tears.
18 You have not come to what you can touch, to *flames*
19 *of fire*, to *mist* and *gloom* and *stormy blasts, to the blare of a trumpet and to a Voice* whose words made those who
20 heard it refuse to hear another syllable (for they could not bear the command, *If even a beast touches the mountain,*
21 *it must be stoned*)—indeed, so awful was the sight that
22 Moses said, *I am terrified and aghast.* You have come to mount Sion, the city of the living God, the heavenly Jeru-
23 salem, to myriads of angels in festal gathering, to the assembly of the first-born registered in heaven, to the God of all as judge, to the spirits of just men made perfect,
24 to Jesus who mediates the new covenant, and to the
25 sprinkled blood whose message is nobler than Abel's. See that you do not refuse to listen to His voice. For if they failed to escape, who refused to listen to their instructor upon earth, much less shall we, if we discard Him who
26 speaks from heaven. Then his voice shook the earth, but now the assurance is, *once again I will make heaven as well*
27 *as earth to quake.* That phrase, *once again,* denotes the removal of what is shaken (as no more than created), to
28 leave only what stands unshaken. Therefore let us render thanks * that we get an unshaken realm; and in this way
29 let us worship God acceptably—but with godly fear † and awe, for our *God is indeed a consuming fire.*

2 **13** Let your brotherly love continue. Never forget to be hospitable, for by hospitality some have entertained
3 angels unawares. Remember prisoners as if you were in prison yourselves; remember those who are being ill-treated, since you too are in the body.
4 Let marriage be held in honour by all, and keep the marriage-bed unstained. God will punish the vicious and adulterous.
5 Keep your life free from the love of money; be content with what you have, for He has said,
Never will I fail you, never will I forsake you.
6 So that we can say confidently,
The Lord is my helper, I will not be afraid.
What can men do to me?
7 Remember your leaders, the men who spoke the word of God to you; look back upon the close of their career, and copy their faith.
8 Jesus Christ is always the same, yesterday, to-day, and

---
* Reading ἔχωμεν.
† Like Jesus himself (v. 7).

9 for ever. Never let yourselves be carried away with a
variety of novel doctrines; for the right thing is to have
one's heart strengthened by grace, not by the eating of
food—that has never been any use to those who have had
10 recourse to it. Our altar is one of which the worshippers
11 have no right to eat. For the bodies of the animals whose
blood is taken into the holy Place by the high priest *as a*
12 *sin-offering, are burned outside the camp;* and so Jesus
also suffered outside the gate, in order to sanctify the
13 people by his own blood. Let us go to him *outside the*
14 *camp*, then, bearing his obloquy (for we have no lasting
15 city here below, we seek the City to come). And by him
let us constantly *offer praise to God* as our *sacrifice*, that is,
16 *the fruit of lips* that celebrate his Name. Do not forget
beneficence and charity, either; these are the kind of
sacrifices that are acceptable to God.
17 Obey your leaders, submit to them; for they are alive to
the interests of your souls, as men who will have to account
for their trust. Let their work be a joy to them and not a
grief—which would be a loss to yourselves.
18 Pray for me, for I am sure I have a clean conscience;
19 my desire is in every way to lead an honest life. I urge
you to this all the more, that I may get back to you the
sooner.
20 May the God of peace *who brought up* from the dead our
Lord Jesus, *the great Shepherd of the sheep, with the blood*
21 *of the eternal covenant,* furnish you with everything * for
the doing of his will, creating in your lives by Jesus Christ
what is acceptable in his own sight! To him be glory for
ever and ever: Amen.
22 I appeal to you, brothers, to bear with this appeal of
mine. It is but a short letter.
23 You must understand that [our] brother Timotheus is
now free. If he comes soon, he and I will see you together.
24 Salute all your leaders and all the saints. The Italians
salute you.
Grace be with you all. Amen.

* Omitting, with ℵ, D*, the Latin and Bohairic versions, etc., the homiletic addition of ἀγαθῷ.

THE EPISTLE OF

JAMES

1 JAMES, a servant of God and the Lord Jesus Christ, to the twelve tribes in the Dispersion: greeting.
2 Greet it as pure joy, my brothers, when you come across
3 any sort of trial, sure that the sterling temper of your
4 faith produces endurance; only, let your endurance be a finished product, so that you may be finished and complete,
5 with never a defect. Whoever of you is defective in wisdom, let him ask God who gives to all men without ques-
6 tion or reproach, and the gift will be his. Only, let him ask in faith, with never a doubt; for the doubtful man is like
7 surge of the sea whirled and swayed by the wind; that man need not imagine he will get anything from God,
8 double-minded creature that he is, wavering at every turn.
9 Let a brother of low position exult when he is raised;
10 but let one who is rich exult in being lowered; for the rich
11 will pass away *like the flower of the grass*—up comes the sun with the scorching wind and *withers the grass, its flower drops off,* and the splendour of it is ruined: so shall
12 the rich fade away amid their pursuits. *Blessed is he who endures* under trial; for when he has stood the test, he will gain the crown of life which is promised to all who love
13 Him. Let no one who is tried by temptation say, 'My temptation comes from God'; God is incapable of being
14 tempted by evil and he tempts no one. Everyone is tempted
15 as he is beguiled and allured by his own desire; then Desire conceives and breeds Sin, while Sin matures and
16 gives birth to Death. Make no mistake about this, my
17 beloved brothers: all we are given is good, and all our endowments are faultless, descending from above, from the Father of the heavenly lights, who knows no change of
18 rising and setting, who casts no shadow on the earth. It was his own will that we should be born by the Word of the truth, to be a kind of firstfruits among his creatures.
19 Be sure of that, my beloved brothers.
   Let everyone be quick to listen, slow to talk, slow to be
20 angry—for human anger does not promote divine righteous-
21 ness; so clear away all the foul rank growth of malice, and make a soil of modesty for the Word which roots itself

22 inwardly with power to save your souls. Act on the Word, instead of merely listening to it and deluding yourselves.
23 For whoever listens and does nothing, is like a man who
24 glances at his natural face in a mirror; he glances at him-
25 self, goes off, and at once forgets what he was like. Whereas he who gazes into the faultless law of freedom and remains in that position, proving himself to be no forgetful listener but an active agent, he will be blessed in his
26 activity. Whoever considers he is religious, and does not bridle his tongue, but deceives his own heart, his religion is
27 futile. Pure, unsoiled religion in the judgment of God the Father means this: to care for * orphans and widows in their trouble, and to keep oneself from the stain of the world.

2 My brothers, as you believe in our Lord Jesus Christ, who is the Glory, pay no servile regard to people.
2 Suppose there comes into your meeting a man who wears gold rings and handsome clothes, and also a poor man in
3 dirty clothes; if you attend to the wearer of the handsome clothes and say to him, "Sit here, this is a good place," and tell the poor man, "You can stand," or "Sit there † at
4 my feet," are you not drawing distinctions in your own minds and proving that you judge people with partiality?
5 Listen, my beloved brothers; has not God chosen the poor of this world to be rich in faith and to inherit the realm
6 which he has promised to those who love him? Now you insult the poor. Is it not the rich who lord it over you and
7 drag you to court? Is it not they who scoff at the noble
8 Name you bear? If you really fulfil the royal law laid down by scripture, *You must love your neighbour as yourself*,
9 well and good; but if you pay servile regard to people, you commit a sin, and the Law convicts you of transgression.
10 For whoever obeys the whole of the Law and only makes
11 a single slip, is guilty of everything. He who said, *Do not commit adultery*, also said, *Do not kill*. Now if you do not commit adultery but if you kill, you have transgressed the
12 Law. Speak, act, as those who are to be judged by the
13 law of freedom; for the judgment will be merciless to the man who has shown no mercy—whereas the merciful life
11 will triumph in the face of judgment. ‡ Do not defame one another, brothers; he who defames or judges his brother defames and judges the Law; and if you judge the Law,
12 you pass sentence on it instead of obeying it. One alone is the legislator, who passes sentence; it is He who is able

* As in Matthew xxv. 36, the word implies personal service and help.
† Reading ἢ κάθου ἐκεῖ with B and some evidence from the Latin version.
‡ Restoring 4¹¹⁻¹² to what seems to have been its original place.

to save and to destroy; who are you, to judge your neighbour?
14 My brothers, what is the use of anyone declaring he has faith, if he has no deeds to show? Can his faith save him?
15 Suppose some brother or sister is ill-clad and short of daily
16 food; if any of you says to them, "Depart in peace! Get warm, get food," without supplying their bodily needs, what
17 use is that? So faith, unless it has deeds, is dead in itself.
18 Someone will object, 'And you claim to have faith!' Yes, and I claim to have deeds as well; you show me your faith without any deeds, and I will show you by my deeds
19 what faith is! You believe in one God? Well and good.
20 So do the devils, and they shudder. But will you understand, you senseless fellow, that faith without deeds is
21 dead? When our father *Abraham offered his son Isaac*
22 *on the altar*, was he not justified by what he did? In his case, you see, faith co-operated with deeds, faith was com-
23 pleted by deeds, and the scripture was fulfilled: *Abraham believed God, and this was counted to him as righteousness*
24 —he was called *God's friend*. You observe it is by what he does that a man is justified, not simply by what he believes.
25 So too with Rahab the harlot. Was she not justified by what she did, when she entertained the scouts and got them away by a different road?
26 For as the body without the breath of life is dead, so faith is dead without deeds.
17 Whoever, then, knows what is right to do and does not do it, that is a sin for him.*

3 My brothers, do not swell the ranks of the teachers; remember, we teachers will be judged with special strict-
2 ness. We all make many a slip, but whoever avoids slips of speech is a perfect man; he can bridle the whole of the
3 body as well as the tongue. We put bridles into the mouths of horses to make them obey us, and so, you see,† we can
4 move the whole of their bodies. Look at ships too; for all their size and speed under stiff winds, they are turned by a tiny rudder wherever the mind of the steersman chooses.
5 So the tongue is a small member of the body, but it can boast of great exploits. What a forest is set ablaze by a
6 little spark of fire! And the tongue is a fire, the tongue proves a very world of mischief among our members, staining the whole of the body and setting fire to the round circle
7 of existence with a flame fed by hell. For while every

* This seems likely to have been the original position of 4¹⁷.
† Reading with C P, the Syriac and Armenian versions, ἴδε (ἰδού), instead of εἰ δὲ.

kind of beast and bird, of creeping animals and creatures
8 marine, is tameable and has been tamed by mankind, no
man can tame the tongue—plague of disorder that it is,
9 full of deadly venom! With the tongue we bless the Lord
and Father, and with the tongue we curse men made *in
10 God's likeness;* blessing and cursing stream from the same
11 lips! My brothers, this ought not to be. Does a fountain
pour out fresh water and brackish from the same hole?
12 Can a fig tree, my brothers, bear olives? Or a vine, figs?
No more can salt water yield fresh.
13 Who among you is wise and learned? Let him show by
his good conduct, with the modesty of wisdom, what his
14 deeds are. But if you are cherishing bitter jealousy and
rivalry in your hearts, do not pride yourselves on that—
15 and be false to the truth. That is not the wisdom which
comes down from above, it is an earthly wisdom, sensuous,
16 devilish; for wherever jealousy and rivalry exist, there dis-
17 order reigns and every evil. The wisdom from above is
first of all pure, then peaceable, forbearing, conciliatory,
full of mercy and wholesome fruit, unambiguous, straight-
18 forward; and the peacemakers who sow in peace reap
righteousness.

4 Where do conflicts, where do wrangles come from, in your midst? Is it not from these
2 passions of yours that war among your members? You
crave, and miss what you want: you envy.* and covet, but
you cannot acquire: you wrangle and fight—you miss what
3 you want because you do not ask God for it; you do ask and
you do not get it, because you ask with the wicked intention
4 of spending it on your pleasures. (Wanton creatures! do
you not know that the world's friendship means enmity to
God? Whoever, then, chooses to be the world's friend,
5 turns enemy to God. What, do you consider this is an idle
word of scripture?—'He yearns jealously for the spirit he
6 set within us.') Yet *he gives grace* more and more: thus it
is said,

The haughty God opposes,
but to the humble he gives grace.

7 Well then, submit yourselves to God;
resist the devil,
and he will fly from you:
8 draw near to God,
and he will draw near to you.
Cleanse your hands, you sinners,
and purify your hearts, you double-minded.
9 Lament and mourn and weep,

* Accepting φθονεῖτε, the conjecture of Erasmus, for the φονεύετε of the MSS.

let your laughter be turned to mourning,
and your joy to depression;
10 humble yourselves before the Lord,
and then he will raise you up.

13 Come now, you who say, "To-day or to-morrow we are
going to such and such a city; we shall spend a year there
14 trading and making money"—you who know nothing about
to-morrow! For what is your life? You are but a mist,
15 which appears for a little and then vanishes. You ought
rather to say, "If the Lord will, we shall live to do this or
16 that." But here you are, boasting in your proud pretensions! All such boasting is wicked.

5 Come now, you rich men, weep and shriek over your impending miseries!
You have been storing up treasure in the very last days; *
2 your wealth lies rotting,
and your clothes are moth-eaten;
3 your gold and silver lie rusted over,
and their rust will be evidence against you,
it will devour your flesh like fire.
4 See, *the wages* of which you have defrauded the workmen who mowed your fields *call out,*
and the cries of the harvesters have *reached the ears of the Lord of Hosts.*
5 You have revelled on earth and plunged into dissipation;
you have fattened yourselves as for *the Day of slaughter;*
6 you have condemned, you have murdered the righteous—
unresisting.
7 Be patient, then, brothers, till the arrival of the Lord. See how the farmer waits for the precious crop of the land, biding his time patiently till he gets *the autumn and the*
8 *spring rains;* have patience yourselves, strengthen your
9 hearts, for the arrival of the Lord is at hand. Do not murmur against one another, brothers, lest you are judged;
10 look, the Judge is standing at the very door! As an example of fortitude and endurance, brothers, take the proph-
11 ets who have spoken in the name of the Lord. See, *we call the stedfast happy;* you have heard of the stedfastness of Job, and you have seen the end of the Lord with him, seen
12 that *the Lord is very compassionate and pitiful.* Above all, my brothers, never swear an oath, either by heaven or by earth or by anything else; let your "yes" be a plain "yes," your "no" a plain "no," lest you incur judgment.

* Transferring the last clause of ver. 3 to what appears to have been its original position.

13 Is anyone of you in trouble? let him pray. Is anyone
14 thriving? let him sing praise. Is anyone ill? let him
summon the presbyters of the church, and let them pray
over him, anointing him with oil in the name of the Lord;
15 the prayer of faith will restore the sick man, and the Lord
will raise him up; even the sins he has committed will be
16 forgiven him. So confess your sins to one another and
pray for one another, that you may be healed; the prayers
17 of the righteous have a powerful effect. Elijah was a man
with a nature just like our own; but he offered prayer that
it might not rain, and for three years and six months it did
18 not rain; then he prayed again, and the sky yielded rain,
the earth brought forth its fruit.
19 My brothers, if anyone of you goes astray from the truth
20 and some one brings him back, understand that he who
brings a sinner back from the error of his way saves his
soul from death and *hides* a host of *sins*.

THE FIRST EPISTLE OF
PETER

1 PETER an apostle of Jesus Christ, to the exiles of the Dispersion in Pontus, Galatia, Cappadocia, Asia, and
2 Bithynia, whom God the Father has predestined and chosen, by the consecration of the Spirit, to obey Jesus Christ and be sprinkled with his blood: may grace and peace be multiplied to you.
3 Blessed be the God and Father of our Lord Jesus Christ! By his great mercy we have been born anew to a life of hope through the resurrection of Jesus Christ from the
4 dead, born to an unscathed, inviolate, unfading inheritance;
5 it is kept in heaven for you, and the power of God protects you by faith till you do inherit the salvation which is all
6 ready to be revealed at the last hour. You will rejoice then, though for the passing moment you may need to suffer
7 various trials; that is only to prove your faith is sterling (far more precious than gold which is perishable and yet is tested by fire), and it redounds to your praise and glory
8 and honour at the revelation of Jesus Christ. You never knew him, but you love him; for the moment you do not see him, but you believe in him, and you will thrill with an
9 unspeakable and glorious joy to obtain the outcome of your
10 faith in the salvation of your souls. Even prophets have searched and inquired about that salvation, the prophets
11 who prophesied of the grace that was meant for you; the Spirit of messiah within them foretold all the suffering of messiah and his after-glory, and they pondered when or
12 how this was to come; to them it was revealed that they got this intelligence * not for themselves but for you, regarding all that has now been disclosed to you by those who preached the gospel to you through the holy Spirit sent from heaven. The very angels long to get a glimpse of this!
13 Brace up your minds, then, keep cool, and put your hope for good and all in the grace that is coming to you at the

* On the basis of Enoch i. 2 (οὐκ εἰς τὴν νῦν γενεὰν διενοούμην ἀλλ' ἐπὶ πόρρω οὖσαν ἐγὼ λαλῶ) Dr. Rendel Harris plausibly reads διενοοῦντο, as above, for the διηκόνουν of the ordinary text.

14 revelation of Jesus Christ. Be obedient children, instead
of moulding yourselves to the passions that once ruled the
15 days of your ignorance; as He who called you is holy, so
you must be holy too in all your conduct—for it is written,
16
17 *You shall be holy because I am holy*. And as *you call upon
a Father* who judges everyone impartially by what he has
done, be reverent in your conduct while you sojourn here
18 below; you know it was *not by* perishable *silver* or gold
that *you were ransomed* from the futile traditions of your
19 past, but by the precious blood of Christ, a lamb unblem-
20 ished and unstained. He was predestined before the foundation of the world and has appeared at the end of the ages
21 for your sake; it is by him that you believe in God who
raised him from the dead and gave him glory; and thus
your faith means hope in God.
22 Now that your obedience to the Truth has purified your
souls for a brotherly love that is sincere, love one another
23 heartily and steadily. You are born anew of immortal, not
24 of mortal seed, by *the living, lasting* word of *God;* for
All flesh is like *the grass,*
and all its *glory like the flower of grass:*
the grass withers
and the flower fades,
25 *but the word of the Lord lasts for ever—*
2 and that is *the word of the gospel* for you.   So off
with all malice, all guile and insincerity and envy and
2 slander of every kind!   Like newly-born children, thirst
for the pure, spiritual milk to make you grow up to salva-
3 tion. You have had a taste of the kindness of the Lord:
4 come to him then—come to that living Stone which men
5 have rejected and God holds choice and precious, come and,
like living stones yourselves, be built into a spiritual house,
to form a consecrated priesthood for the offering of those
spiritual sacrifices that are acceptable to God through Jesus
6 Christ. For thus it stands in the scripture:
Here I lay a Stone in Sion,
a choice, a precious cornerstone:
he who believes in him will never be disappointed.
7 Now you believe, you hold him 'precious,' but as for the
unbelieving—
the very stone the builders rejected
is now the cornerstone,
8 *a stone over which men stumble* and *a rock of offence;*
they *stumble* over it in their disobedience to God's word.
9 Such is their appointed doom. But you are *the elect race,
the royal priesthood, the consecrated nation, the People
who belong to Him,* that *you may proclaim the wondrous
deeds* of Him who has called you from darkness to his

I. PETER III

10 wonderful light—you who once were *no people* and now are *God's people*, you *who* once *were unpitied* and now *are pitied.*
11 Beloved, as *sojourners and exiles* I appeal to you to abstain from the passions of the flesh that wage war upon
12 the soul. Conduct yourselves properly before pagans; so that for all their slander of you as bad characters, they may come to glorify God when you are put upon your trial, by what they see of your good deeds.
13 Submit for the Lord's sake to any human authority;
14 submit to the emperor as supreme, and to governors as deputed by him for the punishment of wrongdoers and the
15 encouragement of honest people—for it is the will of God that by your honest lives you should silence the ignorant
16 charges of foolish persons. Live like free men, only do not make your freedom a pretext for misconduct; live like serv-
17 ants of God. Do honour to all, love the brotherhood, *reverence God, honour the emperor.*
18 Servants, be submissive to your masters with perfect respect, not simply to those who are kind and reasonable
19 but to the surly as well—for it is a merit when from a
20 sense of God one bears the pain of unjust suffering. Where is the credit in standing punishment for having done wrong? No, if you stand suffering for having done right,
21 that is what God counts a merit. It is your vocation; for when Christ suffered for you, he left you an example, and you must follow his footsteps.
22 *He committed no sin,*
 no guile was ever found upon his lips;
23 he was reviled and made no retort,
 he suffered and never threatened,
24 but left everything to Him who judges justly; *he bore our sins* in his own body on the gibbet, that we might break with sin and live for righteousness; and *by his wounds*
25 *you have been healed.* You were *astray like sheep*, but you have come back now to the Shepherd and Guardian of your souls.

3 In the same way, you wives must be submissive to your husbands, so that even those who will not believe the Word may be won over without a word by the behaviour
2 of their wives, when they see how chaste and reverent you
3 are. You are not to adorn yourselves on the outside with braids of hair and ornaments of gold and changes of dress,
4 but inside, in the heart, with the immortal beauty of a gentle and modest spirit, which in the sight of God is of
5 rare value. It was in this way long ago that the holy women who hoped in God adorned themselves. They were
6 submissive to their husbands. Thus Sara obeyed Abraham

by *calling him 'lord'*. And you are daughters of Sara if
7 you do what is right and *yield to no panic*.* In the same
way you husbands must be considerate in living with your
wives, since they are the weaker sex; you must honour
them as heirs equally with yourselves of the grace of Life,
so that your prayers may not be hindered.
8 Lastly, you must all be united, you must have sympathy,
brotherly love, compassion, and humility, never paying
9 back evil for evil, never reviling when you are reviled, but
on the contrary blessing. For this is your vocation, to
bless and to inherit blessing;
10 *he who would love Life*
and enjoy good days,
let him keep his tongue from evil
and his lips from speaking guile:
11 *let him shun wrong and do right,*
let him seek peace and make peace his aim.
12 *For the eyes of the Lord are on the upright,*
and his ears are open to their cry;
but the face of the Lord is set against wrongdoers.
13 Yet who will wrong you if you have a passion for good-
14 ness? Even supposing you have to suffer for the sake of
what is right, still you are blessed. *Have no fear of their*
15 *threats, do not let that trouble you,* but reverence Christ
as Lord in your own hearts. Always be ready with a reply
for anyone who calls you to account for the hope you
cherish, but answer gently and with a sense of reverence;
16 see that you have a clean conscience, so that, for all their
slander of you, these libellers of your good Christian be-
17 haviour may be ashamed. For it is better to suffer for doing
right (if that should be the will of God) than for doing
18 wrong. Christ himself died for sins, once for all, a just man
for unjust men, that he might bring us near to God; in the
flesh he was put to death but he came to life in the Spirit.
19 (It was in the Spirit that Enoch † also went and preached
20 to the imprisoned spirits who had disobeyed at the time
when God's patience held out during the construction of
the ark in the days of Noah—the ark by which only a few
souls, eight in all, were brought safely through the water.)
21 Baptism, the counterpart of that, saves you to-day (not the
mere washing of dirt from the flesh but the prayer for a

* Apparently an allusion to the fear of violence at the hands of their (pagan?) husbands. The language, but not the idea, is that of Proverbs iii. 25.

† Accepting the emendation of Dr. Rendel Harris that 'Ενώχ has been omitted after ἐν ᾧ καί (ΕΝΩΚΑΙ [ΕΝΩΧ]), by " a scribe's blunder in dropping some repeated letters." The story of this mission is told in the Book of Enoch (see above, p. 351).

I. PETER IV

clean conscience before God) by the resurrection of Jesus
22 Christ who is *at God's right hand*—for he went to heaven
after angels, authorities, and powers celestial had been
made subject to him.)

4 Well, as Christ has suffered for us in the flesh, let this
very conviction that he who has suffered in the flesh
2 gets quit of sin, nerve you to spend the rest of your time in
the flesh for the will of God and no longer for human
3 passions. It is quite enough to have done as pagans choose
to do, during the time gone by! You used to lead lives of
sensuality, lust, carousing, revelry, dissipation and illicit
4 idolatry, and it astonishes them that you will not plunge
with them still into the same flood of profligacy. They
5 abuse you, but they will have to answer for that to Him
6 who is prepared to judge the living and the dead (for this
was why the gospel was preached to the dead as well, that
while they are judged in the flesh as men, they may live
as God lives in the spirit).
7 Now the end of all is near. Steady then, keep cool and
8 pray! Above all, be keen to love one another, for *love hides*
9 *a host of sins*. Be hospitable to each other, and do not
10 grudge it. You must serve one another, each with the
talent he has received, as efficient stewards of God's varied
11 grace. If anyone preaches, he must preach as one who
utters the words of God; if anyone renders some service,
it must be as one who is supplied by God with power, so
that in everything God may be glorified through Jesus
Christ. The glory and the dominion are his for ever and
ever: Amen.
12 Beloved, do not be surprised at the ordeal that has come
to test you, as though some foreign experience befell you.
13 You are sharing what Christ suffered; so rejoice in it, that
you may also rejoice and exult when his glory is revealed.
14 If *you are denounced* for the sake of *Christ*, you are
blessed; for then *the Spirit of* glory and *power, the Spirit*
15 of *God himself, is resting on you*. None of you must suffer
as a murderer or a thief or a bad character or a revolu-
16 tionary; but if a man suffers for being a Christian, he must
17 not be ashamed, he must rather glorify God for that. It is
time for the Judgment *to begin with the household of God;*
and if it begins with us,
what will be the fate of those who refuse obedience to
God's gospel?
18 If *the just man is scarcely saved,*
what will become of the impious and sinful?
19 So let those who are suffering by the will of God trust their
souls to him, their faithful Creator, as they continue to do
right.

I. PETER V

5 Now I make this appeal to your presbyters (for I am a presbyter myself, I was a witness of what Christ suffered and I am to share the glory that will be revealed),
2 be shepherds to your flock of God; take charge of them willingly* instead of being pressed to it, not to make a
3 base profit from it but freely, not by way of lording it over
4 your charges but proving a pattern to the flock. Then you will receive the unfading crown of glory, when the chief
5 Shepherd makes his appearance. You younger men must also submit to the presbyters. Indeed you must all put on the apron of humility to serve one another, for

*the haughty God opposes,
but to the humble he gives grace.*

6 Humble yourselves under the strong hand of God, then,
7 so that when it is time, he may raise you; let all your anxieties fall upon him, for his interest is in you.
8 Keep cool, keep awake. Your enemy the devil prowls like a roaring lion, looking out for someone to devour.
9 Resist him; keep your foothold in the faith, and learn to pay the same tax of suffering as the rest of your brother-
10 hood throughout the world. Once you have suffered for a little, the God of all grace who has called you to his eternal glory in Christ Jesus, will † repair and recruit and
11 strengthen you. The dominion is his for ever and ever: Amen.
12 By the hand of Silvanus, a faithful brother (in my opinion), I have written you these few lines of encouragement, to testify that this is what the true grace of God means. Stand in that grace.
13 Your sister-church in Babylon, elect like yourselves,
14 salutes you. So does my son Mark. Salute one another with a kiss of love.

Peace be to you all who are in Christ [Jesus].

* Omitting κατὰ θεόν.
† Omitting θεμελιώσει with A B, the Latin and Ethiopic versions.

THE SECOND EPISTLE OF
PETER

1 SYMEON PETER, a servant and apostle of Jesus Christ, to those who have been allotted a faith of equal privilege with ours, by the equity of our God and saviour Jesus 2 Christ: grace and peace be multiplied to you by the knowl-3 edge of * our Lord. Inasmuch as his power divine has bestowed on us every requisite for life and piety by the knowledge of him who called us to his own glory and 4 excellence—bestowing on us thereby promises precious and supreme, that by means of them you may escape the corruption produced within the world by lust, and par-5 ticipate in the divine nature—for this very reason, do you contrive to make it your whole concern to furnish your 6 faith with resolution, resolution with intelligence, intelli-gence with self-control, self-control with stedfastness, sted-7 fastness with piety, piety with brotherliness, brotherliness 8 with Christian love. For as these qualities exist and in-crease with you, they render you active and fruitful in the 9 knowledge of our Lord Jesus Christ; whereas he who has not these by him is blind, shortsighted, oblivious that he 10 has been cleansed from his erstwhile sins. So be the more eager, brothers, to ratify your calling and election, for as 11 you practise these qualities you will never make a slip; you will thus be richly furnished with the right of entry into the eternal realm of our Lord and saviour Jesus Christ.

12 Hence I mean to keep on reminding you of this, although 13 you are aware of it and are fixed in the Truth as it is; so long as I am in this tent, I deem it proper to stir you up 14 by way of reminder, since I know my tent must be folded up very soon—as indeed our Lord Jesus Christ has shown 15 me. Yes, and I will see to it that even when I am gone, 16 you will keep this constantly in mind. For it was no fabricated fables that we followed when we reported to you the power and advent of our Lord Jesus Christ; we 17 were admitted to the spectacle of his sovereignty, when he was invested with honour and glory by God the Father, and when the following voice was borne to him from †

* Omitting, with P and the Latin Vulgate, τοῦ θεοῦ καὶ Ἰησοῦ.
† Reading with the Syriac and Latin (Vulgate) versions ἀπό instead of ὑπό.

II. PETER II

the sublime Glory, "This is my son, the Beloved, in whom
18 I delight." That voice borne from heaven we heard, we
19 who were beside him on the sacred hill, and thus we have
gained fresh confirmation of the prophetic word. Pray
attend to that word; it shines like a lamp within a darksome spot, till the Day dawns and the daystar rises within
20 your hearts—understanding this, at the outset, that no
prophetic scripture allows a man to interpret it by himself;
21 for prophecy never came by human impulse, it was when
carried away by the holy Spirit that the * holy men of God
spoke.

2 Still, false prophets did appear among the People, as
among you also there will be false teachers, men who
will insinuate destructive heresies, even disowning the
Lord who ransomed them; they bring rapid destruction on
2 themselves, and many will follow their immorality (*thanks*
3 *to them* the true *Way will be maligned*); in their lust
they will exploit you with cunning arguments—men whose
doom comes apace from of old, and destruction is awake
4 upon their trail. For if God did not spare angels who had
sinned, but committing them to pits of the nether gloom
in Tartarus, reserved them under punishment † for doom:
5 if he did not spare the ancient world but kept Noah, the
herald of righteousness, safe with seven others, when he
6 let loose the deluge on the world of impious men: if he
reduced the cities of Sodom and Gomorra to ashes when
he sentenced them to devastation, and thus gave the
7 impious ‡ an example of what was in store for them, but
rescued righteous Lot who was sore burdened by the im-
8 moral behaviour of the lawless (for when that righteous
man resided among them, by what he saw and heard his
righteous soul was vexed day after day with their unlawful
9 doings)—then be sure the Lord knows how to rescue pious
folk from trial, and how to keep the unrighteous under
10 punishment till the day of doom, particularly those who
fall in with the polluting appetite of the flesh and despise
the Powers celestial. Daring, presumptuous creatures!
11 they are not afraid to scoff at the angelic Glories; whereas
even angels, superior in might and power, lay no scoffing
12 charge against these before the Lord. But those people!—
like irrational animals, creatures of mere instinct, born

---

* Reading οἱ ἅγιοι θεοῦ ἄνθρωποι with ℵ A, the Latin version, etc.

† Reading with ℵ A, the Latin and Egyptian versions, and Syr^phil κολαζομένους τηρεῖν instead of τηρουμένους.

‡ Reading ἀσεβέσιν (B P Syr^h) or τοῖς ἀσεβέσιν (sah boh) instead of ἀσεβεῖν. As Weizsäcker renders it, "ein Vorbild des Kommenden gebend für die Gottlosen."

for capture and corruption, they scoff at what they are
ignorant of; and like animals they will suffer corruption
13 and ruin, done out of * the profits of their evil-doing.
Pleasure for them is revelling in open daylight—spots and
blots, with their dissipated revelling, as they carouse in your
14 midst!—their eyes are full of harlotry, insatiable for sin;
their own hearts trained to lust, they beguile unsteady
15 souls. Accursed generation! they have gone wrong by
leaving the straight road, by following the road of Balaam
16 son of Bosor, who liked the profits of evil-doing—but he got
reproved for his malpractice: a dumb ass spoke with human
17 voice and checked the prophet's infatuation. These people
are waterless fountains and mists driven by a squall, for
18 whom the nether gloom of darkness † is reserved. By talking arrogant futilities they beguile with the sensual lure
of fleshly passion those who are just escaping from the
19 company of misconduct—promising them freedom, when
they are themselves enslaved to corruption (for a man is
20 the slave of whatever overpowers him). After escaping
the pollutions of the world by the knowledge of our Lord
and saviour Jesus Christ, if they get entangled and overpowered again, the last state is worse for them than the
21 first. Better had they never known the Way of righteousness, than to know it and then turn back from the holy
22 command which was committed to them. They verify the
truth of the proverb:
"*The dog turns back to what he has vomited,
the sow when washed will wallow in the mire.*"

3 This is the second letter I have already written to you,
beloved, stirring up your pure mind ‡ by way of re-
2 minder, to have you recollect the words spoken by the holy
prophets beforehand and the command given by your
3 apostles from the Lord and saviour. To begin with, you
know that mockers will come with their mockeries in the
last days, men who go by their own passions, asking,
4 "Where is His promised advent? Since the day our fathers
fell asleep, things remain exactly as they were from the
5 beginning of creation." They wilfully ignore the fact that
heavens existed long ago, and an earth which the word
6 of God formed of water and by water. By water the then-
7 existing world was deluged and destroyed, but the present
heavens and earth are treasured up by the same word for
fire, reserved for the day when the impious are doomed and

---

* Reading, with ℵ* B P Syr^{phil} arm ἀδικούμενοι instead of κομιούμενοι.
† Omitting [εἰς αἰῶνα].
‡ A difficult phrase, referring perhaps to freedom from the contamination of heresies. Reuss renders, "votre sain jugement."

8 destroyed. Beloved, you must not ignore this one fact, that *with the Lord* a single day is like a thousand years,
9 and *a thousand years are like a single day*. The Lord is not slow with what he promises, according to certain people's idea of slowness; no, he is longsuffering for your sake,* he does not wish any to perish but all to betake
10 them to repentance. The day of the Lord will come like a thief, when the heavens will vanish with crackling roar, the stars will be set ablaze and melt, the earth and all its
11 works will disappear.† Now as all things are thus to be dissolved, what holy and pious men ought you to be in your
12 behaviour, you who expect and hasten the advent of the Day of God, which dissolves the heavens in fire and makes
13 the stars blaze and melt! It is new heavens and a new earth that we expect, as He has promised, and in them
14 dwells righteousness. Then, beloved, as you are expecting this, be eager to be found by him unspotted and un-
15 blemished in serene assurance. And consider that the longsuffering of our Lord means salvation; as indeed our beloved brother Paul has written to you out of the wisdom
16 vouchsafed to him, speaking of this as he has done in all his letters—letters containing some knotty points, which ignorant and unsteady souls twist (as they do the rest of
17 the scriptures) to their own destruction. Now, beloved, you are forewarned: mind you are not carried away by the error of the lawless and so lose your proper footing;
18 but grow in the grace and knowledge of our Lord and saviour Jesus Christ. To him be the glory now and to the day of eternity: Amen.

* Reading δι' with ℵ A Lat. syr. sah., etc.
† Adding οὐχ before εὑρεθήσεται with the Sahidic version.

THE FIRST EPISTLE OF
JOHN

1 It is of what existed from the very beginning, of what we heard, of what we saw, of what we witnessed and touched with our own hands, it is of the Logos of Life
2 (the Life has appeared; we saw it, we testify to it, we bring you word of that eternal Life which existed with the
3 Father and was disclosed to us)—it is of what we heard and saw that we bring you word, so that you may share our fellowship; and our fellowship is with the Father and
4 with his Son Jesus Christ. We are writing this to you that our own joy may be complete.
5 Here is the message we learned from him and announce to you: 'God is light and in him there is no darkness,
6 none.' If we say, 'We have fellowship with him,' when we live and move in darkness, then we are lying, we are not
7 practising the truth; but if we live and move within the light, as he is within the light, then we have fellowship with one another, and the blood of Jesus his Son cleanses
8 us from every sin. If we say, 'We are not guilty,' we are
9 deceiving ourselves and the truth is not in us; if we confess our sins, he is faithful and just, he forgives our
10 sins and cleanses us from all iniquity; if we say, "We have not sinned," we make him a liar and his word is not within
2 us. My dear children, I am writing this to you that you may not sin; but if anyone does sin, we have an
2 advocate with the Father in Jesus Christ the just; he is himself the propitiation for our sins, though not for ours alone but also for the whole world.
3 This is how we may be sure we know him, by obeying
4 his commands. He who says, 'I know him,' but does not obey his commands, is a liar and the truth is not in him;
5 but whoever obeys his word, in him love to God is really complete. This is how we may be sure we are in him:
6 he who says he 'remains in him' ought to live as he lived.
7 Beloved, I am not writing you any new command, but an old command which you have had from the very begin-
8 ning: the old command is the word you have heard. And yet it is a new command I am writing to you—realized in

him and also in yourselves, because the darkness is passing away and the true light is already shining. He who says he is 'in the light' and hates his brother, is in darkness still. He who loves his brother remains in the light —and in the light there is no pitfall; but he who hates his brother is in darkness, he walks in darkness and does not know where he is going, for the darkness has blinded his eyes.

12 My dear children, I am writing to you,
   because your sins are forgiven for his sake:
13 fathers, I am writing to you,
   because you know him who is from the very beginning:
   young men, I am writing to you,
   because you have conquered the evil One.
   children, I have written to you,
   because you know the Father:
14 fathers, I have written to you,
   because you know him who is from the very beginning:
   young men, I have written to you,
   because you are strong, and the word of God remains within you, and you have conquered the evil One.

15 Love not the world, nor yet what is in the world; if anyone loves the world, love for the Father is not in him. 16 For all that is in the world, the desire of the flesh and the desire of the eyes and the proud glory of life, belongs 17 not to the Father but to the world; and the world is passing away with its desire, while he who does the will of God remains for ever.

18 Children, it is the last hour. You have learned that 'Antichrist is coming.' Well, but many antichrists have 19 appeared—which makes us sure it is the last hour. They withdrew from us, but they did not belong to us; had they belonged to us, they would have remained with us, but they withdrew to make it plain that they are none of us. 20 Now, you have been anointed by the holy One, and you 21 all possess knowledge. I am not writing to you because you do not know the truth, but because you do know it, and know that no lie has any connexion with the truth.

22 Who is the real liar?
   who but he who denies that Jesus is the Christ?
   This is 'antichrist,'
   he who disowns the Father and the Son.
23 No one who disowns the Son can possess the Father:
   he who confesses the Son possesses the Father as well.
24 Let that remain in you which you learned from the very beginning; if what you learned from the very beginning remains with you, then you will remain in the Son and in the Father.

25 Now this is what he has promised you,* eternal life.
26 I am writing to you in this way about those who would
27 deceive you, but the unction you received from him remains within you, and you really need no teaching from anyone; simply remain in him, for his unction teaches you about everything and is true and is no lie—remain in him, as it
28 has taught you to do. Remain within him now, my dear children, so that when he appears, we may have confidence
29 instead of shrinking from him in shame at his arrival. As you know he is just, be sure that everyone who practises
3 righteousness is born of him. 'Born of him!' Think what a love the Father has for us, in letting us be called 'children of God!' That is what we are. The world does not recognize us? That is simply because it did not recog-
2 nize him. We are children of God now, beloved; what we are to be is not apparent yet, but we do know that when he appears, we are to be like him—for we are to see him
3 as he is. And everyone who rests this hope on him,
4 purifies himself as he is pure. Everyone who commits sin
5 commits lawlessness: sin is lawlessness, and you know he appeared to take [our] sins away. In him there is no sin;
6 anyone who remains in him does not sin—anyone who sins has neither seen nor known him. Let no one deceive you,
7 my dear children: he who practises righteousness is just,
8 as He is just; he who commits sin belongs to the devil, for the devil is a sinner from the very beginning. (This is why the Son of God appeared, to destroy the deeds
9 of the devil.) Anyone who is born of God does not commit sin, for the offspring of God remain in Him,
10 and they cannot sin, because they are born of God. Here is how the children of God and the children of the devil are recognized; anyone who does not practise righteousness does not belong to God, and neither does he
11 who has no love for his brother. For this is the message you have learned from the very beginning, that we are to
12 love one another: we are not to be like Cain, who belonged to the evil One and slew his brother. And why did he slay him? Because his own deeds were evil and his brother's
13 just. Do not wonder, brothers, that the world hates you.
14 We know we have crossed from death to life, because we love the brotherhood; he who has no love [for his brother]
15 remains in death. Anyone who hates his brother is a murderer, and you know no murderer has eternal life
16 remaining within him. We know what love is by this, that He laid down his life for us; so we ought to lay down
17 our lives for the brotherhood. But whoever possesses this

* Reading ὑμῖν instead of ἡμῖν.

I. JOHN IV

world's goods, and notices his brother in need, and shuts
his heart against him, how can love to God remain in him?
18 My dear children, let us put our love not into words or
into talk but into deeds, and make it real.
19 Thus it is that we may be sure we belong to the truth
20 and reassure ourselves whenever our heart condemns us;
for God is greater than our heart, and he knows all.
21 If our heart does not condemn us, beloved, then we have
22 confidence in approaching God, and we get from him whatever we ask, because we obey his commands and do what
23 is pleasing in his sight. Now this is what he commands,
that we believe in the name of his Son Jesus Christ, and
24 love one another as he has commanded us to do; he who
obeys his commands remains within him—and He remains
within him. And this is how we may be sure he remains
within us, by means of the Spirit he has given us.
4 Do not believe every spirit, beloved, but test the
spirits to see if they come from God; for many false
2 prophets have emerged in the world. You can recognize
the Spirit of God by this: every spirit which confesses
3 Jesus as the Christ incarnate comes from God, and every
spirit which does not confess Jesus [incarnate] does not
come from God. This latter is the spirit of antichrist;
you were told it was coming, and here it is already in the
4 world. My dear children, you belong to God, and you have
conquered all such, for He who is within you is greater
than he who is in the world.
5 They belong to the world,
   therefore they speak as inspired by the world,
   and the world listens to them:
6 we belong to God—
   he who knows God listens to us,
   he who does not belong to God does not listen to us.
This is how we recognize the spirit of truth and the spirit
of error.
7 Beloved, let us love one another, for love belongs to God,
and everyone who loves is born of God and knows God;
8 he who does not love, does not know God, for God is love.
9 This is how the love of God has appeared for us, by God
sending his only Son into the world, so that by him we
10 might live. Love lies in this, not in our love for him but
in his love for us—in the sending of his Son to be the
11 propitiation for our sins. Beloved, if God had such love for
12 us, we ought to love one another. God no one has ever
seen; but if we love one another, then God remains within
13 us, and love for him is complete in us. This is how we
may be sure we remain in him and he in us, because he has
14 given us a share in his own Spirit; and we have seen, we

can testify, that the Father has sent the Son as the Saviour
15 of the world. Whoever confesses that 'Jesus is the Son of
16 God,' in him God remains, and he remains in God; well, we
do know, we have believed, the love God has for us.
God is love, and he who remains in love remains in God,
17 and God remains in him. Love is complete with us when
we have absolute confidence about the day of judgment,
18 since in this world we are living as He lives. Love has no
dread in it; no, love in its fulness drives all dread away,
for dread has to do with punishment—anyone who has
19 dread, has not reached the fulness of love. We love, be-
20 cause He loved us first. If anyone declares, 'I love God,'
and yet hates his brother, he is a liar; for he who will not
love his brother whom he has seen, cannot possibly love the
21 God whom he has never seen. And we get this command
from him, that he who loves God is to love his brother as
well.

5 Everyone who believes Jesus is the Christ, is born of God;
and everyone who loves the Father, loves the sons *
2 born of him. This is how we are sure that we love God's
3 children, by loving God and obeying his commands (for love
to God means keeping his commands). And his commands
4 are not irksome, for whatever is born of God conquers the
world. Our faith, that is the conquest which conquers the
5 world. Who is the world's conqueror but he who believes
6 that Jesus is the Son of God? Jesus Christ, he it is who
came by water, blood, and Spirit—not by the water alone,
7 but by the water and the blood. The Spirit is the witness
8 to this, for the Spirit is truth. The witnesses are three,
the Spirit and the water and the blood, and the three
9 of them are in accord. If we accept human testimony,
God's testimony is greater; for God's testimony consists
10 in his testimony to his Son. He who believes in the Son of
God possesses that testimony within himself; he who will
not believe God, has made God a liar by refusing to believe
11 the testimony which God has borne to his Son. And the
testimony is, that God gave us life eternal and this life is
in his Son.
12   He who possesses the Son possesses life:
he who does not possess the Son does not possess life.
13   I have written in this way to you who believe in the
name of the Son of God, that you may be sure you have
14 life eternal. Now the confidence we have in him is this, that
he listens to us whenever we ask anything in accordance
15 with his will; and if we know he listens to whatever we

---

* The Greek word is singular. It may be taken strictly, as meaning
" the Son," or generically as above (see the next verse).

ask, we know we obtain the requests we have made to him.
16 If anyone notices his brother committing a sin which is not deadly, he will ask and obtain life for him—for anyone who does not commit a deadly sin. There is such a thing
17 as deadly sin; I do not mean he is to pray for that. All iniquity is sin, but there are sins which are not deadly.
18 We know that anyone who is born of God does not sin; He who was born of God preserves him, and the evil One never catches him.
19 We know that we belong to God, and that the whole world lies in the power of the evil One.
20 We know that the Son of God has come, and has given us insight to know Him who is the Real God; and we are in Him who is real, even in his Son Jesus Christ. This is
21 the real God, this is life eternal. My dear children, keep clear of idols.

THE SECOND EPISTLE OF
JOHN

1 The presbyter, to the elect Lady and her children whom I love in the Truth (and not only I but all who know
2 the Truth) for the sake of the Truth which remains
3 within us and will be with us for ever: grace, mercy, peace will be with us from God the Father and from Jesus Christ the Son of the Father, in truth and love.
4 I was overjoyed to find some of your children leading the true Life, as we were commanded to do by the Father.
5 And now I entreat you, Lady—not as though I were writing you any new command, it is the command which we have
6 had from the very beginning—let us love one another. To live by his commands, that is what love means: and the command is, live in love as you have learned to do from
7 the very beginning. I say this, because a number of impostors have emerged in the world, men who will not acknowledge the coming of Jesus Christ in the flesh; that
8 marks the real 'impostor' and 'antichrist.' Watch yourselves; you must not lose what you have been working for,
9 but gain a full reward. Anyone who is 'advanced' and will not remain by the doctrine of Christ, does not possess God:
10 he who remains by the doctrine of Christ possesses both the Father and the Son. If anyone comes to you and does not
11 bring this doctrine, do not admit him to the house—do not even greet him, for he who greets him shares in his wicked work.
12 I have a great deal to write to you, but I do not mean to use ink and paper; I hope to visit you and have a talk with you, so that your * joy may be unimpaired.
13 The children of your elect Sister greet you.

* Reading with A B and several versions, ὑμῶν, instead of ἡμῶν.

THE THIRD EPISTLE OF
JOHN

1 THE presbyter, to the beloved Gaius whom I love in the
2 Truth. Beloved, I pray you may prosper in every way
3 and keep well—as indeed your soul is keeping well. For I
was overjoyed when some brothers arrived and testified to
the truth of your life, as indeed you do lead the true Life;
4 I have no greater joy than to hear of my children living in
5 the Truth. Beloved, you are acting loyally in rendering
any service to the brothers and especially to strangers;
6 they have testified to your love before the church. Pray
7 speed them on their journey worthily of God; they have
started out for his sake and declined to take anything
8 from pagans; hence we are bound to support such men, to
prove ourselves allies of the Truth.
9   I have written to the church; only, Diotrephes, who likes
10 to take the lead among them, repudiates me. So when I
come, I shall bring up what he is doing, babbling against
me with wicked words—and, not satisfied with words, he
refuses to welcome the brothers, checks those who want to
welcome them, and excommunicates them from the church.
11 Beloved, do not imitate evil but good; he who does good
belongs to God, he who does evil has never seen God.
12   Everybody testifies to Demetrius, and so does the Truth
itself: I testify to him too, and you know my testimony is
true.
13   I had a great deal to write to you, but I do not want to
14 write to you with ink and pen; I am hoping to see you
soon, and we will have a talk.
15   Peace to you! The friends salute you: salute the friends
one by one.

THE EPISTLE OF
JUDAS (JUDE)

1 JUDAS, a servant of Jesus Christ and a brother of James, to those who have been called, who are beloved by God
2 the Father and kept by Jesus Christ: mercy, peace and love be multiplied to you.
3 Beloved, my whole concern was to write to you on the subject of our common salvation, but I am forced to write you an appeal to defend the faith which has once for all
4 been committed to the saints; for certain persons have slipped in by stealth (their doom has been predicted long ago), impious creatures who pervert the grace of our God into immorality and disown our sole liege and Lord, Jesus
5 Christ. Now I want to remind you of what you are perfectly aware, that though the Lord once * brought the People safe out of Egypt, he subsequently destroyed the un-
6 believing, while the angels who abandoned their own domain, instead of preserving their proper rank, are reserved by him within the nether gloom, in chains eternal,
7 for the doom of the great Day—just as Sodom and Gomorra and the adjacent cities, which similarly glutted themselves with vice and sensual perversity, are exhibited as a warning of the everlasting fire they are sentenced to suffer.
8 Despite it all, these visionaries pollute their flesh, scorn
9 the Powers celestial, and scoff at the angelic Glories. Now *the very archangel Michael*, when he disputed the body of Moses with Satan, did not dare to condemn him with scoffs;
10 what he said was, *The Lord rebuke you!* But these people scoff at anything they do not understand; and whatever they do understand, like irrational animals, by mere in-
11 stinct, that proves their ruin. Woe to them! they go the road of Cain, rush into Balaam's error for what it brings
12 them, and perish in Korah's rebellion. These people are stains on your love-feasts; they have no qualms about carousing in your midst, *they look after none but themselves*— rainless clouds, swept along by the wind, trees in autumn
13 without fruit, doubly dead and so uprooted, wild waves

* ἅπαξ must be connected, as in the Syriac and Egyptian versions, with σώσας, not with εἰδότας as in most manuscripts.

foaming out their own shame, wandering stars for whom the nether gloom of darkness has been reserved eternally.
14 It was of these, too, that Enoch the seventh from Adam prophesied, when he said,
> Behold the Lord comes with myriads of his holy ones,
15 to execute judgment upon all,
and to convict all the impious
of all the impious deeds they have committed,
and of all the harsh things said against him by impious sinners.
16 For these people are murmurers, grumbling at their lot in life—they fall in with their own passions, their talk is arrogant, they pay court to men to benefit themselves.
17 Now, beloved, you must remember the words of the
18 apostles of our Lord Jesus Christ; they told you beforehand, "At the end of things there will be mockers who
19 go by their own impious passions." These are the people who set up divisions and distinctions, sensuous creatures,
20 destitute of the Spirit. But do you, beloved, build up yourselves on your most holy faith and pray in the holy Spirit,
21 so keeping yourselves within the love of God and waiting for the mercy of our Lord Jesus Christ that ends in life
22
23 eternal. *Snatch some from the fire*, and have mercy on the waverers, *trembling as you touch them, with loathing for *the garment* which the flesh has *stained*.
24 Now to him who is able to keep you from slipping and to make your stand unblemished and exultant before his
25 glory—to the only God, our saviour through Jesus Christ our Lord, be glory, majesty, dominion and authority, before all time and now and for all time: Amen.

* Reading καὶ οὓς μὲν ἐκ πυρὸς ἁρπάζετε, διακρινομένους δὲ ἐλεᾶτε, with Syr^phil Clement and Jerome.

THE REVELATION

OF ST. JOHN

1 A REVELATION by Jesus Christ, which God granted him for his servants, to show them *what must come to pass very soon*; he disclosed it by sending it through his angel
2 to his servant John, who now testifies to what is God's word
3 and Jesus Christ's testimony—to what he saw. Blessed is he who reads aloud, blessed they who hear the words of this prophecy and lay to heart what is written in it; for the time is near.
4 John to the seven churches in Asia: grace be to you and peace from HE WHO IS AND WAS AND IS COMING, and from
5 the seven Spirits before his throne, and from Jesus Christ *the faithful witness, the first-born* from the dead, and *the prince over the kings of earth;* to him who loves us and
6 *has loosed* us *from* our *sins* by shedding his blood—he has made us *a realm of priests for his God* and Father,—to him be glory and dominion for ever and ever: Amen.
7 *Lo, he is coming on the clouds, to be seen* by every eye, even by those *who impaled* him, and *all the tribes of earth*
8 *will wail because of him:* even so, Amen. "I am the alpha and the omega," saith the Lord God, who is and was and is coming, *the almighty.*
9 I John, your brother and your companion in the distress and realm and patient endurance which Jesus brings, found myself in the island called Patmos, for adhering to God's
10 word and the testimony of Jesus. On the Lord's day I found myself rapt in the Spirit, and I heard a loud voice
11 behind me like a trumpet calling, "Write your vision in a book, and send it to the seven churches, to Ephesus and Smyrna and Pergamum and Thyatira and Sardis and Phil-
12 adelphia and Laodicea." So I turned to see whose voice it was that spoke to me; and on turning round I saw seven
13 golden lampstands and in the middle of the lampstands *One who resembled a human being, with a long robe,* and *a*
14 *belt of gold* round his breast; *his head and hair were white as wool, white as snow; his eyes flashed like fire,*
15 *his feet glowed like burnished bronze, his voice sounded*
16 *like many waves,* in his right hand he held seven stars, a sharp sword with a double edge issued from his mouth, and
17 his face shone like *the sun in full strength.* When I saw him, I fell at his feet like a dead man; but he laid his

371

hand on me, saying, "*Do not be afraid; I am the First and
Last,** I was dead and here I am alive for evermore, holding the keys that unlock death and Hades. Write down your vision of what is and *what is to be hereafter. As for the secret symbol of the seven stars which* you have seen in my right hand, and of the seven golden lampstands—the seven stars are the angels of the seven churches, and the seven lampstands are the seven churches. To the angel of the church at Ephesus write thus:—These are the words of him who holds the seven stars in his right hand, who moves among the seven golden lampstands: I know your doings, your hard work and your patient endurance; I know that you cannot bear wicked men, and that you have tested those who style themselves apostles (no apostles they!) and detected them to be liars; I know that you are enduring patiently and have borne up for my sake and have not wearied. But I have this against you: you have given up loving one another as you did at first. Now, remember the height from which you have fallen; repent and act as you did at first. If not, I will come to you [very soon] and remove your lampstand, unless you repent. Still, you have this in your favour: you hate the practices of the Nicolaitans, and I hate them too. Let anyone who has an ear listen to what the Spirit says to the churches: 'The conqueror I will allow *to eat from the tree of Life* which is *within the paradise of God.*' Then to the angel of the church at Smyrna write thus:—These are the words of *the First and Last*, who was dead and came to life: I know your † distress and your poverty (but you are rich!); I know how you are being slandered by those who style themselves Jews (no Jews are they, but a mere synagogue of Satan!). Have no fear of what you are to suffer. The devil indeed is going to put some of you in prison, *that you may be tested;* you will have a distressful *ten days.* Be faithful, though you have to die for it, and I will give you the crown of Life. Let anyone who has an ear listen to what the Spirit says to the churches: 'The conqueror shall not be injured by the second death.' Then to the angel of the church at Pergamum write thus:—These are the words of him who wields the sharp sword with the double edge: I know where you dwell, where Satan sits enthroned, and yet you adhere to my Name, you have not renounced your faith in me even during the days when my witness, my faithful Antipas, was martyred in your

---

* The words ' and the living One ' (καὶ ὁ ζῶν) have been added as a gloss from the next verse.

† Omitting, as in ver. 13, [τὰ ἔργα καὶ].

14 midst—where Satan dwells. But I have one or two things
against you: you have some adherents there of the tenets
of *Balaam*, who taught Balak how to set a pitfall before
*the sons of Israel by making them eat food which had been
sacrificed to idols and give way to sexual vice.* So even
15 with you; you likewise have some adherents of the tenets
16 of the Nicolaitans. Repent; if not, I will very soon come to
you and make war upon them with the sword of my mouth.
17 Let anyone who has an ear listen to what the Spirit says
to the churches: 'The conqueror *I will allow to share* the
hidden *manna*, and I will give him a white stone inscribed
with *a new name*, unknown to any except him who receives
18 it.' Then to the angel of the church at Thyatira write
thus:—These are the words of the Son of God, *whose eyes
19 flash like fire and whose feet glow like bronze.* I know
your doings, your love and loyalty and service and patient
endurance; I know you are doing more than you did at
20 first. Still I have this against you: you are tolerating that
Jezebel of a woman who styles herself a prophetess and
seduces my servants by teaching them *to give way to sexual
vice and to eat food which has been sacrificed to idols.*
21 I have given her time to repent, but she refuses to repent
22 of her sexual vice. Lo, I will lay her on a sickbed, and
bring her paramours into sore distress, if they do not
23 repent of her practices; and her children I will exterminate.
So shall all the churches know that I am *the searcher of
the inmost heart; I will requite each* of you *according to
24 what you have done.* But for the rest of you at Thyatira,
for all who do not hold these tenets, for those who have
not (in their phrase) 'fathomed the deep mysteries of
Satan'—for you this is my word: I impose no fresh burden
25 on you; only hold to what you have, till such time as I
26 come. 'And the conqueror, he who till the end lays to heart
what I enjoin, *I will give him* authority *over the nations—
27 aye, he will shepherd them with an iron flail,
shattering them like a potter's jars—*
as I myself have received authority from my Father;
28 also I will grant him to see the Morning-star.' Let anyone
who has an ear listen to what the Spirit says to the
churches.

3 Then to the angel of the church at Sardis write thus:
—These are the words of him who holds the seven
Spirits of God and the seven stars: I know your doings,
2 you have the name of being alive, but you are dead. Wake
up, rally what is still left to you, though it is on the very
point of death; for I find nothing you have done is complete
3 in the eyes of my God. Now remember what you received
and heard, hold to it and repent. If you will not wake up,

I shall come like a thief; you will not know at what hour I
4 come upon you. Still, you have a few souls at Sardis who
have not soiled their raiment; they shall walk beside me in
5 white, for they deserve to. 'The conqueror shall be clad in
white raiment; I will never *erase his name from the book
of Life*, but will own him openly before my Father and
6 before his angels.' Let anyone who has an ear listen to
7 what the Spirit says to the churches. Then to the angel of
the church at Philadelphia write thus:—These are the
words of the true Holy One, who holds *the key of David,
who opens and none shall shut, who shuts and none shall
8 open.** Lo, I have set a door open before you which no one
is able to shut; for though your strength is small, you have
9 kept my word, you have not renounced my Name. Lo, I
will make those who belong to that synagogue of Satan, who
style themselves Jews (no Jews are they, but liars!)—lo,
I will have them *come and do homage before your feet* and
10 learn that *I did love you.* Because you have kept the word
of my patient endurance, I will keep you safe through the
hour of trial which is coming upon the whole world to test
11 the dwellers on earth. I am coming very soon: hold to
12 what you have, in case your crown is taken from you. 'As
for the conqueror, I will make him a pillar in the temple
of my God (nevermore shall he leave it), and I will inscribe
on him the name of my God, *the name of the city* of my
God (the new Jerusalem which descends out of heaven
13 from my God), and my own *new name.*' Let anyone who
has an ear listen to what the Spirit says to the churches.
14 Then to the angel of the church at Laodicea write thus:
These are the words of the Amen, *the faithful* and true
15 *witness, the origin of* God's *creation.* I know your doings,
you are neither cold nor hot—would you were either cold
16 or hot! So, because you are lukewarm, neither hot nor
17 cold, I am going to spit you out of my mouth. You declare,
'I am rich, *I am well off*, I lack nothing!'—not knowing
you are a miserable creature, pitiful, poor, blind, naked.
18 I advise you to buy from me gold refined in the fire, that
you may be rich, white raiment to clothe you and prevent
the shame of your nakedness from being seen, and salve to
19 rub on your eyes, that you may see. *I reprove and discipline those whom I love;* so be in warm earnest and repent.
20 Lo, I stand at the door and knock; if anyone hears my
voice and opens the door, I will come in and sup with him,
21 and he with me. 'The conqueror I will allow to sit beside
me on my throne, as I myself have conquered and sat down

---

* Omitting (with Primasius) οἶδά σου τὰ ἔργα, ' I know your doings,' a harmonistic gloss which interrupts the connexion of thought.

22 beside my Father on his throne.' Let anyone who has an ear listen to what the Spirit says to the churches."

4 AFTER this I looked, and there was a door standing open in heaven! And the first voice I had heard talking with me like *a trumpet* said, "Come up here, and I will
2 show you *what must come to pass* after this." At once I found myself rapt in the Spirit; and lo a Throne stood in
3 heaven with *One seated on the throne*—the seated One re-
4 sembled in appearance jasper and sardius—and *round the throne a rainbow* resembling emerald in appearance; also round the throne four and twenty thrones, and on these thrones four and twenty Presbyters seated, who were clad in white raiment with golden crowns upon their heads.
5 From the throne *issue flashes of lightning and loud blasts*
6 *and peals of thunder*. And in front of the throne seven torches of fire burn (they are the seven Spirits of God); also in front of the throne there is like a sea of glass, *resembling crystal. And on each side of the throne, all round it, four*
7 *living Creatures full of eyes* inside and outside; *the first* living Creature resembling *a lion, the second* living Creature resembling *an ox, the third* living Creature with *a face like a man's, the fourth* living Creature like *a flying eagle*.
8 The four living Creatures, *each with six wings apiece, are full of eyes* all over their bodies and under their wings, and day and night they never cease the chant,

"*Holy, holy, holy, is the Lord God almighty,*
who was and is and is coming."

9 And whenever the living Creatures render glory and honour and thanksgiving *to him who is seated on the throne, who*
10 *lives for ever and ever*, the four and twenty Presbyters fall down before *him who is seated on the throne*, worshipping *him who lives for ever and ever*, and casting their crowns before the throne, with the cry,
11 "Thou deservest, our Lord and God,* to receive glory and honour and power,
for it was thou who didst create all things:
they existed and were created by thy will."

5 THEN I saw lying on the right hand of *him who was seated on the throne, a scroll with writing on the back*
2 *as well as inside, sealed* with seven seals. And I saw a strong angel exclaiming with a loud voice, "Who is fit to
3 open the scroll, to break the seals of it?" But no one was fit, either in heaven or on earth or underneath the
4 earth, to open the scroll or look into it. So I began to weep

---

* Omitting [ὁ ἅγιος].

bitterly because no one had been found fit to open the
5 scroll or look into it; but one of the Presbyters told me,
"Weep not; lo, *the Lion of Judah's* tribe, *the Scion* of
David, he has won * the power of opening the scroll and its
6 seven seals." Then I noticed *a Lamb* standing in the midst
of the throne and the four living Creatures and the Presbyters; it seemed to have been *slain*, but it had seven
heads and *seven eyes* (they are the seven Spirits of God
7 sent out *into all the earth*), and it went and took the scroll
out of the right hand of *him who was seated on the throne.*
8 And when it took the scroll, the four living Creatures
and the four and twenty Presbyters fell down before the
Lamb, each with his harp and with golden bowls full of
9 *incense* (that is, full of *the prayers* of the saints), *singing
a new song:*
"Thou deservest to take the scroll and open its seals,
  for thou wast slain and by shedding thy blood hast ransomed for God men from every tribe and tongue and
people and nation;
10   thou hast made them *kings and priests for* our God, and
they shall reign on earth."
11 Then I looked, and I heard the voice of many angels round
the throne and of the living Creatures and of the Presbyters, numbering *myriads of myriads and thousands of thou-*
12 *sands,* crying aloud, "The *slain Lamb* deserves to receive
power and wealth and wisdom and might and honour and
13 glory and blessing." And I heard every creature in heaven
and on earth and under the earth crying, "Blessing and
honour and glory and dominion for ever and ever, to *him*
14 *who is seated on the throne* and to the Lamb!" "Amen,"
said the four living Creatures, and the Presbyters fell down
and worshipped.

6 And when the Lamb opened one of the seven seals, I
looked, and I heard one of the four living Creatures
2 calling like thunder, "Come." † So I looked, and there was
a white horse, its rider holding a bow; he was given a
crown, and away he rode conquering and to conquer.
3   And when he opened the second seal, I heard the second
4 living Creature calling, "Come." And away went another
red horse; its rider was allowed to take peace from the
earth and to make men slay each other; he was given
a huge sword.
5   And when he opened the third seal, I heard the third
living Creature calling, "Come." So I looked and there

---

* Literally, " has conquered (see iii. 21), so that he can open."
 † Addressed either to the seer or, more probably, to the mounted figures.

was *a black horse;* its rider held a pair of scales in his
6 hand, and I heard like a voice in the midst of the four
living Creatures saying, "A shilling for a quart of wheat,
a shilling for three quarts of barley; but harm not oil and
wine!"
7 And when he opened the fourth seal, I heard the voice
8 of the fourth living Creature calling, "Come." So I looked,
and there was a livid horse; its rider's name was *Death,
and Hades* followed him. They were given power over the
fourth part of the earth, *to kill men with sword and famine
and plague and by the wild beasts of the earth.*
9 And when he opened the fifth seal, I saw underneath the
altar the souls of those who had been slain for adhering
to God's word and to the testimony which they bore;
10 and they cried aloud, *"O Sovereign Lord,* holy and true,
how long wilt thou refrain from *charging and avenging* our
11 *blood upon those who dwell on earth?"* But they were
each given a white robe, and told to remain quiet for a
little longer, until their number was completed by their
fellow-servants and their brothers who were to be killed
like themselves.
12 And when he opened the sixth seal, I looked; and a great
earthquake took place, *the sun* turned black as sackcloth,
13 *the full moon* turned like *blood, the stars of the sky dropped
to earth as a fig tree* shaken by a gale sheds her unripe
14 figs, *the sky* was swept aside *like a scroll being folded up,*
and every mountain and island was moved out of its place.
15 *Then the kings of the earth, the magnates,* the generals,
the rich, the strong, slaves and freemen everyone of them,
16 *hid in caves and among the rocks* of the mountains, calling
to the mountains and the rocks, *"Fall upon us* and *hide us*
from the face of *him who is seated on the throne* and from
17 the anger of the Lamb; for *the great Day of* their *anger*
has come, *and who can stand it?"*

7 After that I saw four angels standing *at the four corners
of the earth,* holding back *the four winds* from blowing
2 on the earth or on the sea or on any tree. And I saw
another angel rise up from the east, with the seal of the
living God; he shouted aloud to the four angels who were
3 allowed to injure the earth and sea, "Do no harm to earth
or sea or trees, until *we seal* the servants of our God *upon
4 their foreheads."* And I heard what was the number of
the sealed—a hundred and forty-four thousand sealed from
5 every tribe of the sons of Israel, twelve thousand sealed
from the tribe of Judah, twelve thousand from the tribe of
7 Reuben, twelve thousand from the tribe of Simeon, twelve
thousand from the tribe of Levi, twelve thousand from the
8 tribe of Issachar, twelve thousand from the tribe of

Zebulun, twelve thousand from the tribe of Joseph, twelve thousand from the tribe of Benjamin,* twelve thousand
6 from the tribe of Gad, twelve thousand from the tribe of Asher, twelve thousand from the tribe of Naphtali, twelve thousand sealed from the tribe of Manasseh.
9 After that I looked, and there was a great host whom no one could count, from every nation and tribe and people and tongue, standing † before the throne and before the Lamb, clad in white robes, with palm-branches in their
10 hands; and they cried with a loud voice, "Saved by our God *who is seated on the throne*, and by the Lamb!"
11 And all the angels surrounded the throne and the Presbyters and the four living Creatures, and fell on their faces
12 before the throne, worshipping God and crying, "Even so! Blessing and glory and wisdom and thanksgiving and honour and power and might be to our God for ever and
13 ever: Amen!" Then one of the Presbyters addressed me, saying, "Who are these, clad in white robes? where have
14 they come from?" I said to him, "You know, my lord." So he told me, "These are the people who have come out of *the* great *Distress, who washed their robes* and made them white *in the blood* of the Lamb.
15 For this they are now before the throne of God,
serving ‡ him day and night within his temple.
and *he who is seated on the throne* shall overshadow them.
16 *Never again will they hunger, never again will they thirst,*
never shall the sun strike them, nor any scorching heat;
17 for the Lamb in the midst of the throne *will be their shepherd,*
guiding them to fountains of living water;
and God will wipe every tear from their *eyes.*"

8 And when he opened the seventh seal, silence reigned
2 in heaven for about half-an-hour. Then I saw seven trumpets being given to the seven angels who stand before
3 God. And another angel went and *stood at the altar* with a golden censer; he was given abundant *incense*, to be laid *with the prayers* of all the saints upon the golden
4 altar in front of the throne; and the smoke *of the incense*

---

* The simple transposition of 5c–6 to a place after 8, as Dr. G. B. Gray has pointed out (*Encyclopaedia Biblica* 5209), yields a far more normal list of the tribes.

† In contrast to the dread of vi. 17, and in line with the thought of Luke xxi. 36.

‡ In the sense of worship, as in xxii. 3.

REVELATION IX 379

with the prayers of all the saints rose up from the angel's
5 hand before God. And the angel took *the censer, filled
it with fire from the altar*, and poured it on the earth; then
followed *peals of thunder, loud blasts, flashes of lightning,*
6 and an earthquake. And the seven angels with the seven
7 trumpets prepared to blow their blasts. The first blew, and
there came hail and fire mixed *with blood, falling on the
earth;* a third of the earth was burnt up, a third of the
trees were burnt up, and all the green grass was burnt up.
8 The second angel blew, and *what looked like a* huge *mountain on fire* was hurled into the sea; a third of the sea
9 *turned blood*, a third of the creatures in the sea—the living creatures—perished, and a third of the ships were de-
10 stroyed. The third angel blew, and *a* huge *star* blazing
like a torch *dropped out of the sky*, dropped on a third
11 of the rivers and on the fountains (the name of the star is
Wormwood); a third of the waters became wormwood,
and many people died of the waters, because they had
12 turned bitter. The fourth angel blew; and a stroke fell on
a third of the sun, a third of the moon, and a third of the
stars, so as to darken one third of them, withdrawing
light from a third of the day and likewise of the night.
13 Then I looked, and I heard an eagle flying in mid-heaven
with a loud cry, "Woe, woe, woe to the dwellers on earth,
for the rest of the trumpet-blasts that the three angels
are about to blow!"

9 The fifth angel blew, and I saw a Star which had
dropped from heaven to earth; he was given the key of
2 the pit of the abyss, and he opened the pit of the abyss,
and smoke poured out of the pit, *like the smoke of a* huge
furnace, till the sun and the air were *darkened by* the
3 smoke from the pit. And out of the smoke came *locusts
on the earth;* they were granted power like the power
4 wielded by scorpions on earth, but they were told not to
harm *the grass* on earth *nor any green thing nor any tree,*
only such human beings as had not *the seal* of God *upon*
5 *their foreheads;* these they were allowed, not to kill but
to torture, for five months—and their torture was like the
torture of a scorpion when it stings a man.
6   In those days *men will seek death,*
       but they will not find it:
     they will long to die,
       but death flies from them.
7 *The appearance* of the locusts *resembled horses* armed *for
battle;* on their heads were sort of crowns like gold; their
8 faces were like human faces, their hair like women's hair,
9 and *their teeth like lions' fangs;* they had scales like iron

coats of mail; the whirring of their wings was *like the*
10 *noise of many chariots* rushing to battle; their tails and
their stings were like scorpions', and their power of hurt-
11 ing men for five months lay in their tails; they had a king
over them, the angel of the abyss—his Hebrew name is
Abaddon, but in Greek he is called Apollyon.
12 The first woe has passed:
two woes are still to come.
13 Then the sixth angel blew; and I heard a voice from the
14 four horns of the golden altar before God, telling the sixth
angel with the trumpet, "Let loose the four angels who are
15 bound at *the great river Euphrates.*" So the four angels
were unloosed, who had been kept ready for that hour and
16 day and month and year, to kill the third of men. And
the number of the troops of their cavalry was two hundred
17 millions (I heard what was their number). And this is
how the horses and their riders looked in my vision: they
wore coats of mail red as fire, dark-blue as jacinth and
yellow as smoke; the horses' heads were like lions' heads,
and from their mouths poured fire and smoke and brim-
18 stone. By these three plagues the third of men were killed,
by the fire, the smoke, and the brimstone, that poured out
19 of their mouths; for the power of the horses lies in their
mouths—and also in their tails (their tails are like serpents, they have heads, and it is with their heads that
20 they hurt). But the rest of mankind, who were not killed
by these plagues, did not repent of *the works of their hands
and give up worshipping daemons and idols of gold and
silver and brass and stone and wood, which cannot either*
21 *see or hear or stir;* nor did they repent of their murders
or of *their magic spells* or of *their sexual vice* or of their
thefts.

10 THEN I saw another* strong angel descend from
heaven; he was clad in a cloud, with a rainbow over
his head, his face like the sun, his feet like columns of fire,
2 and a small scroll open in his hand. He set his right foot
3 on the sea, his left upon the earth, and shouted aloud like
a lion roaring; and at his shout the seven thunders gave
4 voice. After the seven thunders had spoken, I was going
to write it down; but I heard a voice from heaven saying,
"*Seal up* what the seven thunders have said, do not write
5 it." Then the angel I saw standing on the sea and the
6 earth *raised his right hand to heaven and swore by Him
who lives for ever and ever, who created the heaven and*

---

* Referring to v. 2, in all probability; but it may simply mean, " another angel, a strong one."

what is in it, the earth and what is in it, and the sea and
7 what is in it, "There shall be no more delay; in the days
of the seventh angel's voice, when he now blows his blast,
then shall *the secret purpose of God* be fulfilled, as he
8 assured *his servants the prophets.*" Then the voice I had
heard from heaven again talked to me, saying, "Go and
take the small scroll which lies open in the hand of the
9 angel who is standing on the sea and the earth." So I
went to the angel, saying, "Give me *the small scroll.*"
"Take it," said he, "and *swallow it;* it will *taste* sweet as
10 honey, but it will be bitter to *digest.*" Then I took *the
small scroll* from the hand of the angel *and swallowed it;
it did taste sweet, like honey,* but when I had eaten it, it
11 was bitter to digest. Then I was told, "*You must prophesy
again of many peoples and nations and languages and
kings.*"

11 And I was given *a reed* like a rod, and told, "Rise up and measure the temple of God and the altar,
2 numbering the worshippers; but omit the court outside the temple, do not measure that, for it has been given over
to *the Gentiles;* and the city will be *under their heel* for
3 two and forty months. But I will allow my two witnesses
to prophesy for twelve hundred and sixty days, clad in
4 sackcloth (they are *the two olive-trees* and the two *lampstands which stand before the Lord of the earth*):
5   whoever tries to harm them,
     fire will issue from their *mouth and consume their
         enemies;*
     whoever should try to harm them,
         so must he be killed."
6 They have power to shut up the sky, *so that no rain falls*
during the days when they are prophesying; and they have
power over *the waters, to turn* them *into blood, and* also
to smite the earth *with all manner of plagues* as often as
7 they choose. But, when they have finished their testimony,
the Beast that ascends from the abyss will make war on
8 them *and conquer them* and kill them, and their corpses
will lie in the streets of that great City whose mystical
name is *Sodom* and Egypt—where their Lord also was
9 crucified. For three days and a half men from all peoples
and tribes and tongues and nations look at their corpses,
10 refusing to let their corpses be buried; and the dwellers
on earth will gloat over them and *rejoice,* sending presents
to congratulate one another—for these two prophets were
11 a torment to the dwellers on earth. But after three days
and a half *the breath of life* from God *entered them; they
stood on their feet (terror fell on* those who saw them)
12 and heard a loud voice from heaven telling them, "Come
up here." So up *to heaven* they went in a cloud, before the

13 eyes of their enemies. At that hour *a great earthquake* took place, a tenth of the City *was destroyed*, and seven thousand souls perished in the earthquake: the rest were awestruck, and gave glory to *the God of heaven.*
14 The second woe has passed:
the third woe soon is coming.
15 Then the seventh angel blew; and loud voices followed in heaven, crying, "*The rule* of the world has passed to our Lord *and his Christ,* and *he shall reign for ever and ever.*"
16 Then the four and twenty Presbyters who are seated on their thrones before God, fell on their faces and worshipped God, saying,
17 "We thank thee, *Lord God almighty, who art* and wast, that thou hast assumed thy great power and *begun to reign;*
18 *the nations were enraged,*
but thine *anger* has come;
the time has come for the dead to be judged,
the time for rewarding *thy servants the prophets,*
and the saints *who reverence* thy name, *both low and high,*
the time for destroying the destroyers of the earth."
19 Then the temple of God in heaven was thrown open, and *the ark of his covenant* was seen *inside his temple;* there were *flashes of lightning, loud blasts, peals of thunder,* an earthquake, and *a hailstorm.*

12 And a great portent was seen in heaven, a woman clad in the sun—with the moon under her feet, and a tiara of twelve stars on her
2 head; she was with child, *crying in the pangs of travail, in*
3 *anguish for her delivery.* Then another portent was seen in heaven! There was a huge red dragon, with seven heads and *seven horns* and seven diadems upon his heads;
4 his tail swept away a third of *the stars of heaven and flung them to the earth.* And the dragon stood in front of the woman who was on the point of being delivered, to devour
5 her child as soon as it was born. *She gave birth to* a son, *a male child,* who is to *shepherd* all *the nations with an iron flail;* her child was caught up to God and to his
6 throne, and she herself fled to the desert, where a place has been prepared for her by God, in which she is to be
7 nourished for twelve hundred and sixty days. And war broke out in heaven, *Michael* and his angels *fighting* with
8 the dragon; the dragon and his angels also fought, but he failed, and there was no place for them in heaven any
9 longer. So the huge dragon was thrown down—that old serpent called *the Devil* and *Satan,* the seducer of the whole world—thrown down to the earth, and his angels thrown
10 down along with him. Then I heard a loud voice in heaven saying, "Now it has come, the salvation and power, the

reign of our God and the authority of his Christ!—for the Accuser of our brothers is thrown down, who accused them
11 before God day and night. But they have conquered him by the blood of the Lamb and by the word of their testimony; they had to die for it, but they did not cling to life.
12 *Rejoice* for this, *O heavens* and ye that dwell in them! But woe to earth and sea! The devil has descended to you
13 in fierce anger, knowing that his time is short." And when the dragon found himself thrown down to earth, he pursued the woman who had given birth to the male child;
14 but the woman was given the two wings of a great eagle for her flight to the desert, to her appointed place, where she is nourished for *a Time, two Times, and half a Time*,
15 safe from the serpent. Then from his mouth the serpent poured water after the woman like a river, to sweep her
16 away with a flood; but the earth came to the rescue of the woman, the earth opened its mouth and swallowed up the
17 river that the dragon had poured out of his mouth. So, enraged at the woman, the dragon went off to wage war on the rest of her offspring, on those who keep God's commandments and hold the testimony of Jesus.

18 **13** Then I stood on the sand of the sea, and I saw *a Beast rising out of the sea* with *ten horns* and seven heads, ten diadems * on his horns, and blasphemous titles
2 on his heads. *The Beast* I saw *resembled a leopard*, his feet were *like a bear's*, and his mouth like *a lion's*. To him the dragon gave his own power and his own throne
3 and great authority. One of his heads looked as if it had been slain and killed, but the deadly wound was healed, and the whole earth went after him in wonder, worshipping the dragon for having given authority to the Beast, and
4 worshipping the Beast with the cry,
"Who is like the Beast?
Who can fight with him?"
5 He was allowed *to utter loud* and blasphemous *vaunts*, and
6 allowed *to exert* authority for two and forty months; so he opened his mouth for blasphemies against God, to blaspheme his name and his dwelling (that is, the dwellers in
7 heaven). He was allowed *to wage war on the saints and to conquer them*, and given authority over every tribe
8 and people and tongue and nation; and all the dwellers on earth will be his worshippers, everyone whose name has not been *written* from the foundation of the world *in the*
9 *book of Life*.† Let anyone who has an ear listen:—

---

* Here, as in xii. 3, an assumption of the royal power which really belonged to God (see xix. 12).

† The words " of the Lamb slain " (τοῦ ἀρνίου τοῦ ἐσφαγμένου) are

10 *Whoever is destined for captivity,*
　　to captivity he goes:
　whoever kills with the sword,
　　by the sword must he be killed.
This is what shows the patience and the faith of the saints.
11 Then I saw another Beast rising from the land; he had
12 two horns like a lamb, but he spoke like a dragon. He exerts the full authority of the first Beast in his presence, causing the earth and its inhabitants to worship the first
13 Beast, whose deadly wound was healed. He performs amazing miracles, even making fire descend from heaven on
14 earth in the sight of men, and by dint of the miracles he is allowed to perform in presence of the Beast, he seduces the dwellers on earth; he bids the dwellers on earth erect a statue to the Beast who lived after being
15 wounded by the sword, and to this statue of the Beast he was allowed to impart the breath of life, so that the statue of the Beast should actually speak. He has everyone put to death *who will not worship the statue* of the Beast,
16 and he obliges all men, low and high, rich and poor, freemen and slaves alike, to have a mark put upon their right
17 hand or their forehead, so that no one can buy or sell unless he bears the mark, that is the name of the Beast
18 or the cipher of his name. Now for the gift of interpretation! Let the discerning calculate the cipher of the Beast; it is the cipher of a man, and the figures are six hundred and sixty-six.

14 Then I looked, and there was the Lamb standing on mount Sion, and along with him a hundred and forty-four thousand bearing his name and the name of his Father
2 written *on their foreheads!* And I heard a voice from heaven *like the sound of many waves* and the sound of loud thunder; the voice I heard was like harpists playing on
3 their harps; they were *singing* * *a new song* before the throne and before the four living Creatures and the Presbyters, and no one could learn that song except the hundred and forty-four thousand who had been ransomed from
4 earth. They have not been defiled by intercourse with women—they are celibates; they follow the Lamb wherever he goes; they have been ransomed from among men, as
5 the first to be reaped for God and the Lamb. And *on their lips no lie was ever detected* † ; they are stainless.

probably a gloss from xxi. 27. The book of Life elsewhere appears without any such addition.
　* Omitting [ὡς].
　† The thought and phraseology of the whole passage should be compared and contrasted with 1 Pet. ii. 21-22.

6 Then I saw another angel flying in mid-heaven with an eternal gospel for the inhabitants of the earth, for every
7 nation and tribe and tongue and people; he cried aloud, "Fear God and give him glory, for the hour of his judgment has come; worship him *who made heaven and earth, the*
8 *sea and the fountains of water.*" And another, a second angel followed, crying, "*Fallen, fallen is Babylon the great, who made all nations drink the wine* of the passion of her
9 vice!" They were followed by another, a third angel, crying aloud, "Whoever worships the Beast and his statue, and
10 lets his forehead or hand be marked, *he shall drink the wine* of God's passion, *poured out untempered in the cup of his anger*, and shall be tortured with *fire and brimstone*
11 before the holy angels and before the Lamb: *the smoke* of their torture *rises for ever* and ever, and they get no rest from it, day and night, these worshippers of the Beast and
12 his statue, and all who are marked with his name." This is what shows the patience of the saints—they who keep God's commands and the faith of Jesus.
13 Then I heard a voice from heaven saying, "Write this:— 'Blessed are the dead who die in the Lord from henceforth! Even so, it is the voice of the Spirit—blessed in resting from their toils; for what they have done goes with them.'"
14 Then *I looked, and there was* a white cloud, and. seated *on the cloud One resembling a human being*, a golden
15 crown upon his head and a sharp sickle in his hand. And another angel came out of the temple shouting aloud to him who sat upon the cloud,
"*Thrust your sickle in* and reap,
the time has come to reap,
the harvest of earth is ripe and ready."
16 So he who sat upon the cloud swung his sickle over the
17 earth, and the earth was reaped. Then another angel came
18 out of the temple, he too with a sharp sickle; and another angel came from the altar—he who has power over fire— and called loudly to the one who had the sharp sickle,
"*Thrust your* sharp *sickle in,*
cull the clusters from the Vine of earth,
for its grapes are fully ripe."
19 So the angel swung his sickle on the earth and culled the clusters from the Vine of earth, flinging the grapes into the
20 great winepress of God's wrath; outside the City *was the winepress trodden*, and blood gushed out of the winepress as high as a horse's bridle for the space of two hundred miles.

15 THEN I saw another portent in heaven, great and marvellous: seven angels with seven plagues—the last

2 plagues, for they complete the wrath of God. And I saw
what was like a sea of glass mixed with fire, and, standing
beside the sea of glass, those who came off conquerors
from the Beast and his statue and the cipher of his name;
3 they had harps of God and *they were singing the song of
Moses the servant of God* and the song of the Lamb—
"Great and *marvellous are thy deeds,
Lord God almighty!
Just and true thy ways,
O King of nations!*
4 *Who shall not fear, O Lord,* and *glorify thy name?*
for thou alone art *holy.*
Yea, all nations shall come and worship before thee,
for thy judgments are disclosed."
5 After that * I looked, and the temple of *the tabernacle of
6 testimony* in heaven was thrown open, and out of the
temple came the seven angels with *the seven plagues, robed
in* pure dazzling *linen,* their breasts encircled with golden
7 belts. Then one of the four living Creatures gave the seven
angels seven golden bowls full of the wrath of God who
8 lives for ever and ever; and *the temple was filled with
smoke from the glory* of God and from his might, *nor could
anyone enter* the temple till *the seven plagues* of the seven

16 angels were over. Then I heard a loud *voice from
the temple* telling the seven angels, "Go and *pour out*
2 the seven bowls of *the wrath* of God *on earth."* So the first
went off and poured his bowl upon the land; *and* noisome,
painful *ulcers broke out on* those who bore the mark of the
3 Beast and worshipped his statue. The second poured out
his bowl upon the sea; it *turned blood* like the blood of a
corpse, and every living thing *within the sea perished.*
4 The third poured out his bowl upon *the rivers* and
5 fountains of water, and *they turned blood.* Then I heard
the angel of the waters cry, *"O holy One, who art* and *wast,*
6 *just art thou* in this thy sentence. *They poured out* the
blood of saints and prophets, and thou hast given *them*
7 *blood to drink!* They deserve it!" And I heard the altar
cry,
"Even so, *Lord God almighty:
true and just are thy sentences of doom."*
8 The fourth angel poured out his bowl upon the sun; and
9 the sun was allowed to scorch men with fire, till men,
scorched by the fierce heat, blasphemed the name of the
God who had control of these plagues; yet they would not
10 repent and give him glory. The fifth poured out his bowl

---

* That is, after the interlude of 2–4. The words always denote a fresh phrase or stage of the vision.

upon the throne of the Beast; his realm *was darkened*, and
11 men gnawed their tongues in anguish, blaspheming *the
God of heaven* for their pains and their ulcers, but refus-
12 ing to repent of their doings. The sixth poured out his
bowl on *the great river Euphrates*, and *its waters were
dried up* to prepare the way for the kings *from the east*.
13 Then I saw issuing from the mouth of the dragon and from
the mouth of the Beast and from the mouth of the false
14 Prophet, three foul spirits like *frogs*—demon-spirits performing miracles, who come out to muster the kings of the
whole world for battle on the great Day *of almighty God*.
15 (Lo, I am coming like a thief; blessed be he who keeps
awake and holds his raiment fast, not to go naked and have
16 the shame of exposure!) * And they were mustered at the
17 spot called (in Hebrew) Harmagedon. The seventh angel
poured out his bowl in the air; then came a loud *voice out
of the temple* of heaven from the throne, crying, "All is
18 over!" followed by *flashes of lightning, loud blasts, peals
of thunder*, and a mighty earthquake, *the like of which
never was since man lived on earth*, such a mighty earth-
19 quake it was; the great City was shattered in three parts,
the cities of the nations fell, and God remembered to give
Babylon the great the cup of the wine of the passion of
20 his anger. Every island fled away, the mountains dis-
21 appeared, *and huge hailstones* fell from heaven on men, till
men blasphemed God for the plague of the hail—for the
plague of it was *fearful*.

17 THEN came one of the seven angels with the seven
plagues and spoke to me, saying, "Come and I will
show you the doom of the great Harlot who is seated on
2 *many waters, with whom the kings of earth have committed vice*, and the dwellers on *earth have been drunk
3 with the wine* of her vice." So he bore me away·rapt in
the Spirit to the desert, and I saw a woman sitting on
a scarlet Beast covered with blasphemous titles; it had
4 *seven heads and ten horns*. The woman was clad in purple
and scarlet, her ornaments were of gold and precious stones
and pearls, in her hand was *a golden cup* full of all abomi-
5 nations and the impurities of her vice, and on her forehead a name was written by way of symbol, "Babylon the
great, the mother of harlots and of all abominations on
6 earth." Then I saw the woman was drunk with the blood
of the saints and the blood of the witnesses of Jesus; and
7 as I looked at her I marvelled greatly. But the angel said

* Ver. 15 interrupts the sequence of thought; it is either a gloss or misplaced, perhaps from the third chapter.

to me, "Why marvel? I will explain to you the mystery of the woman, and of the Beast with the seven heads and the
8 ten horns who carries her. *The Beast* you have seen was, is not, but is to *rise from the abyss*—yet to perdition he shall go—and the dwellers on earth will wonder (all whose names have not been *written* from the foundation of the world *in the book of Life*), when they see that the Beast
9 was, is not, but is coming. Now for the interpretation of the discerning mind! The seven heads are seven hills, on
10 which the woman is seated: also, they are seven kings, of whom five have fallen, one is living, and the other has not arrived yet—and when he does arrive, he can only stay a
11 little while. As for the Beast which was and is not, he is an eighth head; he belongs to the seven, and to perdition he
12 shall go. *As for the ten horns* you have seen, *they are ten kings* who have no royal power as yet, but receive royal
13 authority for an hour along with the Beast; they are of one mind, and they confer their power and authority upon
14 the Beast. They will wage war on the Lamb, but the Lamb will conquer them because he is *Lord of lords and King of kings*—the Lamb and the elect, the chosen, the faithful
15 who are with him." He also told me, "*The waters* you saw, on which the woman is seated, are peoples and hosts,
16 nations and tongues. As for the ten horns you have seen, they and the Beast will hate the harlot, lay her waste, and strip her naked; they will devour her flesh and burn her
17 with fire, for God has put it into their hearts to execute his purpose, by having one mind and by conferring their royal power upon the Beast, until the words of God are
18 fulfilled. As for the woman you have seen, she is the great City which reigns over *the kings of the earth*." *

18 After that I saw another angel descend from heaven,
2 great in might; his radiance lit up the earth, and he shouted aloud with a strong voice,
"*Fallen, fallen is Babylon the great,*
   now she is a *haunt of demons,*
   the den of all foul spirits,
   a cage for every foul and loathsome bird:
3 for *all nations have drunk the wine* of the passion of her vice,
   the kings of the earth have committed vice with her,
   and by the wealth of her wantonness earth's traders have grown rich."
4 And I heard another voice from heaven crying,
"*Come out of her, O my people,*

---

* Possibly xix. 9–10 (" The angel also . . .") originally came at this place in the narrative.

that you share not her sins,
that you partake not of her plagues:
5 for *high as heaven* her sins are *heaped,*
and God calls her misdeeds to the reckoning.
6 *Render to her what she rendered to others,*
aye, double the doom *for all she has done;*
mix her the draught double in the cup she mixed for others.
7 As she gloried and played the wanton,
so give her like measure of torture and tears.
Since *in her heart she vaunts,* '*A queen I sit,
no widow I, tears I shall never know,*'
8 so shall her plagues *fall in a single day,*
pestilence, tears, and famine:
she shall be burnt with fire—
for *strong is God the Lord her judge.*
9 *And the kings of the earth who committed vice* and
wantoned *with her shall weep and wail* over her, as they
10 watch the smoke of her burning; for fear of her torture
they will stand far off, crying,
" 'Woe and alas, thou *great* city!
thou strong city of Babylon!
In one brief hour thy doom has come.'
11 And the *traders* of earth shall *weep and wail* over her;
12 for now there is none to buy their freights, freights of gold,
silver, jewels, pearls, fine linen, purples, silk, scarlet stuff,
all sorts of citron wood and ivory wares, all articles of
13 costly wood, of bronze, of iron and of marble, with cinnamon, balsam, spices, myrrh, frankincense, wines, olive-oil,
fine flour and wheat, with cattle, sheep, horses, carriages,
15 slaves, and *the souls of men.** The *traders* in these wares,
who made rich profits from her, will stand far off for fear
of her torture, *weeping and wailing:*
'Woe and alas, for the great city,
robed in linen, in purple and scarlet,
her ornaments of gold, of jewels and pearl!
And all this splendour gone in one brief hour!'
17 And all *shipmasters* and sea-faring folk, *sailors and all*
18 *whose* business lies *upon the sea, stood* far off as they
watched the smoke of her burning, crying, 'What city
19 *was like* the great City?' *They threw dust on their heads
and cried, as they wept and wailed,*
'Woe and alas for the great City,
where *all shipmen made rich profit by* her *treasures!*
Gone, gone in one brief hour!'

---

* Ver. 14 has been misplaced from its original position in the middle of ver. 23.

20 O *heaven, rejoice* over her!
Saints, apostles, prophets, rejoice!
For God has avenged you on her now."
21 Then a strong angel lifted *a boulder* like a huge millstone *and flung it into* the sea, *crying,*
"*So* shall *the great* city, *Babylon,* be hurled down, hurtling, *and never be seen any more:*
22 *and the sound of* harpists and *minstrels* and fluteplayers and trumpeters
shall never be heard in thee more:
and craftsmen of any craft
shall never be found in thee more:
and the sound of the millstone
shall never be heard in thee more:
23 *and the light of a lamp*
shall never be seen in thee more:
and the voice of the bridegroom and bride
shall never be heard in thee more.
14 Vanished the ripe fruit of thy soul's desire!
Perished thy luxury and splendour!
Never again to be seen.
23 For *the magnates of earth* were thy *traders;*
all nations were seduced *by thy magic spells.*
24 And in her was found the blood of prophets and saints,
of all who were slain upon earth."*

19 AFTER that I heard what was like the shout of a great host in heaven, crying,
"*Hallelujah!* salvation and glory and power are our God's!
2   *True and just are his sentences of doom;*
he has doomed the great Harlot who destroyed earth with her vice,
he has avenged on her *the blood of* his *servants.*"
3 Again they repeated,
"*Hallelujah! And the smoke of her goes up for ever* and ever!"
4   Then the four and twenty Presbyters and the four living Creatures fell down and worshipped God who is *seated on*
5 *the throne,* crying, "So be it, *hallelujah!*" And a voice came from the throne,
"*Extol* our God, *all ye his servants,*
ye who reverence him, low and high!"
6   Then I heard a cry *like the shout of a* great *host* and the sound of many waves and the roar of heavy thunder—
"*Hallelujah! now the Lord* our *God almighty reigns!*

* Ver. 24, like ver. 20, links xvii. 6 to the outburst of xix. 2.

7 *Let us rejoice and triumph,*
let us give him the glory!
For now comes the marriage of the Lamb;
his bride has arrayed herself,
8 Yea, she is allowed to put on fine linen, dazzling white"
(the white linen is the righteous conduct of the saints).
9 Then I was told, "Write this:—'Blessed are those who have been called to the marriage-banquet of the Lamb!' " The angel also told me, "These are genuine words of God."
10 Then I fell before his feet to worship him; but he said to me, "No, not that! I am but a servant like yourself and your brothers, who hold the testimony of Jesus. Worship God" (for the testimony borne by Jesus is the breath of all prophecy).

11 *Then I saw heaven open wide—*
and there was a white horse:
his rider is faithful and true,
yea, *just are his judgments* and his warfare.
12 *His eyes are a flame of fire,*
on his head are many diadems,
he bears a written name which none knows but himself.
13 He is clad in a robe dipped in blood
(his name is called THE LOGOS OF GOD),
14 and the troops of heaven follow him on white horses,
arrayed in pure white linen.
15 A sharp sword issues *from his lips,* wherewith to *smite the nations;*
he will shepherd * *them with an iron flail,*
and *trample the winepress* of the passion of the anger *of God almighty.*
16 And on his robe, upon his thigh, his name is written,
KING OF KINGS AND LORD OF LORDS.
17 Then I saw an angel standing in the sun, who shouted aloud to *all the birds that fly* in mid-heaven, "*Come, gather*
18 *for the* great *banquet* of God, *to devour* the flesh of *kings,* the flesh of generals, *the flesh of the strong,* the flesh of *horses* and their riders, the flesh of all men, free and
19 slaves, low and high alike." And I saw the Beast and *the kings of earth* and their troops *mustered* to wage war on
20 him who was seated on the horse and on his troops. But the Beast was seized, together with the false Prophet who had performed in his presence the miracles by means of which he seduced those who received the mark of the Beast and worshipped his statue; both of them were flung alive into

* The verb had really come to mean no more than "rule" by this time; but the literal rendering may be retained for the sake of the antithesis in vii. 17.

21 the lake of fire that *blazes with brimstone*, while the rest were killed by the sword of him who is seated on the horse, by the sword that issues from his lips. *And all the birds were glutted with* their *flesh*.

20 Then I saw an angel descend from heaven with the
2 key of the abyss and a huge chain in his hand; he gripped the dragon, that old *serpent* (who is the *devil*
3 *and Satan*), and bound him for a thousand years, flinging him into the abyss and shutting and sealing it on the top of him, to prevent him seducing the nations again until the thousand years were completed—after which he has to be
4 released for a little while. And *I saw thrones* with people *sitting on them*, who *were allowed to judge*—saw the souls of those who had been beheaded for the testimony of Jesus and God's word, those who would not worship the Beast or his statue, and who would not receive his mark on their forehead or hand; they came to life and reigned along with
5 the Christ for a thousand years. As for the rest of the dead, they did not come to life until the thousand years
6 were completed. This is the first resurrection. Blessed and holy is he who shares in the first resurrection; over such the second death has no power, they shall be *priests of God* and the Christ, and reign along with him during the thou-
7 sand years. But when the thousand years are over, Satan
8 will be released from his prison, and he will emerge to seduce the nations *at the four corners of the earth, even Gog and Magog*, mustering them for the fray. Their num-
9 ber was like the sand of the sea, and they swarmed *over the broad earth*, encircling the leaguer of the saints and the beloved City; *but fire descended from heaven and con-*
10 *sumed* them, and their seducer, the devil, was flung into the lake of fire and brimstone, where the Beast and the false Prophet also lie, to be tortured day and night for ever and ever.

11   *Then I saw a* great white *throne*,
   and One who was *seated* thereon;
   from his presence earth and sky *fled, no more to be found.*
12   And I saw the dead, high and low, standing before the throne,
   and books were opened—
   also another book, the book of Life, was opened—
   and the dead were judged by what was written in these books, *by what they had done.*
13   The sea gave up its corpses,
   Death and Hades gave up their dead,
   and all were judged *by what each had done.*
14   Then Death and Hades were flung into the lake of fire,
15   and *whoever was not found enrolled in the book of Life*

was flung into the lake of fire—
which is the second death, the lake of fire.*

21 Then I saw *the new heaven and the new earth,* for the first heaven and the first earth had passed away; and
2 the sea is no more. And I saw *the holy City,* the new *Jerusalem,* descending from God out of heaven, all ready
3 *like a bride arrayed* for her husband. And I heard a loud voice out of the throne, crying,
 "*Lo,* God's *dwelling-place* is with men,
 with men will he dwell;
 they shall be his people,
 * and God *will* himself *be with them:*
4 *he will wipe every tear from their eyes,*
 and death shall be no more—
 no more *wailing or crying* or pain,
 for *the first things* have passed away."
5 Then *he who was seated on the throne* said, "Lo, I make all *things new.*" And he said, "Write this: 'these words
6 are trustworthy and genuine.'" Then he said, "All is over! I am the alpha and the omega, the First and the Last. I will let *the thirsty* drink of the fountain of *the*
7 *water of Life without price.* The conqueror shall obtain
8 this, and *I will be his God, and he shall be my son;* but as for the craven, the faithless, the abominable, as for the murderers, the immoral, the sorcerers, the idolaters, and liars of all kinds—their lot is the lake that *blazes with fire and brimstone,* which is the second death."
9 Then came one of the seven angels who had the seven bowls filled with the *seven last plagues;* and he spoke to me thus, "Come, and I will show you the Bride, the wife
10 of the Lamb." So he carried me off, rapt in the Spirit, *to a huge, high mountain,* where he showed me *the City, the holy Jerusalem,* descending from God out of heaven,
11 *with the glory of God.* The sheen of it resembled some rare
12 jewel like jasper, clear as crystal; it has a huge, high wall with twelve *gates,* twelve angels at the twelve gates, and *names* inscribed thereon which are the names *of the twelve*
13 *tribes of the sons of Israel, three gates on the east, three gates on the north, three gates on the south, and three gates*
14 *on the west.* And the wall of the City has twelve foundation-stones, bearing the twelve names of the twelve apostles
15 of the Lamb. He who talked to me had a golden *wand by way of a measuring-rod,* to measure the City and its
16 gates and wall; the City lies *foursquare,* the length the same as the breadth, and he measured fifteen hundred

* Unless this line is to be omitted altogether, it must be placed thus after ver. 15, not after 14 (as in the ordinary text), since there is no question of a second death except for human beings.

miles with his rod for the City, for its breadth and length
17 and height alike; *he made the measure of the wall* seventy-
18 two yards, by human, that is, by angelic reckoning. The
material of *the wall is jasper*, but the City is made of pure
19 gold, transparent like glass. *The foundation-stones* of the
city-wall are adorned with all sorts of *precious stones*, the
first foundation-stone being of jasper, the second of sap-
20 phire, the third of agate, the fourth of emerald, the fifth of
onyx, the sixth of sardius, the seventh of chrysolite, the
eighth of beryl, the ninth of topaz, the tenth of chryso-
prase, the eleventh of jacinth, the twelfth of amethyst.
21 The twelve gates are twelve pearls, each gate made of a
single pearl; and the streets of the City are pure gold,
22 clear as crystal. But I saw no temple in the City, for its
23 temple is *the Lord God almighty* and the Lamb. And the
City needs *no sun or moon to shine* upon it, for *the glory
of God illumines* it, and the Lamb lights it up.
24 *By its light will the nations walk;*
and *into it will the kings of earth bring* their *glories*
25 (*the gates of it will never be shut by day*,
and *night* there shall be none),
26 *they will bring* to it *the glories* and treasures *of the
nations.*
27 *Nothing profane*, none who practises abomination or
falsehood *shall enter*,
but those alone *whose names are written in the Lamb's
book of Life.*

22 Then he showed me *the river of the water of Life,*
bright as crystal, *flowing* from the throne of God and
2 of the Lamb *through* the streets of the City; on both sides
of the river grew the tree of Life, bearing twelve kinds of
fruit, *each month having its own fruit;* and *the leaves*
served to *heal* the nations.
3 *None who is accursed will be there;*
but the throne of God and the Lamb will be within it,
his servants will serve and worship him,
4 *they will see his face,*
and his name will be on their foreheads.
5 Night there shall be none;
they need no lamp or *sun to shine* upon them,
for *the Lord God will illumine* them;
and they will reign for ever and ever.
6 And the angel said to me, "These words are trustworthy
and genuine, for the Lord God of the spirits of the prophets
has sent his angel to show his servants *what must* very
7 soon *come to pass. Lo, I am coming* very soon; blessed

is he who lays to heart the words of the prophecy of this book!"

8 I John saw and heard all this; and when I heard and saw it, I fell down to worship before the feet of the angel
9 who had shown me it all. But he said to me, "No, not that! I am but a servant like yourself and your brothers the prophets, who lay to heart the words of this book. Worship
10 God." Then he said, "Do not *seal up* the words of the prophecy of *this book*, for *the time* is near:
11   Let the wicked still be wicked,
    let the filthy still be filthy,
    let the righteous still do right,
    let the holy still be holy!
12   *Lo, I am coming* very soon, *with my reward,*
    to requite everyone for what he has done.
13   I am the alpha and the omega,
    the First and the Last,
    the beginning and the end.
14 Blessed are those who *wash their robes,** that theirs may be the right to *the tree of Life*, the right to enter the gates
15 of the City! Begone, you dogs, you sorcerers, you vicious men, you murderers, you idolaters, you who love and practise falsehood, every one of you!"
16 "I Jesus have sent my angel to give you this testimony for the churches; I am *the Scion* and offspring of David, the bright star of the Morning."
17   "Come," say the Spirit and the Bride:
    let the hearer too say, "Come";
    and *let the thirsty come*,
    let anyone who desires it, take *the water of Life without price*.
18   I adjure all who hear the words of the prophecy of this book:
    "If anyone *adds to them*,
      God will add *to him the* plagues *described in this book;*
19   and if anyone *removes* any words written in this book,
      God will remove his share in *the tree of Life* and in the holy City described in this book."
20   He who bears this testimony says, "Even so: I am coming very soon." Amen, Lord Jesus, come!
21   The grace of the Lord Jesus Christ be with you all.†
Amen.

* Reading πλύνοντες τὰς στολὰς αὐτῶν with ℵ A, Primasius, the Vulgate, etc.
† Reading πάντων or πάντων ὑμῶν.

www.ingramcontent.com/pod-product-compliance
Lightning Source LLC
LaVergne TN
LVHW091249030126
829014LV00001B/12